Webster's New World

Illustrated Encyclopedic

Dictionary of

Real Estate

THIRD EDITION

Jerome S. Gross

Prentice Hall Press
New York

Published by New World Dictionaries/Prentice Hall Press
A Division of Simon & Schuster, Inc.
Gulf + Western Building
One Gulf + Western Plaza
New York, NY 10023

PRENTICE HALL PRESS, TREE OF KNOWLEDGE, WEBSTER'S NEW WORLD
and colophons are trademarks of Simon & Schuster, Inc.

Manufactured in the United States of America

1 2 3 4 5 6 7 8 9 10

"This publication is designed to provide accurate and authoritative information in regard to the subject matter covered. It is sold with the understanding that the publisher is not engaged in rendering legal, accounting, or other professional service. If legal advice or other expert assistance is required, the services of a competent professional person should be sought."

> From the declaration of Principles jointly adopted
> by a Committee of the American Bar Association
> and a Committee of Publishers and Associations

Library of Congress Cataloging-in-Publication Data

Gross, Jerome S.
    Webster's new world illustrated encyclopedic
dictionary of real estate.

    Rev. ed. of: Illustrated encyclopedic dictionary
of real estate. 2nd ed. 1978.
    1. Real estate business—Dictionaries. I. Gross,
Jerome S. Illustrated encyclopedic dictionary of
real estate. II. Title.
HD1365.G76   1987   333.33'03'21   87-2360
         ISBN 0-13-947318-1

Introduction

"Under all is the land." These few opening words of the Preamble to the Code of Ethics of the National Association of Realtors make a simple statement of fact. Yet, they introduce a very special mystique associated with ownership of real property.

The mystique surrounding land ownership has arisen because of the uniqueness and value of land. Land has certain characteristics typical of nothing else one might own. Every plot of land is unique; it is different from every other plot of land. Each plot has its own soil composition and underlying bedrock, its own water supply and its own drainage, its own vegetation and its own view. Each plot has its own unique location and its unique adjoining lots. Even in a uniform subdivision where it might appear that all lots and, perhaps, all improvements as well, look alike, each plot is unique at least to the extent that it is located in a specific spot and is situated between neighbors unique to itself.

A second major property of the land is its value. Land allows for the production of food and commodities and provides the natural resources and basic ground location for shelter. Land itself, unlike the improvements built upon it, cannot be increased in quantity. Aside from freakish and unusual acts of nature, the amount of land that there is is absolute and finite. Ownership of land represents ownership of something precious indeed.

Because of the inherent value of land itself and because of the singularity of location of each piece of land, a great body of law has grown up regarding land ownership and transfer. Land cannot be moved. It cannot be carried about with ones person nor can it be removed to a safe place. Since land remains in one public spot for all to see, proof of ownership must be established by a means beyond mere obvious possession.

5

Rules regarding land ownership, use and transfer have a history going back to the times people first recognized the value of land. Deeds and wills dating back to the First Century have been uncovered in excavations. In feudal England, only the King owned land. The King granted to certain lords the right to use the land, originating the term *landlord*. In feudal times, however, landlords were tenants of the King, not landowners. Some real estate terminology has drastically altered in meaning over the years. Throughout the long history of interest in the land, a special vocabulary of real estate has evolved and developed. In modern times rules concerning ownership, use, and transfer of property have been codified into law; and legal vocabulary, as the intimidated layman well knows, can be staggering.

However, the language of real estate is not impossible to master. In fact, study of the special meanings of words in their real estate context can be fun. This dictionary will let you know that "quiet enjoyment" of ones property has nothing to do with the neighbor's crying baby, that "running with the land" does not refer to jogging, that "riparian rights" are not related to orchards or their fruits, that ownership in "severalty" is ownership by one person alone. A comprehensive lexicon such as this one brings real estate terminology into the grasp of everyone who has any need or any desire to know.

Thorough knowledge and understanding of the vocabulary of real estate is essential for real estate professionals—brokers, salespersons, appraisers. Likewise, attorneys, mortgage brokers, bankers, builders, land developers and serious, large-scale investors must have a real working knowledge of the language of real estate as well as of the laws which govern their specific activities and dealings in real estate. People who are engaged in these activities should already be conversant with the bulk of the vocabulary. For these people, this book may serve for brush up, as a back-up to fill in gaps in knowledge, as an argument settler and as a handy reference.

Would-be professionals or investors just entering the market place are well-advised to immerse themselves in the vocabulary of the business to prepare themselves for future study, examinations and business dealings. This book as a companion to other texts will keep the student from getting lost among the words. The portfolio of forms towards the back of the volume should also prove extremely useful to this group of readers. Study of the forms involved can serve as a step-by-step introduction to the actual transfer of land, from opening offer through recording of the deed. Prefamiliarity with the forms can save the neophyte from embarrassing unpreparedness at crucial moments. The reader may make a dry run through a real estate transaction by following the forms involved at each stage of the deal.

Finally, this book will serve as an excellent guide and reference for the lay person who is buying or selling a single property for occupancy or investment. The book is very readable. Definitions are clearly written and succinctly stated. The many illustrative diagrams are well drawn and very helpful. These diagrams are a superb adjunct to the text. The lay person who refers frequently to this dictionary will be in a position to converse knowledgeably with real estate professionals and to appreciate the various steps that are being taken in guaranteeing ownership of the property. The buyer, seller, builder, landlord or tenant who understands the language can participate in and feel comfortable with the real estate transactions in which he or she is involved.

CONTENTS

A

AAA TENANT—A nationally known, highly rated tenant whose net worth is calculated to be in excess of one million dollars. A company whose name will lend prestige and importance to the property.

ABANDONMENT—Voluntary renunciation of ownership. Relinquishing any claim or rights to property. Giving up entirely without any intention of regaining possession or interest at a later time. Permanently leave or desert.

A BANKRUPT—(See BANKRUPT.)

ABATE—To decrease; make less; diminish or reduce. Nullify; deduct; subside.

ABATEMENT OF RENT CLAUSE—A clause in a lease that releases a tenant from his obligation to continue to pay rent in the event that the premises are made uninhabitable by fire, flood, hurricane, or other Act of God (See ACT OF GOD.)

ABATEMENT OF TAXES—An authorized cancellation of a portion or all of the taxes. A tax rebate.

ABATOR—One who unlawfully gains possession of an estate upon the death of the owner, thereby, preventing the rightful heirs from obtaining title.

ABEYANCE—1. In real estate law, the temporary suspension of title to property until the proper or competent owner is determined. 2. An interim suspension or inactivity. An undetermined condition.

AB INITIO—(Latin) From the beginning.

ABJURE—To retract or recant. To renounce an oath. To withdraw one's word. The opposite of pledge.

ABLE—Capable; qualified; competent. Financially able, as in the term Ready, Willing, and Able.

ABNORMAL SALE—A sale having irregularities or some unusual feature setting it apart from a normal transaction; a sale that in some way deviates from the ordinary transfer of property.

ABODE—A person's permanent living place. His domicile, habitation or home. One's fixed dwelling.

ABORTION—A common expression meaning an unsightly, poorly designed structure that usually is difficult to sell.

ABROGATE—To annul or nullify. Eliminate by the act of an authority. Abolish or otherwise put to an end.

ABSENTEE OWNER—A person who owns property, but does not reside upon it. One who is continually away from his property and leaves its management in the care of others.

ABSOLUTE FEE—(See FEE: FEE SIMPLE: FEE SIMPLE ABSOLUTE.)

ABSOLUTE SALE—A sale in which all parties to a contract perform as agreed upon, and the property passes to the purchase when title closes.

ABSOLUTE TITLE—An exclusive, complete title. A title without limitations or conditions. A title held by one party or one group.

ABSTRACT: ABSTRACT OF TITLE—A summarized, chronological complication of all the recorded instruments, and a history of ownership that has affected the title to a specific piece of land. A synopsis of its recorded documents.

ABSTRACT COMPANY—(See TITLE COMPANY OR AGENCY.)

ABSTRACTER—One who prepares abstracts. An abstracter can be a lawyer, a public official, or a company that specializes in reading abstracts and preparing title reports.

ABUTTING—Property contiguous to another. Bordering; joining; adjacent; touching.

ACCELERATION CLAUSE—A clause generally found in a mortgage or installment contract stipulating that the payment of the indebtedness must be made in full in the event of a default of any of its covenants. Certain other instruments, such as bonds, leases, and notes may also contain acceleration clauses.

ACCELERATED DEPRECIATION—A method of rapidly taking depreciation benefits of a building in the early years of its existence. In ths manner, a faster recovery of invested capital can be realized over Straight-Line Depreciation. Some depreciation methods utilizing accelerated depreciation include DOUBLE DECLINING DEPRECIATION, COMPONENT DEPRECIATION, and SUM OF THE YEARS' DIGITS. (See those definitions.)

ACCEPTANCE—1. Agreeing to the terms and conditions of an offer making it a binding contract. 2. The receipt of a deed constitutes automatic acceptance of title to property.

ACCESSORY BUILDING—Any building other than the main one; an outbuilding, such as a barn, detached garage, store house, pump house, shed, etc. A secondary building; one used as an adjunct to another building.

ACCESS RIGHT—The vested right of an owner to passage over adjoining public property in order to enter and leave his land.

ACCOUNTANT—A skilled auditor who examines business accounts, makes fiscal recommendations, and prepares statements. (See PUBLIC ACCOUNTANT; CERTIFIED PUBLIC ACCOUNTANT.)

ACCRETION—The gradual acquisition of additional land by the forces of nature, such as occurs when wind or tides add sand deposits to waterfront properties, or when a watercourse is altered by the action of floods.

ACCRUE—An increase or addition. Something that is periodically accumulated. A natural process of growth. To come into existence.

ACCRUED INTEREST—Interest that has already matured. Earned interest. Accumulated interest that is due and payable.

ACCRUING DEPRECIATION—Depreciation that is in the process of building up. Accumulating depreciation.

ACKNOWLEDGMENT—The formal certification of a signature on a document before an authorized officer, such as a Notary Public, or County Clerk. A verification that the document which has been signed is that person's willful act and deed. Some state statutes specify that a particular form of acknowledgment be used. Some uses of the acknowledgment are for contracts and deeds, if they are to be recorded, for leases of more than a year, and for mortgages.

ACQUISITION—The process of obtaining property. The act of acquiring; becoming the owner.

ACQUISITION COST—The sum paid to obtain title to property. In addition to the actual selling price, cost, in this instance, includes closing expenses, such as stamps on deeds and mortgages, survey charges, appraisal fees, title insurance, legal fees, mortgage origination bank charges, and any other moneys expended to obtain ownership.

ACRE—Land measuring 43,560 square feet. 4,840 square yards. 160 square rods. 1/640th of a square mile. Abbreviated as "Ac" or "A", an acre measures

208.75	feet wide by	208.75	feet long
150	" " "	290.04	" "
132	" " "	330	" "
100	" " "	435.6	" "
75	" " "	580.8	" "
66	" " "	660	" "
50	" " "	871.2	" "
33	" " "	1320	" "
16.5	" " "	2640	" "

ACREAGE—Area in acres.

ACREAGE LISTING FORM—A form specifically designed for listing acreage property.

ACTION FOR COMMISSION—Legal action brought to recover a commission.

ACTION ON CONTRACT—Legal action brought to enforce the terms of a contract. The contract itself is used as the evidence.

ACT OF BANKRUPTCY—(See BANKRUPT.)

ACT OF GOD—An event occuring through the unexpected force of nature, as a hurricane, flood, earthquake, tornado or blizzard. An act not created or able to be controlled by human activity.

ACT OF LAW—The performance and application of legal rules by the proper judicial authority, as distinguished from "act of parties."

ACT OF SALE—In Lousiana, it is a formal record of a sale of property. It must be properly signed, witnessed and notarized to be official and binding.

ACTUAL CASH VALUE—The phrase is synonymous with "market value" and "fair market price." It is the price a property will bring on the open market under normal conditions, and not at a distress sale. It is understood that a reasonable, but not a protracted, period of time may elapse to obtain this value.

ACTUAL EVICTION—(See EVICTION.)

ACTUAL FRAUD—An intentional deceit and misrepresentation. Deliberate untruth and trickery. Cunning deception. (See FRAUD.)

ACTUAL POSSESSION—Existing physical control or occupancy of a premises, as distinguished from Constructive Possession, i.e., possession that is assumed by virtue of title.

ACTUAL VALUE—The price that a property will bring on the open market in the ordinary course of business. (See MARKET VALUE.)

ACTUARY—A statistical expert who calculates and charts probability of insurance risk and sets rates. His findings are utilized by insurance management in the setting up of reserve funds and in issuing dividends.

ADDENDUM—(Latin) Additional material attached to a document. An appendix. The plural is addenda. The addendum to a contract is that which is attached to and made a part of it.

ADDITION—1. A portion of a building that is added to an existing structure. A further improvement upon that which is already erected. 2. Acquisition of land that adds to the original parcel, thereby increasing its dimensions and value. 3. A Subdivision.

ADDRESS—The common known description of a property, including its street and number, town, county and state. (See LEGAL DESCRIPTIONS.)

ADEMPTION—The disposal of specific property by a living person who has bequeathed the property in his will. Upon the death of that person, the portion of the will that is unable to be fulfilled is automatically revoked.

AD HOC—(Latin) For a special purpose or end. For this.

ADJACENT—Bordering; neighboring, but it may or may not be in actual contact. Close by.

ADJOIN—To be in actual contact; to abut. To touch at some point. Contiguous.

ADJUDGE—To rule upon; decide or determine by law; legally, award or assign. Adjudicate.

ADJUSTMENTS—As applied to real estate, the credits and debits of a closing statement including such matters as taxes, insurance, rent prorations, escrowed funds, etc. when property is sold. A settlement.

ADMINISTRATOR—A court-appointed person authorized to manage and distribute the estate of one who dies leaving a will in which no Executor is named or of one who dies Intestate (leaving no will). An administrator may also be appointed when an executor is declared legally incompetent, dies before his duties can be performed or refuses to serve.

ADMINISTRATOR'S DEED—A form of deed used by the administrator of an estate to convey the property of one who has died leaving no will or executor.

ADMINISTRATRIX—A female appointed by the court to administrate the estate of a deceased person.

ADOBE—1. Sun-baked brick and clay used for construction in arid areas of the west and southwest. 2. A house or other building made of adobe brick.

AD VALOREM—(Latin) According to the value.

AD VALOREM TAXES—Taxes on real estate assessed according or proportionate to the value of the property.

ADVANCE—The paying of money, or the furnishing of goods or services, beforehand. Giving consideration before it is due.

ADVANCE FEE—A fee paid in advance of completion of services. (See RETAINER.)

ADVERSE LAND USE—The utilizing of land in such a manner that it is detrimental either to itself, the surrounding properties, or both. For example, a factory located in a residential area, or homes constructed too close to one another.

ADVERSE POSSESSION—The acquiring of property by one who does not have title, or who has defective title, to it. That person must be in "actual, open, notorious, exclusive, and continuous" occupancy for a prescribed statutory period. The period of occupancy varies in different states. In some, the period is 5 or 7 years; whereas, in others, it is as long as 20 years. It is also referred to as hostile possession, or notorious possession.

ADVERSE TITLE—Title that is created in opposition to another title to render the former one void, or to defeat a claim by adverse possession.

AEOLIAN SOIL—Soil developed from wind-blown solid materials, as in the formation of sand dunes or volcanic ash deposits. Soil transported by action of the air.

AERIAL MAP—A series of vertical, aerial photographs of the ground that, when assembled in proper sequence, form a map giving a panoramic view of an area.

AESTHETIC VALUE—Value derived from beauty or artistic uniqueness of a property. It could be an unparalleled view, or an original architectural design that creates this special value, but because of its presence it transcends the market value of an otherwise similar piece of real estate.

AFFIANT—The person making an affidavit.

AFFIDAVIT—A voluntary statement, testimony, or declaration in writing, that is sworn to or affirmed before a Notary Public, County Clerk, or other person authorized by law to administer oaths. An affidavit is often required as proof in the absence of other verifying facts or documents. (An example follows.)

AFFIDAVIT

State of _____ County _____, ss:

    Before me, the subscriber, a notary public for the City of _____, State of _____, personally appeared _____, who being duly sworn, deposes and says, that (Here clearly state the matter being sworn to).

_____

    Sworn and subscribed this _____ day of _____, 19_____.

_____
                        Notary Public

AFFIDAVIT OF TITLE—A sworn statement from the seller guaranteeing the purchaser that the title he is conveying is not defective (See page 260).

AFFIRM—Verify; ratify; confirm. To make a declaration. Concur and agree; to accept.

AFFIRMATION—A declaration or pledge in place of an oath. In law, it has the same significance as swearing to a supreme being. It is used when a person objects to taking such an oath because of personal beliefs.

AFFIX—To fasten or add to. To more or less permanently attach. Securely fix to. Inscribing or impressing upon, as a signature or seal to a document. In real estate, certain secured things are a part of the property and said to be affixed to it, as a tree, a fence that is anchored in the ground or a permanently installed chandelier. The affixed material is considered REALTY. Other easily movable objects constitute PERSONAL PROPERTY. (See those terms.)

AFFORESTATION—The creation of a forest cover in an area where one did not exist. The result of converting barren lands into forest and wild life preserves.

A-FRAME CONSTRUCTION—A building of which the front exterior design resembles the form of the letter A.

A-Frame

AFTER-ACQUIRED—Obtaining property subsequent to a specified date or occurrence.

AFTER-ACQUIRED CLAUSE IN MORTGAGES—1. A clause providing for the inclusion in the mortgage of items of chattel and fixtures found on the property. 2. A clause used in certain corporate mortgages stating that all earnings, property, and other assets acquired subsequent to the mortgage shall become subject to it.

AFTER-ACQUIRED TITLE—A title acquired by a grantor who attempts to convey the land to another before it is actually owned by him. Title to land so acquired is automatically returned to the prior grantee.

AGE-LIFE DEPRECIATION—An appraiser's method for estimating depreciation based on the life expectancy of a building, assuming the property receives normal care and maintenance. Depreciation tables are used that forecast physical, economic and functional obsolescence from year to year as the building ages.

AGENCY—An agreement between an agent and his principal wherein the agent represents him in dealing with a third party. An agency exists whether it is expressed or implied, and it need not be designated in writing.

AGENCY COUPLED WITH AN INTEREST—An agency in which the agent also has an interest in the property that he is buying, selling, or leasing.

AGENCY FORM—A contract between an owner and his agent to manage, rent, or sell real property. The instrument that creates the agency. (See LISTING, EXCLUSIVE RIGHT OF SALE, EXCLUSIVE AGENCY, OPEN LISTING and NET LISTING.)

AGENT—An authorized person, who undertakes to manage or transact business for and in place of another; one who represents another and performs in his behalf.

AGRARIAN—Matters relating to the land and soil; its use, ownership, distribution, and acquisition.

AGREEMENT—Accord of two or more people on a given matter. A meeting of the minds, as occurs when people have a like opinion. A real estate contract is called an *agreement*. The contract is the *form* used. However, if a difference of opinion arises and it is contested in a court of law, the form is no longer considered an agreement but is referred to as a contract.

AGREEMENT FOR DEED—A contract stating that if further payments are made on property and if all other terms and conditions are met, the deed will be delivered and title will pass.

AGREEMENT OF SALE: AGREEMENT TO SELL—A contract in which a seller agrees to sell and a buyer agrees to buy under certain specific terms and conditions; a contract.

AGRICULTURAL PROPERTY—Land devoted to and zoned or particularly suited for the raising of crops or livestock.

AIR LOT—(See AIR RIGHTS.)

AIR RIGHTS—The rights to the use of the open space above a property, as occurs in the leasing of air space over highways, railroad tracks or existing buildings. Also, the right to control the air space by *not* building, thereby assuring that light and air will not be blocked out. (See LIGHT and AIR EASEMENT.)

AIT—An islet. A small land formation in a river. A little island.

ALCOVE—Nook. A usually small, recessed area of a room. A vaulted recess. An arched wall opening or niche.

ALEATORY CONTRACT—A contract dependent upon contingencies. A contractual agreement whose benefits or losses to one or all of the parties depend on a future, contingent happening. The performance of the agreement itself is predicated upon the occurrence of the uncertain event. Life and fire insurance contracts and annuity servicing agreements are examples of aleatory contracts. The performance of certain terms and provisions are dependent upon a future occurrence.

ALIENATION—The transfer of interest and title of property to another. There can be voluntary and involuntary alienation. Voluntary alienation occurs in most normal transactions (when an owner of his own free will agrees to sell). Involuntary alienation comes into effect when a person loses his property contrary to his will or choosing, as happens in the event of unpaid taxes, bankruptcy proceedings, or to satisfy a lien.

ALLEY—A narrow roadway or path providing means of access to streets and adjoining properties. A secondary access.

ALLIGATOR PROPERTY—A jargon expression referring to real estate that is difficult for an owner to retain. Excessive taxes, soaring maintenance costs, prohibitively high interest and mortgage payments, or any other onerous operating expense may be the cause.

ALLODIAL SYSTEM—A system of possession of land founded on individual ownership; a free system of ownership. Real property law in the United States is based upon this system. It is the opposite of the FEUDAL SYSTEM which places ownership of all land with the king or sovereign of a country.

ALLONGE—A separate endorsement that is attached to a promissory note, bill of exchange, or other like instrument.

ALLUVION—Nature's process of adding to land by the gradual deposit of sand, clay, silt, gravel, or soil caused by the action of flowing water. Accretion.

ALLUVIUM—A variation in the spelling of Alluvion.

ALTERATION—Modifying; changing. The act of making different. An improvement. Effecting a change without completely destroying the original, as occurs when adding a new wing to a building.

AMENITIES—The pleasure and satisfaction gained from one's surroundings. Features, both hidden and visible, that enhance and add to the desirability of real estate. Frequently used when referring to residential properties, the word embraces the personal, human aspect of livability and pride of ownership, rather than monetary considerations. (See HIDDEN AMENITIES, VISIBLE AMENITIES.)

AMORTIZE—To pay a debt in periodic amounts until the total amount, along with the interest, if any, is paid.

AMORTIZATION TABLE OR SCHEDULE—(See Page 414.)

ANCHOR LEASE—A lease given to an anchor tenant.

ANCHOR TENANT—A TRIPLE-A TENANT, such as a large department or discount store, or a nationally-known chain that forms the nucleus of a modern-day shopping center. The anchor tenant is a mainstay that draws the public and stabilizes the center by assuring a profitable operation for all the other tenants. Developers have long recognized the anchor tenant as a key to success or failure. Consequently, anchor tenants are sought out first and they are often given favorable leases.

ANCILLARY—Supplementary; auxiliary. Something that is subordinate, subservient and ministering to the main. Aiding. An ancillary easement, for example, is the necessary use of land belonging to another for the full use and enjoyment of the original easement.

ANNEX—1. To attach or join to something else that is usually larger, as when an adjoining parcel of land is added to the main tract. 2. A secondary building or one attached to the original structure.

ANNEXATION—The act of joining or uniting one thing to another.

ANNUAL—Once a year. Per annum.

ANNUITANT—A person receiving the payments from an annuity.

ANNUITY—A sum of money received yearly or at other fixed intervals. A fund set up by a grant or will for periodic distribution to one or more persons. If such a fund includes more than one recipient, it is referred to as a JOINT ANNUITY.

ANNUL—To render ineffective; to legally cancel. To void.

ANNUM—(Latin) Year.

ANTE—A prefix meaning in front of, coming prior, or before, as an anteroom, anteporch, anteportico, etc.

ANTICIPATED VALUE—Expected value. Appraisers frequently take future benefits into consideration when formulating the present worth of property. For example, in the instance of raw land ready for development, the appraiser takes into account the cost of adding improvements such as paved roads, sidewalks, utilities, promotional expenses, resulting increased taxes, etc. By adding to a profit for the developer, he then can reach a conclusion as to anticipated market value.

ANTICIPATORY REPUDIATION OR BREACH—An anticipatory breach of contract occurs when a buyer renounces a contract by informing the seller, before the closing of title, that he does not intend to complete the transaction.

APARTMENT HOTEL—A hotel in which the rooms and apartments are designed for permanent occupants, rather than for transients. Utilities, as well as telephone and maid service, are generally provided.

APARTMENT HOUSE—A building containing three or more residential units, each of which contains separate housekeeping facilities and usually certain common, mechanical conveniences, such as a central heating plant, elevator, garbage disposal, etc. Apartment buildings vary from smaller structures, which house a few families, to sprawling garden apartments, covering acres of land, or huge high-rise buildings containing hundreds of separate units.

APARTMENT HOUSE LISTING FORM—A form designed to include all pertinent details when listing apartment houses.

APARTMENT LEASE—A lease form specifically worded for use in renting apartment units.

APPARENT AUTHORITY—The authority that is believed to exist, as for example, the representations made by an agent concerning the principal's property. It is also termed *ostensible authority.*

APPARENT TITLE—(See COLOR OF TITLE.)

APPEAL—To present a case or a cause for rehearing to a higher court, a court of appeals or appellate court.

APPELLANT—A party appealing a court decision or ruling.

APPELLATE COURT—A court for hearing cases appealed from lower courts and for reviewing appeals.

APPELLEE—The party against whom an appeal is directed.

APPOINTMENTS—Furnishings, equipment or fixtures found in a home, office or other building. Accouterments or trappings. Adornments of personal property and fixtures that may enhance or detract from the property.

APPORTIONMENT—A division or partition of property into proportionate parts.

APPRAISAL—Valuation. An expert opinion of the value of the property by one qualified to make such an opinion. Setting a value on an asset. The methods which appraisers use to arrive at an appraisal can be generally classified as: (a) Cost Approach, which is estimated by the replacement value of a property; (b) Market Comparison (or Comparison Approach), comparing a piece of property with other properties and estimating what it will bring on the open market; (c) Income Approach (or Capitalization of Income), which is primarily concerned with the net return that a property will bring (See COST APPROACH TO VALUE APPRAISAL REPORT, MARKET COMPARISON, and INCOME APPROACH.)

APPRAISAL CORRELATION—(See CORRELATION)

APPRAISAL REPORT—An appraisal report can take a variety of forms ranging from a basic one or two-page letter of opinion on the appraiser's letterhead, or the more formal affidavit and certificate (used for court ordered appraisals), to a comprehensive, multi-page, bookbound document.
   The outline presented below lists the essentials one should include in preparing an appraisal document.

   A. Legal and common known description of the property.
   B. For whom the appraisal is being made.
   C. Purpose of the appraisal (Generally market value, but it can be for assessed value, insurance value, liquidation value, litigation value, leasehold value, business value, etc.).
   D. Date of valuation.
   E. Detailed description of the improvements made to the property.
   F. A general history of the property and its surroundings.
   G. Highest and best use.
   H. Comparable values.
   I. Appraisal method(s) used.

        1. Cost Approach
        2. Market Comparison
        3. Capitalization of Income

   J. Surveys, maps, photographs.
   K. Qualifications of appraiser.

APPRAISED VALUE—The worth of a property as estimated by an appraiser.

APPRAISEMENT—The act of setting the value of property. An appraisal.

APPRAISER—An individual who gives his opinoin as to the value of property; usually, a qualified professional skilled in the art of evaluating real estate.

APPRECIATION—Raising of value; increasing in worth; enhance. The opposite of DEPRECIATION.

APPROACHES TO VALUE—The methods which appraisers use to arrive at value can be classified as Cost Approach. Market comparison, Income Approach and Correlation (See APPRAISAL and CORRELATION for definitions of these methods).

APPROPRIATION—1. The taking of private property for public use, as occurs when a governmental body exercises its power of Eminent Domain. 2. Taking without authority or right, as may occur when public property such as a stream or other watercourse is appropriated by an individual. However, under certain circumstances, the law recognizes that the first person to put such appropriated property to a beneficial use has established a right to enjoy its continual benefits. 3. The act of a governmental legislative body authorizing the expenditure of a specified sum of money from its general fund for a specific project.

APPURTENANCE—That which goes with or pertains to the land, but is not necessarily a part of it. An adjunct. Examples include a right of way or an easement (See EASEMENT), as well as physical improvements such as buildings, roads, power lines, fences, etc., Appurtenances pass with the land when it is sold.

AQUATIC RIGHTS—The rights of individuals to use rivers, seas, oceans and other watercourses, as well as the land beneath the water. (See also LITTORAL RIGHTS, RIPARIAN RIGHTS.)

A PRIORI—(Latin) From what went before. A term used when an analogy is being made to deduce what logically follows. A conclusion based on what had previously transpired.

ARCADE—A thoroughfare or passageway open at both ends. It usually contains stores, restaurants, and offices accessible to pedestrians only.

ARCH—An arc-shaped or curved structure providing a passageway or opening in a wall.

Arch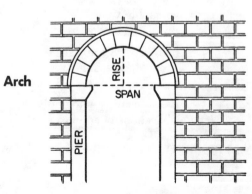

ARCHITECT—A professionally trained designer of buildings and other structures. One also qualified to supervise their construction.

ARCHITECTURE—1. The science and art of structural design. 2. The style of a building.

AREA—Locale; territory; region. General location.

ARM'S LENGTH—A term which clearly implies that a person should approach all business and real estate transactions with due caution. When two parties, each with uncommon interests, undertake an open market transaction, they should proceed with caution; and each at his own risk.

ARPENT—(French) A unit of land measure used in some French sectors of the United States and Canada, equal to approximately one acre. Though only infrequently referred to today, it can be found in early real estate documents. It is also spelled *arpen*.

ARREARS—1. The state of belatedness in paying a debt. 2. Work that is incomplete and overdue.

ARROYO—A gulley formed by a watercourse found in arid areas. A dry gulley. The bed of a stream or rivulet.

ARTICLES OF INCORPORATION—An instrument that states the basic rules and purposes of a private corporation under which it is formed. It is also called a CERTIFICATE OF INCORPORATION or CORPORATION CHARTER.

ARTICLES OF PARTNERSHIP—Provisions in a partnership agreement detailing the terms of the business arrangement.

ARTIFICIAL PERSON—A "person" created by law, and possessed of legal rights and responsibilities. A corporation, for example, is said to be an artificial body which can buy, sell, and inherit property. It is the corporation itself that assumes liabilities, and not the individual officers who comprise it.

ARTISAN—A trained, skilled craftsman. In the building trades, for example, carpenters, plasterers, electricians, plumbers, painters, tile setters, roofers, landscape gardeners, etc. are classified as artisans.

AS IS—When these words are inserted in a contract they mean that no guarantees whatsoever are given regarding the subject property. It is being purchased in exactly the condition in which it is found.

ASKING PRICE—The listed price of real estate; the price at which it is formally offered in a sale. Unlike a FIRM PRICE, the term sometimes denotes a flexible selling price; one from which negotiations can begin.

ASSEMBLING LAND—The combining of adjoining of nearby properties into one tract. Also called PLOTTAGE.

ASSESSED VALUE—An amount assigned to property by an assessor or government board for taxation and other purposes. The value which a property carries on the tax rolls, it usually represents a percentage of the market value of the property.

ASSESSMENT—1. The act of evaluating a property for the purpose of levying property tax. 2. A charge levied against property in the form of a tax. (See SPECIAL ASSESSMENT.)

ASSESSOR—A community official whose duty is to evaluate real estate for the purpose of levying property tax.

ASSET—Something of value owned by a person. A useful item of property.

ASSIGNABILITY—The ability of property to be transferred to another. The state of being assignable.

ASSIGNEE—A person to whom an assignment is made or to whom a property, right, or interest is transferred.

ASSIGNMENT—The transfer of title or interest in writing from one person or group of people to another.

ASSIGNMENT OF CHATTEL MORTGAGE—The transfer of a chattel mortgage from one person to another.

ASSIGNMENT OF CONTRACT—The transfer of a contract from one party to another.

ASSIGNMENT OF LEASE—This type of assignment occurs when a tenant transfers all his interest in a leasehold to another. This distinguishes it from a SUB-LEASE in which some portion of the lease is retained.

ASSIGNMENT OF MORTGAGE—Transfer of a mortgage from one to another.

ASSIGN(S)—The person (or persons) who receives what is assigned.

ASSOCIATE—A person working in conjunction with another in a business or profession. A colleague; partner.

ASSOCIATE BROKER—A broker working in the same office and in conjunction with one or more other brokers.

ASSUME—To take upon oneself. Undertake responsibility.

ASSUMING MORTGAGE—(See ASSUMPTION OF MORTGAGE.)

ASSUMPSIT—(Latin) 1. Legal action to recover damages for failure to perform an oral contract. 2. An understanding, whether expressed or implied, to perform an agreement that is not in writing.

ASSUMPTION OF MORTGAGE—Taking title to property that has an existing mortgage, and being personally liable for its payments. (See SALE OF MORTGAGED PROPERTY.)

AT PAR—At an average. (See PAR.)

ATRIUM—An open patio, around which a house or other structure is built. This area is sometimes enclosed by a roof of glass or other translucent material providing a greenhouse effect for plants and trees.

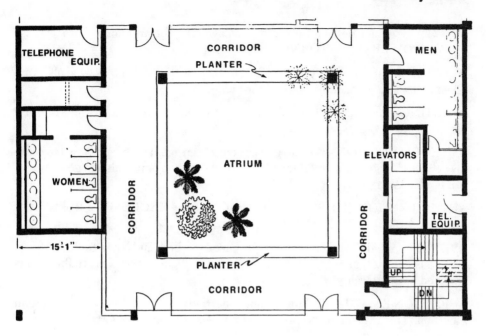

ATTACHMENT—The taking of a debtor's property into legal custody. This usually occurs when a person lives in another part of the country and his property is within the jurisdiction of a specified court. Property may also be attached if it is feared that a person is anticipating leaving an area to avoid payment or responsibility for an obligation.

ATTEST—To be a witness. To certify.

ATTESTATION—(See SUBSCRIBING WITNESS.)

ATTESTING WITNESS—A witness to the signing of any legal instrument.

ATTIC—An upper floor of a home or other structure, located between the ceiling and the roof.

ATOLL—The name given to a coral island consisting of a series of reefs surrounding a lagoon. The term originated in the Maldive Islands of the Indian Ocean, but is in use in describing similar reef formations in the South Pacific Ocean and elsewhere.

ATTORNEY—(See below.)

ATTORNEY AT LAW—A qualified, licensed legal agent. A person who graduates from an accredited law school and practices law in the state in which he was admitted to the bar. A professional member of the bar who may legally represent others. A lawyer. A councilor. In England he is also referred to as a solicitor or barrister.

ATTORNEY IN FACT—One who has the written authority of another to act in his place. This authority is limited by the extent of the written instrument appointing him. One need not be an attorney at law (lawyer) to be an attorney in fact. Also called a POWER OF ATTORNEY.

AUCTION—A specialized form of selling land or chattel, whereby verbal offers are taken and a sale is made to the highest bidder.

AUDITING—An examination and verification of the records of a business or other organization.

AUTHORITY OF AGENT—The power given to an agent by his principal to act in his behalf. The agent's lawful right to act. The delegation or permission given by the principal to an agent.

AUTHORIZATION TO SELL CONTRACT—(See EXCLUSIVE RIGHT OF SALE and EXCLUSIVE AGENCY.)

AVENUE—A dedicated roadway usually paved, curbed, and having sidewalks. An avenue is generally narrower than a boulevard or highway, has less traffic, and is confined to one locality.

AVIGATION EASEMENT—An easement permitting aircraft to fly below a certain elevation. This is common to properties bordering or near airports.

AVULSION—A noticeable shifting of land area from one property to another caused by floods, currents or other movements of a body of water. For example, when a river changes its course.

B

BACKFILL—Returning moved earth to the proximity from which it was taken; as when a builder levels the ground for a foundation and then returns the soil in order to properly grade the area or help support foundation walls.

BACK LAND—Land located back from a roadway or water course. Land that is not easily accessible. Remote, unimproved realty.

BACKWOODS—Sparsely populated, remote area. Back country, rural woodland. In common parlance, the "sticks," or "Boondocks."

BAD FAITH—The willful failure to live up to one's contractual obligations. A breach of faith. The lack of honesty in dealing with another.

BADLANDS—Wastelands. Desolate tracts in remote areas, unsuitable for any known, useful purpose.

BAD TITLE—A defective title. A title that, because of its faults, a purchaser need not lawfully be made to accept. Unmarketable title that does not convey property.

BAILMENT—In law, according to Blackstone, it is the delivery in trust of a contract, expressed or implied, that the trust shall be faithfully executed. Personal property delivered in trust for the fulfilment of an agreement.

BAIL-OUT—A colloquial expression meaning a hasty exit from a property in serious financial or other problems. The term graphically describes the abandoning of a project in "mid-air," with the outgoing party salvaging whatever possible before the impending crash.

BALANCE SHEET—A statement of the financial condition of a business at a certain time, showing assets, liabilities, and capital. A summation of all accounts.

BALLOON LAND—Land lacking frontage on a public road.

BALLOON MORTGAGE—A mortgage that provides for periodic payments which do not completely amortize the loan at the time of its termination. As a consequence, a larger final payment becomes due. Some states require that a balloon mortgage be clearly identified as such on the mortgage instrument in order for it to be valid. Florida statutes, for example, make the following wording mandatory:

"This is a balloon mortgage and the final payment of the balance due upon maturity is $——— together with accrued interest, if any, and all advancement made by the mortgagee under the terms of this mortgage."

BALTIMORE METHOD—A formula for appraising corner lots in which the corner lot is calculated to be worth the total of the inside lots on each side of it. (See CORNER LOT APPRAISAL METHODS.)

BALUSTRADE—Upright supports, usually uniform and decorative, held together by horizontal members to form a railing.

Balustrade

BANK—1. A commercial establishment whose main purposes are: (a) to hold money in safekeeping and pay interest to the depositor for the privilege of doing so; (b) to lend money and receive a higher rate of interest in return, and (c) to exchange money, extend credit, and assist individuals and companies in transmitting funds. 2. Ground bordering a watercourse.

BANK COMMITMENT—(See COMMITMENT.)

BANKRUPT—When liabilities of an individual or a company exceed assets. One adjudged by a court of law to be insolvent. A person unable to meet his financial obligations.

BARE POWER—(See NAKED POWER.)

BARGAIN—1. A mutual agreement between parties setting forth what is to be given and received. To agree; come to terms. 2. To negotiate. Haggle.

BARGAIN AND SALE DEED—A deed in which the seller, for a valuable consideration, "grants, bargains, and sells" specific property to a purchaser. The purchaser receives possession "unto himself and his heirs in fee simple forever." A bargain and sale deed can be with or without covenants against grantor's acts. A deed with covenants assures the purchaser that the grantor has not done or caused to be done anything to encumber the property. Typical wording for this provision is the following: "And the party of the first part covenants that the party of the first part has not done or suffered anything whereby the said premises have been encumbered in any way whatever, except as aforesaid."

BARGAINING—Negotiating. The give and take between buyer and seller before a transaction is made. Each party tries to obtain the best price and terms possible.

BARGEBOARD—The trim at the end of a gabled roof. The bargeboard, sometimes ornamental, serves to cover the timbers that extend over gables. Also referred to as a frieze.

BARN—The building used on a farm to store grain, hay, produce and equipment and to provide shelter for animals. A stable.

BARONY OF LAND—A British term meaning 15 acres.

BARTER—To trade or exchange without the use of money. (See EXCHANGE OF REAL ESTATE.)

BASE—Foundation. The bottom of something that is being supported. The lower portion of a wall, column, pier or other architecural design.

BASEBOARD—A moulding strip situated lengthwise at the base of a wall where it meets the floor.

BASE LINES—Lines running east and west from which township lines are established in GOVERNMENT SURVEY legal descriptions. Base lines are at right angles to meridian lines.

BASEMENT—The level of a building that is wholly or partially below ground. A cellar.

BASIS—1. That which something else is established upon. Foundation. The bottom of something used as support. 2. The amount left after taking depreciation.

BAY WINDOW—A window projecting beyond the main surface of a wall.

BEACH—The portion of a coastline consisting of sand or pebbles. The area located between high and low tides.

BEAM RIGHT AGREEMENT—An agreement for the use of the wall of an existing building, usually as support for the beams of a new building, thus creating a common or party wall. By so doing, material, space, and labor can be saved.

BEARER PAPER—Negotiable commercial paper, such as a draft, check, note, etc. that is payable upon delivery to anyone. The instrument does not state a specific party. It is usually made out "Payable to Bearer."

BEARING WALL—A supporting wall. A wall that helps carry the weight of the structure itself. One that supports the beams.

BEDROOM SUBURB—An area, located within commuting distance of a large city, that functions primarily as a residential community. Also called a Dormitory City.

BENCH MARK—A mark, made at a known elevation point, from which other elevations in a topographical survey are calculated.

BENEFICIAL INTEREST—The beneficiary's interest in property as opposed to the trustee who holds title. A beneficial interest is created when the legal title is held by one party who acts on behalf of another. The one holding the legal interest is the trustee. The recipient of the profits or advantage is the beneficiary.

BENEFICIARY—A party designated in a will, trust, insurance policy, etc. to receive certain proceeds or benefits. One for whom a trust is created.

BEQUEATH—To leave by will.

BEQUEST—Personal property that is given to another by will.

BERNARD RULE—A rule of thumb for appraising a corner lot. The method is simply to appraise the property first as if it were an inside lot fronting on a side street, and then take it as an inside lot fronting on the main street. The total of the two appraisal figures is the value placed on the corner lot. (See CORNER LOT APPRAISAL METHODS.)

BEST AND HIGHEST USE—(See HIGHEST AND BEST USE.)

BETTERMENT—An improvement made to property or its surroundings that enhances the market value, as distinguished from repairs and preventive maintenance. The improvement may be in the form of an additional structure or may actually occur off the property, as when streets, sidewalks, drainage, retaining walls, or utilities are provided. The value of the betterment is calculated in its overall effect and not in its cost.

BID—1. An offer of a specified amount to purchase property. 2. In the construction field, builders compete with one another by submitting estimates, often sealed, for the awarding of a construction contract. It is the price offered in competitive bidding.

BILATERAL CONTRACT—A term used to indicate that both principals have mutually agreed upon and have fully executed a contract, and are bound to fulfill its terms and conditions.

BI-LEVEL HOUSE—Any two-story dwelling.

BILL OF CERTIORARI—(See CERTIORARI.)

BILL OF INTERPLEADER—(See INTERPLEADER.)

BILL OF SALE—An instrument used in a real estate transaction when items other than real property are included in a sale. Furniture, fixtures, appliances, merchandise, motor vehicles and similar items of personalty are found in a bill of sale. The instrument certifies that ownership has been transferred.

BINDER—1. A preliminary agreement in writing, with a valuable consideration given, as evidence of good faith by the offerer. It is an offer to purchase; a unilateral contract. Upon acceptance, it becomes a bilateral contract. Though it contains all the elements of a valid contract, in some areas it is considered to be temporary in nature until a more formal contract can be drawn. (See page 286). 2. A written instrument giving immediate insurance coverage until a regular policy can be issued.

BINDING—Creating or imposing an obligation.

BIRD DOG—An expression referring to a salesman whose sole function is to "flush out" prospects or listings. Once he has obtained a good lead, he turns everything over to his broker, or to another salesman who is more experienced in transacting real estate.

BLACK ACRE AND WHITE ACRE—A generally outmoded means of distinguishing one acre (or other size parcel) of land from another. The purpose is to name the parcel rather than having to recite an entire legal description. It is not unlike today's commonly used reference to "Parcel A" and "Parcel B."

BLANKET INSURANCE—Insurance coverage for more than one type of risk.

BLANKET MORTGAGE—A mortgage covering two or more pieces of property.

BLIGHTED AREA—A neighborhood that has deteriorated in value. One that is nearing slum conditions.

BLOCK—A parcel of land enclosed by streets.

BLOCK BUSTING—The highly unethical real estate practice of creating fear and unrest by moving one or more families of another race or creed into a neighborhood, then exploiting the situaiton by urging residents to sell their homes at deflated prices.

BLUE LAWS—Religious laws passed down from Colonial days restricting the transaction of business on Sundays and certain holidays.

BLUEPRINT—A detailed architectural drawing, plan or map referred to in construction work and real estate, as well as in other fields. It is a permanent, economical, and efficient photographic reproduction process.

BLUE SKY LAWS—Laws designed to regulate companies for the protection of the public. Fly-by-night firms selling securities, land, gold mines, etc. are prevented by these laws from making wild and fraudulent claims.

BOARDING HOUSE—A house that furnishes meals and, usually, lodging to the public.

BOG—Wetland. A moist, spongy swamp.

BOILER-ROOM OPERATION—Unethical and, often, illegal, high-pressure tactics that generally begin with an unsolicited telephone sales pitch. Continual pressure is put on the prospect to buy. Though the term is usually associated with the selling of questionable stocks, it has been carried over into real estate by way of land sale companies that maintain telephone crews to create leads.

BOMB—A derogatory, common expression for a poorly-built structure, or otherwise, faulty parcel of real estate. Any real property that is difficult to sell.

BOARD AND BATTEN—A building technique used for sidings consisting of wide boards protected at the seams by narrow battens.

BOARD OF APPEALS—Known also as Board of Tax Review or Board of Equalization, its quasi-judicial function is to evaluate and adjust real estate assessments and to hear property owners' complaints of tax inequities. The Board's goal is to achieve fair taxation throughout the jurisdiction it serves.

BOARD OF DIRECTORS—The governing members of a corporation or organization.

BOARD OF EQUALIZATION—(See BOARD OF APPEALS.)

BONA FIDE—Made with sincere, good intentions. Honestly and openly done. Without fraud, as when an authentic offer is tended as a show of good faith.

BOND—1. An instrument used as evidence of a debt. It is secured by a mortgage, or other lien, on real estate. 2. An interest-bearing certificate guaranteeing to pay a specified sum of money at a designated time in the future. Bonds are usually issued by corporations or by the government, but they also may be from individuals. 3. A sum of money posted as a guarantee.

BOND AND MORTGAGE—A bond is written evidence of a debt. A mortgage is the pledge of security for the payment of a debt. These legal instruments are sometimes combined into one form.

BOND FOR DEED—The same as CONTRACT FOR DEED. (See that title.)

BONUS—An extra premium or commission. What is given in addition to what is strictly due or expected. A reward for proficiency over and above the basic compensation.

BOOK COST—The value at which an asset is carried on a firm's ledger. All matters pertaining to the acquisition of the asset are totaled, including development costs and mortgage expenses.

BOOK DEPRECIATION—The amount that can be deducted for depreciation purposes from the cost of an asset on the accounting books of the owner of a business. Book depreciation, of particular importance in computing income tax, has no relationship with depreciation as used in appraising.

BOOK VALUE—The amount of an asset as carried on the records of a company, and not necessarily what it could bring in the open market. Book value is computed by the cost of the asset plus additions and improvements, minus accrued depreciation.

BOOM—A sudden increase in activity, value and growth of real estate. A period of great prosperity.

BOONDOCKS—A common term for remote, outlying areas offering few, if any, advantages. Also called *boonies* or *the sticks*.

BOOT—A term used in the exchange of realty when the properties being traded are not exactly equal. Cash, other properties, or services are included in order to bring the transaction to par. That which is given *in addition* is referred to as being "to boot." It serves to compensate for any difference in value.

BORDER—Outer edge or boundary. The perimeter of property. To adjoin.

BORING TEST—A means of studying the contents of the earth below the surface by taking core samples.

BOROUGH—A locally governed area having a charter and similar to an incorporated village, town, or municipality. A land division of a city, such as the five boroughs that divide the city of New York.

BORROWER—A person who receives a fund or something of value with the expressed or implied intention of repayment.

BOTEL—A structure at or near a marina with facilities for room and food accommodations catering to boat travelers.

BOTTOM LAND—1. Lowland situated in a valley, dale, or near a river or creed. 2. Land that is intermittently underwater, such as a tideland, sandbar, or riverbed.

BOTTOM LAND—1. Lowland situated in a valley, dale, or near a river or creek. operating expenses are calculated. It is a reference to the last line of a financial statement.

BOUNDARY—The limit or extent of a parcel of land. Border.

BOUNDARY RIGHTS—The rights or interest one possesses concerning the borders of his property.

BOUNDS—1. The limits of property lines. Boundaries; enclosures; borders. 2. As in the METES AND BOUNDS legal description, the word refers to direction. It is a method of describing property through terminal points and angles. (See METES AND BOUNDS.)

BOUNTY LANDS—A generally obsolete term referring to public lands given to individuals for rendering a service to their country.

BRANCH OFFICE—An additional office for conducting business, as distinguished from the main, or home office.

BREACH OF CONTRACT—Not living up to the terms and conditions of a contract; refusal to carry out the provisions therein. Failure to perform without legal justification. (See ANTICIPATORY REPUDIATION OR BREACH.)

BREACH OF TRUST—A failure on the part of a trustee to properly protect or perform regarding that with which he was entrusted. The breach may be willful, fraudulent or merely through an oversight.

BREEZEWAY—A partially enclosed area connecting garage and house.

Breezeway

BRIDGING—A cross-bracing used as added support for beams, joists, floors, ceilings, etc.

Bridging

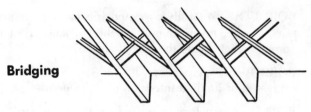

BRIEF—A summarized, written statement. A condensation of a more complete document.

BRIEF OF TITLE—The summary of all documents (liens, encumbrances, satisfactions, conveyances, etc.) affecting a particular piece of real property.

BRITISH THERMAL UNIT (B.T.U.)—A unit of measure used to gauge the effectiveness of heating and air conditioning systems. It is the amount of heat needed to be generated to raise the temperature of one pound of water one degree Fahrenheit at approximately 39.2°F.

BROKER—A licensed person who, for compensation, acts as an intermediary in real estate transactions. An agent.

BROKER AND SALESMAN CONTRACT—A written instrument between a broker and his salesman outlining their obligations and duties to one another.

BROKERAGE—1. The business of a broker. 2. The amount charged for a broker's service.

B.T.U.—(See BRITISH THERMAL UNIT.)

BUDGET LOAN—A mortgage loan that provides, in each periodic payment, for a proportionate amount of tax, insurance, and assessment to be held in escrow, along with the principal and interest payment.

BUFFER ZONE—1. A strip of ground separating two parcels of land. 2. An area between two different land uses.

BUILDABLE AREA—The actual footage of a property that can be built upon, after deducting front, rear, and side setback regulations, parking requirements, height restrictions, etc.

BUILDER—One who constructs. A person who undertakes the erection and supervision of construction of a building.

BUILDER'S ACRE; BUILDER'S HALF ACRE—An exaggerated, promotional term used by builders to describe property that is something less than stated. For example, it is common practice for a builder to subdivide a 50-acre tract into 100 homesites, proclaiming that each home is on a builder's half acre. The actual land sold with each house is substantially less as some of it is utilized for roads, sidewalks and drainage basins. Because it is misleading, ethical-minded building industry spokesmen and many communities are discouraging this inaccurate form of promotion.

BUILD FOR LEASE—A building erected to the specifications of a particular tenant who agrees to lease the premises when completed.

BUILDING—Any enclosed structure used for shelter, commercial purpose, or storage, such as a house, barn, store, warehouse, shed, factory, office building, apartment house, etc.

BUILDING AND LOAN ASSOCIATION—An incorporated, mutual organization with the prime purpose of investing a member's funds in residential mortgages and repaying him in the form of stocks or periodic dividends. (See FEDERAL SAVINGS AND LOAN ASSOCIATION.)

BUILDING AREA—The actual area occupied by the building. (See BUILDABLE AREA.)

BUILDING CODE—A standard of construction rules and regulations which must be conformed to before a structure can be completed. (See also NATIONAL BUILDING CODE, UNIFORM BUILDING CODE.)

BUILDING LEASE—1. A lease agreement for the occupancy of a building. 2. A lease for the ground upon which a building is situated. (See GROUND RENT.)

BUILDING LIEN—A builder's charge or encumbrance upon property.

BUILDING LINE—An established line, parallel to the front lot line, within which a building must be constructed. The rear, and side, yard lines, as well as the height of a structure, must also conform to ordinance regulations before all dimensional requirements of a building are met.

BUILDING LOAN—A loan given to a builder generally for the duration of construction of a building. Most building loans provide for periodic payment to the builder as each phase of construction is completed. A building loan precedes a permanent mortgage that is given when the building is completed. Also called an interim loan. Some instruments used in conjunction with building loans are: Building Loan Bond, Building Loan Mortgage, Building Loan Mortgage Note. (See Portfolio of Forms.)

BUILDING MAINTENANCE—(See MAINTENANCE; PREVENTIVE MAINTENANCE.)

BUILDING PERMIT—1. A written form by the proper government agency allowing construction work to proceed according to the plans and specifications submitted with an application. 2. A permit granting the right to build or make alterations upon property.

BUILDING RESTRICTIONS—Zoning, regulatory requirements, or clauses in a deed limiting the type and size of a building.

BUILDING SITE—The land on which a building can or will be erected.

BUILD UP—Periodic increases. To develop by increments. In mortgage parlance, for example, an *equity build up* is the principal payment of a loan which gradually lessens the indebtedness and increases the mortgagor's equity.

BUILT-INS—Certain stationary equipment, such as kitchen appliances, wall-oven, counter-top range garbage disposal, dishwasher;, book case, furniture, wall safe, etc. Something permanently affixed to a house and understood to be included with it when sold. Also, a garage that is under the same roof as the structure it serves.

House with

Built-In Garage

BULKHEAD—A wall erected to retain water or soil. A seawall.

BULK ZONING—Zoning that regulates the number of buildings and their size, shape, and location within an area. By so doing, the physical characteristics and the overall density of population of a neighborhood can be controlled.

BUNDLE OF RIGHTS—All the legal rights that go with ownership of property. The rights to sell, lease, mine, build, mortgage, improve, will to another, etc. that one possesses with ownership of real estate. Rights within the framework of the law to control one's property.

BUNGALOW—A small, one, or one-and-a-half story dwelling.

BUREAU OF LAND MANAGEMENT—A federal bureau within the Department of Interior that has charge of the management, sale surveying, and leasing of government-owned land; also, the execution of all actions relating to these lands. This bureau was formerly known as the GENERAL LAND OFFICE.

BURN-OFF—A common expression used when someone ceases to make payments on an installment sales contract, and the sale is "burned-off," or terminated. The property reverts to the deedholder.

BUSINESS CHANCE—(See BUSINESS OPPORTUNITIES.)

BUSINESS BUILDINGS—A generalized term meaning commercial buildings of every description, including retail stores, gas stations, office buildings, professional buildings, garages, warehouses, restaurants, theaters, and others.

BUSINESS CERTIFICATE—A certificate of registration required by certain states when doing business under an assumed name.

BUSINESS DISTRICT—An area zoned for a commercial purpose.

BUSINESS LEASE—A lease specifically designed for the renting of business property.

BUSINESS OPPORTUNITIES—As applied to real estate, this term has come to mean businesses of every description that are for sale.

BUSINESS PROPERTY—(See COMMERCIAL PROPERTY.)

BUSINESS PROPERTY LISTING FORM—A form designed to cover pertinent details when listing commercial properties.

BUSINESS TRUST—An unincorporated business association in which title to property is given to trustees to hold, manage, or sell. It is similar to the usual corporate organization in that a transferable certificate is issued to a shareholder, but unlike a corporation, the trustees must be principals and hold office in the trust on a permanent basis. In real estate, this type of business structure is sometimes used when a tract of land is subdivided, improved, and sold. It is also referred to as a MASSACHUSETTS TRUST or COMMON LAW TRUST.

BUTTERFLY ROOF—A roof style that is concave in the middle with outer sides higher at the eaves. An inverted gable roof design. Also referred to as a double-pitch roof.

BUTT LOT—(See KEY LOT.)

BUTTS AND BONDS—In legal descriptions of land, it is length and direction of property lines. It means the same as METES AND BOUNDS. (See that definition.)

BUYER—A purchaser. One who buys.

BUYERS' MARKET—A business condition in which the type of property for sale is plentiful. Consequently, sellers are forced to lower their prices and make concessions in their terms in order to make a sale.

BY-BIDDING—Fictitious bidding at an auction by a "shill." The one making the by-bid has no intention of purchasing. This fraudulent practice is used to spur the bidding. He is also referred to as a "puffer," "decoy," or "sham bidder."

BY-LAWS—Rules and regulations of corporations or other organized bodies for conducting their activities. Private statutes for governing and managing the affairs of an association.

C

CALL—1. In property law, a natural landmark used in legal descriptions. 2. A banking term meaning loaned money that is payable on demand.

CANAL—An artificial waterway used for navigation, irrigation, water power, drainage, logging, flood control, etc.

CANCELLATION CLAUSE—A provision written into some contracts and leases giving one or both of the parties the right to cancel the agreement in the event of a specified occurrence. (Also see RELEASE CLAUSE and TRANSFER CLAUSE.)

CANONS OF ETHICS—(See CODE OF ETHICS.)

CANTILEVER—An overhanging portion extending past its support. A projecting surface secured or fastened at one end.

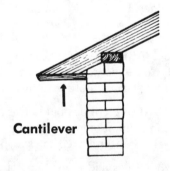

Cantilever

CAP—The highest point of a building. (Also see CHIMNEY CAP; TOPPING-OFF.)

CAPACITY—1. In the legal sense, one's qualifications, power and fitness to enter into agreements, such as being competent, of sound mind, over age 21, etc. 2. Ability. Potentiality.

CAPE COD HOUSE—A popular style of architecture used in moderate-priced house building. A simple, rectangular design with peaked roof, it offers economy and efficiency in construction.

Cape Cod

CAPITAL—1. Pertaining to wealth. Money or accumulated assets, such as goods, stocks, bonds, equipment or other valuable material used in business. 2. In construction terminology, the top part of a column, frequently ornamental.

CAPITAL GAIN—1. Profit gained from the sale of a capital asset in excess of its cost or appraised value. The amount of the selling price above the acquisition cost. 2. Appreciation in value over a period of time on money invested in an asset.

CAPITALIZATION METHOD—A means of appraising real property arrived at by deducting the estimated normal expenses from the amount of income the property should bring. The resulting calculated net profit does not necessarily represent the actual figures of the property.

CAPITALIZE—1. To provide with cash; to furnish capital. 2. To establish the value of an asset.

CAPITALIZATION RATE—The rate of return, expressed in percentage, that is considered a reasonable profit one should expect for his investment. It is used by investors and appraisers in establishing commercial real estate values.

CAP RATE—Abbreviation for CAPITALIZATION RATE.

CARPORT—A partially enclosed area used as a shelter for a car.

Carport

CARRYOVER CLAUSE—The clause, found in an exclusive listing, that protects the broker for a specified time (beyond the expiration date of the listing). By this clause a broker would still be considered the procuring cause of a transaction, if someone, who was shown the property when the exclusive listing was in force, later should decide to purchase.

CARTEL—A group of business enterprises that controls the market by limiting production, pooling techniques, setting prices, and otherwise limiting or eliminating competition. The word implies a monopoly that is international in scope.

CASH—Currency. Ready, liquid funds. Negotiable instruments that can be promptly converted into usable money. That which is accepted as legal tender.

CASH FLOW—The net income. The usable cash after all expenses are paid.

CASH ON THE BARREL HEAD—A common expression meaning money that is put up immediately, such as a complete cash payment or a deposit.

CASH ON THE LINE—(See CASH ON THE BARREL HEAD.)

CASH TENANT—Any tenant who pays his rent in advance with money or its equivalent.

CASH VALUE—The actual money that an asset will bring on the open market without a lengthy delay. The preferred term is MARKET VALUE.

CASUALTY INSURANCE—Coverage for loss from known damages. An ACT OF GOD, such as a hurricane, earthquake, flood, lightning, or windstorm, is covered by casualty insurance, as are fire, theft, sonic boom, etc.

CAUSE—To bring about an effect or result. Make happen. A broker is said to be the PROCURING CAUSE of a transaction when he produces a ready, willing and able buyer upon acceptable terms and conditions.

CAVEAT—(Latin) Let him beware. A warning to be on the alert. Act cautiously against misrepresentation.

CAVEAT ACTOR—(Latin) Let the one who acts beware.

CAVEAT EMPTOR—(Latin) Let the buyer beware. Under the throry of this legal maxim, the buyer is expected to judge and evaluate property carefully before purchasing. As long as there is no misrepresentation, a person buys at his own risk.

CAVEAT VENDOR—(Latin) Let the seller beware.

CBS—An abbreviation meaning a building made of concrete, block, and stucco.

CEDE—Assign. Transfer. To grant, typically by treaty.

CEILING PRICE—1. The highest price obtainable in the current market. 2. When referring to rentals, it means the highest price that a landlord can charge, or in the case of a tenant, the maximum that he will pay.

CEMETERY LOT—A small plot used as a burial ground. The purchaser of a cemetery lot may, or may not, have title to it. Usually he possesses only an easement rather than absolute ownership. He may visit, care for, or place a monument or headstone upon the site, but if it is abandoned, the rights to it can be forfeited.

CENTERING—A builder's term meaning the framing of an arched structure during its erection.

CENTRAL BUSINESS DISTRICT—The concentrated area of a city or town containing some of the following: Financial district, governmental area, professional center and a concentration of retail stores. It is frequently referred to as the downtown district.

CERTIFICATE—A document certifying or attesting to something. An award for successfully completing certain requirements permitting the recipient to participate in a specialized field, skill, or profession. A license.

CERTIFICATE LANDS—Lands in western Pennsylvania that were first obtained from the government by redeeming certificates. The certificates were given to Revolutionary Army soldiers from that state in lieu of cash.

CERTIFICATE OF ELIGIBILITY—A certificate issued by the government bearing evidence of an individual's eligibility for a VETERANS ADMINISTRATION (G.I.) loan. To obtain this certificate a veteran must submit his discharge papers along with a statement that he intends to occupy the property he is purchasing as his residence.

CERTIFICATE OF EQUITABLE OWNERSHIP—(See LAND TRUST CERTIFICATE.)

CERTIFICATE OF NO DEFENSE—An estoppel certificate signed by the borrower, when the mortgage is sold or assigned, that states the full mortgage indebtedness. (See ESTOPPEL CERTIFICATE OR LETTER.)

CERTIFICATE OF OCCUPANCY—A certificate or permit issued by a building department verifying that all work on the project complies with local zoning ordinances and is completed (or so nearly completed) that people may occupy it. Also referred to as a COMPLETION ORDER. Abbreviated as C. O.

CERTIFICATE OF PARTICIPATION—(See LAND TRUST CERTIFICATE.)

CERTIFICATE OF REDUCTION OF MORTGAGE—(See ESTOPPEL CERTIFICATE (OR LETTER.)

CERTIFICATE OF RELEASE—A certificate signed by the lender indicating that a mortgage has been paid and its indebtedness fully satisfied.

CERTIFICATE OF TITLE—In real estate, a certification issued by a title company or an opinion rendered by an attorney that the seller has good, marketable and/or insurable title to the property. If a title company has issued such a certificate and a defect in the title is later found, the title company will cure the defect or indemnify the title holder.

CERTIFIED CHECK—A check guaranteed to be good by the bank that it is drawn on. It is immediately debited against the drawer's account and the bank will honor it upon presentation.

CERTIFIED PUBLIC ACCOUNTANT (CPA)—A person holding a state certificate to practice and be recognized as a *certified* accountant. It is issued only after a candidate has met educational requirements, passed a qualifying examination, and demonstrated through experience his professional knowledge and ability. (See also PUBLIC ACCOUNTANT.)

CERTIFY—To declare something as being true or correct. To guarantee, assure or attest to. Confirm.

CERTIORARI—(Latin) The proceedings of a higher court reviewing actions of a lower one or those of a board (such as a real estate commission or industrial commission) acting in its judicial capacity.

CESSION DEED—This form of deed is used to convey street rights of privately owned property to a municipality.

CESSPOOL—An underground, porous pit used to catch and temporarily contain sewage and refuse, where it decomposes and leaches into the soil. (See also SEPTIC TANK.)

CESTUI QUE TRUST—(Latin) An estate's beneficiary who is acting as trustee, even though title is vested in another.

CHAIN—A lineal measurement equal to 66 feet. A chain is divided into 100 links of 7.92 inches each. Sometimes referred to as Gunther's Chain, it is a unit of length for surveys of U.S. public lands.

CHAIN OF TITLE—The history of ownership, conveyances and encumbrances, both recorded and unrecorded, that have affected the title of a specific parcel of land. (See ABSTRACT: ABSTRACT OF TITLE.)

CHALET—A house style originating in the Swiss Alps and found principally in mountainous areas. Its design prominently features large, overhanging eaves that offer protection from heavy winter snows.

Chalet

CHANCERY—The law of equity. (See EQUITY.)

CHARTER—A written instrument of authority that serves as evidence of a franchise, grant or right.

CHATTEL—Personal property. Tangible property other than real estate. Furniture, automobiles, goods, leases, money, livestock, etc. are chattels. Chattels are classified as either personal or real: Chattels *personal* include property that can be transported (jewelry, domestic animals, merchandise); Chattels *real* are any possessory interest in real property (leases, estates for life, for years, at will, etc.).

CHATTEL MORTGAGE—A mortgage encumbering personal property.

CHECKS—1. Written instruments used to authorize banks to pay money. 2. In GOVERNMENT SURVEY legal description, squares of land 24 miles by 24 miles are also referred to as "checks."

CHECK KITING—(See KITING.)

CHIMNEY CAP—A layer of concrete or other finishing material used to secure a chimney in place. This is generally the highest point of construction. (See page 412.)

CIRCUIT COURT—A court of law whose jurisdiction extends over several counties or districts.

CITY—An urban, populated area. A self-governed municipality usually larger in population and size than a town, village or hamlet.

CITY PLANNING—A city government's plans for the future development of the community.

CITY REAL ESTATE—1. Land located within the limits of a city. Urban property. 2. Real estate owned and in use by the municipal government.

CIVIL LAW—National, state and municipal laws concerned with the rights of the individual, as distinguished from criminal law.

CIVIL RIGHTS—The basic rights of freedom and liberty guaranteed every United States citizen by the Thirteenth and Fourteenth Amendments to the Constitution.

CIVIL WRONG—(See TORT.)

CLAIM OF LIEN—A legal claim for payment, made by one who performed labor, services or furnished material. A MECHANIC'S LIEN.

CLAIM OF TITLE—(See COLOR OF TITLE.)

CLASSIFIED PROPERTY TAX—The classification of properties by ownership and usage for the purpose of setting variable levels of assessment with respect to market value and tax rates. A tax of property according to its zoning classification (industrial, agricultural, residential, etc.) and value.

CLEAR ANNUAL INCOME—The annual income remaining from a property after all fixed and operating expenses are paid.

CLEAR MARKET PRICE—The fair and equitable market price.

CLEAR MARKET VALUE—(See MARKET VALUE.)

CLEAR TITLE—Good title. Marketable title. Title to property of which an owner can be assured of quiet enjoyment. Merchantable title. One that is free from incumbrances.

CLEARING TITLE—The process of checking the recorded and unrecorded instruments affecting a property and taking the necessary action to clear any defects, in order that it may become good, marketable or insurable. The act of curing or removing a "cloud" from the title.

CLERESTORY—Derived from the words *clear story*, it refers to an outside wall of a structure, containing windows, that rises above the roof line.

CLERK OF THE COUNTY COURT—Throughout most areas of the country, the Clerk of the County Court is the officer who records legal instruments (deeds, mortgages, contracts, etc.) concerning title transfers and other legal matters.

CLIENT—The person who employs a broker, lawyer, appraiser, etc. and is responsible for payment of their commissions or fees. In reference to a real estate broker, the client can be either the buyer, the seller or both. (As a matter of actual application, it is the seller who most often employs the broker.)

CLOSE—To complete a transaction; when real estate formally changes ownership. A settlement. However, in some areas of the country, "close" means the *agreement* to do so, which occurs when the contract is made and there is a meeting of minds, the actual change in ownership following at a later date. (In Boston and vicinity, the change in real estate ownership is called a "passing.")

CLOSED-END MORTGAGE—A mortgage that has no provisions for increasing the balance. This is the opposite of an OPEN-END MORTGAGE which permits the mortgagor to continue borrowing from it, in amounts up to the original sum.

CLOSED MORTGAGE—A mortgage that cannot be paid off until maturity.

CLOSER—A person having the responsibility of getting the contract signed and the transaction consummated. The one whose job is to successfully complete a sale; the one who closes the deal.

CLOSING—(See CLOSE.)

CLOSING COSTS—The numerous expenses buyers and sellers normally incur in the transfer of ownership of real estate. See typical list below:

Buyer's Expenses at Closing	*Seller's Expenses at Closing*
State Stamps on Notes	Abstracting
Recording Deed & Mortgage	State Stamps on Deed
Escrow Fees	Real Estate Commission
Attorney's Fee	Recording Mortgages
Title Insurance	Survey Charge
Appraisal & Inspection Fees	Escrow Fee
Survey Charge	Attorney's Fee

CLOSING STATEMENT—A detailed financial account of all the credits and debits that the buyer and seller receive when completing a real estate transaction.

CLOSING TITLE—The formal exchange of legal documents and money when real estate is transferred from one owner to another.

CLOUD ON TITLE—A claim, encumbrance or apparent defect that impairs the title to real property. Any evidence appearing in the abstract which could place in dispute the FEE SIMPLE title to the property.

CLUSTER DEVELOPING—1. The construction of buildings in close proximity to one another. 2. A group of similar or related structures advantageously assembled for mutual benefit. By so doing, the open space around the buildings can be utilized to best advantage. Result: convenience, extra and closer parking facilities, overall efficiency and economy of operation, highest and best use of the land, beauty, etc. (See COMPLEX, ROW HOUSING.)

CLOVERLEAF—A highway network that passes one roadway over another permitting exit and entrance by merging traffic lanes instead of direct crossings.

C.O.—An abbreviation for Certificate of Occupance.

CO—A prefix meaning in conjunction with; jointly; together. It is frequently used in real estate terminology as co-operating broker, co-assignor, co-venturer, co-insurance, co-executor, co-heir, etc.

CO.—Abbreviation for company.

CODE—A system of rules and regulations. A collection of laws, on a specified subject, arranged for clarity and understanding.

CODE OF ETHICS—Rules and principles governing the relationship of members of a professional group and expressing a standard of accepted conduct. In the real estate profession, the National Association of Realtors, with over 550,000 member Realtors, subscribes to a Code of Ethics consisting of thirty-five separate canons or articles. This code is their accepted standard of professional conduct and behavior in transacting real estate. The underlying theme, as with any worthwhile code of ethics, is embodied in the golden rule, "Do unto others as you would have them do unto you." (For complete Code of Ethics, see page 415.)

CODICIL—A written addition or change in a will made subsequent to the original document.

CO-EXECUTORS—(See JOINT EXECUTORS.)

COGNOVIT—(Latin) 1. A written confession of a debtor that authorizes the entering of a judgment against him. 2. In the state of Ohio it refers to a type of PROMISSORY NOTE.

CO-INSURANCE—A type of insurance policy requiring the insured to carry coverage of at least 80% of the replacement value of the property; and in turn the insurance company agrees to either charge a reduced premium or give the policy holder the full amount of any loss.

COLD CANVASS—A method of obtaining listings by canvassing from door to door asking each owner to list his property. Real estate salesmen use this method when they are seeking listings in a specific area or property having certain features.

COLLATERAL—Anything of value that a borrower pledges as security. In business, collateral can take the form of bonds, certificates of deposit, stocks, accounts receivable, inventory, etc. In real estate, the collateral for a mortgage is the mortgaged property itself.

COLLECTIONS—The receiving of moneys that are due and payable. A method followed to receive payments.

COLLECTOR OF DECEDENT'S ESTATE—A court-selected person who, on a temporary basis, collects rents, pays bills, and generally cares for the assets of a decedent's estate until an executor or administrator is appointed.

COLONIAL HOUSE—A one or two-story house design reminiscent of the early American period.

Colonial

COLOR OF TITLE—That which appears to have the semblance of good title, but actually has a defect that renders it invalid. It is also termed APPARENT TITLE.

COLUMN—A pillar used as a structural supporting member or for decorative purposes.

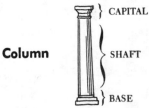

Column

COMMERCIAL BANKS—State and federally chartered banks that obtain the bulk of their funds from their depositor's checking accounts. Commercial banks are traditionally known for giving short-term loans, though their charters permit amortized mortgages of up to 20 years in amounts as high as 80% of appraised value. However, the bulk of their real estate financing is in short-term loans. They give builders interim loans until a project is completed when other lending institutions furnish the permanent financing. Commercial banks also administer to trust funds.

COMMERCIAL LAW—Law that relates to business activities.

COMMERCIAL PAPER—Any negotiable instrument. An endorsed document payable on demand or a specific sum at a specified future time. It is made payable to order or to bearer. Commercial paper includes checks, notes, certificates of deposit and bills of exchange.

COMMERCIAL PROPERTY—Income property which is zoned for business purposes, as distinguished from residential, industrial, or agricultural properties. Commercial properties include office buildings, hotels, motels, apartment houses, parking lots, warehouses, lofts, gasoline stations, shopping centers and stores of all descriptions.

COMMINGLE FUNDS—To combine escrow money with personal or business funds in a common account. In most states this is illegal as far as real estate brokers are concerned. They are required to keep a separate escrow account for all moneys given them in trust.

COMMISSION—1. The fee paid a broker for his services in transacting real estate business. Generally a commission is agreed upon beforehand and an agreement paragraph is inserted in the contract or a separate commission letter is drawn. However, in the absence of such an agreement, the accepted rate of the area should determine the amount. 2. A group of people formed into a unit to perform a specific function.

COMMISSION AGREEMENT—An agreement between the broker and his client stating the amount of commission to be paid if he is successful in bringing about a sale or lease.

COMMISSION RATES—Established, recommended rates in a given locale that are considered fair and equitable compensation for a broker's services. Typical is the schedule below:

For selling or exchanging improved property up to and including
$100,000 . . . . 7½%
On the excess over $100,000, up to and including $1,000,000 . . .5%-6%
On the excess over $1,000,000 up to and including $2,000,000 . .4%-5%
On the excess over $2,000,000 . . . . .3%-4%
For selling vacant land 10%
For leasing property 10%
For the sale of a business 10%
Management Fee . . . . .6% of gross rental income
Appraisal Fee . . . . $100-$200 per day

COMMITMENT—A pledge or promise to do something in the future. Lending institutions generally give written commitment letters stating specific terms of mortgage loans they will give. Commitments can be either "firm" or "conditional." Conditional commitments may be contingent upon such factors as determining a mortgagor's credit, completion of construction or that a certain percentage of occupancy be obtained.

COMMITTEE DEED—A form of deed used when the property of an infant or one of unsound mind is to be conveyed. A committee is appointed and court approval must be obtained before the transfer can be made.

COMMON AREA—Areas used by the public in general. An area that is used in conjunction with other individuals, for example, the portions of a building that consists of corridors, lavatories, lobby, and stairways.

COMMON ENTERPRISE—(See JOINT ENTERPRISE.)

COMMON LAW—Old English law that was handed down through the centuries. It was founded on custom and based on justice and reason rather than inflexible rules. Law that is guided by previous decisions in similar cases. Much of the old English common law is incorporated in the American system of jurisprudence, either by custom or by statute.

COMMON LAW TRUST—(See BUSINESS TRUST.)

COMMON PASSAGEWAY—A way or passage area between two properties mutually dedicated by the owners for common usage.

COMMON PROPERTY—Land for use of the public at large. Common property permits usage by one person of land belonging to another, as may occur when the public is permitted to utilize a shoreline for fishing purposes, or when pasture lands are open for general use. It also may give a lessee the limited right to harvest a portion of that which is upon the property such as timber, peat moss, etc.

COMMON STOCK—A classification of corporate stock that is inferior to PREFERRED STOCK in dividend payments and distribution of assets in the event of dissolution. Dividends are divided among common stockholders only if there is sufficient profit remaining after preferred stockholders receive their share. Common stockholders, however, receive all benefits of surplus income and stock growth.

COMMON, TENANTS IN—(See TENANTS IN COMMON.)

COMMON WALL—(See PARTY WALL.)

COMMUNITY PROPERTY—Property owned jointly by husband and wife. Though the law differs in various states, it generally refers to property obtained during their marriage. Property owned before or after termination of a marriage, or acquired by inheritance, is individually owned.

COMMUNITY SHOPPING CENTERS—Larger shopping centers that may serve several populated areas and cater to more than the basic needs provided by small neighborhood centers. When located outside of downtown city areas, they are called SUBURBAN SHOPPING CENTERS. (See SHOPPING CENTER.)

COMPANY—An organization of individuals combining their skills for the purpose of transacting business. An association of people working together for a common objective. An unincorporated business concern.

COMPARABLE VALUE, COMPARISON APPROACH, COMPARATIVE APPROACH TO VALUE or MARKET COMPARISON—All are terms for a method of appraising real estate which compares one property with as many similar surrounding properties as possible. By careful study of the condition of the various parcels and of recent known sales, a logical appraisal conclusion can be drawn.

COMPASS POINTS—The 32 positions on a compass along the 360 degrees of a circle for measuring directions. It is used when recording Metes and Bounds and other legal descriptions.

COMPENSABLE DAMAGES—In law it is the actual money for damages an owner is awarded by the government or a public utility as compensation for property taken for public use. If all his property is not expropriated, he will be given an additional sum for damages to the remaining parcel.

COMPETENCY OF PARTIES—(See CAPACITY.)

COMPETENT—Legally able and qualified to transact business. Capable. Fit. For example, one is competent by being of legal age and mentally able to enter into agreements.

COMPLETED TRANSACTION—A sale of property that has closed. One in which all the financial and legal details have been accounted for and title to the property has transferred from the seller to the buyer. (See CLOSE.)

COMPLETION BOND—A performance bond posted by a contractor as a guarantee that he will satisfactorily complete a project and that it will be free of any liens. It is sometimes called a PERFORMANCE BOND.

COMPLETION ORDER OR CERTIFICATE—1. A document certifying that work on a construction project has been completed in accordance with the specifications and the terms of the contract and is satisfactory as to workmanship. (See CERTIFICATE OF OCCUPANCY.) 2. For FHA Title I financing, which covers repairs and improvements to homes, a completion certificate must be signed by the homeowner before the contractor receives payment.

COMPLEX—1. A concentration of like or related buildings within a given area, as a group of hospital buildings, apartment houses or an industrial park. 2. A combination of related business firms, such as when a number of independent companies combine talents and facilities and work toward a common interest.

COMPLIANCE INSPECTION—1. An inspection of a building to see that all codes and specifications have been complied with. 2. In government insured or guaranteed loans (FHA and VA), it is an inspection of the construction work before payment of the mortgage is made. In the case of resale homes, it is the inspection of the premises before approval of the new mortgage is given. 3. In conventional financing, it is a bank appraiser's inspection of the building to see that it complies with all of their requirements.

COMPONENT BUILDING—A building that has prefabricated portions. Completed sections of walls, beams, floors, roofs, trusses and other parts are delivered to a building site ready to be assembled and secured into place. Commonly known as a prefabricated building.

COMPONENT DEPRECIATION—A technique for depreciating a real estate asset such as a building by breaking it down into its component parts. The Internal Revenue Service recognizes that certain portions of a structure have a shorter life span than others, and the useful life of one portion may be twice or three times that of another. The suggested list below will further illustrate the component depreciation theory.

Component Part	Assigned Useful Life
Air condition Compressor	5 years
Elevator	10 "
Heating Plant	10 "
Ceiling Tiles	10 "
Paving	11 "
Floor	15 "
Wiring	12 "
Plumbing	15 "
Roof	15 "

COMPOUND INTEREST—Interest computed on both the principal amount and the accruing interest as the debt matures. (See also SIMPLE INTEREST.)

COMPREHENSIVE COVERAGE—An insurance policy that covers many possible contingencies.

CONCESSION—1. Conceding a point. Relenting from an opinion or position held. In negotiating real property, concessions in price and terms are often made before deals are finalized. 2. A grant. The government concedes land to citizens in return for services or for their agreement to use the land given them for a certain purpose. 3. A lease for a portion of a store or other property. The lessee is called a concessionaire. A leased department.

CONCURRENT AUTHORITY—Concurrent authority automatically occurs when any number of brokers are given an open listing. After a sale is consummated, this authority is similarly automatically terminated.

CONDEMNATION—1. The taking of private property for public use. There must be a need for the government to acquire it; that condemnation is in the best interest of the general public. The owner is entitled to just compensation for that which is taken, and if it is determined that loss in value in the remaining property was sustained, he will likewise receive an equitable payment for it. Condemnation is exercising the power of eminent domain. 2. A government's right under its police powers to declare a structure unsafe or unfit for use or for human habitation and a menace to public safety. Its use can thus be prevented until the defects have been remedied.

CONDEMNATION APPRAISAL—An estimate of the value of property that is undergoing condemnation proceedings.

CONDITIONAL COMMITMENT—(See COMMITMENT.)

CONDITIONAL FEE—(See FEE UPON CONDITION.)

CONDITIONAL SALES CONTRACT—A contract whereby possession is given the buyer, but title remains with the seller until certain specific conditions of the contract have been fulfilled, such as full payment of the consideration. A conditional sales contract is used primarily in installment sales transactions, and is variously referred to as an INSTALLMENT CONTRACT, AGREEMENT FOR DEED, CONTRACT FOR DEED or a LAND CONTRACT.

CONDOMINIUM—Individual ownership of a portion of a building that has numerous other units similarly owned. Each owner possesses a deed and a good and marketable title to it. He pays his taxes independently of the other owners and may buy, sell, mortgage, lease or will the portion that he holds. The common areas such as halls, lobby, elevators, heating plant, public lavatories, storage rooms, etc. and the land itself are owned jointly with the other owners. In addition to residential apartments, office and industrial buildings are offering condominium ownership and this form of real estate possession is increasingly in evidence throughout the country.

CONFIDENCE—The trust and reliance one has in another, as when a condition of mutual understanding and assurance exists between a real estate agent and his client.

CONFIDENTIAL RELATION—(See FIDUCIARY.)

CONFIRMATION—A written statement affirming what was orally agreed upon. Establishing or proving the truth of a statement; substantiation.

CONFIRMATION DEED—(See DEED OF CONFIRMATION.)

CONFISCATION—The seizing of privately held property for public use without payment of just compensation. Though the property is appropriated by the government, title to it remains with the owner.

CONGLOMERATE—A corporation that controls a group of other corporations or companies in unrelated businesses. As long as a monopoly does not exist, such a business structure is not in violation of antitrust laws. If the companies acquired by a conglomerate are in related fields and monopolistic practices such as controlling prices are proved, strict antitrust laws are in force to eliminate such practices.

CONSENT—The approval of a proposal, as when an offer that has been made is accepted or agreed upon.

CONSEQUENTIAL DAMAGES—Devaluation of property as a result of a change taking place in nearby land. For example, damages may occur when road grading impairs ingress and egress, or when the addition of fill to adjoining land causes flooding.

CONSERVATION—Preserving areas from decay or waste. Protecting rivers and fields for their natural resources.

CONSERVATOR—One appointed by a court to administer the property of a person found to be incapable of managing his own affairs. A temporary protector or guardian of another's assets.

CONSIDERATION—Something of value given to influence a person to enter into a contract. It usually is money, but need not be. Personal services, merchandise or nothing more than love and affection can be the inducement or consideration.

CONSPIRACY—An agreement between two or more persons to harm or take unfair advantage of a third party or to commit an illegal act.

CONSTANT—Fixed. Uniform. Without variation. In real estate financing, for example, the words *constant percentage rate* refer to the combined principal and interest paid periodically to extinguish a mortgage. If the interest is, say, 10 percent and the amortization 3 percent, the constant percentage rate is 13 percent.

CONSTRUCT—To build.

CONSTRUCTION—The art and process of erecting and building; the manner in which it is being completed. The act or result of something being built. The building of roads, towers, bridges, fences, structures and buildings of all kinds.

CONSTRUCTION LOAN OR MORTGAGE—(See BUILDING LOANS.)

CONSTRUCTION TERMS—Terms used in the building industry.

CONSTRUCTIVE—1. A legal declaration or interpretation. (See also CONSTRUCTIVE NOTICE.) 2. Toward improvement and development. Promoting.

CONSTRUCTIVE EVICTION—1. In law, any disturbance by a landlord that renders a property unfit for its intended use constitutes constructive eviction (as when he shuts off water or electricity to the premises). 2. The inability of a purchaser to obtain clear title to property constructively evicts him from taking possession.

CONSTRUCTIVE FRAUD—A fraud relating to a breach of fiduciary relationship, as when a person who has gained another's confidence takes an unconscionable advantage of this relationship. (See FRAUD.)

CONSTRUCTIVE NOTICE—Notification by the recording of documents in public records or by publication; by so doing the public is presumed to have notice. Also called LEGAL NOTICE.

CONSTRUCTIVE POSSESSION—Having legal possession by virtue of title, but not necessarily occupying the property.

CONSUMMATE—To bring a matter to a successfully conclusion. This occurs in real estate, for example, when a sale is completed and all rights, title and ownership are transferred from one party to another.

CONTIGUOUS—1. Physically adjoining, as between two or more properties. 2. In close proximity.

CONTINGENT—Dependent or conditioned upon a future event with no certainty that it will occur. It is liable to happen, but not known for sure.

CONTINGENT REMAINDER—(See REMAINDER ESTATE; REMAINDER-MAN.)

CONTINUANCE—When an ABSTRACT is brought up to date by a search being made of the public records, noting any changes in ownership, new liens and encumbrances, etc., the process is referred to as a continuance. The abstract is *continued* to the present time.

CONTINUOUS POSSESSION—Uninterrupted possession.

CONTOUR MAP—A map showing the different elevations of an area of land by means of a series of lines connecting all points of equal elevation. It is also called a TOPOGRAPHIC or RELIEF MAP.

Contour Map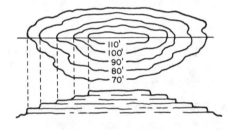

CONTRACT—A binding agreement between competent parties, with sufficient consideration given, to do or refrain from doing something. An agreement, written or oral, that is enforceable by law.

In dealing with real property a valid contract must contain five essential points. a) The principals must be competent; that is, mentally capable in the eyes of the law. b) Valuable consideration must be given. Consideration usually takes the form of money, but it need not be. Personal services, merchandise, other real estate or simply love and affection (as when one member of a family transfers property to another) are valuable considerations. c) An offer and an acceptance. This occurs when the price, terms and conditions are all agreed upon. A meeting of minds takes place. d) Legality of object. The use of the property under contract must be for a lawful purpose. For example, a building sold to be used as a gambling house, where such activity is illegal, would render the contract void. e) In writing and signed. In general, real estate sales contracts must be written and signed by both buyer and seller to be enforceable.

Contracts in real estate take many forms. Refer to the specific type of contract under study. (See INTERPRETATION OF CONTRACTS.)

CONTRACT BREACH—(See BREACH OF CONTRACT.)

CONTRACT DEFAULT—(See DEFAULT.)

CONTRACT FOR DEED—(See INSTALLMENT SALES CONTRACT.)

CONTRACT FOR SALE—(See CONTRACT.)

CONTRACT OF BENEVOLENCE—A contract drawn to benefit only one of the parties.

CONTRACT OF RECORD—The contract recognized by a court as having jurisdiction. The one used to carry out the decisions of a court. The recognized legal document.

CONTRACTOR—One who contracts to do something for another. In the construction industry a contractor is one who contracts to erect buildings or portions of them. There are also contractors for the many other phases of construction such as heating, electrical, plumbing, air conditioning, road building, bridge and dam erection and others.

CONTRACT RENT—The rent specified in a lease agreement.

CONTRACTUAL OBLIGATION—(See OBLIGATION OF CONTRACT.)

CONTROL—In charge of managing the administration of a business or property.

CONVENTIONAL LOAN—The type of mortgage loan that is customarily granted by a bank or savings and loan association. A loan based on real estate as the security, as distinguished from one guaranteed or insured by an agency of the government.

CONVERSION—1. The act of changing a property from one use to another, as for example when a residence is renovated and partitioned into offices. 2. The illegal converting of funds or appropriating another's assets for one's own use.

CONVERSION COMMITMENT PROGRAM—A program devised by the FHA for speeding the processing of mortgage loans. Applications that heretofore took many weeks and sometimes months to process, now are promptly "converted" or changed into acceptances or rejections. By this method much time-consuming, unnecessary "red tape" has been eliminated. Because it was first tested in Greensboro, North Carolina on a limited scale, before it was adopted throughout the country, it is often referred to as the GREENSBORO PLAN.

CONVEYANCE—An instrument, in writing, used to transfer title to property from one to another. A CONTRACT and DEED are two forms of conveyances.

CO-OBLIGOR—One of two or more persons who are bound by an agreement or obligation. A joint obligor.

COOPERATING BROKERS OR CO-BROKERS—Two or more brokers working together in a joint venture to successfully bring about a real estate transaction. Their work, expenses and any commission received are shared.

COOPERATIVE APARTMENT OR BUILDING—In a cooperative type of ownership the tenants of the building become stockholders in a corporation that owns the real estate. They are part owners of the corporation. In lieu of rent, each pays a proportionate monthly or quarterly fixed rate to cover operating costs, mortgage payments, taxes, salaries, etc.

COOPERATIVE SALE—(See COOPERATING BROKERS or CO-BROKERS, JOINT VENTURE.)

CO-ORDINATE—On equal terms with the same order, or rank. Not subordinate. A co-ordinate mortgage, for example, is of equal dignity or rank. One does not receive precident over the other.

CO-OWNER—1. One of two or more persons who jointly own an asset either equally or in proportionate amounts. 2. One of the owners of a partnership.

CO-PARTNER—Synonymous with partner. One who is part-owner of a business, property or a profession.

CORNER INFLUENCE—The additional value of a lot because of its being on the corner or located near to it. (See CORNER LOT APPRAISAL METHODS.)

CORNER LOT—A lot located on the corner of a block and having frontage on two streets.

CORNER LOT APPRAISAL METHODS—Normally corner lots are considered to be worth more than others, though this does not always hold true. The actual additional amount that it may be worth is based on a number of factors. For appraisal purposes, particularly by assessors doing mass appraisals, several formulas have been adopted. In the BALTIMORE METHOD, for example, a corner lot is worth the total of the inside lots on each side of it.

For commercial properties, the ZANGERLE CURVE (formulated by John A. Zangerle) is a method that shows the percentage of side street frontage value to be added to main street frontage value to arrive at an estimated worth of the corner lot. Professional appraisers, it should be noted, have questioned the accuracy of this formula and it is not widely used today.

Another method of appraising corner lots is the BERNARD RULE. By this formula a lot is first evaluated as if it were a side street (inside) lot, then as a main street (inside) lot. The total of the two is the appraised value. At times, appraisers use ¼, ½, or ¾ of the side street value in making their computations. This is because corner lot values vary in different areas.

Good appraisal practice does not rely solely on formulas in reaching conclusions. They are merely tools to the expert appraiser. Sound appraisals always take into consideration such factors as market conditions, the future of the property, salability, etc.

CORNER LOT RULES—Rules of thumb applied by appraisers when evaluating corner properties. (See CORNER LOT APPRAISAL METHODS.)

CORNERSTONE—A stone forming the quoin or external corner of a structure's outer wall. (See QUOIN.)

CORNICE—The horizontal trim located along the top of a building.

CORPORATE VEIL—The legal shield or curtain that protects a corporation where an individual would be liable. Because of this protection individuals sometimes choose the corporate structure when going into a business venture, so that in the event of failure, they will not be personally accountable.

CORPORATION—An association of individuals, formed within the framework of law, to act as a single person. A corporation is said to be an artificial body created by law. Its officers, directors and stockholders are not responsible for the debts of the corporation in case of default or bankruptcy. Corporations are registered with and chartered under state statutes and must conform to their numerous regulations. Officers and directors have to be registered with the state, and most require that an annual financial statement be filed. While most corporations are formed for commercial and industrial purposes, many are founded for charitable, scientific, fraternal, educational or political endeavors.

CORPORATION NOT FOR PROFIT—(See NON-PROFIT CORPORATION.)

CORPORATION SOLE—A non-profit, ecclesiastic corporation organized for the purpose of running a church organization. Headed by a priest or minister, it holds title to church property. Title descends to the successor in office and not to heirs of the priest or minister.

CORPOREAL HEREDITAMENT—Tangible property that is capable of being inherited. (See HEREDITAMENT.)

CORPOREAL PROPERTY—Real or personal property having body or form; relating to or having physical substance such as a house, furniture, fixtures or land. Something tangible; a material body.. It is the opposite of INCORPOREAL PROPERTY such as franchises, stocks, bonds, accounts receivable, rents, etc.

CORRECTION DEED—(Same as DEED OF CONFIRMATION.)

CORRECTION LINES—In Government Survey legal descriptions, correction lines are adjustments made to compensate for the curvature of the earth's surface. (See GOVERNMENT SURVEY.)

CORRELATION—1. In appraising real property it is common for professional appraisers to separately take the three accepted appraisal methods (COMPARISON, COST, and CAPITALIZATION), evaluate the property from each standpoint and, by correlating these conclusions, arrive at a knowledgeable, single estimate of value. This is referred to as APPRAISAL CORRELATION. 2. Bring into proper relation with one another. The act of being in mutual relationship.

COST—1. That which is paid in money, goods or services. An outlay or expenditure. The price paid. 2. Loss; sacrifice. 3. Expenses sustained in litigation, such as attorney's fees and court costs. (See CLOSING COSTS.)

COST APPROACH TO VALUE—A method of estimating the value of property by deducting depreciation from the replacement cost, then adding the value of the land to the remainder. Depreciation, as used in the cost approach, is the difference between replacement cost and the market value of the improvements. Also called SUMMATION APPRAISAL. (See APPRAISAL.)

CO-STIPULATOR—One who jointly promises to do or refrain from doing something.

COST OF LIVING INDEX CLAUSE—(See INDEX CLAUSE)

COST PLUS—The term refers to a construction contract in which the builder is reinbursed for the cost of all materials and labor, plus an additional fee for his services.

CO-TENANCY—Two or more persons owning property jointly. (See JOINT TENANCY; TENANCY IN COMMON.)

COTTAGE—A small house or bungalow.

COUNSELOR OR COUNSELLOR—An attorney. An advisor. In most states the term is used interchangeably with any member of the legal profession. A lawyer who gives council and advise.

COUNSELOR AT LAW—An attorney. Lawyer.

COUNTER OFFER—A new offer as to price, terms and conditions, made in reply to a prior, unacceptable one. The counter offer terminates the original offer.

COUNTERPART—The duplicate copy of an agreement. Though there is only one original from which copies are made, when each copy is individually signed and witnessed they are interchangable with the original and the law considers them all originals.

COUNTERSIGN—The second signature on a document by an authorized subordinate to vouch for the authenticity of the principal signer.

COUNTRY—1. An expanse of land. A region. 2. The land where one is a citizen. A sovereign state; a nation. 3. A rural area as distinguished from an urban community.

COUNTY—A geographical and political land area normally containing rural and urban sections and encompassing cities, towns and villages. It is usually the largest administrative division within a state.

COUNTY COURT—A court of law having jurisdiction over trials for the county in which it is located. Its powers cover civil cases as well as those involving legal guardianship, probate, criminal cases, trusteeships, appeals and others. In some states it is referred to as a Circuit Court.

COUNTY DEED—A deed used when county-owned property is conveyed.

COUNTY JUDGE'S COURT—(See PROBATE COURT.)

COUNTY PROPERTY—Property owned or controlled by a county government.

COUNTY RECORDER—(See RECORDER OF DEEDS.)

COUNTY TAX—The taxes levied and collected by a county government used exclusively for county purposes.

COUPLED WITH AN INTEREST—A real estate agent's interest in a property he is negotiating, separate and above the normal commission he is to receive. His special fiduciary relationship as a broker requires that he openly reveal such interest to all parties.

COURSE—The path from one point to another. In a land survey it is the direction of a line as it relates to a meridian. Land descriptions frequently refer to water courses which serve as natural boundaries or reference points.

COURT—1. An open area covered on two or more sides by walls or buildings. 2. An official session for the administration of justice. A court of law. 3. A street that is not a main thoroughfare.

COVENANT—An agreement between parties, written into legal instruments, promising to do or refrain from doing certain acts. (See DISCRIMINATORY COVENANTS, CONVENANTS FOR TITLE, RESTRICTIVE COVENANTS.)

COVENANT FOR QUIET ENJOYMENT—(See QUIET ENJOYMENT.)

COVENANT OF SEISIN—(See SEISIN.)

COVENANT OF WARRANTY—(See WARRANTY DEED.)

COVENANT RUNNING WITH THE LAND—(See RUN WITH THE LAND.)

COVENANTS FOR TITLE—Agreements in a deed, put there by the grantor, that assure the grantee absolute ownership in quiet enjoyment. Also called COVENANTS FOR QUIET ENJOYMENT.

COVERTURE—A woman's legal status during marriage. Unlike the single person, a wife is placed at a certain legal disadvantage.

CRAWL SPACE—An unfinished half basement. The space below the main floor that is less than the height of a full story. A space that can be entered only by crawling.

CREAM-PUFF—In real estate sales, an expression meaning property easy to sell. It is usually applied to a house, but may be used when referring to any type of real estate that has many desirable features. A real estate agent's prime listing.

CREATIVE REAL ESTATE—Imaginative real estate selling or developing. Having the quality of originality rather than imitative. Developing a market for real estate through one's creative powers.

CREDIT—The balance in one's favor. As used in closing statements, what is due either the buyer or seller. The opposite of debit.

CREDITOR—The one to whom a debt is owned. A person who gives credit.

CREDIT REPORT—A report covering the credit history of a person or business.

CROFT—A term used primarily in England meaning a small, enclosed field or farm.

CROPLAND—Farmland used or set aside for crop production.

CROP SHARE RENT—(See SHARECROPPING.)

CROSS—The mark made by a person unable to write his name. (See X.)

CROWN LANDS—In England and Canada, government-owned land. (See also DEMESNE LAND.)

CUBAGE—Cubic content. (See CUBIC.)

CUBIC—A three-dimensional measurement obtained by multiplying the length by the width by the height. It is used to determine the volume of space occupied by a building or other structure.

CUBIC FOOT COST—1. A building's cubic foot cost is found by dividing the total amount expended for its construction by the amount of cubic feet in the structure. 2. As an appraisal technique, it is a means of estimating a building's value when the cubic foot construction cost of a comparable building is known. It is arrived at by finding the cubic foot content of the building being appraised and multiplying it by the cubic foot cost of the building being used for comparison.

CUL-DE-SAC—A short dead-end street, usually having a circular "turnaround" area for convenient entrance and exit.

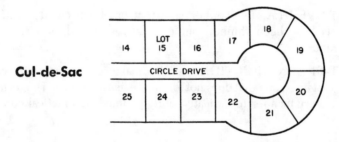

Cul-de-Sac

CURABLE DEPRECIATION—Depreciated property that is nevertheless economically sound. Property in which the cost to repair or remodel would sufficiently enhance its value and more than repay the owner. The opposite of Incurable Depreciation.

CURING THE TITLE—The act of removing a cloud or claim from a title and rendering it marketable and insurable.

CURRENCY—Money; cash. That which is accepted as a medium of exchange. Coin and paper money that is in circulation.

CURRENT ASSETS—(See LIQUID ASSETS.)

CURTAIL—To lessen. Reduce. A mortgage, for example, is said to be curtailed as periodic payments are made and the principal reduced.

CURTESY—A husband's interest for the duration of his life in his wife's estate. Like

Dower (the wife's interest), state laws vary as to the right of curtesy. Most states have abolished this form of estate. (See DOWER.)

CURTILAGE—A fenced, yard area also enclosing a house, out-building and the surrounding property.

CUSHION—A term used in business meaning a financial margin of safety against hidden or unforeseen costs. A reserve fund or contingency allowance for a sudden loss in revenue or a sharp increase in expenses.

CUSTODIAL ACCOUNT—(See ESCROW ACCOUNT.)

CUSTOM BUILDER—One who builds houses or other structures "to order" or who builds one or two at a time on speculation; as distinguished from a developer whose method of operation is mass production. Also called an operation builder, speculative builder or spot builder.

CUSTOMER—One who buys; the purchaser. A prospective buyer.

CUSTOMER RECORD CARDS—An alphabetical system of keeping a file of prospective buyers, it serves as a ready reference of their requirements, what properties have been shown them, their reactions, the amount of cash they have to invest, etc. Also called PROSPECT CARDS.

CUT-OVER LAND—Timber land that has been cut down. Land upon which forests have been thinned out or totally removed as a result of a lumbering operation.

CUT-UP CONSTRUCTION—A colloquial term for a building having irregular wall and roof lines; one that does not follow the usual pattern. The term is often used in a derogatory manner to indicate poorly planned, impractical construction.

D

DAMAGES—1. Loss sustained or harm done to a person or property. 2. Loss in value to the remaining property when, under the theory of eminent domain, a portion of one's property is expropriated. 3. That which a party recovers when he has suffered a loss through the acts or failure to act of another.

DAMNUM ABSQUE INJURIA—(Latin) An injury or loss in which there are no grounds for a legal claim against the party who was the cause of its occurance.

DARK STORE CLAUSE—A colloquial term referring to a lease provision requiring the tenant's store to be open and operating during the entire term of the lease. The advantage of this clause to the landlord is the assurance that the appearance of his property does not deteriorate. It also reduces the probability of the tenant's opening at a nearby location during the concluding months of a lease. Without this provision, when a Percentage Lease is involved, an empty store could result in loss of income to the landlord.

DATA SHEET—(See INFORMATION SHEET.)

DATE—The day, month and year that a document is written or an event occurs.

DAYS OF GRACE—(See GRACE PERIOD.)

D.B.A.—An abbreviation meaning "doing business as".

DEADLINE—A set date for something to be done or refrained from being done.

DEAD PLEDGE—An expression for a mortgage that is being paid on time, as pledged. It is said to lie "dead" or dormant in the files. However, on failure to make payments as agreed, it "comes to life" and steps are taken to receive the due payment or recover the property.

DEAL—An agreement between two or more parties to transact business; indicates a "meeting of the minds." A transaction in real estate, usually in writing. A business arrangement.

DEALER—In real estate, an individual who buys property with the prime object of reselling it for profit as soon as possible, rather than retaining it as an investment for the future.

61

DEBENTURE—A bond given as evidence of a debt, but unsecured by a specific asset. The security a debenture holder has is the credit standing and worth of the company. Debentures usually extend over a period of years.

DEBIT—1. A charge. A debt. The opposite of CREDIT. 2. In double-entry bookkeeping, it is the column used to record what is owed.

DEBT INSTRUMENT—The document creating the debt. In the case of mortgaged property, it is the note or bond that the borrower signs, and not the mortgage itself. The mortgage pledges the property as collateral. Other examples of debt instruments are PROMISSORY NOTES, DEBENTURES and STOCK CERTIFICATES.

DEBTOR—A person who is in debt; the one who owes money to another.

DEBT SERVICE—The amount of money required periodically to make the payments necessary to amortize a debt and interest charges; the principal and interest payments.

DECEDENT—One who has died.

DECEIT—The act of lying. The use of a trick. Dishonest behavior. The practice of deceiving.

DECLARATION OF NO SET-OFF—(See CERTIFICATE OF NO DEFENSE.)

DECLARATION OF TRUST—An acknowledgment, made by one holding title to property, that he is keeping it in trust for another.

DECLARATORY JUDGMENT—1. A binding legal decree. 2. In real estate it is the court ruling sought by a third party holding money in trust, when a dispute concerning it arises between the principals. When so doing the third party does not relinquish his interest, but is held responsible for court costs.

DECLINING BALANCE DEPRECIATION—(See DOUBLE DECLINING BALANCE.)

DECREE—A court order to do or refrain from doing a specific thing.

DECREE OF FORECLOSURE—The court's decision and disposition of a foreclosure action.

DECREMENT—A decrease or loss in value. A loss in property value due to social and economic changes. The opposite of INCREMENT.

DEDICATION—The appropriation of private property for public use. A grant of land that is open to public use or purpose. The acceptance of private property by a public agency for general public use, such as streets and highways, public schools and historic sites.

DEDUCTIBLE—1. Able to be taken from; subtracted. An amount that can be taken away. 2. For income tax purposes, that sum which is allowed to be taken off, thereby reducing the payment.

DEED—An instrument under seal, signed by the grantor, transferring title to another. To be valid a deed must a) be made between competent parties, b) have a legally sound subject matter, c) contain a good and valuable consideration, d) correctly state what is being conveyed, e) be properly executed, and f) be delivered.

There are many types of deeds used for various specific purposes, such as: Executor's Deed, County Deed, Referee's Deed in Partition, Referee's Deed in Foreclosure, Grant Deed, Administrator's Deed, Gift Deed, Deed of Release, Deed of Surrender, Guardian's Deed, Committee's Deed, Cession Deed, Deed in Lieu of Foreclosure, Deed in Trust, Mineral Deed, Deed of Confirmation, Support Deed, Sheriff's Deed (Master's Deed), as well as numerous others. The ones primarily used to convey real property are the following:

General Warranty Deed—sometimes referred to as a Full Covenant and Warranty Deed, this deed conveys a covenant of warranty. By it the grantor will warrant and defend the title against *all* claims. From the grantee's standpoint, it is the best form of deed he can receive.

Special Warranty Deed—used when the grantor warrants only claims against him or his heirs, and not that of previous owners. It is frequently used to convey tax title. (In the state of Michigan, the term Warranty Deed is used in place of Special Warranty Deed).

Bargain and Sale Deed, *with* Covenants Against Grantor's Acts—contains covenants stating, "the party of the first part (grantor) has not done or suffered anything whereby the premises have been encumbered in any way whatsoever."

Bargain and Sale Deed, *without* Covenants Against Grantor's Acts—used to convey all the rights, title and interest of the grantor and nothing more. This is one of the simplest forms of a deed and carries with it no promises by the grantor.

Quit Claim Deed—in which the grantor states that he releases all rights, title and interest he may have in the property, but gives no warranties. It is usually used to relinquish a claim. In certain sections of the country, quit claim deeds are used when there is a questionable interest, or to remove a cloud upon the title. In other areas it is more commonly used in ordinary transactions.

(For further detailed definitions and exhibits of deeds, refer to the specific deed under study.)

DEED IN FEE—A deed conveying fee simple ownership. Such a deed transfers complete possession without conditions, and is free of encumbrances. Absolute ownership of good and marketable title. (See FEE: FEE SIMPLE: FEE SIMPLE ABSOLUTE.)

DEED IN LIEU OF FORECLOSURE—A mortgagor's act of conveying title to the mortgagee to prevent foreclosure of the property.

DEED OF CONFIRMATION—The deed used to correct mechanical errors in another deed. An incorrect legal description, errors in the spelling of names and places, and improper execution can be rectified by this instrument. It is also known as a CORRECTION DEED or REFORMATION DEED.

DEED OF PARTITION—(See PARTITION DEED.)

DEED OF RELEASE—Used to release property or a portion of it from the lien of a mortgage, this form is often used when a mortgage covers more than one parcel.

DEED OF SURRENDER—This instrument is used to convey an ESTATE FOR LIFE or an ESTATE FOR YEARS to a remainderman or one who will receive it in reversion. (For further study see ESTATE IN REVERSION.)

DEED OF TRUST—This instrument is used in some areas of the country, notably Missouri, Illinois, California, Virginia and Washington, D.C., (as well as in other locales) as a mortgage. The deed is placed in trust with a third party to insure payment of the indebtedness or assure that some other condition of the transaction is met. Upon payment of the debt, or when all other conditions are satisfied, the third party delivers the deed to the purchaser, which frees him of further responsibilities. It is also called a TRUST INDENTURE and a LONG-TERM ESCROW.

DEED POLL—A deed executed by, and obligatory to, a single party.

DEED RESTRICTIONS—Clauses in a deed limiting the future uses of the property. Deed restrictions take many forms: they may limit the density of buildings, dictate the type of structures that can be erected, prevent buildings from being used for certain purposes or used at all. Deed restrictions may impose a myriad of limitations and conditions.

Until recently restrictions against persons of certain races, colors, religion or national origin owning or occupying real property in a given area was not uncommon. This form of deed restriction has been declared unconstitutional by the United States Supreme Court. (See DISCRIMINATORY COVENANTS.)

DE FACTO—(Latin) In actual fact. In reality. Indeed. Actually but not specifically qualified in law to act. The acts of an officer *de facto*, however, are frequently considered valid. *De Facto* refers to a matter of common practice not necessarily founded in law.

DEFAULT—The breach of an obligation. Failure to perform the covenants of a contract. Omitting something that should be done; not fully discharging an obligation; not doing something agreed upon.

DEFAULT JUDGMENT—(See JUDGMENT BY DEFAULT.)

DEFEASANCE CLAUSE—A clause reciting certain provisions and conditions which, when fulfilled, will make the document, or a portion of it, null and void. A defeasance clause in a mortgage, for example, stipulates the terms and the amount of the indebtedness and that the mortgage automatically becomes void when the amount outstanding is paid.

DEFEASIBLE—Capable of being defeated, revoked or being made null and void. Defeasible title, for example, is one that can be voided. A defeasible fee is an estate that can be defeated by a future occurance or contingency.

DEFECT—Deficiency, that which is faulty; imperfection. The absence of a legal requirement; insuffiency; flaw.

DEFECTIVE TITLE—A flaw in the title. As an example, if an otherwise good title is illegally obtained, or an illegal consideration was used, it is a defective title. Until the defect is eliminated, it is looked upon as no title at all.

DEFENDANT—The person being sued or charged with committing an illegal act. The party from whom recovery or compensation is being sought.

DEFERRED MAINTENANCE—Maintenance to a building that should be done but is postponed, thereby causing a decline in the physical condition of the structure. That part of a building in need of repair and maintenance in order to restore it.

DEFERRED PAYMENTS—Provisions in a mortgage allowing for the postponement of principal or interest payments. This is frequently done with mortgages on new commercial buildings or apartment houses. It affords the owner a grace period, in which to obtain tenants, in order to build the income.

DEFICIENCY—A shortage; an insufficiency. That which is lacking in standards, money, performance, etc.

DEFICIENCY DECREE—(See DEFICIENCY JUDGMENT.)

DEFICIENCY JUDGMENT—A judgment issued when the security for a loan is insufficient to satisfy the debt upon its going into default. It is the awarding of the amount still due on a foreclosed mortgage, after applying the sum received for the sale of the property.

DEFUNCT—No longer in existence. Dead.

DEGREE—A unit of circular measurement that is 1/360th part of the circumference of a circle. It is further divided into 60 minutes, each of which is divided into 60 seconds. In METES AND BOUNDS legal descriptions, degrees are used to indicate directions and as a means of measuring the length of arcs.

Degrees

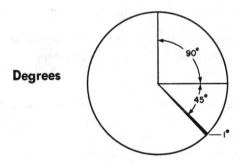

DE JURE—(Latin) Lawful title. Under authority of law. By right.

DELINQUENT DEBT—An overdue debt or loan. That which is late in being received, thereby not complying with the agreed upon terms. An omission of payment.

DELIVERY—The absolute act of exchanging legal title by the delivery of a properly executed deed. The transfer of ownership.

DEMAND NOTE OR MORTGAGE—A note or mortgage that can be called in for payment at any time without prior notice, upon the demand of the holder.

DEMISE—1. Lease. Conveyance of an estate to another for life, years or at will. To let. 2. Death.

DEMOLITION OF BUILDINGS—The process of destroying buildings, usually for the purpose of clearing the land to make way for new construction, or to level old buildings as unfit for habitation.

DENSITY ZONING—The limiting of land use to control population rather than controlling density by limiting the number of families per building.

DEPARTMENT OF HOUSING AND URBAN DEVELOPMENT (HUD)—This federal agency came into existence November 9, 1965, absorbing all of the programs formerly administered by the Housing and Home Finance Agency and its constituents. Through seven regional offices throughout the United States and Puerto Rico, and some 76 local offices (at least one in each state), HUD administers programs which include:

Large-scale urban renewal efforts to eliminate slum and blight by making loans and grants to communities to tear down or rehabilitate housing and other buildings.

Granting funds for building recreational and service centers, beautification projects, playgrounds, parks, etc.

Colleges may borrow from HUD to erect student housing, dining halls and other facilities.

Helping people buy homes by insuring loans through the Federal Housing Administration (FHA).

Under HUD the Federal National Mortgage Association (FANNIE MAE) helps banks and other lending institutions get more money to loan by buying up some of the mortgages they hold.

HUD helps communities create better sub-divisions and improve mass transportation facilities by preparing comprehensive, long-range development plans for both city and suburb and by giving grants to metropolitan transportation systems to modernize equipment and facilities.

HUD's Model Cities program is a direct step to solve ghetto conditions and related city problems. Within this program a number of selected cities across the country are being used as "laboratories" in an effort to learn how to effectively improve the quality of city life. Model cities will strive to:

* Remove blight and decay in whole neighborhoods.
* Increase the supply of housing for low and moderate income families.
* Develop jobs for people in the area who need work.
* Upgrade job skills and education levels in the area.
* Offer the social services needed by the poor and disadvantaged in slum areas.

* Encourage self-help by those being served.
* Improve the quality of life for people living in model neighborhoods.
* Advance the sound development of the whole city.

HUD also strives to bring equal opportunity to all Americans by eliminating discrimination in housing.

DEPENDENT—Someone who relies upon another for support.

DEPLETION—Reduction in size or quantity. The exhausting of an asset, as can occur when drilling for oil, cutting timber, mining, etc. To lessen in value and amount.

DEPONENT—One who gives evidence in writing under oath. A witness.

DEPOSIT—1. Commonly the amount of money placed in trust as evidence of good faith for the future performance of a real estate transaction. Money given as a pledge to do something at a later time. EARNEST MONEY; down payment. 2. A mass of a mineral found in rock or in the ground.

DEPOSIT RECEIPT—An instrument used to submit a written offer for the purchase of property. It serves as a receipt of money deposited. Upon acceptance of the offer it becomes a binding contract. In various parts of the country it is referred to by different names. Some of them are: BINDER, PROPOSITION, OFFER, OFFER TO PURCHASE, PURCHASE OFFER.

DEPOSITION—Testimony of a witness, usually in writing, as ordered by a court. A formal declaration. A deposition is used primarily when a court appearance is not absolutely necessary, such as for a witness residing out of the area or a person who is not able or available to testify in court.

DEPRECIATION—1. A lowering of value. A reduction; lessening. The decline in value of property. Loss in market value. Deterioration over a period of time. The opposite of appreciation. 2. In appraising, depreciation is the reduction in value of a property as measured from the cost to replace it. It is the difference between the replacement cost and the market value. 3. In accounting, it is a writeoff (usually computed annually) of a portion of an asset on the records. (See DOUBLE DE-CLINING BALANCE, STRAIGHT LINE DEPRECIATION, OBSOLES-CENCE, PHYSICAL DEPRECIATION.)

DEPTH INFLUENCE—An appraiser's term referring to the effect depth has on the value of a parcel of land. For example, a lot having a greater depth than that of a standard lot is evaluated at a certain percentage greater. (See 4-3-2-1 DEPTH RULE.)

DEPTH TABLE—A fixed evaluation for various portions of a parcel of land, front footage having the greatest value with the center and rear proportionately less. It is used primarily in assessing parcels of land of varying depths, so that a uniformity of value can be reached. (See 4-3-2-1 RULE, HOFFMAN RULE, HOFFMAN-NEIL

RULE, CORNER LOT APPRAISAL METHODS.) Other known rules for evaluating depth of land are the following (the names of which are derived from the community where they originated or for the individual who developed them): Newark Rule, Milwaukee Rule, Cleveland Rule, Somers Rule and Martin Rule.

DERELICTION—1. The intentional abandonment or renunciation of property. 2. Neglect of duty, either express or implied. 3. The addition of land that was once under water due to the lowering of the water level. (See RELICTION.)

DESCENT—To obtain something by inheritance. To receive from one's ancestors. The passing on of property to an heir or heirs. The transfer of property by inheritance. Receiving an estate by succession.

DESCRIBE—To give a legal or physical description of property.

DESCRIPTION OF PROPERTY—The legal description of property as well as the commonly known street and number address. (See LEGAL DESCRIPTIONS.)

DETACHED RESIDENCE—A dwelling not attached to another by a common wall. A home separated from others.

DETAINER—The prevention of a person from possessing what is legally his. As an example, when a tenant refuses to vacate after his lease has terminated, he is repudiating the owner's right to the property. Thus, by unlawfully remaining in possession he is detaining the owner from use and enjoyment of his land.

DETERIORATION—The lowering of value of property. Physical depreciation; degeneration. A neighborhood may deteriorate as buildings are neglected or abandoned.

DETERMINABLE FEE—(See FEE DETERMINABLE.)

DETERMINE—To decide; to bring to a conclusion. Reach a decision.

DEVALUATE—A lowering in value. A reduction.

DEVELOP—To expand by steady growth. To cause to unfold more fully and completely.

DEVELOPED LAND—Improved land. Any man-made additions to real property that add to its value. Land that has been improved in such ways as road building, grading, bringing in utilities, constructing buildings, adding sidewalks and sewers, landscaping, etc.

DEVELOPER—A person who, for profit, subdivides land into homesites, builds roads, houses and shopping centers, as well as all other facilities required to serve the community he has created. One who attempts to put land to its highest and best use by the construction of improvements upon it.

DEVELOPMENT—An improved area of streets, homes, shopping centers, schools and churches. The installment of utilities, sewers, parks and recreation areas; a subdivision. An area in the process of being developed.

DEVEST: DIVEST—To relinquish. To deprive; free. To give up something, such as real or personal property. Strip; rid. Take away title to. The opposite of invest.

DEVISE—A gift of real property under a will. It is contingent upon some future occurrence (such as the death of the devisor).

DEVISEE—The receiver of a gift of real property by will.

DEVISOR—The donor of real property by will.

DEVOLUTION—The passing of rights, title or liabilities from one individual to another. That which accrues from one party to a successor automatically without the recipient having to do anything positive to obtain it.

DEVOLVE—To pass from one to another by succession or transmission as a title or right. Real property is said to devolve when an estate is transfered from a dying person to his successor.

DIEM—(Latin) Day.

DILUVION—The erosion of land by water, such as by the flow of streams, rivers and tides.

DIMINISHING ASSETS—(See WASTING ASSETS.)

DIRECTIONAL GROWTH—The direction in which a community is expected to grow. In developing regions, a trend can usually be seen as to which way future expansion can reasonably be expected to follow. This directional growth plays an important part in the present and future market value of property.

DIRECTOR—1. A member of the governing board of a corporation or other organization. 2. One who leads or directs.

DIRECT REDUCTION MORTGAGE—A mortgage loan in which the periodic payments are applied to the outstanding principal balance. Only when this sum is completely satisfied is interest or other charges deducted.

DISBURSEMENTS—1. Money paid out. Expenditures. 2. At a real estate closing, the necessary moneys expended by buyer and seller in order to transfer ownership. (See CLOSING COSTS.)

DISCHARGE—In contracts it refers to canceling the obligation. If all terms and conditions of a contract were met, it would be terminated or discharged by perform-ance. A contract is also said to be discharged if all the terms and conditions are *not* met, as in the case of a resulting lawsuit that eventually is settled.

DISCLAIMER—1. Renunciation or rejection of an estate; refusal to acknowledge an interest in it. Denial of ownership. 2. A statement denying legal responsibility. A written disavowal of the accuracy or correctness of the presented facts. The following are two examples of disclaimers:

  a) Any information herewith given is obtained from sources we consider reliable. However, we are not responsible for misstatements of fact, error, omission, prior sale, withdrawal from market or change in price without notice.

b) This property is listed for sale on the following terms and conditions only:

(1) although material herein is from sources deemed reliable, its accuracy is not guaranteed. (2) Subject to change in terms or price, prior sale or withdrawal at any time, for any reason whatsoever, without notice. (3) No offer or solicitation of employment is made to anyone. No liability of any kind is to be imposed on the brokers herein. (4) No representations or warranties, express or implied, relating to any matter herein above or the condition of the premises or parts thereof, are made to any purchaser who is deemed not to rely on any representations but is relying solely on his own investigation. (5) No waiver or amendment of any of the foregoing shall be effective unless in writing and signed by the brokers herein.

DISCLAIMER OF ESTATE—The refusal to accept an estate that has been conveyed. A renunciation of one's right to possess and claim title.

DISCONTINUANCE—Interruption or cessation of a legal action. The voluntary suspension of proceedings by the plaintiff. Such terms as *discontinuance of an estate* (termination or interruption of an estate) *discontinuous easement* (a noncontinuous right to another's property as may occur with a right of way or a right to obtain water) are part of real estate nomenclature.

DISCLOSURE—Something revealed. A public statement of subject matter. Opening to view. Making known what previously was private knowledge.

DISCOUNT—1. That which can be taken off the established amount. Mortgages, for example, are frequently discounted when paid in advance of maturity. 2. A sum paid to obtain certain preferred mortgages, as the payment of points to a lending institution for FHA and VA mortgages.

DISCRIMINATORY COVENANTS—Agreements made for reasons other than individual merit. Unfair covenants, running with the land, created to bar a particular group or race of people. Discrimination by category rather than on an individual basis. Discriminatory covenants have been declared unconstitutional by the United States Supreme Court.

FHA regulations require that housing provided with FHA assistance be made available without discrimination because of race, color, creed, or national origin.

The regulations prohibit any person, firm, or group receiving the benefits of FHA mortgage insurance or doing business with FHA from practicing such discrimination in lending or in the sale, rental, or other disposition of the property. Violations may result in discontinuation of FHA assistance.

One-or two-family dwellings which have been occupied by the owner are exempt from the regulations; but if the purchaser of such a home wishes to finance it with an FHA-insured mortgage the lender may not refuse to make the loan because of the buyer's race, color, creed, or national origin.

The Veterans Administration requires that all veterans purchasing property through this program sign a nondiscrimination statement before taking title. The statement, in form of a certificate, reads as follows:

To ensure equal housing opportunity for all as provided by the Federal fair housing law, I hereby certify that neither I, nor anyone authorized to act for me, will refuse to sell or rent, after receiving a bona fide offer, or refuse to negotiate for the sale or rental of, or otherwise make unavailable or deny the dwelling or property covered by this loan to any person because of race, color, religion, sex or national origin.

I recognize that any restrictive covenant on this property relating to race, color, religion, sex or national origin is illegal and void and any such covenant is hereby specifically disclaimed.

I understand that civil action for preventive relief may be brought by the Attorney General of the United States in any appropriate U.S. District Court against any person responsible for violation of the applicable law.

_____   _____
     (Date)   (Signature of Veteran)

DISPENSATION—An exception made to a rule or law.

DISPOSSESS—Forcing an individual to vacate property. Putting one out of possession or occupancy. To legally oust.

DISPOSSESS NOTICE—A notice to a tenant to vacate the premises.

DISPOSSESS PROCEEDINGS—A landlord's legal recourse through which a tenant can be removed from the premises for failing to comply with the lease agreement.

DISSEISIN—The loss of possession of property by one claiming ownership. Dispossession; forcible expulsion of an owner from his land.

DISSOLUTION—Termination by dispersing. The process of dissolving. A dissolution of a contract is its cancellation by the parties to it. The dissolution of a corporation occurs when its existance is terminated. It is the act of nullifying a legal instrument or proceeding.

DISTINCT POSSESSION—One of the requirements in obtaining property by adverse possession is to have distinct possession of the property for a specified period of years; that is, to have complete control and to be in exclusive possession of it. It is sometimes referred to as OPEN and NOTORIOUS POSSESSION.

DISTRAIN—To seize another's property as security or a pledge for an unfulfilled obligation.

DISTRAINT FOR RENT—The receiving of personal property, as a pledge of security from a tenant who is delinquent in his rent payments. (See also LANDLORD'S WARRANT.)

DISTRESSED PROPERTY—Property that is bringing an inadequate return to the owner, or is in difficulty for other reasons. For example, real estate which has to be sold off at a lower price because it is undergoing a change to a less desirable usage, is located in a blighted area, or for whatever the reason, the market value is diminishing.

DISTRIBUTEE—An heir; the person entitled to the estate of a deceased person. The receiver of inherited property. Also, the recipient of property from one who dies without leaving a will.

DISTRICT—An area or territorial division. A region containing distinguishing characteristics such as a residential district, financial district, school district, etc. A district court, for example, has jurisdiction over a specific territory. It may cover an entire state or a certain area within it.

DIVEST—The opposite of invest. To dispossess or rid oneself of property title. In law, *divestiture* is a court ordered remedy for a party to give up property.

DIVIDEND—The distribution of money or stock to shareholders of a corporation. A method of distributing a portion of profits.

DIVISIBLE CONTRACT—A contract that, by its nature and intent, can be readily divided.

DIVISION—The separation of land into subdivisions or smaller units, such as homesites. (See DEVELOPMENT.)

DOCK STAMPS—An abbreviation for Documentary Stamps.

DOCUMENTS—Legal instruments such as deeds, contracts, mortgages, bills of sale, acknowledgments, options, depositions, wills and the myriad of legal forms that furnish information or serve as proof of some fact.

DOCUMENTARY EVIDENCE—Authoritative evidence in writing.

DOCUMENTARY STAMPS—A state tax, in the form of stamps, required on deeds and mortgages when real estate title passes from one owner to another. The amount of stamps required varies with each state.

DOMAIN—Absolute ownership of land. Complete, ultimate right of possession of land. EMINENT DOMAIN, for example is the right a governmental body has in claiming and controlling private property. (See that term.)

DOMESTIC CORPORATION—A corporation having its home offices in the state where it was incorporated or where issued its charter, regardless of where it does business. (See also FOREIGN CORPORATION.)

DOMICILE—A person's place of residence. His permanent home, as distinguished from a temporary residence. The place a person designates as his home for tax, voting, and similar established purposes.

DOMINANT ESTATE (TENEMENT)—An estate in which the holder is allowed to utilize certain benefits of another's property. As an example, when land is subdivided, and the owner of one portion is granted an easement to use of the other, his is the dominant estate. The other is referred to as the SERVIENT ESTATE.

DOMINION—Ownership of property, and the freedom and right to use or dispose of it as one sees fit.

DONATION LANDS—Public lands first given to soldiers returning from war during colonial times. Later, to encourage settlement of the west, large areas of land were donated by the government to those citizens who laid claim to it. In similar fashion today, certain remote western and Alaskan tracts are given to people who agree to work and develop the land for a specified period of years.

DONATIVE TRUST—A gift of property by its legal owner to be held in trust for the recipient. No consideration is required to be paid by the beneficiary.

DONEE—One who receives a gift.

DONOR—The originator of a gift. One who gives an estate. The one who grants or presents something to another. Also called the *donator*.

DORMANT PARTNER—A silent partner. A person who does not actually participate but maintains a monetary interest in a business and receives some of its profits, if any.

DORMER—A vertical window protruding from a roof and making its own roof line.

Dormer

DOTAL PROPERTY—Property a woman owns and brings with her upon marriage.

DOUBLE-DECKING—The illegal act of selling the same property twice. A practice of disreputable land operators.

DOUBLE DECLINING DEPRECIATION—A method wherein the owner of improved property can deduct more for depreciation in the early years of a building, than would normally apply if distributed over the life of the asset. If the title holder is the original owner, he can elect to deduct up to double the regular depreciation the first year, and slightly lesser amounts each succeeding year. When acquiring resale property, one can begin by deducting no more than one and one-half times the STRAIGHT LINE DEPRECIATION.

DOUBLE DWELLING—A two-family house. (See DUPLEX.)

DOUBLE INSURANCE—Two insurance policies covering the same asset or risk.

DOUBLE RENT—A practice whereby a tenant, given notice to leave by a certain date, is charged double the usual rental for staying beyond that time.

DOUBTFUL TITLE—Title to property where a legal doubt exists as to its validity. Clouded title; questionable title. Title that leaves the owner vulnerable for litigation.

DOWER—The legal rights that a widow possesses to her husband's estate. In some states she holds an estate for life in his property. State laws vary as to dower rights, with many of them having absolished this form of interest entirely. In other states, under common law, a wife owns $1/3$ of her deceased husband's real estate. (See CURTESY.)

DOWNEY—A slang expression meaning DOWN PAYMENT.

DOWN PAYMENT—The money deposited as evidence of good faith for purchasing real estate upon signing the contract. The deposit. The portion of a contract applying to the down payment often reads as follows:

> RECEIPT is hereby acknowledged of the sum of $_____ from _____ _____ as a deposit on account of the purchase price of the following described property upon the terms and conditions as stated herein.

DRAFT—A written order, from one person or bank to another, for the payment of a stipulated amount of money.

DRAINAGE—1. Man-made provisions for the controlled flow of water from a parcel of land. 2. The natural flow of water from the surface of land, or the sub-surface flow through the soil.

DRIVEWAY—A private road connected to a public thoroughfare.

DRUMLIN—An elongated ridge or oval hill of glacial drift. A lenticular mound.

DRY MORTGAGE—A mortgage that creates a lien upon property without imposing the mortgagor to personal liability. The mortgagee must look to the property only as security should a default occur.

DRY RENT—Rental payments not secured by the personal liability of the tenant.

DRY TRUST—A trust that requires no action by the trustees other than to furnish funds or property. The parties to the trust play a passive role.

DRY WALL CONSTRUCTION—Wall sections made of prepared materials such as sheetrock, gypsum, plywood, styrofoam, pressed fiber. Any wall construction made without using mortar.

DUAL EMPLOYMENT—Employment of a broker by both a buyer and a seller. As long as both parties are made aware of this double employment, there is nothing illegal or unethical about such an arrangement. Both principals pay a brokerage commission. One serving in such a dual capacity is sometimes called a MIDDLEMAN.

DUE—1. That which is proper and fair. 2. Something owed and payable. A matured debt. Often a fixed debt that periodically becomes due.

DUE PROCESS OF LAW—Impartial legal procedure. The Constitution of the United States guarantees that every person will receive a fair and impartial hearing through our courts of justice. The Fifth Amendment to the Constitution states that no person shall "be deprived of life liberty or property without due process of law." It is also embodied in the Fourteenth Amendment, Section I, which refers to the fact that no State may deprive a person of these fundamental rights.

DUMMY—A person who buys property for another to conceal the identity of the true purchaser. This may be done, for example, when a well-known company or individual is involved, to insure that the price will not be arbitrarily changed. A party acting in such a capacity is also known as a STRAW MAN. He is said to hold naked legal title until the real owner takes over.

DUPLEX—1. A house that provides living accommodations for two families by having separate entrances, kitchens, bedrooms, porches, living rooms and baths. A two-family dwelling. (See page 329, for a typical Duplex Listing Form.) 2. A single apartment unit that has two floor levels.

DURABLE LEASE—A long-term lease. One that prevails for an extended period of years without significant change. Such a lease has been described as extending "for as long as the grass grows or water runs."

DURATION OF LEASE—The lease period. The remaining time for which the property is leased. The length of a lease.

DURESS—Forcing a person to do something against his will by threat, implication or by inflicting physical harm. Any agreement that is so made is automatically void.

DUTCH COLONIAL—A variation of the traditional Colonial style house. The Dutch Colonial features a slightly pitched roof, giving it a boxlike, but trim appearance.

DWELLING—A residence. A structure occupied exclusively for living purposes. The building in which a person resides.

E

EARNED INCREMENT—An increase in property value due primarily to an owner's initiative, skill and good judgment in managing and operating his property, rather than from outside factors such as economic and social changes. When these later factors favorably affect a property's value, they are referred to as UNEARNED INCREMENT. (See that term.)

EARNEST MONEY—A purchaser's partial payment, as a show of good faith, to make a contract binding. A deposit; a down payment.

EARNING-PRICE RATIO—A ratio of the net income of property to the selling price. As an example, if a building nets $100,000 profit and is sold for $800,000, the earning-price ratio is 8 (8 times the income). In computing earning-price ratio, net income refers to the sum remaining after all expenses are deducted, except mortgage payments.

EARNINGS—1. The amount remaining after deducting expenses from the gross income of a business. Profits for one's labors. 2. Wages or salary paid an employee.

EARNINGS APPROACH—An appraiser's approach to valuation of real estate by considering its present and anticipated (future) income. (See INCOME APPROACH TO VALUE.)

EASEMENT—A limited right to use another's property in a specified manner. The right given to travel on, over, or through adjoining land, or to use it for a specific purpose. An easement can be permanent or temporary. Utility right-of-ways, pole easements and party walls are examples of permanent easements. The temporary right to cross a neighbor's land to reach one's own, until roads are repaired, is a temporary easement. Generally, easements pass with the land when it is sold, unless prohibited by deed restrictions. Easements can take many forms. (See OVERFLOW RIGHTS, AVIGATION EASEMENT, AIR RIGHTS, SUBSURFACE EASEMENT, EASEMENT IN GROSS.)

EASEMENT BY PRESCRIPTION—(See PRESCRIPTION.)

EASEMENT IN GROSS—The granting of a personal interest in real estate, rather than some right in the land itself. Such an easement is usually not assignable, nor able to be inherited. As an example, when an owner permits a small portion of his property, such as a wall or a portion of a roof, to be used for a billboard, the courts have ruled it to be an easement in gross and not a lease.

EAST—A description of direction; toward the east. Ninety degrees to the right of north. One of the four cardinal points of direction.

EAVES—The overhanging portion of a roof projecting beyond the sides and serving to protect the building from the elements.

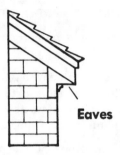

Eaves

ECCLESIASTICAL PROPERTY—Church-owned property. Church buildings, cemeteries and lands given to the church, as distinguished from privately held, or government property.

ECONOMIC APPROACH—(See INCOME APPROACH TO VALUE.)

ECONOMIC DEPRECIATION—(See ECONOMIC OBSOLESCENCE.)

ECONOMIC LIFE—The time remaining during which a property can be profitably and feasibly used.

ECONOMIC OBSOLESCENCE—A decline in the market value of property due to any external influence. An environmental decline that limits the highest and best use to which the property can be put.

ECONOMIC RENT—The estimated income that a property should bring in the current rental market. The economic rent may be above or below that which is actually received. It represents a rental rate that comparable properties are bringing.

ECONOMIC VALUE—Value based on the monetary return, or its equivalent, that a parcel of real estate brings.

EDIFICE—A large, imposing building.

EFFECTING A SALE—Completing a sale. The bringing about of a sale.

EFFECTING LOAN—The renewal or extension of a previous loan without lending additional money, such as the extension of period for paying a bank loan.

EFFECTIVE AGE—A building's physical condition, not its actual age, determines its effective age. For appraisal purposes, it is an assumed age that would be equivalent to the physical condition of the structure; the better the condition, the lower the effective age. For example, some well-maintained 35-year-old buildings may be assigned an effective age of 20 or 25 years. It is used to indicate to the prospective purchaser or appraisal client that the structure is in better or worse condition than the average building of similar vintage.

EFFECTIVE DATE—The date something commences or ceases. The origination date.

EFFECTIVE PROCURING CAUSE—(See PROCURING CAUSE.)

EFFECTS—Personal property. Movable property not affixed to the ground. CHATTEL. GOODS. PERSONALTY.

EFFICIENCY—1. A small, compact apartment consisting of a combination living room-bedroom, kitchen and bath. Also referred to as a studio apartment or pullmanette. 2. Accomplishment without waste. Effective operation. The maximum productivity with the minimum cost and time expended.

EGRESS—A passageway leading from property. The means of exiting. The opposite of INGRESS.

EJECT—To evict from the premises; expel. Physically remove someone or something from property.

EJECTMENT—Legal action brought to regain possession of real property and receive payment for damages from the one who illegally retained it.

ELEEMOSYNARY CORPORATION—(See NON-PROFIT CORPORATION.)

ELEVATION—1. Height above sea level. 2. A raised area. 3. A side-view architectural drawing of a structure.

EMBEZZLEMENT—Stealing. Unlawfully appropriating the benefits of another's property or money. One entrusted with something of value who fraudulently takes it for himself. Larceny.

EMBLEMENT—That which a lessee may take from the land after the term of his lease has expired. As an example, a tenant farmer whose tenancy has ended may still keep the harvest of a crop that has not yet matured.

EMINENT DOMAIN—The right or power of the state or a public utility to expropriate private property for public use, upon paying just compensation. For this right to be exercised, it must be in the best interest and security of the general public (as in times of war the government may take over privately held lands). In peacetime the government can obtain private property for roadways, right-of-ways, railroads, channels or similar public benefits. (See CONDEMNATION.)

EMPLOY—1. To use as an agent to act for another. Engage to manage one's affairs. 2. Hire. To give a person work.

EMPLOYMENT CONTRACT BETWEEN BROKER AND SALESMAN—(See BROKER AND SALESMAN CONTRACT.)

EMPLOYMENT OF BROKER—The retaining of a broker to perform a service concerned with real estate.

EMPTOR—(Latin) A purchaser. Buyer. Part of the phrase *Caveat Emptor*, meaning, "let the buyer beware."

ENAJENACION—Meaning "transfer of property," the word is of Spanish origin. The act of transferring title by gift or, in the instance of onerous title, by sale or an exchange. Alienation.

ENCLOSED LAND—(See INCLOSED LAND.)

ENCROACHMENT—An intrusion or infringement upon the property of another without his consent. As an example, a portion of a building that protrudes beyond its property line and onto another. Encroachments that continue for a great length of time without objection may be adjudged an implied easement. Encroachments can be written into a contract of sale with the buyer aware of and accepting the risk. If, however, an encroachment is not known and a further study reveals that one exists, it may render the title unmarketable.

ENCUMBRANCE—A legal right or interest in land that diminishes its value. It can take numerous forms, such as zoning restrictions, easements, claims, mortgages, liens, charges, a pending legal action, unpaid taxes or in the form of restrictive covenants. It does not prevent transfer of the property to another.

ENDORSEMENT—1. Approval by signing one's name to a document. 2. Guaranteeing a loan in case a debtor fails to make payment. 3. Formally sanctioning.

ENDOW—1. To furnish a DOWER. The valuable personalty or realty a wife brings with her upon marriage. 2. To bestow an income upon, as when one provides funds for an institute of learning.

ENFEOFF—To give someone a gift of ownership to property. Giving fee simple possession without receiving compensation.

ENHANCE—To increase or grow in value. To make greater. By appreciation or improvements made to property, its market value is raised or enhanced. Intensify.

ENJOIN—To impose by authority. Prohibit by a court order; forbid. To regulate by a legal order.

ENTAIL—The restricting of inherited property to the lineal heirs or to a select portion of them, such as to a male or female heir.

ENTIRETY—Complete. Sum total. A form of joint possession, as when land is owned equally by husband and wife. (See TENANCY BY THE ENTIRETY (ENTIRETIES.)

ENTITLE—To give title to another. Designate. Provide sufficient rights to claim title to something.

ENTITLEMENT—To be legally entitled to something. The giving of a right or title.

ENTREPRENEUR—A sole proprietor of a business. An individual who builds a commercial enterprise taking all the risks and responsibilities, suffering any loss or enjoying any profit that may result.

ENURE—To accrue. (See INURE for more complete definition.)

EQUAL DIGNITY—A reference to mortgages, liens or other legal obligations that are equally ranked in status, so that one does not take precedence over the other.

EQUAL OPPORTUNITY IN HOUSING—(See DISCRIMINATORY COVE-NANTS.)

EQUALIZATION OF ASSESSMENTS—In taxation, it is the process of adjusting assessments in a particular taxing district in order to bring them in line with surrounding areas. The purpose of the adjustment is to assure an overall uniformity between the assessed value and the market value of property, as well as to maintain an adequate tax base.

EQUITABLE LIEN—1. A lien arising or existing in equity (fairness). It can evolve from a written contract, where intent to create a lien on a particular property is clearly indicated, or by a court of equity, where right of justice and fair play is applied. 2. A debtor's right to have an asset he possesses applied in whole or part to the payment of the debt.

EQUITABLE TITLE—1. The right that exists in equity to obtain absolute owner-ship to property when title is held in another's name. 2. An interest in title to land that may not amount to a fee simple estate, but a right of which a court will take notice and seriously consider.

EQUITY—1. The difference between the current market value of a property and the liens that exist against it. Equity can also refer to the difference between the cost of the property and the liens against it. 2. In law, equity refers to natural justice. Something that is fair, just and morally right, after all facts are carefully considered. The law of equity is different from and generally overrides statute law. It covers reason, natural rights and ethics, rather than a strict interpretation of the written law.

EQUITY BUILD-UP—A mortgage term referring to the principal repayment in loan amortization which decreases the debt and increases the owner's equity.

EQUITY KICKER—The ownership interest a lender obtains in the property he finances. (See KICKER.)

EQUITY OF REDEMPTION—A mortgagor's right to redeem an estate after it has been forfeited for non-payment, but before it is foreclosed. Title to the property remains with the mortgagor. He may, at a specified time and place, pay the debt along with paying interest, legal fees and any other accumulated costs. This differs from the right of redemption in that equity of redemption must take place *before* foreclosure and is not granted by statute. (See RIGHT OF REDEMPTION.)

EQUITY PARTICIPATION—(See INCOME PARTICIPATION.)

EROSION—The gradual wearing away of land by water, wind and general weather conditions.

ESCALATOR CLAUSE—A clause providing for increased payments in the event of specified occurrences, as for example, in leases of long duration where such matters as taxes, insurance and increased operating costs can appreciably change. So that the lease will continue to be an equitable one for years after it is drawn, the rental amount is proportionately adjusted to the increases. It is also called a GRADED LEASE or STEP-UP LEASE. Escalator clauses can be applied to contracts as well, providing for an increase in price when materials and labor are appreciably advanced.

ESCAPE CLAUSE—A clause is an agreement allowing one or more of the parties to modify it or to withdraw completely. The opposite of an ironclad agreement.

ESCARPMENT—A long, steep slope. A cliff that divides more level surfaces. Escarpments are generally the result of erosion.

ESCHEAT—The reversion of property to the government when a person dies without leaving a will and having no heirs, or when it is abandoned.

ESCROW—Something of value left in trust to a third party. It can take the form of money, a deed, a bond, or real property itself. Upon fulfillment of the conditions, and a mutual agreement by the principals, the escrow may be released.

ESCROW ACCOUNT—A special bank account maintained by brokers, attorneys, trustees, banks, etc., who are authorized to hold money in trust for others. Most state laws require that special escrow accounts be maintained by anyone acting in this capacity and that its funds be kept strictly separate from any other account. Escrowing funds plays an important role in transacting real estate. By placing money or other valuables in the care of a mutually acceptable third party, the sincerity and good faith of the one making an offer are shown. Also called a TRUST ACCOUNT.

ESCROW AGENT—A party holding funds or something of value in trust for another.

ESCROW ANALYSIS—A study of a mortgagor's escrow fund to see if it will be adequate to cover anticipated expenditures, such as for tax and insurance increases, special assessments, furniture and appliance replacements, and others.

ESQUIRE—Abbreviated as Esq. Used as a title of respect following the name of a person admitted to practice law. A courtesy title used for English gentry.

ESTATE—1. A party's possessory interest in land and the improvements upon it. His real estate holdings. The rights, title and ownership one possesses in real and personal property. 2. The assets left by a deceased person and distributed to his heirs or in the absence of a will, given to the state.

ESTATE AT SUFFERANCE—This type of estate exists when one who was rightfully in possession, or had lawful title, keeps it beyond the termination period of the agreement or after title was vested in another. (See TENANT AT SUFFERANCE.)

ESTATE AT WILL—An estate of indefinite duration allowing the lessee possession as long as both lessor and lessee mutually agree to it. If this reciprocal agreement is changed by either party, the estate at will may be terminated. A month to month tenancy is an example of this type of estate.

ESTATE BY THE ENTIRETY—A single estate held by both husband and wife jointly. An estate in which husband and wife are as one. They are each in possession of the entire estate and when one dies the surviving spouse does not inherit the other's interest, but automatically comes into sole ownership and use.

ESTATE FOR LIFE—(See LIFE ESTATE.)

ESTATE FOR YEARS—An estate established for a definite period of time, longer than a person's lifetime, for a year, or even less.

ESTATE IN FEE SIMPLE—(See FEE: FEE SIMPLE: FEE SIMPLE ABSOLUTE.)

ESTATE IN LAND—The property or interest one has in land.

ESTATE IN REMAINDER—(See REMAINDER ESTATE.)

ESTATE IN REVERSION—The remaining part of an estate that the grantor holds after certain interests in it have been transferred to another, such as the relinquishing of rights and possession under a lease. After expiration of the lease, the property automatically reverts to the grantor or his heirs. That which takes place when an estate is returned to the grantor upon the death of the grantee.

ESTATE IN SEVERALTY—An estate held by one person only. No one else has any part or interest in it.

ESTATE IN TAIL—(See ENTAIL.)

ESTATE OF FREEHOLD—A real estate interest no less than an estate for life.

ESTATE TAX—An excise tax imposed by the federal or state government upon an estate for transferring property from the deceased to his heirs. This is separate and distinct from an inheritance tax which is levied against the heirs for receiving the estate.

ESTIMATE—1. To approximate or set a value. Evaluate; appraise. To fix or assign the size or worth of something. 2. A written statement of the approximate charges to do a specified job.

ESTOP—To impede; stop; bar; obstruct.

ESTOPPEL CERTIFICATE (OR LETTER)—An instrument used when assigning a mortgage to another, setting forth the exact remaining balance of the indebtedness. It can be signed by the mortgagor or mortgagee, but the one so doing is held responsible for the representations made. It is variously known as a Certificate of No

Defense, Declaration of No Set-off, Waiver of Defense, Owner's Estoppel Certificate and Reduction of Mortgage Certificate.

ESTREPEMENT—The wasting of land, as when a tenant makes the ground barren through improper farming methods. The landlord or the heirs who hold a reversionary interest would be detrimentally effected.

ETHICS—Accepted standards of right and wrong. Moral conduct, duty and behavior. (See CODE OF ETHICS.)

ET AL—(Latin) The term means "and another" or "and others." It is used in legal documents when a list of names is given that has to be repeated later in the instrument. Rather than state again the entire roster, the first name or two on the list are given followed by *et al.*

ET UXOR—(Latin) It means "and wife." It is frequently abbreviated *et ux.*

EURODOLLAR—A United States dollar deposited in a European bank.

EVALUATION—To find or fix the value; to estimate; to appraise.

EVICTION—The act of dispossessing a person from property. Forcing out; ejection, expulsion. Eviction can take three forms: actual, constructive or partial. Actual or *total eviction* is physical expulsion from the premises. Constructive eviction occurs when a landlord's acts render the property unfit for use, such as shutting off water, heat or electricity. Partial eviction takes place when the one in possession is deprived of a portion of the leased or occupied premises.

EVIDENCE—That which furnishes proof; testimony. Grounds for belief or disbelief. Facts established in a court of law.

EXAMINATION OF TITLE—A search of the records relating to a property to determine the status of the title as to its marketability and insurability, and to ascertain if any liens, easements, encumbrances and possible "clouds" on the title exist.

EXCEPTION TO TITLE—An apparent defect or insufficiency in the title brought to light as a result of an examination of title or through other research.

EXCHANGE OF REAL ESTATE—A real estate transaction in which two or more properties are traded either at equal (par) value or when a sum of money is used to balance the exchange. Both principals simultaneously become buyers and sellers. This form of dual sale has become increasingly popular in recent years, mainly because of the attractive capital gains tax benefits it affords. In commercial real estate, as well as residential, (unlike in a normal sale) tax obligations are indefinitely deferred when properties are exchanged.

   Another frequently used form of exchanging real estate occurs in conjunction with the sale of new homes. Builders, to expedite or insure a sale, often take in trade the purchaser's present residence.

EXCISE TAXES—This tax takes the form of licensing fees to practice one's trade, occupation or profession; also, taxes on manufactured and consumed products, but it does not include taxation of property or the income received from real estate. Excise taxes are established by federal, state and local agencies. Examples: license fees, document recording fees, gasoline taxes, severance taxes, sales taxes, estate taxes, etc.

EXCLUSIVE AGENCY—An agreement, generally in writing, employing a broker for a specified period of time to the exclusion of all other brokers. In the event another broker makes the sale, the one possessing the exclusive agency is also entitled to a commission. In an exclusive agency the only time a broker will *not* receive a commission upon a sale being made is when the owner sells the property himself. (See also EXCLUSIVE RIGHT OF SALE, EXCLUSIVE LISTING.)

EXCLUSIVE AUTHORITY TO LEASE FORM—(See PORTFOLIO OF FORMS, page 332.)

EXCLUSIVE LISTING—A property listing held by one real estate agency to the exclusion of all others. There are two types of exclusive listings: EXCLUSIVE AGENCY and EXCLUSIVE RIGHT OF SALE. (See those terms for the distinction between them.)

EXCLUSIVE POSSESSION—Having complete control and being in distinct, sole possession of the property.

EXCLUSIVE RIGHT OF SALE—An agreement (usually written) employing a broker for a specified period of time to the exclusion of all others. In this form of exclusive listing, not only is the broker protected in the event of a sale by another broker, but he is also entitled to a commission even if the owner sells the property himself.

EXCULPATE—To excuse from fault or responsibility. Free from blame. Vindicate. Absolve.

EXCULPATORY CLAUSE—A clause often included in leases that clears or relieves the landlord of liability for personal injury to tenants as well as for property damages. It does not always protect him, however, against injury to a third party.

EXECUTED CONTRACT—A signed contract.

EXECUTION—1. Performance; the act of completing or accomplishing. In real estate it is the signature on an instrument and the delivery of same. Different documents require various further verifications, however, such as being notarized, acknowledged, attested to, and sealed. 2. A legal order directing an authorized official to enforce a judgement against the property of a debtor.

EXECUTOR—A man appointed under the terms of a will to execute its provisions and dispose of the property as written or implied. (See also ADMINISTRATOR.)

EXECUTOR'S DEED—This deed conveys title to a testator's property. If authorization to convey property is not given the executor in the will, permission of the court must be obtained.

EXECUTORY CONTRACT—A contract where there remains something to be done by either party before title can pass. A contract not completely performed. When that which remains to be done is completed it becomes an "executed" contract and the transfer of title may then take place.

EXECUTORY DEVISE—An executory devise comes into force when, under the terms of a will, a future contingency arises necessitating a delay in exercising the will. This contingency must take place, if it occurs at all, during the lifetime of the heir or within 21 years and 9 months of the testator's death.

EXECUTRESS—A female EXECUTOR.

EXECUTRIX—A woman appointed under the terms of a will to execute the provisions therein and dispose of the property as written or implied.

EXEMPTION—1. Release or immunity from a liability, obligation or duty. 2. Immunity granted from a tax. (See HOMESTEAD EXEMPTION.)

EXERCISE—To motivate by doing something. To put into use. Activate by signing a document. As an example, one exercises an option by depositing funds and writing a letter of acceptance.

EXISTING MORTGAGE—A mortgage that is presently encumbering a property. It may or may not remain on the property after being sold.

EXPANSION ATTIC—An attic having a sufficiently high roof line to be adaptable for finishing into a habitable room.

EXPENSES—Disbursements. The expending or outlay of money or credit. Costs; charges incurred; business operating payments. An amount that is expended.

EXPIRATION—Termination. Coming to the end.

EXPOSURE—The situation of a property regarding compass direction or its access to air or light, as a building having southern or eastern exposure.

EXPRESS—Directly stated or written. Not represented by implication but clearly brought out. To represent in words or acts; explicit. The opposite of imply.

EXPRESS CONTRACT—A contract where all terms and conditions are openly mentioned and explicitly agreed upon by the principals.

EXPRESS EASEMENT—An easement written into a deed or other document.

EXPROPRIATE—To take over possession or ownership rights, as when the government assumes control of privately held land under the right and power of eminent domain.

EXTENDED COVERAGE—Additional insurance at an extra premium for coverage not generally found in the normal insurance contract. Insurance for the coverage of certain specified risks, such as smoke damage, windstorm, hail, lightning, vehicle damage, riots, aircraft accidents, explosions, civil disorders, etc.

EXTENSION—1. An increase in the length of time. The act of being extended. The granting of additional time in which to perform some act. 2. A section forming an addition, as a new wing of a building is an extension of the exisiting structure.

EXTENSION AGREEMENT—An agreement to extend the terms of an instrument. An extension agreement in a mortgage, for example, grants additional time to perform one or more of its provisions.

The extension agreement document can take the form of a detailed separate instrument, or it can be simply endorsed on the original agreement as follows:

> The time of the foregoing agreement is extended to the ___ day of _____, 19 ___. In all other respects this agreement shall be modified and in full force. Time still is of the essence of this agreement.

EXTENSION OF LEASE—An agreement extending or renewing the terms of a lease for a period beyond the expiration date. (See LEASE RENEWAL.)

EXTENSION OF MORTGAGE—An agreement extending the terms of a mortgage.

EXTINGUISHMENT—Removing or discharging an obligation, contract or any portion of one. To cause to nullify. Abolish. A mortgage, for example, is said to be satisfied, and the obligation extinguished when it is paid.

EXTORTION—Unlawfully obtaining money, property or a promise from another. Extracting funds by the threat of bodily injury, loss of property or damaged reputation.

EXTRAPOLATE—The taking of known, proven facts to project or determine other conclusions. To predict by an extension of facts at hand and experience.

EXTRAS—A term referring to additional items put into a building. They represent extra materials or appliances not stipulated in the plans, specifications or the contract itself.

EXURBAN—A contrived word applied to the region between the outer reaches of the suburbs and the truly rural areas. The territory between rural and suburban. (See RURAL, RURBAN, SUBURBAN, URBAN.)

EYE APPEAL—The outward attractiveness of property that adds to its value. The visual appeal of any parcel of real estate that contributes to its salability.

F

FABRIC—Something structured or put together. That which is fabricated. A building, edifice.

FABRICATE—To construct; build. Make by assembling.

FABRIC LAND—In early English law this was the name given to lands that were donated to religious orders. The purpose of such gifts was to improve the strength and substance (the fabric) of the church.

FACADE—The exterior face or front side of a building. The front of a structure that often has an imposing or distinctive architectural design or flair.

FACE VALUE—The apparent value. Value indicated on the outside. The value shown on the face of any instrument such as stock certificates, bonds, bills or currency. Par value. In some areas the face value of an instrument, such as a note, is the principal amount, plus the accrued interest.

FACIA—(See FASCIA.)

FACSIMILE—An exact replica. A faithfully reproduced copy preserving all the marks of the original. A likeness of a first document.

FACTO—(Latin) In fact. By an act. By an actual deed or accomplishment. (See also *DE FACTO, IPSO FACTO.*)

FAILURE OF CONSIDERATION—When the consideration given in a contract or other instrument has lost its value or even lessened in value from what it was originally. For example, a check given as a deposit that is returned for insufficient funds.

FAILURE TO PERFORM—Failure of one of the parties to a contract to perform what was agreed upon. This can occur by wilful design or because of subsequent circumstances beyond control, preventing performance.

FAIR—Equitable; reasonable; impartial; just. Free from favoritism; unbiased. This word is frequently used in real estate in such forms as Fair Consideration, Fair Contract, Fair Dealings, Fair Market Value, Fair Rent, Fair and Equitable Settlements, Fair Compensation, Fair Housing, etc.

FALCIDIAN LAW—The legal premise that no one can bequeath more than a certain proportion of his estate in legacies to other than his heirs. Dating back to early Roman law, which provided that at least one-quarter of an estate must be retained by the heirs, this principal of testamentary disposition prevails today in many parts of the world.

FALL OF LAND—A parcel of land measuring approximately six yards square.

FALLOW LAND—1. Plowed land allowed to go unseeded for a year or longer. 2. Inactive, dormant land, idle land. Unproductive property.

FANNIE MAE—A common name for the Federal National Mortgage Association (FNMA).

FARM BROKER—A real estate broker who specializes in the sale and leasing of farm properties.

FARM LAND—Land devoted to agricultural purposes either in crop production or the raising of livestock.

FARM LEASE—A lease especially written and adopted for the renting of farm properties.

FARMSTEAD—The main structure and nearby areas that comprise a farm. The center of farm living and working activity.

FARTHING OF LAND—One-quarter acre. A rood. Also called a farthingdeal.

FASCIA—A flat strip of wood or metal used as moulding for finishing and decorative purposes. Also spelled FACIA.

FATE—A banking term used when a special inquiry is made concerning the disposition of a specific check. A check being good only at the bank drawn on, a business man in one part of the country may have to know immediately if it will be honored in another. He can wire or phone the bank asking "what is the fate" of the check.

FEALTY—Fidelity. The quality of being faithful. Allegiance. Loyalty.

FEASIBILITY STUDY—The study of an area or neighborhood to determine all possibilities for putting it to its highest and best use.

FEDERAL ESTATE TAX—(See ESTATE TAX.)

FEDERAL HOME LOAN BANK SYSTEM—A network of Federal Home Loan Banks having eleven regional offices throughout the country. Their function is to provide reserve funds for Federal Savings and Loan Associations. They also serve as a control and regulatory body. Each member institution is a shareholder having capital stock in its regional Federal Home Loan Bank.

FEDERAL HOUSING ADMINISTRATION (FHA)—The FHA was founded in 1934 by the National Housing Act to provide mortgage insurance to approved lending institutions for financing homes and apartments. FHA insures the lending institution 97% of the first $15,000 plus 90% of the next $5,000, plus 80% of the remainder. FHA mortgages can be as high as $30,000 on one-family homes, and may even exceed this amount in Alaska, Hawaii and Guam because material and labor costs are appreciably higher there. The FHA will insure the bank up to 97% of the money it lends, if the property and mortgage are approved by them. In this manner the FHA is able to control and raise housing and living conditions and act as a stabilizing influence on the national mortgage market. Interest rates vary in the mortgage field, but FHA loans invariably bear a slightly lower interest rate than prevailing conventional loan rates. The loans extend up to 30 years and in cases where a house is built under FHA inspections, a mortgage up to 35 years duration is permitted. The FHA does not lend money itself, nor does it construct housing.

To counteract the lower-than-market interest rates under this program, lending institutions are charging discounts or points before they will make an FHA loan. (A point is 1% of the amount borrowed). The amount of points charged varies with the changing mortgage market.

The two classifications of the FHA loan insurance program are known as Title I and Title II. Title I covers repairs and improvements made to homes. The amount of the loan cannot exceed $3,500. Title II encompasses the entire remaining FHA loan insurance program. Included in it are mortgages for both new construction and resale homes as outlined above, as well as insuring loans for rehabilitating older properties. For rehabilitation under Ttile II the loan can go as high as $10,000.

FEDERAL LAND BANK SYSTEM—The purpose of this government agency is to make available long-term mortgage loans, at equitable terms, to farmers, so they may own their own farms. The Federal Land Bank System is the largest holder of farm mortgages in the world and hundreds of thousands of farmers have become independent land owners through this system.

FEDERAL LANDS—Land owned by the federal government. All such properties are under the control and supervision of the Bureau of Land Management, an agency of the Department of Interior.

FEDERAL NATIONAL MORTGAGE ASSOCIATION (FNMA)—More popularly known as FANNIE MAE, formerly a branch of the U.S. Department of Housing and Urban Development (HUD). Its prime function is to purchase mortgages from banks, trust companies, mortgage companies, savings and loan associations and insurance companies, to help them further facilitate the distribution of funds for home mortgages. Occasionally Fannie Mae provides mortgage money directly, where by so doing improved housing and economic stability result. Fannie Mae is a privately owned corporation subject to the strict supervision of the Secretary of HUD. Some of its earlier functions such as financing government sanctioned, low-rent housing and in management and liquidation have been taken over by its offshoot, the GOVERNMENT NATIONAL MORTGAGE ASSOCIATION (GNMA). (See that title.)

FEDERAL REVENUE STAMPS—(See FEDERAL STAMPS.)

FEDERAL SAVINGS AND LOAN ASSOCIATION—A financial institution that is federally chartered and privately owned either by stockholders or by depositors. Federal Savings and Loan Associations' prime functions are twofold: 1. Financing homes and, to a more limited degree, commercial properties, through conventional loans and FHA and VA mortgages. And, 2. providing interest bearing savings accounts (which are government insured to $20,000). All Federal Savings and Loan Associations are required to be members of their regional Federal Home Loan Bank.

FEDERAL STAMPS—In the transfer of title to real property, up until January 1, 1968, a federal tax was levied in the form of stamps required to be placed on the deed. (The rate was 55¢ per $500, or a fraction thereof, on the purchase price over the existing mortgage.) Federal stamps are no longer required on real estate transactions.

FEE: FEE SIMPLE: FEE SIMPLE ABSOLUTE—All three terms are synonymous and mean that the owner has absolute, good and marketable title to the property conveyed to him. It is complete ownership without condition. Fee simple is the largest and highest possible estate one can possess in real estate. The owner of an estate in fee simple has every legal possession with unconditional power and right to dispose of it in his lifetime or retain it for his heirs upon death.

FEE APPRAISER—A professional appraiser whose services are available to the general public for a fee.

FEE CERTIFICATE—(See LAND TRUST CERTIFICATE.)

FEE CONDITIONAL—(See FEE UPON CONDITION.)

FEE DETERMINABLE—The holder of a fee determinable has a fee simple estate with the limitations upon it of a contingency. If that contingency occurs the property will automatically revert to the grantor.

FEE OWNER—(See FEE: FEE SIMPLE: FEE SIMPLE ABSOLUTE.)

FEE TAIL—An estate left only to the heirs of one's body.

FEE UPON CONDITION—The holder possesses a fee simple estate with a conditional provision. If the specified condition occurs it may then be clarified, in which case the fee will remain with the current holder and not revert to the prior owner.

FEME: FEMME—A woman.

FEME COVERT—A married woman.

FEME-SOLE—A single woman.

FEN—Low, marshy land. Boggy ground.

FEOFFARE—The giving or bestowing of a fee.

FEOFFEE—The receiver of a fee.

FEOFFEE TO USES—A person receiving and holding a fee in trust for a third party.

FEOFFMENT—Granting as a gift ownership to property with actual delivery of possession.

FEUD—The early European right to the use and occupancy of land being held by a superior or soverign for the rendering of services. (See FEUDAL SYSTEM.)

FEUDAL SYSTEM—A European and English system of land ownership that prevailed during the eleventh, twelfth and part of the thirteenth centuries. It maintained the ancient concept that all land is in the name of the king or soverign. Anyone living upon the land or putting it to use does so in return for services. They were said to have a "feud" to the land. The feudal system is directly opposed to the allodial system which is the American concept of free land ownership. (See ALLODIAL SYSTEM, FEUD.)

FHA—Abbreviation for Federal Housing Administration. (See FEDERAL HOUSING ADMINISTRATION.)

FIAT—(Latin) A decree. A short, authoritative sanction. A directive from a legally recognized source that an act be done.

FIDELITY—Fealty. The obligation one has to his employer to faithfully perform his duties. Loyalty.

FIDELITY BOND—(See SURETY BOND.)

FIDES—(Latin) Faith. Honesty. Trust. (See BONA FIDE).

FIDUCIARY—A position of trust and confidence. One who transacts business for another and by so doing establishes a relationship of great faith. A broker is automatically put in such a position when he is employed to act for another in real estate. A person performs in a fiduciary capacity when he is given authorization to act for the best interests of another.

FINANCES—That which pertains to money matters. Money or other liquid resources. Relating to money and business; the management of money.

FINANCIAL STATEMENT—A formal written statement of an individual's or company's assets, liabilities and net worth as of a specified date.

FINDER'S FEE—As applied to real estate brokerage it is generally understood to mean a fee paid to another for furnishing a buyer or a property listing. For example, it is not uncommon for a broker specializing in one phase of real estate to have prospects referred to him. If a sale results, the specializing broker would pay the referring broker a fee for "finding" the customer for him.

FIRE INSURANCE—An insurance policy indemnifying the holder against loss by fire.

FIRE WALL—A wall constructed of fireproof material installed to check the spread of fire into other areas of a building or to adjacent properties.

FIRM CONTRACT—A valid, binding contract.

FIRM COMMITMENT—(See COMMITMENT.)

FIRM PRICE—A selling price that leaves no room for negotiations. The price quoted is the price the owner will accept and nothing less.

FISCAL YEAR—The business year as distinguished from the calendar year. A twelve-month period in which accounts of a business are calculated and income taxes computed. Companies use various periods as their fiscal year, the most commonly used period ending June 30.

FIRST DEED OF TRUST—The deed of trust that is recorded first and is the first lien. (See DEED OF TRUST, SECOND DEED OF TRUST.)

FIRST DEVISEE—The first recipient of an estate by the terms of a will.

FIRST LIEN—The lien that takes legal priority over any other charges or encumbrances upon property. It is the one that must be completely satisfied before others are paid. A FIRST MORTGAGE.

FIRST LOAN—First mortgage.

FIRST MORTGAGE—The mortgage on property that is superior to any other. The one that takes precedence over a junior or second mortgage. A FIRST LIEN. (See MORTGAGE.)

FIRST MORTGAGE BOND—A bond that has a first mortgage as security.

FIRST PAPERS—A term used extensively in some areas of the country (notably New England) referring to a BINDER or DEPOSIT RECEIPT. It is literally the first documentation of an agreement.

FIRST PRIVILEGE TO BUY—(See FIRST REFUSAL.)

FIRST REFUSAL—The right given a person to have the first privilege to buy or lease real estate, or the right to meet any offer made by another.

FIRST RIGHT TO BUY—(See FIRST REFUSAL.)

FIXED ASSETS—Assets necessary for the general operation of a business. Assets that are permanent in nature and have an economic life extending over years, such as tools, machines, office equipment, the factory or warehouse and the land it is on.

FIXTURE—Any fittings or furnishings that are attached to a building and considered a part of it. What is annexed to real property and legally goes with it when sold.

FLASHING—Sheet metal used on roof joints, around dormers, chimneys, drainspouts, etc. for waterproofing.

Chimney Flashing

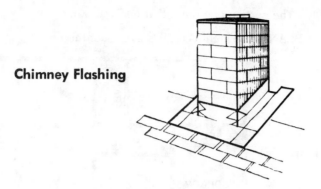

FLAT—1. An apartment unit or suite of rooms on one floor used for residential purposes. 2. Any land of even surface. Level ground.

FLAT LEASE—A lease with regular, equal, periodic payments. One in which the amount and the time for payment (monthly, quarterly, yearly) remain constant throughout the term of the lease. Also called a straight lease.

FLAT LOAN—(See STRAIGHT LOAN.)

FLOAT—A banking term indicating a check that has not been cleared for collection. When banking within a local area, checks may float for approximately three days before clearance, with out-of-town and out-of-state checks taking as long as ten days or more.

FLOATER POLICY—An "all risk" insurance policy covering the personal property in a house.

FLOATING INTEREST RATE—A variable interest rate that changes with the mortgage market. One such sample clause in a mortgage agreement follows.

> The interest rate shall, from the date hereof until maturity, bear interest equal to _____ Bank's prime rate subject to a maximum of _____% percent per annum and a minimum of _____% percent per annum, calculated on the daily outstanding principal balance, payable monthly, commencing _____ _____, 19____, and on the first day of each month thereafter; all accrued and unpaid interest being due and payable on maturity. Changes in the interest rate on said indebtedness shall be effective on the day of a change in said bank's prime rate.

FLOATING ZONE—A zoning provision allowing a change in regulations for an area in return for certain compensating facilities or controls. This frequently occurs when the builder of a large, planned community seeks to develop an entire neighborhood. As an example, it may be mutually agreed that in return for the right to build closer to a property line, a portion of the land will be set aside for parks and recreational facilities.

FLOOR—The portion of a room that one walks upon.

FLOOR PLAN—The architectural drawings of the floor layout of a building.

Floor Plan

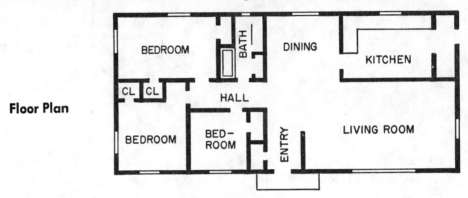

FLOWAGE RIGHT OR EASEMENT—(See FLOWING LANDS.)

FLOWING LANDS—The raising and lowering of water onto another's land by means of a dam or by dredging. (See OVERFLOW RIGHTS.)

FLUID ASSETS—Assets that are readily convertible into cash.

FLY-BY-NIGHT-OPERATION—A company that operates on the fringe of the law, often resorting to unethical or illegal methods of doing business. It is so named because such operations go in and out of business under the protective cover of darkness.

FLYSPECKING—A jargon word referring to the careful scrutiny of a document, particularly in reference to an abstract of title, to uncover every technical defect; the inference being that even a flyspeck will be detected and examined by the diligent searcher.

FOOT-FRONTAGE—(See FRONT FOOT VALUE.)

FORAGE ACRE—An acre of land that can be totally utilized for grazing animals.

FORCED SALE—A forced sale occurs when one sells or loses his property without actually wanting to dispose of it, as in bankruptcy proceedings or to satisfy unpaid taxes or liens. (See ALIENATION.)

FORECLOSURE—A legal action instituted by a mortgage holder, when a mortgage goes into default, to end all rights and possession of the mortgagor. The subject asset then becomes the property of the mortgagee.

FORECLOSURE SALE—A sale in which the property pledged as security for a debt is sold to pay the debt.

FOREIGN CORPORATION—A corporation conducting business outside the state in which it has been granted its charter. If the company's home office is in another state or country, it is considered a foreign corporation.

FORESHORE LAND—Land that is above sea level only at low tide. Visible land between high and low tide.

FOREST—A tract of land covered with trees. Wooded land.

FORFEIT—To give up the right to or physical possession of something. Loss of anything of value because of failure to act or otherwise do what was agreed upon.

FORGERY—To fabricate, counterfeit or imitate with intent to deceive or defraud. Fraudulently signing, writing or otherwise altering an instrument.

FORMAL CONTRACT—A contract that is in writing and signed under seal.

FORMS—Printed or typed documents, for specific purposes, having blank spaces for filling in variable information.

FOUNDATION—The masonry substructure of a building upon which the upper portion is supported.

4-3-2-1 DEPTH RULE—An appraisal method once used primarily by assessors in mass-appraising for evaluating different portions of a parcel of land. By this rule, property is divided into four equal parts from front to rear, with 100' depth taken as standard. The first quarter having street frontage is evaluated at 40 per cent of the total value; the next quarter is assigned 30 per cent of value; the next 20 per cent and the rear portion 10 per cent. Today, with more refined depth tables developed for specific communities and neighborhoods, the 4-3-2-1 Rule is generally conceded to have limited application for mass-appraising as well as individual appraisals.

FRAME CONSTRUCTION—A building constructed of wood framing. The studs, walls and partitions are also primarily of wood, as are the supporting roof and floors.

FRAMED OUT—A building term meaning the completion of the outer skeleton or framework of a structure.

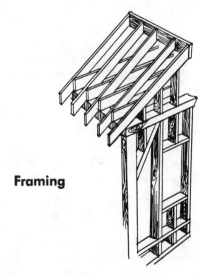

Framing

FRANCHISE—A special, usually exclusive right or privilege granted a person, individual or company.

FRANK-TENANT—An owner of property. A FREEHOLDER.

FRAUD—Deceiving; misrepresenting. An untruth in order to obtain an illegal advantage of or something of value from another. Wilful deceit to deprive someone of his rights or to otherwise injure him. Fraud can follow three forms: 1. actual fraud, which has to do with an intentional untruth, direct deceit or cunning and outright trickery; 2. constructive fraud, which is less direct and relates to a person's conscience or to a breach of fiduciary relationship; and 3. legal fraud, which refers to a misrepresentation made without knowingly doing so.

FRAUDS, STATUTE OF—(See STATUTE OF FRAUDS.)

FRAUDULENT CONCEALMENT—Failure to disclose a material fact that should legally and morally have been disclosed. The intent of the party must be to mislead or defraud. Fraudulent concealment in real estate transactions is grounds for rescinding a contract.

FRAUDULENT CONVEYANCE—Transferring property with intent to avoid or delay payment of an obligation, or to defraud someone. Conveying property to another in order to put it beyond the reach of a creditor.

FRAUDULENT REPRESENTATION—Misrepresentation of a material fact with the intent of deceiving another. If by such planned, purposeful misrepresentation one is induced to act to his detriment, fraudulent representation will have occurred and grounds for rescission of the agreement may result. Likewise, a promise to perform without intention of so doing constitutes fraudulent representation.

FREE AND CLEAR—A reference to ownership of property that is free of all indebtedness. Property that never had a mortgage encumbering it, or in which the mortgage has been paid in full.

FREEDEALER—In some states a married woman dealing in real estate on her own behalf must register with the state as a freedealer. After being declared as such, she no longer needs her husband's signature or consent to buy, sell or lease property.

FREE ENTERPRISE—The inherent right of an individual to conduct business for profit in any manner he sees fit, as long as he abides by the law. Under the free enterprise system, in force in the United States and other industrial nations of the free world, a businessman may conduct his affairs freely and openly and with as few restrictive governmental regulations as possible.

FREE ENTRY—The right of an individual to go on land as often as he requires or sees fit to do so.

FREEHOLD—A real estate interest in fee simple or one that is not less than an estate for life. For an estate to be a freehold, it must have a) the qualities of immobility, meaning land or an interest that is derived from land, and b) ownership of indeterminate duration; that is, the length of time for the estate to endure cannot be fixed.

FREEHOLDER—A person who owns property. One who holds legal or equitable title to property. The possessor of a freehold estate.

FREEHOLD ESTATE—(See FREEHOLD.)

FREEWAY—A super-highway designed to allow many vehicles to travel rapidly into and around heavily populated areas. A highway that is free of "stop" and "go" traffic signals.

FREE WILL—The ability to choose freely. A conclusion or action voluntarily reached. Free choice. The right and power to make a decision without fear or restraint.

FREEZING PRICES—Keeping prices or rentals as they exist, either by choice or by law; not raising or lowering them.

FRONTAGE—The distance land or a building extends on a street, watercourse, etc. Where a building faces.

FRONT ELEVATION—The front view of a structure in architectural plans.

FRONT FOOTAGE RULE—A rule applied by assessors establishing a uniform front footage value regardless of the property's depth.

FRONT FOOT VALUE—The value of property measured per linear foot fronting on a street or watercourse. The price for which land sells per foot of such frontage. Land so measured is understood to mean its extension to the rear of the property line.

FRONT MAN—A person acting as a front or dummy for another. Also called a STRAW MAN.

FRONT MONEY—Money required to get a project underway. Funds used for such matters as the down payment, feasibility study, preliminary plans, appraisal, survey, test borings, etc.

FRUCTUS—(Latin) Literally, the fruits of a thing. The rights or benefits one receives for use and enjoyment of his property. As an example, the rent an owner receives for the use of his land.

FULL COVENANT AND WARRANTY DEED—(See WARRANTY DEED.)

FUNCTIONAL DEPRECIATION—(See FUNCTIONAL OBSOLESCENCE.)

FUNCTIONAL OBSOLESCENCE—Defects in a structure that detract from its marketability and value. When a building begins to outlive its usefulness through antiquated equipment, such as inadequate electrical wiring, outmoded elevator system, lack of or poor air-conditioning, impractical design, faulty heating plant, etc., it becomes functionally obsolete. It cannot compete with more modern facilities.

FUNCTIONAL UTILITY—The use of a property for what it was intended. When a structure complies with safety, zoning and other governmental standards, and its design is not obsolete, it is referred to as being functionally useful. When such standards are lacking and a building becomes antiquated, its practional utility diminishes. Its usefulness is impaired, and it is referred to as having reached a state of FUNCTIONAL OBSOLESCENCE.

FUNDING—The act of providing funds. Financing.

FURLONG—One-eighth of a mile.

FURTHER ASSURANCE WARRANTY—A warranty put into a deed by the grantor stating that if at a later date an error is found to render the title imperfect, he will do whatever is necessary to correct it.

FUTURE ACQUIRED PROPERTY—Property that is not transferred in the usual manner, but at a later, specified time, or is contingent upon some event occuring in the future. (See FUTURE INTEREST.)

FUTURE DEPRECIATION—Anticipated depreciation of an asset. The loss from present value that a property presumably will experience as time diminishes its value. This term, frequently used when making appraisals, takes into account a structure's loss of attractiveness and the ensuing, inevitable FUNCTIONAL OB-SOLESCENCE.

FUTURE ESTATE—An estate created with the distinct purpose of possession being taken at a specified later date or upon the occurance of a future event. It is legally referred to as a NONPOSSESSORY ESTATE.

FUTURE INTEREST—An interest in real or personal property that does not become effective until sometime in the future. For example, a will that stipulates that the recipient is to receive property upon reaching the age of 21.

G

GABLE—A building term meaning the triangular end-wall of a ridged roof. (See HOUSE CROSS SECTION, page 412.)

GABEL—See LAND GABEL.

GAIN—A benefit; increase in value; profit. To obtain possession. Achieve. To get an advantage.

GAMBREL ROOF—A roof design having a comparatively flat upper section with the lower portion more steeply pitched. (See ROOF illustrations.)

GAP FINANCING—Interim financing of any kind, as may occur when a builder obtains a short-term loan for a project until a more permanent loan or mortgage can be secured.

GAP INSURANCE—An insurance policy that would protect the lender from any liens placed on a subject property between title closing and the recording of the deed.

GARDEN APARTMENT—A style of multiple-dwelling building, usually no more than two or three stories high, that provides for lawn and garden areas.

GARNISHEE—The person who legally retains assets until a court decision is reached to determine who is entitled to the asset. The one garnished.

GARNISHMENT—1. A legal notification for a creditor to keep in his possession assets belonging to a debtor until a court decision is reached regarding its disposition. 2. A notification for a third party to stand ready to appear and give information in a court of law.

GARRET—An attic. A room, frequently unfinished, situated just below the roof.

GENERAL AGENT—(See AGENT.)

GENERAL BENEFITS—(See GENERAL IMPROVEMENT.)

GENERAL BUILDING SCHEME—(See DEVELOPMENT.)

GENERAL CONTRACTOR—(See CONTRACTOR.)

GENERAL ESTATE—The entire estate. This term refers to the whole estate that a person possesses.

GENERAL FEE CONDITIONAL—(See FEE TAIL.)

GENERAL IMPROVEMENT—A public improvement that benefits many property owners in a given area, such as water and power lines, sewers, etc. Unlike special benefits, general improvements cannot be directly charged to property owners.

GENERAL LAND OFFICE—(See BUREAU OF LAND MANAGEMENT.)

GENERAL LIEN—A lien against an individual rather than real property. This lien gives the right to detain personal property until a debt is satisfied. The asset involved does not have to be that which created the debt.

GENERAL MORTGAGE—A mortgage covering all of the properties of a debtor and not restricted to a specific parcel. (See BLANKET MORTGAGE.)

GENERAL PARTNER—(See PARTNER)

GENERAL RELEASE—(See RELEASE.)

GENERAL SERVICE ADMINISTRATION (GSA)—Created in 1949, this independent federal agency manages, leases and sells buildings belonging to the United States government. Among its other functions, it distributes and warehouses strategic building and other materials. Regional offices are maintained throughout the country, with headquarters at the General Services Administration Building, 18th and F Streets, N.W. Washington, D.C. 20405.

GENERAL WARRANTY DEED—(See WARRANTY DEED.)

GENTLEMEN'S AGREEMENT—A private agreement between individuals or companies. It sometimes takes the form of monopolizing prices or excluding minority groups from an area. By its nature it is a secretive, verbal agreement.

GEODESIC DOME—A round structure made of small, straight elements that form a series of connecting triangles. When properly attached, the tensile strength thus created provides a structurally-sturdy surface. Also referred to as an O-DOME.

GEODETIC SURVEY—A survey of large land areas that provides allowances for the earth's curvature. The United States Coast And Geodetic Survey System has latitudinal and longitudinal monuments or bench marks located throughout the country. These identify governmental lands as well as private tracts.

GEOGRAPHY—The science of describing the earth's surface, including land and sea areas. The geographic features that comprise a place or region.

GEOLOGIC MAP—A map that shows the surface material and mineral composition of the ground immediately below it. Rock formations, faults, dips and strikes are depicted.

GEOLOGY—A study of the earth's surface and the various layers beneath it. The science dealing with rock formations, fossils, rock movements, and the chemistry of rocks at the earth's crust.

GEORGIAN ARCHITECTURE—A Colonial design frequently featuring high ceilings, high chimneys and balanced windows. Formal in concept, straight lines predominate, providing overall simplistic beauty. The style was copied from eighteenth century English architecture.

GHETTOS—Specific sections of a city in which people of a particular race or national origin are heavily concentrated. Originating in Italy and Eastern Europe, they were the areas where the Jewish population were forced to live.

GIFT—The giving of something of value without receiving or expecting to receive anything in return. A transfer of personal or real property without consideration.

GIFT DEED—A deed given free of charge or for a nominal sum. The consideration given for a gift deed is love and affection.

GIFT TAX—A tax imposed by the federal government on property given as a gift during the donor's lifetime. Some states also impose such a tax.

G.I. LOAN—A Veterans Administration guaranteed loan available to honorably discharged veterans (or an unremarried widow of a veteran who died as a result of service) at a minimum or no down payment. Interest rates on G.I. loans vary with the changing mortgage market, but most are slightly less than those in conventional financing. The loan can be used for buying, building, repairing and improving a home or farm, or to buy land or a building for business purposes. The veteran can obtain the loan for supplies, equipment or working capital to go into a business or profession.

The veteran is protected by a VA appraisal before the loan is approved. There is a limit also on the amount of guarantee that can be issued for a loan. Loans eligible for insurance for real estate purposes may not exceed $26,666. For non-real estate the amount is $13,333 or $6^2/_3$ times the amount of entitlement authorized by the veteran.

A real estate home loan can be made for up to 30 years; for farms, up to 40 years, and for non-real estate, up to 10 years.

Real estate loans for home purposes may be guaranteed up to a maximum of $7,500. For farms or businesses the maximum guarantee is $4,000.

The Veterans Administration also makes direct loans to veterans who are satisfactory risks in certain housing credit-shortage areas. These areas, designated by the VA, are generally confined to rural locales and smaller towns that do not have nearby private lending institutions. (See also VETERANS ADMINISTRATION.)

GINGERBREAD—Fancy, sometimes unnecessary ornamentations added to a building for show.

GINNIE MAE—Colloquial for GOVERNMENT NATIONAL MORTGAGE AS-SOCIATION (GNMA).

GIRDER—A large, main beam; one into which other beams usually meet.

GIVE NOTICE—Informing someone in a proper legal manner, of an impending action. Notification.

GOOD AND VALUABLE CONSIDERATION—(See CONSIDERATION.)

GOOD FAITH—Having honorable intentions. This term denotes integrity in conducting oneself beyond technicalities of law. Acting in good conscience.

GOOD FAITH MONEY—Earnest money; deposit; down payment. Money deposited in trust with a third party to show the good intention of the depositor to go through with a transaction.

GOOD RECORD TITLE—Title to property that is free of recorded encumbrances. If, after a thorough title search, the subject property is found to be unencumbered in a way that a fee simple title can be transferred, the property is said to have good record title.

GOOD TITLE—Title to property sufficiently free of defects and significant objections that it is marketable and the owner can be assured of quiet enjoyment. Also called CLEAR TITLE, MARKETABLE TITLE, MERCHANTABLE TITLE, PERFECT TITLE.

GOODWILL—The intangible part of a business earned by favorably treating the public. It assures future, repeat business and becomes a significant factor when selling. It is an extra increment beyond the value of the stock, current profits, and the property itself. Goodwill is good reputation, resulting in steady trade, that a business maintains by fair and honorable dealings.

GOODS—Items of personal property other than animals. In business, goods refer to merchandise, inventory and stock.

GORE—A small wedge-shaped parcel of land.

GOUGING—The exacting of something improper; overcharging. Receiving of excessive compensation.

GOVERNMENT LAND—Land owned by the government. (See BUREAU OF LAND MANAGEMENT.)

GOVERNMENT LOTS—Parcels of land not divided into regular sections by Government Survey because they were isolated or made irregular in shape by bodies of water. They are identified by being assigned lot numbers.

GOVERNMENT NATIONAL MORTGAGE ASSOCIATION (GNMA)—An Agency of the Department of Housing and Urban Development (HUD), GNMA is an outgrowth of the Federal National Mortgage Association (FNMA) which functions in the Secondary Mortgage Market. GNMA's prime objective is in the area of government sanctioned, special housing programs. It offers permanent financing for low-rent housing in a program to provide better living accommodations for lower- and moderate-income citizens. *Ginnie Mae*, as it is nicknamed, also performs in a management and liquidation capacity when this becomes necessary to protect the government's investment. See also FEDERAL NATIONAL MORTGAGE ASSOCIATION (FNMA).

GOVERNMENT PATENT—The term refers to the original grant of United States government lands to individuals.

GOVERNMENT SURVEY—The federal government in 1785 adopted the Government or Rectangular Survey method of describing land. It is currently in use in 31 states. By this method large or small tracts of land can be easily described and rapidly located. It employs a fixed, imaginary line running east and west across a state, called the Base Line, and another, bisecting it and running north and south, called the Prime or Principal Meridian. See typical map below showing the locations of the Prime Meridians and their Base Lines in the California area.

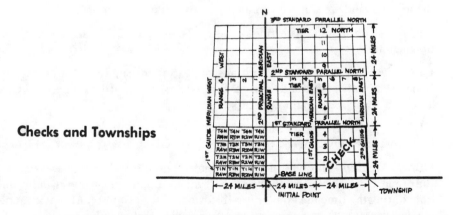

Government or Rectangular Survey

Where the Prime Meridian and Base Line intersect as the point of origin, surveyors divide the land into squares, 24 miles by 24 miles, called "checks." The dividing lines, running east-west and forming the checks, are called Standard Parallels. The lines running north and south are called Guide Meridians.

The squares are further divided into smaller squares, six miles on each side, called Townships. The lines running east and west forming the townships are called Range Lines. The lines running north and south are referred to as Township Lines.

Checks and Townships

With the slight corrections to allow for the earth's curvature, each township is still further divided into 36 Sections one mile by one mile (640 acres).

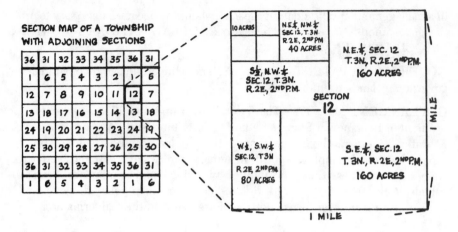

SECTION MAP OF A TOWNSHIP
WITH ADJOINING SECTIONS

Sections may be divided into still smaller half-, quarter-, eighth-, sixteenth-sections, and so on; thus providing an accurate description for even the smallest parcel. This method is also known as Section, Township and Range Description, Rectangular Survey, and U.S. Government Public Land Description.

GRACE PERIOD—A period when a mortgage payment or other debt becomes past due, and before it goes into default. Most mortgages provide for a specified period of time when it can be paid without penalty or default.

GRADE—1. The elevation of a hill, slope, road or sidewalk. The degree it inclines from level ground. 2. To level and even off any sloping surface.

GRADED LEASE—(See ESCALATOR CLAUSE.)

GRADUATED LEASE—A lease agreement providing for periodic increases (or conceivably, decreases) in rent over the term of the lease.

GRAIN RENT—The payment of rent in the form of grain or other crops for the right to farm the land. It is more commonly known as Sharecropping.

GRANT—The act of transferring property. To bestow an interest in real property upon another.

GRANT AND DEMISE—This phrase, appearing in long-term leases, means an implied warranty of title and the right to quiet enjoyment of the property. It creates an estate and not the right of occupancy.

GRANT, BARGAIN AND SELL—This phrase is used in deeds when conveying encumbrance-free property. (See GRANTING CLAUSE.)

GRANT DEED—This type of deed is popularly used in California. It warrants that the property is free of encumbrances made by the grantor or anyone claiming under him, during the time the grantor was the owner of the property. Also, it guarantees any further right to the property that the grantor may acquire.

GRANTEE—The recipient of a grant.

GRANTING CLAUSE—The clause in a deed reciting what is being conveyed. It usually appears just before the description and states "grant, bargain and sell." Also called the Premises.

GRANTOR—1. The donor of a grant. 2. The seller of real estate. The one who relinquishes title to real property.

GRANTOR-GRANTEE INDEX—(See CHAIN OF TITLE.)

GRANTOR'S LIEN—(See VENDOR'S LIEN.)

GRASSLAND—Open farmland covered primarily with grass.

GREENSBORO PLAN—A nickname for the FHA's Conversion Committment Program. First tested and perfected in Greensboro, North Carolina, it is a speeding-up method of processing loan applications.

GRID—Grating. A network of horizontal and vertical lines used to locate specific points or areas on a map.

GRIEVANCE PERIOD—A custom in many sections of the country whereby once a year a specified day or week is designated for the public to register objections to the tax assessment of their property or other claim of inequity.

GROSS—The whole amount with nothing taken out; total. The word is often used in matters related to real estate, with terms such as gross estate, gross profit, gross revenue, gross sales, gross loss, gross lease, gross income, gross earnings, etc. The opposite of net.

GROSS INCOME—The total of money, received from income property or a business, before operating expenses, taxes, depreciation, commissions, salaries, fees, etc. are deducted.

GROSS INCOME MULTIPLIER—A method of estimating the value of certain types of income properties by multiplying the gross income by an established multiplier. If, as an example, an apartment house is valued at 6 X the gross income, and the gross income is $100,000, then the estimated value would be $600,000. Appraisal experts agree that this method, at best, should be used as a rule-of-thumb, and only taken into account in conjunction with other appraisal techniques.

GROSS LEASE—A lease whereby the landlord pays for all repairs, taxes and operating expenses incurred through ownership. It is the opposite of a NET LEASE in which these costs are borne by the tenant.

GROSS RECEIPTS—The total aggregate amount of money received from property.

GROUND—The land itself. The earth's surface. Terra firma; soil.

GROUND FEE—(See GROUND RENT.)

GROUND LANDLORD—The holder (lessor) of a ground lease. The party who grants an estate on which ground rent payment is reserved.

GROUND LEASE—A contract for the possession and use of land. (See GROUND RENT.)

GROUND RENT—Rent for the possession and use of the land, often with a lease of long duration. The length can be for any span of time, but grounds on which buildings are erected customarily have 49 year leases, 99 year leases or longer. Buildings that are constructed on land leased in this manner sometimes have a recapture clause providing for outright purchase of the ground at a fixed price and terms, after a specified number of years have elapsed. Ground rents have numerous variations and refinements to fit specific situations. (See MARYLAND GROUND RENT, PENNSYLVANIA GROUND RENT.)

GROUND WATER—Surface water level that represents the water table.

G.S.A.—GENERAL SERVICE ADMINISTRATION. (See that definition.)

GUARANTEE—The recipient of a guaranty.

GUARANTEED LOAN—A loan in which the lender is guaranteed payment in the event of a default. G. I. loans (Veterans Administration) for example, are guaranteed by the government.

GUARANTEED TITLE POLICY—(See TITLE POLICY.)

GUARANTOR—The one making the guaranty.

GUARDIAN—An individual entrusted with the care of another person or property. A custodian.

GUARDIAN DEED—The form of deed used to convey the property of an infant or an incompetent. Both the transfer of property and selection of a guardian must meet court approval.

GUIDE MERIDIANS—As used in Government Surveys, they are survey lines running due north and south, twenty-four miles apart. (See GOVERNMENT SURVEY.)

H

HABENDUM CLAUSE—The clause in a deed or mortgage that defines the extent of the estate being transferred. It generally reads: "To have and to hold the premises herein granted unto the parties of the second part, his heirs and assigns forever."

HABENDUM ET TENENDUM—(Latin) Found in old deeds and meaning "to have and to hold." (See *HABENDUM* CLAUSE.)

HABITABLE—Capable or fit to be lived in. The word denotes not only a dwelling that would sustain life, but also one that may be occupied in reasonable comfort, safety and enjoyment.

HALF BATH—A room with a toilet and wash basin, but without bathing facilities.

HALF SECTION—Three hundred and twenty acres. (See GOVERNMENT SURVEY.)

HAND MONEY—(See HARD MONEY.)

HANDSHAKE DEAL—A deal closed or sealed with a handshake and without written documents to verify the transaction.

HARD MONEY—Earnest money; down payment; good faith money. Hand money; deposit. The actual money invested, as opposed to SOFT DOLLAR, which refers to deferred payments, mortgages, notes, etc.

HARDPAN—A compact subsoil layer consisting of clay and other elements, almost rock-like in firmness, that prevents the seepage of water.

HARD SELL—Applying high-pressure, strongly persuasive methods in attempting to bring about a sale. The opposite of SOFT SELL.

HAVE AND TO HOLD—The phrase, used in the *habendum* clause of deeds and leases, which defines the extent and quality of what is being conveyed.

H-BEAM—A structural steel beam generally used for piles or columns.

HEAVY INDUSTRY—A zoning classification generally given to industries that, by their nature, are noisy, odorous, cause air pollution or are otherwise undesirable to residential and commercial areas. Certain large manufacturing plants, such as oil refineries, foundaries, and shipbuilding facilities, are usually thus calssified. Because of the type of production activities utilized in heavy industry, planning boards generally set aside outlying areas, away from the path of real estate growth and development, for this class of industry. (See also LIGHT INDUSTRY, MEDIUM INDUSTRY.)

HECTARE—Land measuring 2.47 acres.

HEIR—The individual who has or will inherit property. The receiver of an inheritance.

HEIRESS—A female heir.

HEIRS AND ASSIGNS—Part of the phraseology found in deeds, contracts and other documents when transferring title. Heirs are recipients of an inheritance; assigns are parties who may be subsequently designated by the assignor. The phrase is used when an estate can be conveyed to the heirs of the purchaser or one designated by him. Without its inclusion the estate could revert to the seller upon the purchaser's death.

HEIRS AT LAW—(See LEGAL HEIRS.)

HEREDITAMENT—Property that can be inherited. It may be real, personal; tangible or intangible property, or the combination of these. (See CORPOREAL HEREDITAMENT, INCORPOREAL HEREDITAMENT.)

HIATUS—A gap. A break in continuity. Lapse, as may occur when there is a break in the chain of title, or when referring to an unclaimed strip of land between property lines.

HIDDEN AMENITIES—The favorable features of a property that may not always be noted at first inspection, but nevertheless are present and serve to enhance its value. High quality of workmanship, superior materials, originality and excellence of design are examples. (See also AMENITIES, VISIBLE AMENITIES.)

HIGHEST AND BEST USE—When land is being put to its most logical and productive use. Such factors as beauty and utility to the surrounding community are considered, as well as the highest income it can bring the owner.

HIGHLAND—Upland. An elevated or hilly terrain. A plateau or mountainous area.

HIGH RATIO FINANCING—Obtaining financing that represents a large percentage of an assets value.

HIGH-RISE (HI-RISE)—An indefinite term, but generally understood to mean an apartment house or other structure higher than three or four stories requiring heavy construction methods. When referring to large office buildings the term "skyscraper" is more applicable.

HIGHWAY—A main public road. Generally, a direct, major route.

HIGHWAY EASEMENT—A right to the use of, or to maintain, property for purposes of a thoroughfare.

HILL—An elevation of land situated above the surrounding countryside, but not reaching the height of a mountain.

HIPPED ROOF—A roof design having hips. The angled roof surface formed by two sloped sides. (See ROOF illustrations.)

HOFFMAN RULE—An old formula for evaluating portions of lots 100 feet deep, whereby the first 50 feet is assigned a worth equaling $2/3$ of the entire value. The first 25 feet of the front 50 feet is worth $2/3$ the value of *that* 50 feet. The first 12½ feet of the front 25 feet is worth $2/3$ the value of *that* 25 feet, and so on. This rule, developed in 1866 by Judge Murray Hoffman and now generally recognized as being inaccurate, is rarely used to appraise property.

HOFFMAN-NEILL RULE—An elaboration on the principle of the Hoffman Rule for assigning values to various portions of the land, it was formulated by Henry Harmon Neill. Like the Hoffman Rule, it is considered by most professional appraisers as being outdated and generally invalid.

HOLD—To keep in one's possession; to have lawful title; to retain. To maintain control and ownership. The word is frequently used in real estate terms such as FREEHOLD, LEASEHOLD, HAVE AND TO HOLD, HOLDOVER TENANT, HOLDING COMPANY, etc.

HOLD HARMLESS CLAUSE—A clause in an agreement that frees a party of all responsibility or obligation regarding a specified matter.

HOLDING—Property in which one has legal title and possession. Owned property. The word is frequently used in plural.

HOLDING COMPANY—A corporation that owns or directs the operations of various other companies. Holding companies "hold" or control the stock in other corporations.

HOLDOVER TENANT—One who remains in possession of the premises after the term of his lease has expired. Also called a TENANT AT SUFFERANCE.

HOLOGRAPHIC INSTRUMENT—An instrument, such as a will, contract or deed, completely written in the testator's or grantor's own hand.

HOME—An individual's dwelling place; residence; where one lives; house; the homestead. The place in which one resides, intends to reside or has resided. Legal residence.

HOME BUILDING—1. The construction of a dwelling. 2. That segment of the building industry devoted to producing homes.

HOMEOWNER—A person possessing title to a home. One who owns a home.

HOMEOWNER'S POLICY—An overall "package" insurance policy for the home covering fire, theft, personal liability, flood, windstorm damage and numerous other contingencies.

HOMESITE—A suitable parcel of land on which a home will or can be built.

HOMESTEAD—1. The home and property of an individual and his family; their fixed residence. One's homestead is protected by state and federal laws from being attached or sold from under him by his creditors. 2. Certain unreserved public lands, from 80 to 180 acres, given free to United States citizens who agree to live on and cultivate the land or otherwise improve it for a minimum of five years. 3. Homestead laws vary in different states. There are homestead exemption acts covering rural and urban homeowners, and business homesteads (notably in Texas) in which a family head may declare his place of business exempt from certain property taxes. (See HOMESTEAD EXEMPTION.)

HOMESTEAD ESTATE—The real estate that is owned and occupied as a residence and cannot be seized for the payment of a debt.

HOMESTEAD EXEMPTION—A tax exemption offered by certain states for all or a portion of taxes on one's home, and the exemption of his home from being foreclosed for non-payment of debts.

HOSTILE POSSESSION—(See ADVERSE POSSESSION.)

HOTEL—An establishment providing rooms, meals and personal services to the traveling public or to those remaining for a relatively short period of time. An inn.

HOUSE—(See HOME.)

HOUSE CONSULTANT—An expert on house construction and prevailing values who will, for a fee, examine the construction and condition of a house and submit a report of his findings and recommendations to a prospective buyer. Also referred to as a HOUSE INSPECTOR.

HOUSE CROSS SECTION—(See page 412.)

HOUSE INSPECTOR—(See HOUSE CONSULTANT.)

HOUSE LEASE—A lease for a private residence.

HOUSE LISTING FORM—(A form specially designed for taking housing listings. (See page 346.)

HOUSING AND HOME FINANCE AGENCY—This federal agency was taken over by the Department of Housing and Urban Development (HUD) in 1965. (See DEPARTMENT OF HOUSING AND URBAN DEVELOPMENT.)

HOUSING PROJECT—A development of homes or apartments. A residential subdivision.

HUD—Abbreviation for DEPARTMENT OF HOUSING AND URBAN DEVELOPMENT (See that title.)

HUNDRED PERCENT LOCATION—An area, usually in the center of a downtown business district, that offers the busiest central location. It is generally indicative of an area having the highest traffic and pedestrian count, highest rentals and, consequently, the highest land values.

HUSBANDRY CLAUSE—A clause in a lease or other document that provides for the cultivation and production of edible crops, or farm animals.

HYPOTHECATE—The pledge of property as security for a debt, without giving up possession of it. To mortgage.

I

I-BEAM—A structural steel beam formed in the shape of the letter I.

ILLEGAL—Unlawful; not according to law; unauthorized by law.

ILLEGAL CONTRACT—A contract made for an unlawful purpose. It may be correctly drawn and executed, but its illegality renders it void. As an example, a lease of a house used for gambling (where gambling is illegal) is unenforceable.

ILLUVIATION—The accumulation of soil from one area to another by natural causes, such as the movement of rivers, floods or tides.

IMMORAL CONTRACT—A contract in which the consideration or the purpose itself is based on something morally wrong and not in keeping with accepted concepts of human behavior. The contract is automatically void.

IMPERFECT TITLE—A defective title. One which does not pass on the complete fee or is not, for some reason, marketable or insurable.

IMPLIED CONTRACT—A contract that is deduced or inferred by the actions of the principals. An agreement not expressed either by word or in writing. One determined by the conduct of the parties. A contract in which the terms are not stated but are understood and agreed to.

IMPLIED EASEMENT—An encroachment upon property that has been left unchallenged for a long period of time. One that is apparent by long and continued use.

IMPLIED LISTING—A listing obtained without the owner's oral or written consent, but with his knowledge. The listing arises by implication. If a broker effects a sale from such a listing, the owner may be required to pay him for his services.

IMPLY—To infer; to assume by inference, conduct and association, rather than by a statement or in writing. Imply is contrary to the word EXPRESS, which means directly stated or written. (See IMPLIED CONTRACT, IMPLIED EASEMENT and IMPLIED LISTING, above.)

IMPROVED LAND—Man-made additions *to* and *on* real property that enhance its value. Improvements *to* land are grading, roadbuilding, irrigating, draining, installing water lines, cultivating farmland, building sidewalks, bringing in electricity, etc. And improvements *on* land include the construction of buildings, bridges, structures of all kinds, fencing, etc.

IMPROVEMENTS—(See IMPROVED LAND.)

IMPUTE—Attribute; ascribe; charge. To fix responsibility. In real estate usage, for example, to impute interest is to assign an interest rate where none is indicated. Attribute vicariously.

IN—This preposition is frequently used in real estate law to denote one's interest, i.e., in possession, in contract, *in invitum,* in trust, in fact, in gross, in perpetuity, etc.

INC.—Abbreviation for Incorporated. (See CORPORATION.)

INCHOATE—Partially completed; unfinished; incomplete. Recently begun. As yet imperfect. (See INCHOATE DOWER, INCHOATE INSTRUMENTS and INCHOATE INTEREST, below.)

INCHOATE DOWER—The dower interest a wife has in her husband's estate while he is alive. This interest vests in her upon his death.

INCHOATE INSTRUMENTS—Incomplete legal papers. Documents that are not fully executed, or those that are required to be recorded, are inchoate instruments until they are recorded.

INCHOATE INTEREST—A future interest in real estate. As an example, a minor having been left an estate, title to which would pass only upon his reaching a specified age.

INCLOSED LAND—Fenced land. Land surrounded by man-made or planted material. Same as ENCLOSED LAND.

INCLUSIVE RENT—Rent that includes certain specified utilities and other charges, such as gas, electricity, water, parking, etc.

INCOME—The financial benefits from business, labor, capital invested or property. The monetary return or other advantageous benefits of an investment. The amount of gain received in money, goods or services over a period of time.

INCOME APPROACH TO VALUE—A method of appraising property basing the value upon the net amount of income produced by the property. It is calculated by subtracting the total income of the property from the expenses to determine the net profit. Also known as the CAPITALIZATION METHOD. (See APPRAISAL.)

INCOME AND EXPENSE STATEMENT—A statement of income received from a property and an itemized list of expenses incurred in its operation.

INCOME MULTIPLIER—The associaton between the price of property and the net income it generates. As an example, an income-producing property that nets the owner $20,000 per year and sells for $100,000 has an income multiplier of 5. This relationship between price (or value) and income is also referred to as the NET INCOME MULTIPLIER.

INCOME PARTICIPATION—A reference to the mortgagee receiving a share of profits of a project. It is also referred to as EQUITY PARTICIPATION, or colloquially, as a KICKER.

INCOME PROPERTY—Property owned or purchased primarily for the monetary return it will bring. It may be classified as commercial, industrial or residential.

INCOME TAX—Federal, state and sometimes local taxes that are levied against the annual income of an individual or a corporation.

INCOMPETENT—A person who is not legally qualified to reach proper decisions. One who is unable to come to a sound conclusion or to manage his affairs by reason of insanity, feeble-mindedness or other mental deficiency. A person for whom a guardian must be appointed to legally act in his place.

INCORPORATED—(See CORPORATION, INCORPORATION.)

INCORPORATION—1. The act of forming a legal corporation. (See CORPORATION.) 2. The process of making one document or property a part of another. Joining or merging with something else.

INCORPOREAL HEREDITAMENT—(See HEREDITAMENT.)

INCORPOREAL PROPERTY—Intangible, personal property. Property rights, such as copyrights, mortgages, leases, patents, etc., rather than those having form or substance. Without body; not corporeal. That which is neither visible nor can be touched. Things that are perceived by the mind.

INCREMENT—An increase or enlargement in number and value. Something gained; growth; one of a pattern of similar increases. Augmenting. Opposite of DECREMENT. *Earned increment*, for example is the increase in value due to the skill and labor of the owner, or by improvements made to property, such as adding an annex to a building. *Unearned increment* is an increase due to natural causes, such as a build-up of land by the deposit of sand or soil. Also, the normal appreciation of real estate that might be the result of population increases and favorable economic conditions.

INCUBATOR BUILDING—A structure erected and maintained expressly as a model for studying and improving techniques for future buildings. One used to test both construction and practicality in actual use. An experimental building.

INCUMBRANCE—A variation in spelling of ENCUMBRANCE. (See that term.)

INCURABLE DEPRECIATION—Depreciation of property that is beyond rehabilitating. Property in which the cost to repair or remodel would be uneconomical and therefore prohibitive.

INCURABLE TITLE—A cloud or other encumbrance on the title to property that cannot be removed, consequently preventing the transfer of ownership.

INDEFEASIBLE—That which cannot be altered or defeated. Not liable to be made void. An indefeasible estate is one in fee simple, that is absolute and denotes having as near to perfect title as can be obtained. It is one that cannot be overturned or undone.

INDEMNITY—1. Reimbursement or compensation for a sustained loss or for that which was expended. 2. A bond or other form of security given as assurance of compensation for an anticipated loss, or one that has already occurred.

INDEMNITY LANDS—1. Federal lands granted to a state in exchange for or to replace state property given over to the U.S. government. 2. Lands granted to railroads or utility companies that were already in the public domain.

INDENTURE—A formal, legal instrument. A binding contract or deed between two or more parties. An official document. The opening words in deeds often begin with the words, "This indenture made the _____ day of _____, between "_____, etc.

INDENTURE DEED—A deed, made between two or more parties and signed by the grantor, but in which each undertakes reciprocal obligations toward one another.

INDEPENDENT CONTRACTOR—A contractor who undertakes to perform a specialized service for another, but is under his own supervision. He manages his operation and affairs and is completely independent to the extent that he need not answer to anyone for his work or the method in which he carries it out. Upon completion, however, the results must meet the standards set forth in his contract of employment.

INDEX CLAUSE—A clause in a lease that provides for an increase or decrease in rent according to the rise and fall in the cost of living. Most index clauses are governed by the United States Department of Labor's regularly published COST-OF-LIVING INDEX. One such typical clause reads as follows:

> Should the Cost of Living Index rise or fall during the term of this lease from the cost of living figure for the year 19__,, the monthly rent will be adjusted each January 1. The advance or decrease shall be in the same proportion as the Cost of Living Index which is published annually by the United States Department of Labor.

INDICTMENT—A formal document, by an authorized legal body, presented to a grand jury charging a person with an offense. An accusation. In some states, when charges are preferred by a public prosecuting office (without the intervention or approval of a grand jury), it is called an INFORMATION.

INDORSEMENT—A variation in spelling of Endorsement. (See ENDORSE-MENT.)

INDUCEMENT—Something of value offered to a person in order to have him do or refrain from doing something. The act of persuading; influencing one's reason.

INDUSTRIAL BROKER—A real estate broker specializing in the listing, selling and leasing of industrial properties; one primarily engaged in industrial real estate.

INDUSTRIAL BUILDING—A building designed and used primarily for industrial and commercial purposes. Any structure used for manufacturing and general business purposes, such as a factory, assembly plant, warehouse, etc.

INDUSTRIAL PARK—A development of industrial plants, warehouses, factories and wholesale distributing firms. Many modern industrial parks are the result of comprehensive planning and study. Adequate public utilities, wide streets, ample railroad siding, professional landscaping and the modern plants themselves contribute to attractive, carefully conceived and coordinated industrial areas.

INDUSTRIAL PROPERTY—Land specifically suited to and zoned for the use of factories, warehouses and similar industrial purposes.

INDUSTRIALIZED BUILDING—This is a term familiar to the prefabricated building industry. An industrialized building is a structure in which the major parts are factory made and assembled, and then transported to the site for erection into a complete building. It differs from the conventional methods of on-site, stick-by-stick construction.

INFANT—A minor in the eyes of the law. In most states a person under the age of twenty-one.

IN FEE—(See FEE, FEE SIMPLE, FEE SIMPLE ABSOLUTE.)

INFORMATION—A written accusation of a crime by an authorized legal body. (See INDICTMENT.)

INFORMATION SHEET—1. A compilation of facts concerning a particular real estate offering. A brochure; leaflet; flyer. 2. A form used as a ready reference for factual data concerning a transaction.

INFRINGEMENT—1. An encroachment upon another's property; trespassing. 2. A violation of a right or privelege, such as a copyright or patent.

INGRESS—Entrance or access to property. The ability to enter upon land. The opposite of EGRESS, which means going out; exit.

INHABIT—Dwell; to occupy as a residence. Live in; reside; stay.

INHERITANCE—The act of acquiring property by descent. An estate that passes to the heir or heirs.

INHERITANCE TAX—The tax levied on the transfer of an estate to the heirs. It is not a tax on the property itself, but the taxing of the heirs for their right to acquire it by succession.

IN INVITUM—(Latin) Something uninvited and done against another's will. Proceedings or taxes imposed against one who does not consent to them.

IN INVITUM LIEN—(See LIEN *IN INVITUM*.)

INJUNCTION—A writ or court order either compelling or restraining one or more parties from doing a particular act that could prove injurious or otherwise detrimental to others. An injunction can be temporary or permanent.

INLAND—In the interior. Not being on the coast.

IN LIEU OF—Substituting for; in place of. An alternative.

IN-LOT—A lot lying within the city or incorporated limits of a town. One that was surveyed and platted when the community was originally formed.

INN—A house for sleeping, eating and the general comfort of transient, paying guests. A commercial place where travelers are accommodated. A hotel.

INNOCENT PURCHASER—One who obtains title to property in good faith believing there are no hidden title defects.

IN PERSONAM—(Latin) An action directed against a specific person. The opposite of *IN REM*.

IN RE—(Latin) In regard. In the matter of.

IN REM—(Latin) An action directed against no particular person, but against the property itself. The opposite of *IN PERSONAM*.

INSIDE LOT—A lot situated between the two corner lots of a block. Any lot that is not a corner lot.

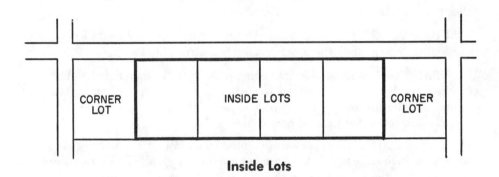

Inside Lots

INSOLVENT—The state of being unable to meet one's financial obligations as liabilities exceed assets. Impoverished.

INSPECTION—Examination; a close study. A careful scrutiny of something. An examination to ascertain certain information.

INSTALLMENT—One of a series of payments of an obligation. Periodic, partial payments of a debt.

INSTALLMENT NOTE—A promissory note which provides for a series of periodic payments of principal and interest, if any, until the amount borrowed is paid in full.

INSTALLMENT SALES CONTRACT—A contract for the sale of property in which the buyer receives possession of the property, but not title to it, upon signing the contract. The buyer makes regular installment payments until the purchase price is reached. Only then does he receive the deed and title.

One reason for an installment contract being used, instead of a mortgage, is the ease and speed with which the property can be repossessed in the event of a default. This type of contract is also referred to as an AGREEMENT FOR DEED, CONTRACT FOR DEED, CONDITIONAL SALES CONTRACT and a LAND CONTRACT.

INSTITUTIONAL LENDERS—Banks, Federal Savings and Loan Associations and Life Insurance Companies, that invest depositors' and clients' funds in mortgages and other loans, are called institutional lenders; as distinguished from individual or private lenders who invest their own money.

INSTITUTIONAL PROPERTY—Property that is maintained primarily in the interest of the public, and not necessarily to generate a profit. Educational facilities, hospitals, museums, jails, and government buildings are examples.

INSTRUMENT—A written, legal document, such as a deed, bill of sale, contract, option, bond, lease, affidavit, will, mortgage, acknowledgement, or any other formal document used in the day to day transacting of legal business.

INSURABLE—Capable of being insured.

INSURABLE TITLE—Land that a title insurance company will issue a policy for, after making a thorough search of the abstract.

INSURABLE VALUE—The amount of insurance a property should carry in order to adequately indemnify the owner against a destructable loss.

INSURANCE—A method of guaranteeing or indemnifying an individual or company against loss from a specified hazard. For the payment of an agreed sum (premium), the insurer or underwriter issues a policy to the insured that gives financial protection for a stated period of time.

INSURANCE AGENT—A person appointed by an insurance company as its representative in the sale of policies. An agent is more closely allied to a company as its representative than is an INSURANCE BROKER, whose function is mainly as a middleman.

INSURANCE BROKER—A person engaged in the sale of insurance protection by acting as an independent middleman between the company he has been authorized to represent and the general public.

INSURANCE OF LOANS—(See INSURED LOAN.)

INSURANCE OF TITLE—(See TITLE INSURANCE.)

INSURANCE ON MORTGAGED PROPERTY—An insurance policy on mortgaged property that is generally made mandatory by the lender to protect his equity in the property in the event of a fire or other loss.

INSURED—The indemnified person or company who receives the insurance policy. The one who will be the recipient of the proceeds in the event of damages.

INSURED LOAN—A loan in which the lender is assured payment in the event of a default by the borrower. As an example, the Federal Housing Administration (FHA) insures payment to the lending institution should the borrower become unable to pay. (The Veterans Administration's G. I. Loan *guarantees* that a certain percentage of the mortgage will be paid the lender in the event of a default. Technically, it does not *insure* that the periodic payments will continue).

INSURER—The one who issues an insurance policy indemnifying another. An insurance company or underwriter.

INTANGIBLE ASSETS—Assets of a business that are evidence of property rights, but which have variable substance and value. The part of a business that includes goodwill, franchises, leaseholds, licenses, patents, trademarks and similar benefits that may be an integral part of a firm's success but on which an accurate dollar value cannot always be placed.

INTANGIBLE TAX—The tax levied on intangible assets.

INTEGRATED—United; incorporated into the whole; desegregated, such as a neighborhood that has both white and black residents.

INTEREST—1. A portion, share or right in something. A partial but not complete ownership. Having an interest does not necessarily indicate possessing title, as for example, in a leasehold interest or mortgage. 2. The charge or rate paid for borrowing money; the compensation received for loaning it. (See COMPOUND INTEREST, SIMPLE INTEREST.)

INTEREST ONLY LOAN—(See STRAIGHT LOAN.)

INTEREST RATE—The percentage of the principal amount that is charged periodically for the use of money.

INTERIM FINANCING—Short-term, temporary financing that is generally in effect during a building's construction or until a permanent, long-term loan can be obtained. (See BUILDING LOAN.)

INTERIM LOAN—(See BUILDING LOAN.)

INTERIOR LOT—(See INSIDE LOT.)

INTERMINGLE FUNDS—To commingle money. When funds that should be kept in a separate escrow account are combined or used with another account. This is an illegal act, as far as real estate brokers are concerned. A separate escrow account must be maintained that is always available for inspection by the state licensing authority.

INTERPLEADER—The filing in the proper court, by a third party holding disputed funds in trust. By so doing, the third party divests himself of liability. The funds in trust are turned over to the court. The purpose of a Bill of Interpleader is to force the conflicting principals to litigate the dispute between themselves and not the third party. The third party relinquishes any claim to the money and in turn is relieved of any court costs or fees. If the third party desires to lay claim to all or part of the money in his trust, he should file for a DECLARATORY JUDGMENT.

INTERPRETATION OF CONTRACTS—A judicial procedure for giving meaning to the terms and conditions of a disputed contract. There are a number of general rules to determine the intent of the parties. Sound court interpretations are based on good faith and common sense. If, for example, words are omitted from a contract, but the meaning is quite obvious, these words are furnished. Accepted customs and procedure in an area, or what is common practice in a business, trade or profession, are taken into consideration, as are local laws. When two contradictory statements exist in a contract, the first one is more often accepted. When no time is specified, a reasonable time is substituted. Written portions take precedence over printed. In areas of doubt, where one party will definitely benefit, that portion in question is most thoroughly studied and carefully judged before an interpretation is given. In this manner it falls upon a judge to exercise logic in reaching equitable solutions in interpreting contracts.

INTER-VIVOS TRUST—(Latin) A trust formed by living people. It is the opposite of one that is created upon death.

INTESTATE—A person who dies without having made a will. Also, one who dies leaving an invalid will. His estate is given to administrators for settlement.

INTRINSIC VALUE—Actual, true worth. The essential value of an asset. Inherent value.

INTRUSION—1. Forcefully seizing and taking possession of property belonging to another. 2. A court order obtained by an owner of property against a trespasser. An Intrusion Writ.

INURE—To vest. To bring to a certain condition. To result, accrue. Habituate. To take effect to the benefit of someone.

INVALID—Unfounded in law. Not of binding force. Lacking authority to be enforced. Not valid; null and void.

INVENTORY—An itemized list of real or personal property for the purpose of determining the quantity or its value. A detailed listing of items; a compilation of articles.

INVESTMENT—An amount of money, property or other valuable asset expended for the purpose of making a profit at a later time.

INVESTMENT PROPERTY—Real property acquired for the purpose of bringing a profitable return at some future date.

INVESTOR—An individual who puts money into a business or real estate venture with the intention of realizing a satisfactory financial return on the capital invested.

INVOICE—A written account of the amount of money due for itemized services rendered or materials furnished. A bill.

INVOLUNTARY—Something done without will, desire or choice. If done under duress, it is an involuntary act. The opposite of volition or desire.

INVOLUNTARY ALIENATION—A forced sale of real estate. (See ALIENATION.)

INVOLUNTARY LIEN—A lien imposed upon property without the choice or will of the owner. Tax increases, and sidewalk or sewer assessments are examples of involuntary liens.

IN WITNESS THEREOF (OR WHEREOF)—These words appear on deeds, contracts and many other legal instruments and signify before whom a document is signed.

IPSO FACTO—(Latin) By the fact in or of itself; by the very fact. For example, a properly drawn, executed and recorded deed should "ipso facto" end any doubt as to the rightful owner of the property.

IPSO JURE—(Latin) By the operation of law.

IRONCLAD AGREEMENT—An agreement that cannot be broken or evaded by the parties to it. The term applies to precise and specific written agreements, expressly made more definitive and binding so that there can be no escape from its provisions. The opposite of an ESCAPE CLAUSE.

IRREDEEMABLE GROUND RENT—A reference to ground rents that do not provide for the lessee to purchase or recapture the land. (See also RECAPTURE CLAUSE.)

IRREVOCABLE—That which cannot be changed or recalled. Not revocable; unalterable.

IRRIGATION DISTRICT—A specified taxing district set up under state auspices for the purpose of providing water for human consumption and irrigation to residents of an area. Such districts usually have authority to levy a charge against the consumers as well as the right to make additional special assessments.

ISLAND—Land completely surrounded by water.

ISLET—A small island. A tiny piece of land consisting of physical elements different from that which surrounds it, as solid land surrounded by marshes, or a land area amid a stream.

ISTIMRAR LEASE—An infrequently used term meaning a perpetual lease. A lease without an expiration period.

J

JALOUSIE—A window consisting of a number of adjustable, horizontal glass slats which, when opened or closed, control the air flow and, if tinted, the amount of light.

JERRY-BUILT—A jargon term familiar to those in the construction industry meaning a poorly built, hastily put together building. Any cheaply built structure done in a slipshod manner.

JOG—An irregular change in direction of a property line creating a small corner or pocket of land.

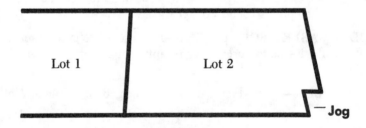

JOHN DOE—A fictitious name used in legal instruments when the correct name is not known or when citing an illustration.

JOINT ADVENTURE—(See JOINT VENTURE.)

JOINT AND SEVERAL LIABILITY—The term is used when compensation for liability may be obtained from one or more parties either individually or jointly, whichever may be most advantageous. Partners, for example, are jointly and severally liable for each other's actions in business transactions. Similarly liable are the obligors of a bond or mortgage.

JOINT ANNUITY—An annuity created for more than one recipient.

JOINT ENTERPRISE—An enterprise where the associates have the authority to act for one another in reaching a common purpose or goal. All have a voice in the management and control, and they act together for the mutual benefit of the undertaking. A joint venture.

JOINT ESTATE—(See JOINT TENANCY.)

JOINT EXECUTORS—Two or more persons who have been designated as executors by a court of law to execute the terms of a will. They function as co-executors.

JOINT LIABILITY—Liability that is shared by more than one person.

JOINT OWNERSHIP—Ownership of property by two or more persons. (See JOINT TENANCY, TENANCY IN COMMON, CO-TENANCY.)

JOINT TENANCY—An estate held by two or more people with equal and undivided interest and ownership. Upon the death of one, his interest automatically passes to the surviving owner or owners.

JOINT VENTURE—The joining of two or more people to carry out a specific business venture; a cooperative endeavor. If more than one or two separate business deals are transacted, the association is no longer considered a joint venture, but becomes a partnership. A joint venture is of limited duration. Also referred to as a JOINT ADVENTURE.

JOISTS—Small, parallel beams that are horizontal supports in roofs, floors and ceilings. They are made of wood, steel and sometimes precast concrete. (See page 412, House Cross Section.)

JUDGMENT—1. A considered opinion; a formal pronouncement; an estimate or evaluation. The ability to make sound decisions. 2. A decree or finding handed down from a court of law following litigation. An order or pronouncement of a court.

JUDGMENT BY DEFAULT—A judgment given when a defendant fails to appear in court, to file necessary pleadings or to otherwise take proper legal steps. Also referred to in reverse as DEFAULT JUDGMENT.

JUDGMENT CREDITOR—A lender who has obtained a court order directing the debtor to make payments to him.

JUDGMENT DEBTOR—The one against whom a judgment is being brought.

JUDGMENT D.S.B.—*D.s.b.* is the abbreviation for the Latin *debitum sine brevi*. It means a judgment without suit being brought, as for example, one made evident by a written confession.

JUDGMENT LIEN—A lien that binds the land of a debtor so that its proceeds can be used to satisfy a debt. The holder of the lien may prevent the owner from using the property or cause it to be sold at a public auction; the purpose being to force him to pay the amount due or to apply the proceeds of a sale to satisfy the lien. A judgment lien does not transfer title interest in the land, but confers the right to levy against it. The first holder of a judgment lien has priority over such subsequent liens that may be issued.

JUDICIAL—Of or relating to the administration of justice. The judiciary process. The function and province of a judge.

JUDICIAL MORTGAGE—In Louisiana, it is an automatic lien created by a judgment given in favor of one bringing an action. It need not be in writing or orally agreed to. Also called a TACIT MORTGAGE and a LEGAL MORTGAGE.

JUDICIAL SALE—A sale of real or personal property ordered by a court or other authorized legal body.

JUDICIARY—1. That branch of government responsible for the administration of justice and the trying of government cases. 2. The court system.

JUNIOR FINANCING—(See JUNIOR MORTGAGE.)

JUNIOR MORTGAGE—A second or third mortgage (or any other) that is subordinated to the first or prior mortgage.

JUNKER—An unusual expression for an old, run-down building that should be junked or demolished. Any structure in extremely delapidated condition.

JUNK VALUE—The salvage value of an asset. In the case of a building, it is the value placed upon it for removal from the premises.

JURAT—A clause found at the end of an affidavit, acknowledgement or any other legal instrument stating when, before whom, and where the document was sworn to. A sample *jurat* reads as follows:

WITNESS my hand and official seal at _____, County of _____, State of _____, this _____ day of _____, A.D. 19__.

My commission expires: _____

Notary Public State of _____

JURE—(Latin) By right. By law.

JURISDICTION—1. The power and the right by law to render a legal decision. 2. The territory within which a court's power and authority extend; also, the type of case that can be heard.

JURISPRUDENCE—The study and philosophy of common law and its practice. A civilized state's body of laws and their application.

JUST COMPENSATION—Impartial, legitimate, fair compensation. For example, when land is appropriated for public use, every effort is made to compensate the owner justly by paying the market value plus added payment for damages sustained to remaining property, if any exist.

JUST TITLE—Good and proper title; one that will stand up against all claimants. In cases of PRESCRIPTION (title by Adverse Possession) the term refers to title received by a grantee from one honestly believed to be the true owner.

JUSTIFIED PRICE—A sum that a knowledgeable buyer would pay for property. Warranted price; a fair market price.

K

KAME—A small mound or knoll made of sand or gravel particles and formed by stratified glacial drift.

KEY LOT—1. A lot that is strategically located and thus has added market value. 2. A lot adjoining a corner lot at the corner lot's rear property line and fronting on the secondary street. Also referred to as a BUTT LOT.

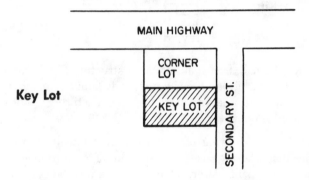

KEYSTONE—The wedge-like, main stone in a structure so designed that other stones are dependent upon it for added support.

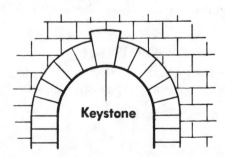

KICK-BACK—The unauthorized, secret payment of money to an individual or group in return for a favorable decision, information or assistance.

KICKER—A slang term meaning a mortgage holder's participation in the profits of a property in addition to the agreed upon interest rate. This can take a variety of forms. It is something extra received by the mortgagee, and is also referred to as "a piece of the action."

KING POST—A vertical beam extending from the base beam to the peak. (See also QUEEN POSTS.)

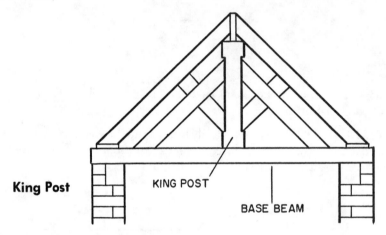

King Post

KING POST

BASE BEAM

KIOSK—A small, free-standing, light-structured building, usually having an open side. This type of one-room structure is familiar to shopping centers and other business areas for newsstands, key manufacturing, photo-film sales, and other specialized products.

KITING—The drawing of a check against uncollected bank funds or against a balance that is falsely raised, then obtaining funds from another bank to cover it. In this manner a skilled kiter, relying on the time it takes for one bank to clear a check from the other, can have large sums of money floating back and forth between banks for extended periods of time.

KNOCK-DOWN CONSTRUCTION—Unassembled, factory-built construction materials that are delivered to a site ready for installation. Prefabricated building parts.

KNOCK-DOWN PRICE—Reduced price.

KNOW ALL MEN—The opening words found in many legal documents. The term dates back to the earliest known written instrumentation.

L

LABORER'S LIEN—(See MECHANIC'S LIEN.)

LACHES—Neglect or an undue lapse of time in bringing about a legal claim or asserting a right. As a long delay can change conditions and cloud memories, a court often dismisses an action that is not pursued with at least reasonable diligence.

LAKELAND—A land area predominant with lakes.

LAND—In the general sense, land encompasses the entire solid portion of the earth's crust. It means all real property. No matter what the surface—soil, rock, mineral, clay, shale, sand—if it is of solid substance, it is classified as land. Land includes everything that is permanently affixed to it. (Also see PUBLIC LANDS.)

LAND CERTIFICATE—A document given to the owner of land upon properly registering for it. It contains a legal description of the property and the name and address of the owner of record. Its purpose is to serve as written proof of ownership.

LAND CONTRACT—(See INSTALLMENT CONTRACT.)

LAND COP—An early English method of proving the transfer of ownership of land before public records of title were kept. During a court proceeding, a notched stick was given by the seller to a middleman, who in turn formally presented it to the buyer. Its purpose was to furnish *prima facie* evidence of the transfer.

LAND COURT—A specialized court whose authority is limited to real estate and related matters.

LAND DEPARTMENT—1. A division of a real estate office that handles the sale and leasing of land. 2. A bureau of the federal government devoted to the sale, leasing, acquisition and management of United States government lands. (See BUREAU OF LAND MANAGEMENT.)

LAND DEVELOPMENT—(See DEVELOPMENT.)

LAND DISTRICTS—The federal government's geographic divisions located throughout the country, each containing a government land office. Their function is to supervise, acquire and sell federal lands within their jurisdiction.

LAND ECONOMICS—The study of land and how it may be put to its highest and best use.

LAND GABEL—A nearly obsolete real estate term meaning GROUND RENT.

LAND GRANT—A gift of government land to a university, public utility, railroad or the like that would be in the best interest and benefit of the general public.

LAND IMPROVEMENT—(See IMPROVEMENT.)

LANDLOCKED—A piece of land lacking public road frontage. Such parcels require an easement over adjoining property in order to be reached.

LANDLORD—The owner of leased property. The LESSOR.

LANDLORD AND TENANT—The area of real estate law dealing with leasing. It covers the entire contractual relationship that exists between lessor and lessee.

LANDLORD'S DISTRESS—(See LANDLORD'S WARRANT.)

LANDLORD'S WARRANT—A landlord's legal recourse in obtaining back rental payments or from losses sustained due to a tenant's default of the lease. This warrant allows the landlord to take possession of the lessee's personal property within the leased premises and hold it as security until the debt is satisfied, or to sell it at public auction.

LANDMARK—1. A stake, monument or other object designating a property line. A mark denoting land boundaries. 2. Something familiar to the general public that identifies an area. It can have historical interest or be a predominant feature of the landscape that serves as a guide.

LAND OFFICE—(See LAND DEPARTMENT, BUREAU OF LAND MANAGEMENT.)

LAND PATENT—A proof of title to land, issued by the government to private interests, for the transfer of ownership of public property.

LAND POOR—A reference to a person who possesses land but, because of taxes, assessments, interest payments on a mortgage or other obligations, is continually short of money.

LAND RECLAMATION—(See RECLAMATION.)

LAND REVENUE—Money received as rent, a share of the crops, mineral or timber royalties or any other form of income derived from ownership of the land.

LANDSCAPE—1. The land formation of a countryside. A view of the scenery and terrain of the land, 2. The lawn and shrub placement created by a landscape architect and planted and maintained by a gardener that adds beauty and amenities to property. The plants, trees, shrubs, bushes and grasses that abound in an area.

LANDSCAPE ARCHITECT—A professional who specializes in beautifying property by creating a design and arrangement for the planting of trees, shrubs and lawns.

LANDSCAPE GARDENER—A person who plants and cares for trees, shrubs and grasses. An expert in the art of landscaping property and beautifying the surroundings.

LANDS, TENEMENTS, AND HEREDITMENTS—A term referring to the whole BUNDLE OF RIGHTS that constitute ownership of land. It includes the land itself and other property affixed to it that cannot readily be moved and therefore passes with it when a transfer of ownership occurs.

LAND SUBDIVISION—A tract of land divided into residential, industrial or commercial sites. (See DEVELOPMENT.)

LAND TAX—A tax levied for the ownership of real property, the rate of which is determined by the assessed valuation. A more preferred term is *AD VALOREM* TAX or PROPERTY TAX.

LAND TITLE AND TRANSFER ACT—This act was the basis for England's method of recording title to land and keeping a history of the transfer of ownership. Our American system of abstracting and recording was based on this and today is in many ways similar.

LAND TRUST—Title to land held by a trustee in the interest of the beneficiaries under the terms of a trust.

LAND TRUST CERTIFICATE—An instrument used in financing certain larger real estate transactions. The investor receives a trust certificate as evidence of his share in the enterprise. He holds an interest in the trust similar to that of a stockholder in a corporation. Land trusts were used extensively in the mid-west (notably Ohio), but have given way to other methods of financing and are not in frequent use today. It is also known as a CERTIFICATE OF EQUITABLE OWNERSHIP, CERTIFICATE OF PARTICIPATION and a FEE CERTIFICATE.

LAND USAGE—The use being made of land or the uses permitted under zoning ordinances. Zoning ordinances act to control land usage in a community by establishing building codes and set-back requirements. Some divisions for land usage are commercial, residential, multi-family, public, semi-public, industrial, institutional, agricultural and so forth. Proper land usage attempts to assign the highest and best use of each parcel.

LAND WARRANT—A document given by the government to anyone purchasing public land, as proof that he is the owner of record.

LAPSE—The discontinuance of a right or privilege by the passage of time, as when a grace period ends in a mortgage or when the expiration date of a lease has passed.

LARCENY—Theft. Illegally obtaining personal property from the rightful owner.

LAST WILL AND TESTAMENT—(See WILL.)

LATE CHARGE—A charge levied against installment loans and mortgage payments when not paid on time. It may take the form of a flat penalty fee or it can be a percentage of the periodic payment. The amount of the late charge is stated in the original instrument of indebtedness.

LATENT—Not visible or apparent; hidden; concealed. Not discernible. What does not appear on the face.

LATERAL SUPPORT—1. The natural support given to land by the adjoining property. (An owner is protected by law from excavation work to neighboring lands that could prove detrimental to his parcel.) 2. In construction, any parallel support given another beam or column.

LATITUDE—The angular distances measured in degrees running north and south of, and parallel to, the Equator.

LAW—Rules of conduct and action by which men live. Conduct controlled by government for maintaining an orderly society. The whole series of precepts, codes and guides binding upon civilized man and by which he conducts himself. Authorized rule or order; jurisprudence. (See COMMON LAW; EQUITY; STATUTORY LAW.) 2. The enforcement of the rules for governing men's actions. 3. The profession of judges and lawyers.

LAWFUL—Legal; authorized or sanctioned by law; in conformity with the law; established by law; not forbidden; rightful.

LAWFUL AGE—The age at which one is no longer considered a minor. Generally at age 21 a person is recognized as having reached his majority and is legally adjudged an adult, though in some states 18 years is the lawful age for females. Lawful age may be full or partial. A person not yet 21, after judicially proving his competency, can enter into binding contracts, transact business and (in some states) be licensed in real estate. (See MAJOR, MINOR.)

LAWYER—An attorney at law; a qualified, licensed legal agent trained in the law and admitted to the bar of his state. A person who transacts legal business for others for a fee. COUNSELOR. In England he is called a solicitor or barrister. Most states require that only a lawyer represent another person before a court.

LEAD—A vernacular term meaning a prospective buyer or (less frequently) seller. A customer is sometimes referred to as a lead, as is one who may be considering selling his property. A prospect.

LEAN-TO—A small building having a single pitched roof and "leaning" against the side of another structure.

LEASE—A contract between the owner of property (lessor) and a tenant (lessee) for the possession and use of the property for a stipulated period of time, in consideration for the payment of an agreed upon rent or for services rendered. (Page 350.)

LEASEBACK—The term refers to a seller who remains in possession as a tenant after completing the sale and delivering the deed (See SALE-LEASEBACK.)

LEASE BROKER—A real estate broker who specializes in the leasing of real property.

LEASE INSURANCE—A lease guarantee policy that protects the landlord against a default in rental payments on the remaining portion of a lease. Used primarily in store and office leasing, it raises the credit position of the smaller tenant so that he can obtain space that a landlord might otherwise reserve for a highly rated or national company. It acts as a relief for the tenant in the event financial difficulty prevents his making the payments. The premium for such a policy is usually paid by the landlord. Also found in apartment house leases, it insures against loss in rental payments in the event of a tenant's death.

LEASE-PURCHASE AGREEMENT—An agreement which provides that a portion of a tenant's rent be applied to the purchase price. Upon an agreed equity being reached, the title will then be conveyed.

LEASE RENEWAL—By an extension agreement or endorsement, the terms of a lease may be renewed. A typical lease renewal reads as follows:

> By mutual consent, this lease is hereby extended for a term of _____ years beginning _____ and ending _____ for a total rental of $_____ payable $_____ per month. All terms and conditions in the original lease shall remain in full force and effect.

LEASED DEPARTMENT—The renting of a portion of a store by an outside firm or individual; a concession. Also called a concession lease. This type of lease arrangement is commonly done in larger department stores and retail discount operations to firms specializing in one type of merchandise or service.

LEASED FEE—A property that is owned in fee simple and is conveyed to another by a ground lease. At the termination of the lease, the property is repossessed by the fee holder. (See GROUND RENT.)

LEASED FEE INTEREST—The owner's interest in a leased property.

LEASEHOLD—The estate or interest in realty a tenant holds for a term of years in the property he is leasing. It is less than a fee interest.

LEASEHOLD APPRAISAL—An appraisal of the value of a lease from the points of view of both the lessee and the lessor. (See also LEASEHOLD VALUE.)

LEASEHOLD IMPROVEMENTS—The structural improvements and additions made to property by the lessee.

LEASEHOLD INSURANCE—1. A form of insurance coverage that protects a lessee who has subleased to another. It guarantees that rental payments will be made by the sublease holder. (See also LEASE INSURANCE.) 2. A leasehold policy is a title insurance policy furnished the tenant insuring that the owner has clear title to the leased premises.

LEASEHOLD VALUE—As economic conditions change, a lease may be worth more or less with the passing of time. Leasehold value is that increase in the market value of a lease over what is being paid. (See ESCALATOR CLAUSE.)

LEASING DEPARTMENT—A division of a real estate brokerage company devoted exclusively to the leasing of real property. (See LEASE BROKER.)

LEAVE—1. Devise. Bequeath. A gift by will. 2. Permission. Authorization to do something. Consent to take action.

LEGACY—A gift of personal property by will.

LEGAL—Founded on law and order; according to the principles of law; recognized by law; lawful.

LEGAL ACTION—Resorting to a court of law to uphold one's legal rights.

LEGAL AGE—(See LAWFUL AGE.)

LEGAL AID—1. Legal help or assistance. 2. Free legal council given by attorneys to those in need of a lawyer but who cannot afford to pay for his services.

LEGAL ASSETS—Any property that can be used for the payment of a debt.

LEGAL CONSIDERATION—(See CONSIDERATION.)

LEGAL DESCRIPTIONS—Methods of identifying the location of land and defining its boundaries. Legal descriptions take the following forms: 1. Lot, Block and Subdivision (also called Recorded Map). 2. Metes and Bounds. 3. Government Survey (also called Section, Town and Range Description, Rectangular Survey, or U.S. Government Public Land Description). 4. Monuments. (See those titles, for further information.)

LEGAL ENTITY—Legally existing.

LEGAL ESTOPPEL—To stop by the use of a court order, deed or by record, rather than by one's actions or conduct. (See ESTOPPEL.)

LEGAL FRAUD—A misrepresentation made without knowingly doing so, as for example, in a vaguely worded, misleading contract or an unintentionally incorrect representation. (See FRAUD.)

LEGAL GUARDIAN—A court-appointed or approved individual who is entrusted with the care of another's property.

LEGAL HEIRS—A decedent's kin who normally would receive his estate.

LEGALITY OF OBJECT—Having a legal purpose. It is an essential element of every contract. If the purpose is not legal, a contract is automatically void.

LEGAL MORTGAGE—A term used in Louisiana indicating that in certain cases a creditor has an automatic mortgage on the property of a debtor. Nothing written or oral need transpire to create the mortgage. It is also called a **TACIT MORTGAGE** or **JUDICIAL MORTGAGE**.

LEGAL NOTICE—1. Notice required to be given by law. The type of notice that must be furnished for the specific legal matter involved. 2. Notification by publicly recording documents, as when deeds, mortgages and other instruments are filed in the County Clerk's office or other proper place and made a part of the public records. Also called **CONSTRUCTIVE NOTICE**.

LEGAL OWNER—The true owner of record. (See OWNER.)

LEGAL RATE OF INTEREST—The maximum rate of interest that can be charged for the use of money as permitted by state laws or regulations of federal agencies.

LEGAL REPRESENTATIVE—A person who, by proper authorization, represents and stands in place of another. An Executor, Administrator, Attorney, Attorney-In-Fact, Power Of Attorney, Guardian and Trustee, all are legal representatives of others.

LEGAL RESIDENCE—Where a person lives; one's permanent home; his domicile. A legal residence is said to be a state of mind and therefore the law does not require that one spend a majority of his time in a certain place to be so recognized. In this sense, it is the place which the individual represents to be his residence and where he intends to return. The law recognizes only one legal residence.

LEGAL RIGHTS—Rights existing by law; one's natural rights.

LEGAL TENDER—The money of a country. What is accepted as a medium of exchange.

LEGAL TITLE—Title to property that will be recognized in a court of law. Title that appears to be good; however, one in which the holder may not necessarily be able to benefit.

LEGATEE—The recipient of a legacy. The one to whom a gift is bequeathed.

LEGISLATIVE—The branch of the government that is empowered to make laws, levy taxes and appropriate funds.

LEISURE HOME—A week-end or vacation home. A U.S. Commerce Department survey revealed that approximately three million American families own a country or seashore home.

LENDER PARTICIPATION—When the mortgagee shares in the profits of the property in addition to receiving the customary loan interest, lender participation occurs. It is referred to in the vernacular as a KICKER LOAN.

LESSEE—A tenant. The one to whom a lease is given to occupy premises for a given length of time and at a specified rate.

LESSOR—A landlord. The grantor of a lease. The one who leases property to a tenant.

LET—1. Lease. The word is usually prefixed by "to," as "to let" or "to lease" property. 2. Concerning construction contracts for public works or private enterprise, it refers to the awarding or "letting" of a contract to an individual or a firm following open bidding.

LETTER OF COMMITMENT—(See COMMITMENT.)

LETTER OF CREDIT—A letter, from a company or bank in one area of the country to a similar business establishment in another, introducing the person named and vouching for him and specifying a sum of money to be extended to him. If the person being introduced paid the maker of the letter the amount stipulated, the letter of credit is the same as a SIGHT DRAFT or BILL OF EXCHANGE. If given as one vouching for another with no money having been posted, it represents a guarantee of payment by the maker.

LETTER OF INTENTION—An agreement in letter form. It is also frequently used as a DEPOSIT RECEIPT until a more formal, detailed contract can be prepared. When properly drawn, such a document has all of the legal requisites of a binding contract. Also called MEMORANDUM OF AGREEMENT.

LETTING—Leasing.

LEVEE—A man-made embankment constructed to control water or to avert flooding.

LEVEL PAYMENT MORTGAGE—In this type of mortgage payment schedule, a like amount is paid periodically. However, the amount of the payment credited to the interest gradually decreases while the amount for amortizing the principal gradually increases as each payment is made.

LEVERAGE—In real estate, the term means effective use of money. It is usually accomplished by investing the least amount of capital possible when acquiring property in order that it may bring the maximum percentage of return. This can be done by mortgaging to the highest amount that is practical. As long as the mortgage payments and operating expenses are not prohibitively high, the greatest yield on capital invested can generally be obtained.

LEVY—1. To assess, raise or collect; to impose a tax upon a person or property. (See ASSESSMENT.) 2. In law, to seize property when following out a court order to do so.

LIABILITY—Any drawback, debt or obligation. Something that acts as a disadvantage. An obligation or duty that must be performed. The opposite of ASSET.

LIABILITY INSURANCE—A policy that financially protects the insured against loss or damages for which he is responsible. Indemnity against loss.

LIABLE—Responsible for; an obligation according to law. Accountable for; chargeable; legally answerable.

LIBER—(Latin) Book. Lot book. Plat records in some jurisdictions are referred to as liber volumes.

LIBERTY OF CONTRACT—The freedom to make or refrain from making a contract. The condition of not being required to become a party to an agreement if one chooses not to. The right to act as one's judgment dictates in contractual matters, as long as it is within the law.

LICENSE—Permission by a recognized authority to act or to engage in business, a profession or other activity. A certificate or document which gives the right to perform some service. Conferring a power or authorization without which it would not exist.

LICENSEE—A person who is licensed. The holder of a license.

LIEN—A charge or claim upon property which encumbers it until the obligation is satisfied. The property serves as the security. (See ASSESSMENT; ATTACHMENT; EQUITABLE LIEN; INHERITANCE TAX; JUDGMENT LIEN; LIEN *IN INVITUM;* MECHANIC'S LIEN; MORTGAGES; STATUTORY LIEN; TAXES; VENDEE'S LIEN; VENDOR'S LIEN.)

LIEN AFFIDAVIT—An affidavit stating there are no liens or other encumbrances against a particular property, or if liens do exist, they are itemized and described.

LIENEE—The one whose property has a lien upon it, or to which a lien can be placed.

LIEN *IN INVITUM*—(Latin) A lien placed on property without the consent of the owner. An "uninvited" lien.

LIEN OF COMMISSION—A charge or claim upon property for non-payment of a commission.

LIENOR—The holder of a lien.

LIEN THEORY STATES—States offering more legal protection to the mortgagor than the mortgagee. Lien-theory states hold that the lender has only a lien on property and possesses no title interest whatsoever. In certain other states the reverse is true and thus more chance of financial recovery is assured the lender in the event of a default. These states are called TITLE THEORY STATES. Where the lender finds it difficult to enforce the terms of the mortgage, it is necessary to charge higher interest rates to compensate for the additional risk. Understandably, large national lenders (such as insurance companies) give priority to loans from states having mortgage laws more favorable to them. Construction and real estate activity in general, dependent upon favorable financing, are affected. Most states follow a middle course in their lien laws so that neither the lender nor the borrower is excessively protected.

LIEU LAND—Land granted to a party in place of appropriated property. For example, an owner of land taken for public use may receive compensation in the form of a similar tract of equal size and value.

LIFE ESTATE—Any estate in real or personal property that terminates upon the death of the owner. A life estate can also be for the length of another's life, or it can be contingent upon some future event, such as being terminated when the recipient is married. The person holding a life estate, in return for the use of the property, must maintain and pay all taxes and liens. He ordinarily cannot dispose of any part of the property during his lifetime or after death. The disposition of the property after death is often provided for when the estate for life is made.

LIFE INSURANCE FOR MORTGAGOR—Insurance carried by the mortgagor which provides for paying off the mortgage at the time of his death. Mortgages sometimes require that this type of life insurance policy be issued. In the absence of such a provision, the mortgagor may nevertheless elect to take out a policy of this kind as protection for his heirs.

LIFE INTEREST—(See LIFE ESTATE.)

LIFE-LAND OR LIFE-HOLD—Leased land held for a period of lives.

LIFE RENT—(See LIFE ESTATE.)

LIFE TENANT—The one who holds a LIFE ESTATE.

LIGHT AND AIR EASEMENT—An easement that provides for open space in a specified area. For example, an owner of a building might obtain an easement from the owner of adjoining property that another building will not be erected on the property line, thereby assuring him light and air that otherwise would have been blocked out. (See AIR RIGHTS.)

LIGHT INDUSTRY—An industrial zoning classification for those industries whose production processes are "clean," do not create hazards or cause air or water pollution and are not objectionable to their neighbors. The following types of industries are typical of those falling into this classification: baking, food processing, yacht repairing, ice manufacturing, milk distributing, dry cleaning, motion picture production. etc.

LIKE-KIND PROPERTY—1. Property that similarly corresponds to another. That which is alike in quality, quantity and degree. 2. In the exchanging (trading) of real estate, the federal government offers a somewhat different definition. In order to qualify for deferred tax treatment, the Internal Revenue Service explains the term as follows:

"The words 'Like-kind' have reference to the nature of the property and not to its grade or quality. The fact that any real estate involved is improved or unimproved is not material, for such fact relates only to the grade or quality of the property and not to its kind or class."

LIMITATION—A specified period of time within which something must be done or refrained from being done. A time period fixed by statute in which a legal matter must be litigated. (See STATUTE OF LIMITATIONS, LACHES.)

LIMITED ACCESS LAND—1. Land that is difficult to reach. Property that is partially or almost totally inaccessible. 2. Land that is made more inaccessible, as when interstate or major throughways, with relatively few exits and entrances, restrict the right of access to abutting property owners.

LIMITED DIVIDEND HOUSING—Subsidized, privately owned public housing. The term refers to an owner who builds and rents property under public supervision. In return for obtaining a government (state or federal) contract and operating under government control, the builder agrees to limit rents and keep profits to a certain percentage of his investment. Government-controlled housing projects for lower-income citizens are often constructed in this manner.

LIMITED PARTNERSHIP—A partnership arrangement which limits certain of the partner's liability to the amount invested and likewise places a limitation on the amount of profit he can make. Usually a limited partner is not permitted to have a voice in managing the company. His role is primarily that of an investor. Most states require that such a partnership agreement be registered with the state.

LINE—The border between two parcels of land. Property line. Boundary demarkation. A thin, elongated mark that defines the shape of land.

LINE OF SIGHT EASEMENT—An easement that prohibits altering the terrain or construction if by so doing the view is obstructed or obliterated.

LINEAL—1. Of or pertaining to direct line descendants; hereditary; belonging to a single lineage. 2. Relating to a line. Having length only. A lineal measure. Also *linear*.

LINTEL—A horizontal beam or girder over an opening to support the structure above.

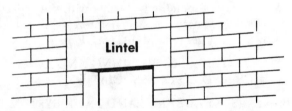

LIQUID ASSETS—Cash on hand or other assets that can be readily turned into cash. It is also called QUICK ASSETS or CURRENT ASSETS.

LIQUIDATE—1. To settle or pay off an indebtedness or other obligation. Turning assets for cash or exchanging them for the satisfaction of a debt. 2. To wind up the affairs of an individual or a business.

LIQUIDATED DAMAGES—The sum agreed upon as payment for a breach of contract.

LIQUIDATION VALUE—The amount of cash that could be raised if an asset was sold at a forced sale.

LIQUIDITY—A reference to the amount of capital a person can quickly raise. One's cash position.

LIS PENDENS—(Latin) A pending legal action.

LISTER—1. A broker or salesman who takes real estate listings. 2. In Vermont, the name by which an ASSESSOR is known.

Listing **138**

LISTING—A broker's authority to sell or lease real property for an owner. Listings take various forms, such as EXCLUSIVE RIGHT OF SALE, EXCLUSIVE AGENCY, IMPLIED LISTING, OPEN LISTING, MULTIPLE LISTING and NET LISTING. (See those titles.)

LITIGATE—To seek a lawful decision; to carry on a suit in a court of law; contest in a legal manner.

LITTORAL LAND—Land bounded by a large body of water such as an ocean, sea or great lake. Property lines for littoral land are usually determined by the high water mark of the tide.

LITTORAL RIGHTS—The legal rights that owners of land abutting an ocean, sea or great lakes possess in the water and the right to make use of it. (See RIPARIAN RIGHTS; WATER RIGHTS.)

LIVABILITY—The desirability of a home as a place of residence; its amenities and comforts that make it pleasing and desirous to live in.

LIVING TRUSTS—(See TRUSTS.)

LOAD-BEARING WALL—(See BEARING WALL.)

LOAN—1. Delivery of something of value with the expectation of repayment or return. 2. Money given to another at interest. 3. A loan on real property is evidenced by a mortgage. (See MORTGAGE.)

LOAN ASSOCIATION—(See BUILDING AND LOAN ASSOCIATION; FEDERAL SAVINGS AND LOAN ASSOCIATION.)

LOAN BANK—(See FEDERAL LAND BANK SYSTEM.)

LOAN CLOSING CHARGES—Expenses that normally arise when a mortgage loan is closed. Mortgage origination costs, legal fees for preparing the instruments, documentary stamps, appraisal fees, recording fees, as well as other fixed expenses that are charged by the lending institution.

LOAN MODIFICATION PROVISION—A clause in a mortgage which permits the borrower to skip one or more payments in the event of financial hardship without the loan going into default. (See GRACE PERIOD.)

LOAN POLICY—A title insurance policy issued by a title insurance company to a holder of a mortgage. (See TITLE INSURANCE.)

LOAN RELIEF—1. A payment reduction or moratorium granted to a mortgagor either of the principal payments, interest payments or both. 2. The settlement of an outstanding loan, thereby relieving the mortgagor of further obligation.

LOANS ON REAL ESTATE—(See MORTGAGES.)

LOAN TRUST FUND—An escrow account in which the periodic payments made to cover taxes, insurance and certain other anticipated expenses are deposited.

LOAN VALUE—The amount a lending institution will lend on the property.

LOAN VALUE OF LIFE INSURANCE—Life insurance policies that have a cash surrender value are often used as collateral for loans. The loan value is that amount which a lender would advance when the life insurance is given as security.

LOAN VALUE RATIO—The ratio of the appraised value of property in proportion to the amount of the mortgage loan.

LOBBY—1. A public room serving as a waiting area or meeting place in hotels, motels, apartment houses, office buildings or other structures. 2. Individuals engaged in putting forth the views of a particular group.

LOCAL ASSESSMENT—A tax levied to pay for improvements in an area. The properties in the immediate area are proportionately assessed for the cost.

LOCATION—Property site; a specific tract of land; an area; place.

LOCK, STOCK AND BARREL—In real estate, an expression used in contracts for the sale of businesses indicating that everything on the premises is included in the sale.

LOCUS SIGILLI—(Latin) Abbreviated "L.S." and found at the end of signature lines on legal documents, it means "under seal" or "the place of the seal" and appears as follows: _____ L.S.

LODGING HOUSE—A rooming house. A house where sleeping and living accommodations are rented to the public.

LOFT—A room or enclosed area above the ground floor. An open, upper floor of a warehouse, factory or barn, such as an attic. A large, unpartitioned area in a building.

LONG FORM MORTGAGE CLAUSE—This clause in a mortgage provides for the mortgagor to *assume* responsibility for its satisfaction when he takes title and not just acquire the property *subject to* it, which carries no personal responsibility in the event of defaulting. (See SALE OF MORTGAGED PROPERTY.)

LONGITUDE—The angular distances, measured in degrees running east and west of, and parallel to, the prime meridian at Greenwich, England.

LONG-TERM ESCROW—(See DEED OF TRUST.)

LONG-TERM LEASE—A lease of long duration. What is considered "long," however, is relative. It varies with the type of lease being dealt with. As an example, a three or four-year lease for an apartment would be considered of long duration (most are drawn for one or two years), while for a business lease it would not. Twenty-five year leases for commercial purposes are considered long, as are GROUND RENTS for ninety-nine years.

LONG-TERM LOAN—In banking, mortgage loans for real estate made for 20 years or more are considered long-term loans.

LOOPHOLE—A means of getting out of an agreement. An omission, unclarified statement or indefinite phrase or clause in a contract that may allow one of the parties to avoid his legal obligation or responsibility under it. The opposite of what is found in an IRONCLAD AGREEMENT.

LOST PROPERTY—The relinquishing of property either voluntarily or involuntarily. Property can be lost by insolvency, abandonment, inadvertence, or neglect.

LOT—A parcel of land having fixed measurements. A part of a survey. A form of legally describing property by LOT, BLOCK, and SUBDIVISION. (See also DESCRIPTION OF PROPERTY; GOVERNMENT LOTS.)

LOT, BLOCK AND SUBDIVISION—In subdividing land, the tract is first assigned a name, and each block and lot within that subdivision is numbered or lettered. A map of the subdivision is then recorded with the proper governmental (usually County) authority. It then becomes officially recognized when legally describing the property. Also called RECORDED MAP. A typical Lot, Block and Subdivision description might read as follows: Lot 15, Block 8, Mountain View Park Subdivision of the City of *Steepdale*, as recorded in Plat Book Number *100*, page *50*, records of *Mountainair* County, state of *California*.

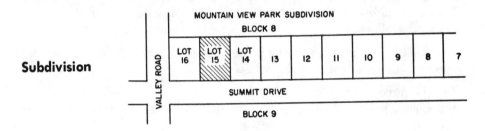

LOT BOOK—(See PLAT BOOK, *LIBER*.)

LOT LINE—The boundary line of a lot.

LOT SPLIT—The division of a plot into two or more parcels.

LOUVER—An opening on the wall of a building having slanted, sometimes movable, thin slats for ventilation, preventing rain or sunlight from entering. Also spelled Louvre.

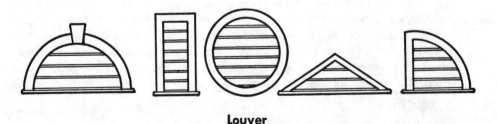

Louver

LOVE AND AFFECTION—The valuable consideration sometimes used when real estate is conveyed between members of a family with no money being exchanged. The law recognizes this as being consideration that is legally as good as any other form.

LOW-PRESSURE SELLING—Selling by employing logic and reasoning rather than high-pressure, overly aggressive tactics. It is sometimes referred to as SOFT SELL.

L. S.—An abbreviation for the Latin *Locus Sigilli*, meaning "under seal," or "the place where a seal is to be affixed." See *LOCUS SIGILLI*.

LTD.—An abbreviation for *limited*. Used extensively by the British, it means that the stockholders or partners of a company are limited as to their liability.

LUCRATIVE TITLE—Title that is acquired by someone paying less than the true market value. Also, title to property that is obtained by gift.

M

MADE LAND—Land formed by the addition of fill.

M.A.I.—Member Appraisal Institute. This coveted professional designation is the most prestigious in the appraisal field. It is conferred upon qualified members by the American Institute of Real Estate Appraisers which is an affiliate of the National Association of Realtors. In order to be awarded the M.A.I. certificate, applicants must pass comprehensive, technical examinations, demonstrate their professional qualifications, and have a minimum of five years practical appraisal experience. Members pledge to adhere to a strict code of ethics.

MAIL BOX RULE—A rule of law providing that the acceptance of an offer is binding at the exact time that it is mailed. If, for example, an offerer seeks to rescind his offer, it must be done *before* acceptance. In the case of the acceptance being mailed, it is necessary to determine when the communication was actually placed in the mail. The Mail Box Rule prevails, provided the time of mailing can be established; and that the acceptance of the agreement in this manner is a reasonable means of responding under the circumstances.

MAINTENANCE—The painting, cleaning and general repair work done to property and equipment to keep it productive and useful. Care given a building and its fixtures to remedy deterioration and maintain it in effective operating order. The continual work required to offset the physical decline of a property. Upkeep.

MAINTENANCE RESERVE—An amount of money allocated for the upkeep of property. A fund reserved to cover maintenance. The purpose of a maintenance reserve fund is to regularly set aside money to cover expenses that may occur at irregular intervals. As an example, it is often necessary to paint a structure every five years. If one-fifth of this cost is set aside each year in a maintenance reserve fund, it will not present an economic hardship when required to be done.

MAJOR OR MAJORITY—One who has attained legal age in the eyes of the law. A person capable of managing his own affairs, can legally enter into contracts and has acquired his civil rights. One who is no longer a minor. Most states recognize age 21 for a person to be considered an adult. In a few states the age is reduced to 18 for females.

MAKE A CONTRACT—A meeting of the minds that results in the writing and signing of an agreement. Concurring to all the terms and conditions of a contract and the signing of it by both parties. (See CONTRACT.)

MAKE AN ASSIGNMENT—The act of transferring property or personal assets to another.

MALA FIDES—(Latin) Something done with bad intentions. Clandestinely and secretly accomplished with fraud or other illicit purpose intended. The opposite of *Bona Fide.*

MALFEASANCE—Wrongdoing. Unlawful conduct that interferes with a person's official duties. The commission of a wrongful deed. Committing an act that one has no legal right to do. The breaking of the law by a public official. The word differs from MISFEASANCE, which is the improper performance of a lawful act, and NONFEASANCE which is nonperformance in the course of carrying out required duties. (See those terms for more detailed definitions.)

MALL—1. A landscaped public area set aside for pedestrian use. 2. A median strip consisting of pavement or a landscaped area as a traffic divider between two roadways. 3. The enclosed public area found in today's larger, modern shopping centers which connects the stores that make up the center.

MANAGEMENT—1. The supervision of property for others. See PROPERTY MANAGEMENT.) 2. The act of controlling and directing a business and its affairs.

MANAGEMENT AGREEMENT—A contract between an owner and agent for the management of property. (See page 356.)

MANAGING AGENT—One authorized to manage the business affairs in connection with the property of another.

MANDAMUS—A writ issued from a higher court ordering or prohibiting the performance of some action by a lower court, body, or person. It is the result of a prior legal proceeding to enforce a right.

MANSARD—A rectangular roof style having two degrees of pitch with the lower half of the roof more steeply inclined than the upper. (See ROOF for illustration).

MANUFACTURED HOME—(See COMPONENT BUILDING, PREFABRICATE, SHELL HOUSE.)

MAP—A pictorial representation of the earth's surface or a portion of it usually drawn to scale. A drawing depicting an area of land.

MARGINAL LAND—Land that is of little economic value due to such factors as inaccessibility, poor quality of soil, steep terrain, lack of rainfall, etc. Economically, only the barest income, if any at all, can be derived from it.

MARINA—A mooring and docking area for boats affording repair facilities, gas, water, supplies and other conveniences to boat owners.

MARK DOWN—A reduction in the asking price.

MARK UP—An addition to the cost which is intended to cover overhead and profit for the seller.

MARKER—A boundary mark. A stake or other visible evidence set in place to indicate a perimeter point of real property.

MARKET—1. The rate or price of something offered for sale. 2. To expose for sale. The place where goods or property are offered for sale and where people go to buy.

MARKET COMPARISON—(See COMPARABLE VALUE, COMPARISON APPROACH, COMPARATIVE APPROACH TO VALUE, or MARKET COMPARISON.)

MARKET RENT—An established rental income a property would be able to generate. (See ECONOMIC RENT).

MARKETABLE—Salable. Property sought by purchasers and which can be sold within a reasonable period of time; merchantable.

MARKETABLE TITLE—Good title; clear title. Title to property that is free of significant defects and which a purchaser will accept without objections. Title under which an owner can be assured of quiet and peaceful enjoyment and that he can convey to others. It is marketable title in the sense that it is good enough not to present a valid objection to the sale of the property; merchantable title.

MARKET PRICE—(See MARKET VALUE; PRICE.)

MARKET VALUE—The price that a property will bring under normal conditions on the open market. The amount that an owner, under no obligation or compulsion to sell, is willing to sell for and the amount a buyer is freely willing to pay. The highest price an asset will bring under normal market conditions within a reasonable period of time.

MARL LAND—Land containing loose, easily crumbled earth deposits of clay and calcium carbonate.

MARSHALING—The ranking or arranging of property according to proper order, sequence or value.

MARSH LAND—Soft, wet grassland. Land heavily saturated with stagnant or slowly moving water. Spongy in texture, marshes are usually covered with plant life.

MARYLAND GROUND RENT—The method of GROUND RENT provides for ninety-nine year land leases with perpetual renewal provisions. The lessee usually pays a semi-annual or annual rent. In the event of a default, the lessor may void the lease. Interest accrued for the lessee is considered personal property. Also no dower rights exist. The Maryland system contains a recapture clause at some point during the term of the lease whereby the lessee can pay a specified sum and become the owner of the fee. The lessee, in fact, is much like the owner of the property throughout the lease, as he must pay all taxes as well as any maintenance and operating expenses normally incurred by the owner. Though the lessee has the right to redeem the fee, he does not have to exercise that right. This has also been referred to as the Baltimore system of ground rent as it had its origin in that city. (See GROUND RENT; PENNSYLVANIA GROUND RENT.)

MASONRY—Construction with stone, brick, concrete, rock or a similar material.

MASSACHUSETTS TRUST—(See BUSINESS TRUST.)

MASS APPRAISING—The appraising of whole areas or a large number of properties at one time. It is commonly used by ASSESSORS when a reappraisal of a jurisdiction is made or when appraising right-of-way acquisitions.

MASTER: MASTER IN CHANCERY—An officer of the court judicially appointed to act as its representative for the performance of a specific transaction. Sometimes called a Special Master, the appointed person frequently has to hear testimony or supervise the sale of real property under a decree. When the Master In Chancery's acts and reports are approved by the presiding judge they become the legal, binding decision of the court. The function of the Master is performed by such individuals as referees, appraisers, assessors, commissioners, court clerks, auditors, etc.

MASTER LEASE—The original lease. Any SUBLEASE or ASSIGNMENT OF LEASE must be based on the master lease.

MASTER PLAN—A long-range, overall concept of an area's development generally proposed by the planning department of a city or other community. By projecting population changes and growth trends, it becomes possible to prepare plans for adequate highways, parks, housing and the overall highest and best usage of the land. A well prepared master plan can do much toward eliminating blighted and slum areas, inadequate public transportation facilities, insufficient and improper housing, overcrowded and congested business and residential areas. Proper master planning can result in important and lasting improvements made to America's cities and towns, thereby permanently enriching our standard of living.

MASTER'S DEED—(See SHERIFF'S DEED).

MATERIALMAN—The individual or firm furnishing the construction materials used in a building or other improvement.

MATERIALMAN'S LIEN—A MECHANIC'S LIEN.

MEAD—Meadow land. Lush grassland sometimes covered with wild flowers.

MEADOW—A level or gradually sloping tract of grassland. An open field.

MEANDER LINE—The uneven, winding property line formed by the natural turning of streams, rivers, brooks and other water courses.

MECHANIC'S LIEN—A statutory lien levied on property by those who furnish material and labor for the construction of a building or other improvement. The lien attaches to the land as well as the structures upon it and establishes a priority of payment. In most states a mechanic's lien is created by statute.

MECHANIC'S LIEN AFFIDAVIT—A sworn statement, made by a property owner, that there are no unpaid bills or liens encumbering the personal property on the premises.

MEDIAN—1. Being in the middle; the average. 2. A strip of pavement or seeded area serving as a barrier separating two or more lanes of a highway.

MEDIUM INDUSTRY—An industrial zoning classification for firms whose manufacturing and production processes are not as objectionable in terms of noise, air pollution, odor, etc. as HEAVY INDUSTRY, but more so than LIGHT INDUSTRY.

MEETING OF THE MINDS—When two or more parties are in complete agreement as to price, terms and conditions of a sale, a common understanding or meeting of the minds is said to take place. It comes about as a result of their expressed purpose and intentions.

MEGALOPOLIS—A large, heavily populated urbanized area sometimes extending over hundreds of miles. With cities and suburbs in huge industrial centers merging into other cities and their suburbs, the term has come to mean entire regions that sometimes cross state lines.

MEGASTRUCTURE—A large multi-purpose structure usually found in or near major U.S. cities. Most contain (under one roof, or in close proximity) all or some of the following facilities: department stores, shops, theaters, restaurants, hotels, offices, recreation areas and enclosed parking. In an attempt to counter building trends away from metropolitan areas, megastructures may prove a major factor in revitalizing urban communities.

MEMBER APPRAISAL INSTITUTE—(See M.A.I.)

MEMORANDUM OF AGREEMENT—An informal, written agreement outlining the essentials of a transaction. It is generally binding upon both parties and remains in force until a more formal contract is drawn. Even though in letter or memorandum form and written in non-legal terminology, when properly written it should contain all the elements of a valid contract. (See also BINDER, CONTRACT, and DEPOSIT RECEIPT.)

MERCANTILE LAW—1. Commercial Law. Law dealing with business transactions. 2. Rules and customs of the business community to regulate and govern their activities.

MERCHANTABLE TITLE—(See MARKETABLE TITLE.)

MERGED LOT—A parcel of land having frontage on two streets. A Through Lot.

MERGE LINE—1. The property line that divides a Merged Lot. 2. A technique for appraising MERGED LOTS accomplished by visualizing an imaginary line at a point between the two street frontages. The line reflects the most logical division of the land and therefore the most value for each lot.

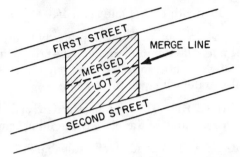

Merge Line and Merged Lot

MERGER—1. To consolidate two or more companies into one. 2. In real property law, it is a principle that when two estates join to become the assets of one person, the lesser estate is merged in the greater. Also, in documentation, a contract merges and is extinguished by the deed upon its delivery and acceptance.

MERIDIAN LINES—Longitudinal lines running north and south on a map. (See GOVERNMENT SURVEY, PRIME MERIDIAN, LONGITUDE.)

MESSUAGE—A house with adjoining or nearby accessory buildings which are used in conjunction with the dwelling.

METER—A unit of measure equaling 39.37 inches or 3.28083 feet.

METES AND BOUNDS—A means of describing property, often used where a high degree of accuracy is required. Length (metes) and directions or boundaries (bounds) start at a known point of beginning and, using 360 degrees of the compass for directions, with each degree divided into minutes, 1/60 of a degree, and seconds 1/3600 of a degree, a highly accurate description of land can be reached. Degrees are shown as °, minutes as ' and seconds as ".

METROPOLIS—The area occupied by a large city and its immediate suburbs. (See also MEGALOPOLIS.)

METROPOLITAN AREA—Of or relating to a metropolis. Urban; the area in and around a city.

MICRO-RELIEF—Slight variations or irregularities in the earth's surface. Hummocks, dunes, ridges, sink holes and caverns are examples.

MIDDLEMAN—As applied to real estate, an agent employed by both buyer and seller. It is an ethical and legal business arrangement provided both principals are aware of his dual employment. When a sale is made, the broker is entitled to commissions from both parties.

MILE—A measure of distance 5,280 feet (1760 yards) long.

MILITARY CLAUSE—A clause providing for cancellation of a lease when the lessee is a member of the armed forces and is transferred. (See TRANSFER CLAUSE.)

MILL—One-tenth part of one cent; 1/1000th of a dollar.

MILLAGE—In conjunction with property taxes, it is the factor generally used to state the rate of taxation and compute the taxes. One mill per thousand is equivalent to $1 of taxes per thousand of assessed value. Thus, the assessed value multiplied by the millage rate will equal the tax rate.

MINERAL DEED—The severance by deed of the mineral rights to one's property. An owner's granting of the oil, gas and other mineral rights to his property.

MINERAL LAND—Land chiefly valuable for containing mineral deposits.

MINERAL LEASE—A lease which permits the lessee to explore for and extract minerals from the land. Such leases are usually payable on a royalty basis.

MINERAL RIGHT—The right given to a lessee to take minerals from the land. (See MINERAL DEED.)

MINIMUM LOT ZONING—A zoning requirement that states the minimum lot size on which a building may be erected.

MINIMUM RENTAL—A term applicable to PERCENTAGE LEASES. It is the base rent that must be paid no matter what volume of business is achieved by the tenant. (See OVERAGE.)

MINING—The extraction of minerals from land.

MINOR—One who has not reached the age required to be legally recognized as an adult. An infant in the eyes of the law and as such not legally responsible for contracting debts or signing contracts. An individual under the age of 21 (except in a few states that consider females at age 18 no longer minors).

MINUTE—As used in measuring degrees of a circle in directions for Metes and Bounds legal descriptions, it is 1/60th of a degree of an angle or 1/21,600th of a circle.

MISCELLANEOUS INCOME—Incidental income brought in from other than regular receipts. As for example, the money received for allowing a signboard on a property or from coin machines.

MISDEMEANOR—A minor crime less serious than a felony; one not usually punishable by imprisonment. A misdeed.

MISFEASANCE—A misdeed in the carrying out of a lawful act. Improper performance of one's duties, especially by a public official. The wrongful exercising of lawful authority.

MISPLACED IMPROVEMENT—A poorly planned improvement; one that is too costly for, or otherwise incongruous with its location. As an example, an expensive residence in a blighted or slum neighborhood.

MISREPRESENTATION—A false presentation of the facts. A statement made with the express purpose of deceiving or misleading; an untrue representation; a fraud.

MISSION ARCHITECTURE—An architectural design fashioned after the Spanish missions found mostly in California during early settlement days.

MIXED ESTATE—GROUND RENT for ninety-nine years that is renewable forever. Though a leasehold in form, in reality it has more of the characteristics of fee ownership.

MOBILE HOME PARK—An area zoned for and set up to accommodate house trailers. (See TRAILER PARK.)

MODEL—A typical house or apartment designated as the showpiece or facsimile of others being built.

MODEL CITIES PROGRAM—(See DEPARTMENT OF HOUSING AND URBAN DEVELOPMENT (HUD).)

MODERN ARCHITECTURE—A contemporary design of a building. A new style relating to the present.

MODERN ENGLISH ARCHITECTURE—A style of architecture that includes features of the Tudor and Elizabethan era. Steep roof lines with stucco exterior walls are characteristic.

MODERNIZATION—The act of remodeling; bringing up to date; to modernize. To repair and renovate a building so it has more of the characteristics of contemporary design.

MODULE CONSTRUCTION—Construction containing standardized, component parts and materials. Prefabricated, mass-produced members that offer uniformity of quality and economy.

MOLDING—A decorative strip, usually of wood, used to finish and beautify. Also spelled Moulding.

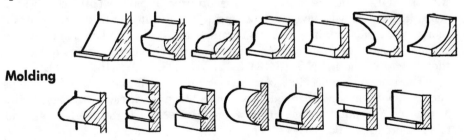

Molding

MONETARY—Pertaining to money.

MONEY—Currency; what is accepted as a medium of exchange; cash as distinguished from notes, stock certificates, bonds or other negotiable instruments or valuable assets.

MONEY MARKET—The current availability of bank money and the rate of interest being charged to borrow it. Like any commodity, the money market fluctuates with its availability and the demand. When in short supply, the interest rates become higher, and vice versa.

MONITOR ROOF—A saw-tooth roof design used in industrial buildings. It serves the dual purpose of increasing light and ventilation. (See ROOF illustrations.)

MONOPOLY—The exclusive control or ownership of so much in one industry, field or product as to be in a position to limit or exclude competition. Power to stifle competition and restrain trade.

MONTHLY TENANCY—The tenancy of one who rents for a month at a time.

MONTH-TO-MONTH TENANCY—A tenant for one month. Also, when a tenant with an expired lease, a month-to-month lease, or no lease at all continues paying rent and remains in occupancy from one month to another.

MONUMENT—A fixed boundary mark identifying the extent of a parcel of land. The monument can be a man-made cement slab, a mound of stones, a stake, a wood or steel post or natural objects such as a boulder, a notched tree or the MEANDER LINE of a water course.

MORAL OBLIGATION—An obligation not necessarily binding by law, but one inspired by conscience and ethics.

MORAL TURPITUDE—(See TURPITUDE.)

MORATORIUM—An authorized postponement in meeting an agreed obligation during a period of financial distress; temporary suspension of payments. A legal delay in paying an obligation; an officially granted waiting period.

MORE OR LESS—Approximately; about; a qualifying term used in describing the extent of property when the precise fractional measurements are uncertain or unknown. In contracts it implies that both buyer and seller are aware that a small difference can and probably does exist. It is often shown on surveys as follows: ±.

MORTGAGE—A pledge of property as security for the payment of a debt. In some states it is the actual conveyance of land to the creditor until the terms of the mortgage are satisfied. In others it is regarded as just a lien and does not create an estate. The mortgagor retains possession and use of the property during the term of the mortgage. (See LIEN THEORY STATES, TITLE THEORY STATES.)

There are numerous kinds of mortgages for different purposes and situations, such as Government Insured Mortgages, Conventional Mortgages, First Mortgages, Second Mortgages, Third Mortgages (etc.), Chattel Mortgages, Equitable Mortgages, Purchase Money Mortgages, Private Mortgages, Blanket Mortgages, General Mortgages, Special Mortgages, Legal, Judicial or Tacit Mortgages and others. Refer to the specific mortgage term for definition. (See also MORTGAGE DEED.)

MORTGAGE BANKERS—Firms that furnish their own funds for mortgage loans.

Some mortgage bankers specialize in short-term building loans, which they later sell to permanent investors. Others hold the mortgage through both stages of development. They also refinance mortgages for existing buildings. In most instances they continue to service the loans for a specified fee.

MORTGAGE BOND—A bond that is secured by a mortgage. (See BOND.)

MORTGAGE BROKER—An individual or company that obtains mortgages for others by finding lending institutions, insurance companies or private sources that will lend the money. Mortgage brokers sometimes service the account by making collections and handling disbursements.

MORTGAGE CERTIFICATE—When one mortgage is shared by a number of investors their proportionate, undivided interests are sometimes documented by certificates. Each certificate states for whom the mortgage is being held and outlines the extent of that party's interest. The basic terms and conditions of the mortgage are sometimes also detailed. The mortgage certificate itself does not serve as evidence of monies to be paid (as in a note or bond). It functions only as proof of the interest held in the mortgage.

MORTGAGE COMMITMENT—(See COMMITMENT.)

MORTGAGE COMPANY—(See MORTGAGE BROKER; MORTGAGE INVESTMENT COMPANY.)

MORTGAGE CONSTANT—The annual percentage paid on a loan including the interest rate and the amortization. If, for example, the interest rate is 9 percent and the rate of principal reduction is 2 percent, the annual mortgage constant would be 11 percent.

MORTGAGE CORRESPONDENT—An authorized agent for institutional lenders who is empowered to make loan commitments. A mortgage correspondent sometimes services the loan once it is granted.

MORTGAGE DEBT—An indebtedness created by a mortgage and secured by the property mortgaged. Personal liability may or may not be a part of the obligation. If the terms of the agreement do not hold the debtor personally liable, the property mortgaged is the security. A mortgage debt is made evident by a bond or note.

MORTGAGE DEED—A mortgage. Some areas of the country refer to the instrument used as a mortgage deed.

MORTGAGE DISCOUNT—(See DISCOUNT.)

MORTGAGE-EQUITY—In evaluating income property the influence of the existing mortgages to its market value is loosely referred to as mortgage-equity. Mortgages play a vital role in investment realty because they have the greatest influence on cash flow, which is perhaps the most important single factor in determining value. The mortgage amount, interest rate, the term, debt service, prepayment privileges or penalties are just some of the mortgage factors to be considered when reaching a conclusion as to a property's true value.

MORTGAGE INSURANCE POLICY—A title policy issued by a title insurance company to a holder of a mortgage. (See TITLE INSURANCE.)

MORTGAGE INVESTMENT COMPANY—A company that buys mortgages for investment purposes, such as insurance companies, trust companies, banks, savings and loan associations and private organizations formed expressly for investing their funds in mortgages.

MORTGAGE LIEN—A mortgage given as security for a debt serves as a lien upon the property after it is recorded. The mortgage is sometimes referred to as a mortgage lien.

MORTGAGE LOAN INSURANCE—(See INSURED LOANS.)

MORTGAGE MONEY—The amount of funds invested in the mortgage by the lender.

MORTGAGE MORATORIUM—(See MORATORIUM.)

MORTGAGE NOTE—A note, secured by a mortgage, that serves as proof of an indebtedness and states the manner in which it shall be paid. It is the actual amount of the debt that the mortgage secures and renders the mortgagor personally responsible for repayment.

MORTGAGE ON LEASEHOLD—The mortgaging of a leasehold interest. A lease creates a valuable interest and unless the lease agreement prohibits, it can be used as security for obtaining a mortgage.

MORTGAGE ORIGINATION FEE—(See ORIGINATION FEE.)

MORTGAGE PREMIUM—An extra fee charged for placing or originating a mortgage; points. This is an expense in addition to normal closing costs and comes about when: 1. the legal interest rate (as in the case of FHA and VA mortgages) is less than the prevailing mortgage market rate; and 2. there is a scarcity of readily available mortgage money.

MORTGAGE REDLINING—(See REDLINING.)

MORTGAGE REDUCTION CERTIFICATE—(See ESTOPPEL CERTIFICATE.)

MORTGAGE REGISTRATION TAX—A tax in effect in some states when a mortgage is filed.

MORTGAGE VALUE—The value placed upon property for mortgage purposes. As a practical matter, this usually means the MARKET VALUE.

MORTGAGEE—The one who holds the mortgage as security for the money he has loaned on property. The lender or creditor.

MORTGAGEE IN POSSESSION—To protect his interest a mortgagee sometimes takes possession of property about to be dispossessed. Usually this is done when dealing with income properties where rental money, management and disbursements continue whether or not the property is in default. It must be with the consent of the mortgagor or, in cases of foreclosure, by a court order.

MORTGAGOR—The giver of a mortgage as security for money he borrows on his property.

MORTMAIN—An early-English term denoting the obtaining of lands or tenements by the church. As such property is generally kept in perpetuity, it is said to be alienated or "dead" for any other purpose.

MOTEL—A building used to rent rooms to the transient public and designed to afford accessbile parking and convenient, informal accommodations.

MOTHER HUBBARD CLAUSE—A provision in a mortgage allowing a lender, upon default of its terms and conditions, to foreclose on the delinquent mortgage as well as any *other* mortgages the lender may have given the borrower. The legality of the clause is regarded as highly questionable in most areas of the country.

MOTIF—The predominant design of a building's interior or exterior. The style or theme of a structure.

MOTION TO QUASH—A court request for dismissal made by the defendant. The reasoning as to why the charges should be quashed as it applies to the law are set forth in the motion.

MOVABLE ESTATE—Personal property. That which is not affixed to the land and can be removed upon transfer of ownership. Personalty.

MOVABLE FREEHOLD—Land that is capable of being increased or diminished as is the case of ocean-front property or river banks.

MUCK LAND—Soft, muddy lowland; land with high moisture content.

MULTIPLE DWELLING—Any building designed to house two or more families. (See APARTMENT HOUSE; DUPLEX; TENEMENT.)

MULTIPLE FAMILY—A zoning classification for residential areas. (See also MULTIPLE DWELLING.)

MULTIPLE LISTING—An exclusive listing, for the sale or lease of real estate, given to one broker for distribution to others. Many local real estate boards have a central clearing house where multiple listings are submitted by member brokers. Photos and brochures are printed and sent to participating agents for cooperative sales. In this way a client is assured his property will receive wide market exposure.

MULTIPLE NUCLEI DEVELOPMENT—The term refers to a community's real estate development, where the population growth is formed around numerous separate centers of construction activity, rather than only one.

MULTIPLE TRANSACTION—A multiple transaction exists when the exchange, lease or sale of real estate involves more than one property.

MULTIPLIER—A rule-of-thumb number for finding the value of investment property. It is the multiplier X the income. For example, if the annual income of the property under study is $50,000, and the multiplier for this type and condition of property in the area is 6, then the estimate of value is $300,000. (See also GROSS INCOME MULTIPLIER, NET INCOME MULTIPLIER.)

MULTI-STORY BUILDING—A building having two or more stories.

MUNICIPAL—A general term encompassing all forms of local government, but most commonly applied to a city.

MUNICIPALITY—A self-governing city or town.

MUNICIPAL LIEN—A lien, created by a local government, against a property owner to obtain funds in order to make improvements to his and immediately surrounding properties. A lien to give special benefits to the properties assessed. A SPECIAL ASSESSMENT LIEN.

MUNICIPAL ORDINANCE—A law adopted by a local government for the protection and best interest of its people. Zoning requirements and building codes are examples of municipal ordinances.

MUNIMENT OF TITLE—Written proof that enables an owner to defend his title to property. Instruments such as deeds and contracts that serve as documentary evidence of ownership.

MUTUAL—Something in common shared by two or more individuals. Reciprocal. Interchangeable. A mutual insurance company, for example, is one in which the members are both the insured and the insurors. The term is used in real estate parlance with such words as account, agreement, bank, contract, credit, debit, enterprise, testaments, wills, etc.

MUTUAL SAVINGS BANK—(See SAVINGS BANK.)

N

NAKED CONTRACT—A contract in which there is no consideration given, and therefore unenforceable. Also called a Nude Contract.

NATIONAL BANK—A bank that is chartered by and doing business under federal law. National banks are distinguished from state lending institutions, which are governed and regulated by the state in which they are located.

NATIONAL BUILDING CODE—Published by the American Insurance Association and used primarily by certain cities in eastern United States, it is the first model building code ever adopted. The purpose of this and other building codes that followed is to create construction standards in the best interest of safety, health, property and public welfare. Also, to create uniformity in regulations pertaining to the building industry. (See also UNIFORM BUILDING CODE.)

NATURAL AFFECTION—Affection that exists between close relatives such as husband and wife, mother and child, brother and sister. When real estate or other valuable property is given to a near relative, it is considered good consideration in law.

NATURAL FINANCING—A real estate transaction that requires no outside financing or mortgages, as evidenced in an all-cash sale. When properties are traded, it occurs when no third party financing is required, as when the parties assume each other's mortgages.

NATURAL PERSON—A human being. The term is contrasted with an ARTIFICIAL PERSON, which is a "person" created by law such as a corporation.

NATURAL RESOURCE PROPERTY—Land upon or under which the natural resources can be used for commercial purposes. Property containing sufficient quantities of usable timber, sand, gravel, clay, gas, coal, oil or minerals are thus classified.

NEGATIVE EASEMENT—An easement which relinquishes some valuable right and acts to curtail the complete use of the property. Building restrictions or covenants preventing lots from being fully utilized are examples.

NEGATIVE LEVERAGE—When the cost to borrow money (interest) exceeds the return that money would bring, the resulting loss becomes leverage in reverse. (See LEVERAGE).

NEGOTIABLE INSTRUMENT—Any readily transferable written instrument such as a check, promissory note, government bond, a public stock, etc.

NEGOTIATE—The transacting of business through discussion, compromise and reasoning, or the attempting of same. A real estate broker's function is to aid in the negotiating process in order to bring about a MEETING OF MINDS. (See that term.)

NEGOTIATION—The process of attempting to create a meeting of the minds between two or more parties in an effort to bring about a sale or other agreement; bargaining.

NEIGHBORHOOD—1. A community of people living in a general vicinity. 2. The immediate proximity of property; the land that surrounds another parcel. A section; area.

NEIGHBORHOOD SHOPPING CENTER—A relatively small group of stores devoted to the basic needs of the immediate neighborhood. (See SHOPPING CENTER.)

NET ESTATE—The portion of an estate left after all expenses to administer it have been taken out.

NET FLOOR AREA—The actual rentable floor space of a building, excluding such areas as halls, lobby, lavatories, elevator shafts, heating plant, etc. Rentable floor area is measured to the center line of the walls.

NET INCOME—The money remaining after expenses are subtracted from the income. The profit.

NET INCOME MULTIPLIER—(See INCOME MULTIPLIER.)

NET LEASE—A lease requiring the tenant to pay all the costs of maintaining the building, including taxes, insurance, repairs and other expenses normally required of the owner.

NET LISTING—A listing stating the minimum amount the seller will accept for himself. Commissions and sometimes other expenses to close the transaction have to be added to the net price.

NET NET INCOME—In real estate dealings the word net is sometimes repeated for emphasis, stressing actual profit for *all* expenses are paid including mortgage reduction payments (principal and interest). What remains is usable cash. The cash flow.

NET PROFIT—(See NET INCOME; NET NET INCOME.)

NET RENT—The income a landlord retains after expenses.

NET RENTAL—(See NET LEASE.)

NET SPENDABLE INCOME—Cash flow. Usable income after all expenses are paid.

NET WORTH—The current market value after totaling assets and subtracting liabilities.

NEW—Having recently been completed or initiated; never existing before. In real estate the word is frequently used in such terms as new construction, new acquisition, new listing, new mortgage, new management, new assets, new lease, etc.

NEW ENGLAND COLONIAL ARCHITECTURE—Colloquially referred to as a "salt box," its features include a square plan with two stories at the front elevation, plus a long, steep roof that slopes to one story at the rear. The exterior materials usually are of clapboard, and the chimneyed roof is often wood-shingled.

NIHIL—(Latin) Not at all. In no respect. Nothing. More commonly contracted to *Nil.*

NO DEAL, NO COMMISSION CLAUSE—A broker earns his commission when an agreement has been reached by the parties to the transaction, and it is due and payable at once. However, variously worded clauses are sometimes inserted in contracts that provide for the commission to be paid only when and if title passes. These contingency provisions are called "no deal, no commission" clauses.

NO LIEN AFFIDAVIT—A statement by an owner that work is completed on the subject property and that no liens or chattel mortgages encumber it. (See OWNER'S AFFIDAVIT OF NO LIENS.)

NOMINEE—A person designated or appointed. The one proposed to act for another as his representative. An ASSIGNEE designate. The party who is to receive an ASSIGNMENT OF CONTRACT.

NONBEARING WALL—A wall that does not help support the structure. The opposite of a BEARING WALL, which is built to hold the weight of the floors above. Also referred to as a Nonload Bearing wall.

NONCONFORMING USE—The lawful use of land or improvements upon it that does not comply with current zoning regulations. It is allowed to remain as it was before the zoning ordinance was passed. Generally such properties cannot be replaced, remodeled or enlarged.

NONCONTINUOUS EASEMENT—An easement that must be granted each time a property changes ownership; one that does not automatically occur. Easements as a rule are continuous and pass with the land when sold, but when this is not the case the new owner must seek renewal of the right given by the easement or it may discontinue.

NONDISCLOSURE—The courts refer to nondisclosure as "misrepresentation by silence." When certain material facts of a property are withheld from the buyer and are later discovered, he may sue for nondisclosure.

NONFEASANCE—1. Nonperformance. In the law of agency, it is the omission or failure of an agent to perform the duties he and his principal have agreed would be done. 2. The neglect or refusal of an officer to substantially perform what it is legally his duty to do. It differs from MALFEASANCE (wrongdoing), and MISFEASANCE (improper performance). (See those titles for complete definitions.)

NON-INVESTMENT PROPERTY—Residential, church, vacation property or land obtained for the purpose of living and enjoyment only, rather than for income that can be derived from it.

NON-MERCHANTABLE TITLE—Faulty title; title to real property that cannot be sold because of a cloud or other encumbrance upon it. Title that would be legally unsound to accept because of its defects. Unmarketable title.

NONPOSSESSORY ESTATE—(See FUTURE ESTATE.)

NON-PROFIT CORPORATION—A corporation formed for the specific purpose of furthering charitable, benevolent, scientific, fraternal, political or educational endeavors, and not for a profit motive. Its legal term is ELEEMOSYNARY CORPORATION.

NONRECURRING EXPENSE—An expense that does not regularly or periodically occur. Repairs necessitated by vandalism, theft or an Act of God are examples.

NON-RESIDENT—One who does not live in a specified area.

NOOK—1. A secluded corner of a parcel of land. Also, an alcove or corner of a room. 2. English law refers to a nook of land as being 12½ acres.

NORMAL SALE—A routine real estate transaction in which a fair price and terms are agreed to and duly carried out. No abnormal or irregular situations develop and both buyer and seller are satisfied.

NORMAL VALUE—The price a property will bring, under ordinary conditions, on the open market. (See MARKET VALUE.)

NORTH—A directional description that is due north; pointing toward the north pole. The 0 and 360th degree on a compass. One of the four cardinal points of direction.

NOTARIAL—Performed by a notary public. Pertaining to a notary. Executed by a notary, as evidenced by the seal and signature.

NOTARY: NOTARY PUBLIC—One who notarizes documents; a bonded officer licensed by the state to "acknowledge and attest" to the signatures and statements of others.

NOTE—An instrument used as tangible proof that a person owes a certain sum of money to another and that he agrees to pay it under the specified terms and conditions. It is also called a PROMISSORY NOTE.

NOTICE—(See LEGAL NOTICE.)

NOTICE OF COMPLETION—A notice, filed by the owner of a building that is officially recorded with the proper county agency, stating that all construction bills have been paid. By publicly recording such an instrument, suppliers, sub-contractors and service companies are constructively put on notice. They then have a specified period of time (which varies from one jurisdiction to another) to file a LIEN in the event that they desire to make claim for bills unpaid.

NOTICE OF LIS PENDENS—(See LIS PENDENS.)

NOTICE OF SALE—A notice from a broker or owner that a particualr property has been sold and is no longer on the market. Also called a SOLD NOTICE.

NOTICE OF UNPAID RENT—A formal notification of a sum of money due for non-payment of rent and a demand for its payment.

NOTICE OF UNPAID RENT

Date _____

From _____

_____

To _____

_____

You are hereby notified that you are indebted to me in the sum of _____ _____, Dollars, for the rent and use of the premises _____ County, State of _____, now occupied by you, and that I demand the payment of the said rent or the possession of said premises within three days from the date of this notice, to-wit: on or before the _____ day of _____, A.D. 19___

_____

NOTICE TO QUIT—A landlord's notice to his tenant to give up possession of the leased premises at the end of the term of the lease. As a common practice, many jurisdictions require that the notice be delivered three months prior to the lease's expiration. If upon receipt of the notice the tenant agrees to vacate, he waives any claims to an extension of the lease. If the landlord, on the other hand, accepts rent that may accrue for the period after the date to quit, it will serve as recognition of the extended occupancy.

NOTORIOUS POSSESSION—Possession of land that is obvious and common knowledge to the neighbors or the public in general. It is a legal requirement before one can obtain property by ADVERSE POSSESSION.

NOVATION—The exchange or substitution of a new obligation or debt for an old one by mutual agreement.

NUDE CONTRACT—(See NAKED CONTRACT.)

NUISANCE VALUE—The price someone will pay for property because of annoyances or damage caused by the current owner. The value is abnormal and does not relate to its worth under usual circumstances, and therefore is not true value.

NULL AND VOID—Canceled; invalid; having no legal force or effect; not binding; not enforceable.

O

OATH—A declaration appealing to God to be a witness of the truth of a fact, statement or act; a solemn affirmation or serious pledge.

OBJECTION TO TITLE—Grounds for disapproval of the title; opposition to it. A fault or flaw in the title that needs clarification or correction.

OBJECTIVE—Arriving at a conclusion by studying the facts and not letting personal feelings or prejudices interfere. The opposite of subjective.

OBLIGATION BOND—A bond signed by the mortgagor that is in excess of the amount of the mortgage. It creates a personal obligation that serves as a further safeguard to the lender for payment of taxes, assessments, and any overdue interest that may accrue over the amount of the mortgage.

OBLIGATION OF CONTRACT—The binding, legal requirements of a contract by the parties. The civil obligations and duty a party has assumed upon signing a legal document. His contractual obligations. Except where SPECIFIC PERFORMANCE is a remedy, actual performance of the terms of a contract is not required, but rather, one is liable for the damages caused by not performing as agreed.

OBLIGEE—A party to whom something is owed; the creditor. One to whom another has an obligation to perform.

OBLIGOR—One who has an obligation to fulfill; the debtor.

OBSOLESCENCE—Passing out of style; outmoded; out of date. Older buildings are said to gradually reach a point of economic or functional obsolescence. ECONOMIC OBSOLESCENCE occurs when it is no longer profitable to keep a building operating. FUNCTIONAL OBSOLESCENCE is when defects in the structure limit its usefulness, thereby lessening its marketability and value.

OCCASIONAL OVERFLOW RIGHTS—An easement to occasionally overflow water onto another's land during periods of high water.

OCCUPANCY—Having possession of property. Physically taking and holding it and residing thereon as a tenant or owner.

OCCUPANCY CLAUSE—The clause in a lease stating when occupancy of the property is to be given.

OCCUPANCY EXPENSE—The landlord's expenses to maintain a premises in habitable condition, such as for light, heat, water and repair costs.

OCCUPANCY RATE—The ratio of the square footage that is leased to that of the entire building. Also, the rate of rented apartments or offices as compared to the total number. It is usually expressed in percentages (a 100 unit apartment house with 7 vacancies has a 93 percent occupancy rate).

O-DOME CONSTRUCTION—A "house-in-round" style of vacation shelter, featuring 360° living space. Made of lightweight paneling with no supporting beams or walls, it is generally built to be easily relocatable.

OFFER—An expression of one's willingness to purchase property at a specified price and terms; a proposal; a readiness to enter into an agreement; A unilateral contract.

OFFER AND ACCEPTANCE—A willingness to buy, under stated terms, by the purchaser and an approval of those terms by the seller; a contract. (See CONTRACT; INTERPRETATION OF CONTRACT.)

OFFER TO BUY—(See OFFER.)

OFFER TO SELL—The offering of property for sale to the public (See LISTING.)

OFF-GRADE LOT—A lot that requires the addition or removal of fill to be effectively utilized. One that has to be made level with the surrounding terrain before construction can begin.

OFFICE BUILDING—A building principally used by companies to conduct business; one divided into offices.

OFFICIAL—1. Approval by a recognized authority. 2. An individual holding a position of responsibility, trust and authority.

OFFSETTING BENEFITS—(See SPECIAL BENEFITS.)

OIL AND GAS LEASE—A lease granting the right to extract oil or gas from beneath the surface of the land.

OMITTED ASSESSMENT—An assessment made after the dates specified by the authorities for the assessment period. Also called a Retrospective Assessment.

ON DEMAND—When asked for. When the amount is requested. An obligation payable in this manner is called a DEMAND NOTE OR MORTGAGE. No specific due date is stated in the instrument, but it can be "called in" for payment at any time without prior notification.

ONE-AND-A-HALF STORY—A building having the second floor walls about three or four feet high with a substantial portion of the ceiling conforming to the angle of the roof.

ONEROUS—Oppressive; burdensome; exacting; troublesome. In real estate law, the terms onerous cause, onerous contract, onerous deed, onerous gift and onerous title are sometimes used to indicate that the consideration given is of more value than that which is received.

ONE-THIRD, TWO-THIRDS RULE—An old appraisal formula once used by assessors to uniformly evaluate land. This rule holds that 50 percent of the land value is assigned to the front one-third of the property and 50 percent to the remainder. It is not always valid and experts agree that it no longer should be used to appraise land.

ON OR ABOUT—A term used in documents when an exact date is to be specified or is not known for certain. It represents an approximation of the time.

ON OR BEFORE—A term used in instruments when a deadline is given for something to be fulfilled or refrained from being done. As long as it is complied with any time on or before the date specified, the condition will have been met.

OPEN—1. To make accessible or available, as an open house, open listing, open mortgage, etc. 2. Apparent; visual; patent.

OPEN AND NOTORIOUS POSSESSION—Conspicuous possession that is common knowledge to the public. The term is most frequently used to indicate the type of possession an individual holds when attempting to acquire land by ADVERSE POSSESSION.

OPEN-END MORTGAGE—A mortgage which permits the borrower to reborrow the money paid on the principal, usually up to the original amount.

OPEN HOUSING—Housing free of racial or religious discrimination of any form. Dwellings that are made available to anyone that can afford them.

OPEN HOUSING LAW—A federal law prohibiting discrimination in housing because of one's race, religion, color or national origin. Such practices as discriminatory advertising, changing purchasing terms, BLOCKBUSTING and falsely stating that a property is off the market, when in reality it is not, are unlawful. The law covers discrimination in making mortgage loans whether through banks, institutions or private sources and in the sale of vacant land as well. In addition to the federal open housing laws, a majority of the states have passed their own equivalent fair housing bills.

Discrimination in renting or selling of all housing units is unlawful, with the following exceptions: (a) One-family dwellings, provided the owner does not own more than three such homes. If the owner does not himself occupy the home, he is exempt from the open housing law for only one sale within a two-year period. (b) Owners of four-unit apartments or less, if they occupy one of the apartments. (One-family homes are no longer exempt from the provisions of the open housing law if sold through a real estate agent.)

OPEN LISTING—A listing made available to more than one broker. The first one who procures a buyer READY, WILLING AND ABLE for the price and terms of the listing, is the one who receives the commission. The listing is then automatically terminated.

OPEN LOT—A parcel of land having all sides fronting on streets.

Open Lot

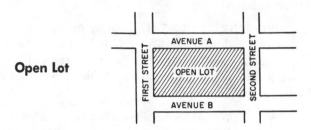

OPEN MORTGAGE—1. A mortgage that can be paid off at any time before maturity without penalty. 2. When mortgage payments are overdue, it is sometimes referred to as an "open mortgage," in that it is open for a foreclosure action.

OPEN OCCUPANCY—Occupancy of a neighborhood or building that is open to all people regardless of race, creed or color.

OPEN POSSESSION—(See ADVERSE POSSESSION; NOTORIOUS POSSESSION.)

OPERATING EXPENSES—The actual expenses incurred keeping property in usable or rentable condition, to protect it against hazards and to pay taxes. Such items as management, maintenance, repairs, utilities, furniture replacement, taxes and insurance are included. Not included as operating expenses are principal and interest mortgage payments, depreciation and interest on money invested.

OPERATING INCOME—Income received directly from property or from the operation of a business before expenses are deducted.

OPERATING PROFIT—The financial gain realized from conducting a business after operating expenses have been paid. The return received on a investment after all direct operational charges have been deducted.

OPERATING PROPERTY—Property that is currently utilized. One that is not being held for possible future needs or for speculation.

OPERATING RATIO—The ratio of the expenses of running commercial property or a business to its gross income.

OPERATIVE BUILDER—(See SPECULATIVE BUILDER.)

OPERATOR—A person skilled in real estate who knows the ins and outs of transactions. A prudent, knowledgeable individual acting for his own account.

OPINION OF TITLE—An attorney's opinion as to how good the title to a specified piece of property is after studying the ABSTRACT. He renders a judgment as to whether the seller has good and marketable title, defective title or any title at all.

OPTION—A right given, for a valuable consideration, to purchase or lease property at a future date for a specified price and terms. The right may or may not be exercised at the option holder's discretion. If he does not choose to exercise the option the consideration is forfeited.

OPTIONEE—The holder of the option. The prospective buyer or tenant.

OPTIONER—The owner of the property. The seller or landlord.

ORAL—By mouth; not written; spoken.

ORAL CONTRACT—A contract that may be partly in writing and partly verbal, or one that is completely verbal; a PAROL CONTRACT. Though oral contracts are said to be binding, they are considered virtually unenforceable. (See STATUTE OF FRAUDS.)

ORDINANCE—A law or rule of order established by a recognized, authoritative agency. A local government's code, regulation or statute.

ORGANIZATION—The management and structure of a business. The act of organizing in order to properly conduct affairs. The condition or state of being organized.

ORIGINAL—The initial one; the first; that from which copies are made. Number one of its kind and completely independent of anything that came before.

ORIGINAL ASSESSMENT—The first authorized assessment made of a newly constructed building.

ORIGINAL COST—The initial cost; the amount paid to build or acquire the property. In new construction, it is the total outlay for material, labor and land.

ORIGINAL PLAT—The first plat or survey made of a city, town, village or other specified area. Subsequent additions use the original plat as reference. (See PLAT.)

ORIGINATION FEE—In reference to mortgaging, it is a charge for establishing and processing a new mortgage loan.

OSTENSIBLE PARTNERS—Individuals who give an outward appearance of being business partners, though this may or may not be consistent with the fact.

OUTBUILDING—Any building other than the main one on a particular parcel of land. A secondary or accessory building, as, for instance, a garage, barn, outhouse, guest cottage or storage house.

OUTDOOR LIVING SPACE—The remaining, open area of a residential lot that is not occupied by the house, garage or other building.

OUTLOT—An unimproved lot located away from a developed area. It is generally larger in size than a normal building lot.

OVERAGE—Retail store leases are sometimes established at a minimum figure with a percentage of the volume of business the store does over a specified amount going to the landlord as additional rent. This amount is referred to as overage. (See also PERCENTAGE LEASE.)

OVERALL PROPERTY TAX LIMITATION—A legal tax limit that may be levied against a given parcel of real estate during any one year. It represents a fixed percentage of the overall value of the property, and is distinguished from taxes imposed on separate portions of the property.

OVERDUE—Past an agreed upon time; something delayed; due yet unpaid; extended beyond a specified period.

OVERFLOWED LANDS—Lands that are occasionally or periodically flooded. Shoreline property that is daily covered and uncovered by the rise and fall of the tides. Such lands are generally swampy and not navigable. Property that requires drainage or embankments before it can be utilized.

OVERFLOW RIGHT—The right, either permanent or temporary, to flood or submerge another's land.

OVERHANG—A wall or roof projecting beyond a lower wall; cantilever.

OVERHEAD—The general cost of operating a business or property; fixed expense.

OVER-IMPROVEMENT—An improvement to land that is more extensive or costly than needed. As an example, the erection of a thirty-story office building where fifteen would have been adequate for the present and foreseeable future needs of the business community. The resulting empty space provides no return to the owner. The market value of the property, as well as the surrounding land, is correspondingly lessened. Also called a MISPLACED IMPROVEMENT; the opposite of UNDER-IMPROVEMENT.

OVERRIDE—A percentage of the commission an office manager receives from sales made by the salesmen in his charge.

OVERT—Open; in view; evident; public.

OVERZONED—1. An excessive amount of land zoned for a specific use. 2. Zoning too restrictive for land to be put to its HIGHEST AND BEST USE.

OWE—To be indebted; to be obligated to pay or render service to another.

OWNER—The one possessing dominion or title to property. A person having a lawful interest in the land; the holder of the fee.

OWNER'S AFFIDAVIT OF NO LIENS—An affidavit stating that any work that was being done to the subject property has been completed, that the owners are in undisputed possession and that there are now no liens or chattel mortgages encumbering it.

OWNER'S ESTOPPEL CERTIFICATE—(See ESTOPPEL CERTIFICATE.)

OWNER'S, LANDLORD'S AND TENANT'S PUBLIC LIABILITY INSURANCE—A specialized policy covering liability for accidents or death occurring on an owner's or tenant's property. This type of policy covers judgments against the insured and may also include damages done to the premises. It is often referred to in abbreviation as "O. L. & T."

P

PACKAGE DEAL—A builder's term meaning a complete construction job from architecture, to financing, to the final structure. A package deal differs from a TURN-KEY JOB in that financing is included in the former. A turn-key job involves just the construction and sometimes the design.

PACKAGE MORTGAGE—A type of mortgage used in home financing that covers both the realty and certain appliance and equipment items such as air conditioner, kitchen range, laundry machine, garbage disposal unit, refrigerator, dryer, etc.

PAPER—A jargon reference to the taking of a note or mortgage in lieu of cash. When there is limited money being put down in a real estate transaction, the seller may agree to take the balance in "paper."

PAPER PROFIT—An anticipated profit. A proposed or prospective profit. The estimated return on an investment after anticipated income and expenses are calculated.

PAPER STREET—A plotted street that is not yet in existence. A planned street that is currently only on paper; one that a developer or the government intends to construct.

PAPER TITLE—Legal documents that appear to give evidence of title ownership, but in fact may not convey proper title.

PAR—Average; face value; equal. The accepted standard of comparison. The common level. Such matters as mortgage interest rates, closing costs, price paid, etc. are referred to as being at par, below par or above par, as the case may be.

PARALLELS—(See STANDARD PARALLELS.)

PARAMOUNT TITLE—Title that is superior to all others, such as being the original title from which another evolved; foremost title.

PARAPET—A low, exterior, protective wall along a roof, terrace, balcony or similar structure.

PARCEL—A specified part of a larger tract of land: a lot. A description of property setting forth the boundaries.

PARITY CLAUSE IN MORTGAGE—A clause in a mortgage providing equal

167

priority for all notes secured by the mortgage. No note is senior to or takes precedence over another; they are said to have "equal dignity." This clause takes on added significance due to the variance in state laws concerning lien priorities.

PARK—1. An area of grass, shrubs and woodland partially kept in its natural state for public recreation and enjoyment. 2. Land set aside for special usage, such as an industrial park or mobile home park.

PARKING LOT—A parcel of land used for parking cars.

PARKING RATIO—The ratio of required parking spaces to the number of units or square footage area in an office, apartment house or other building.

PARKWAY—A broad, attractively landscaped highway with off-roadway parking and planted median strips.

PAROL—Oral; verbal. A parol agreement is one not in writing.

PAROL GIFT—The transfer of property when no consideration is given. The grantor must describe the property given and the grantee, upon receiving and making improvements to it (which is treated as the consideration), becomes the true title holder.

PARTIAL EVICTION—Eviction that deprives one of a portion of his rights. As an example, partial eviction occurs when one area of leased premises becomes uninhabitable through no fault of the tenant, or because of the landlord's negligence. If this occurs, the tenant need not vacate the habitable portion.

PARTIAL RELEASE CLAUSE—A clause found in some mortgages and deeds providing for the release of a portion of the property when certain prescribed stipulations are met.

PARTIBLE LAND—Land that is readily divisible. Property that lends itself to being divided.

PARTICIPATE—To partake; share in; to be an active part of.

PARTICIPATION CERTIFICATE—(See LAND TRUST CERTIFICATE.)

PARTICULAR LIEN—A lien that gives the holder the right to retain property for claims growing out of the specific property. Liens that emanate for labor, material or money expended are examples. The lien may arise by an express contract or by implication. Also called a SPECIAL LIEN.

PARTICULARS—Details. The listing of the facts concerning specific property.

PARTIES—Those taking part in a transaction. The principals; participants. In contracts and other instruments, the "party of the first part" refers to the seller or lessor; the "party of the second part" to the buyer or lessee.

PARTITION—1. The division of jointly owned real estate among principals in proportion to their interests. Partitioned property may be held in joint tenancy or tenancy in common. Partitioning of real estate is generally determined by judicial decree. 2. An interior wall separating rooms or areas of a building.

PARTITION DEED—The instrument used when joint tenants, co-owners or tenants-in-common divide land so that each can individually own specified portions.

PARTNER—The co-owner of a company; an associate; a colleague. One who is part owner in a business or profession. A partnership can be formed by oral or written agreement. (See LIMITED PARTNER; OSTENSIBLE PARTNERS; SILENT PARTNER; SPECIAL PARTNER. For a sample partnership agreement form, see Exhibit P-1.)

PART PERFORMANCE—Completing only a portion of an agreement, such as a contract, and leaving something still to be done.

PARTY DRIVEWAY—A driveway built on both sides of a property line and used as a common drive by each owner.

PARTY WALL—A wall built between two adjoining parcels. One built on the property line as a common part of two structures separately owned. Each owner has an equal interest in it, which may not be disturbed without joint consent.

PASSING TITLE—The change in ownership of real property. The actual handing over of title to the new owner. A closing.

PATENT—1. On the surface; visible; open to view; evident; not hidden. The opposite of LATENT. 2. An instrument, showing proof of title to government land, given to private interests and to be used for public benefit.

PATIO—A paved area adjoining a home for outdoor living. Also, an inner courtyard open to the elements.

PAVILION—1. A projecting wing of a building. A partially connected portion of a building. 2. A small structure found in public parks or gardens for shelter.

PAYEE—The person who is to receive or has received a payment.

PAYER—The person who is to make or has made a payment. It is also spelled Payor.

PAYMENT—Compensation; recompense; the act of paying; remuneration.

PEDIMENT—The triangular surface formed by a pitched roof and found over doors, windows and porticos.

Pediment ⟶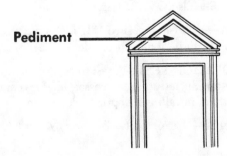

PENALTY—A loss sustained for not fulfilling an agreement. The punishment imposed for not complying with the terms of an agreement, after having made a commitment to do so.

PENDENS—(Latin) Pending. *LIS PENDENS* is a notice of a pending legal action.

PENINSULA—A projection of land having three sides exposed to water. A land formation nearly surrounded by water but connected to the mainland.

PENNSYLVANIA GROUND RENT—A variation of the usual form of ground rent in that the grantor conveys the land in fee simple, but reserves in the deed periodic rental payments to himself and his heirs. Subsequent owners must continue to make payments but, with the exception of the first grantee, are not liable for them in the event of a default. Unless otherwise provided for in later deeds, only the first grantee or his heirs remain responsible for the payments. If a default occurs, the land and all the improvements upon it revert to the original owner or his heirs. Pennsylvania laws require that ground rents be recapturable; that is, the agreement must provide for the grantee to be able to buy the land outright, at a specified price and within a stipulated period of time. (See GROUND RENT; MARYLAND GROUND RENT.)

PENSION FUNDS—Trust funds belonging to company or union pension programs. They are frequently invested in large mortgages and other forms of real estate.

PENTHOUSE—1. An apartment built on a portion of the roof of a building. Typically, such units are larger and more luxurious than most apartments. 2. A shed or other small building joined to a larger structure.

PEPPER AND SALT AREA—A jargon term meaning a mixed racial neighborhood. Any area populated by black and white people.

PER—(Latin) By; by means of. Words such as per annum, per capita, percent, per diem are familiar in real estate terminology.

PER ANNUM—(Latin) Yearly. By the year.

PERCENT—One part of one hundred (1/100).

PERCENTAGE LEASE—A lease in which the rental is based upon a percentage of the volume of sales. With the advent of discount houses, large chain stores and modern shopping centers, this has become an increasingly popular method of leasing. (See also OVERAGE.)

PERCH—A unit of measure 16½ feet long; a rod. The word is infrequently used today, but can be found in old deeds, surveys, contracts and other documents.

PERCOLATION TEST—A test to determine how well the ground will absorb and drain water. Such tests are necessary, before construction begins, to determine the suitability of installing a septic tank system.

PER DIEM—(Latin) Daily. By the day. An allowance per day.

PERFECT INSTRUMENT—Any recorded instrument. It is said to be "perfect" upon recording because it then becomes good for all the world to see.

PERFECT TITLE—Title without defects. Good and marketable title; flawless title; clear title. Property showing absolute right of ownership.

PERFORMANCE—The completion of an agreement or contract. Fulfilling of a required function or obligation. Performance means accomplishing a purpose.

PERFORMANCE BOND—A bond posted to guarantee that the builder will satisfactorily complete a construction contract and that it will be free of liens. It is also referred to as a COMPLETION BOND.

PERIMETER—The boundary limits of land or of a building.

PERIODIC TENANCY—A tenancy that exists without a written lease and is generally on a month to month basis. A tenancy at will. (See MONTH-TO-MONTH TENANCY.)

PERIPHERY—The perimeter or external boundary lines of land, buildings or other objects; the outer limits.

PERMANENT FINANCING—A long-term loan in the form of a mortgage. The opposite of short-term financing as used in a building loan. It is an amortized mortgage usually extending over 15, 20 or more years with a fixed interest rate.

PERMIT—1. Written permissoin endorsed by someone having authority to grant such permission. A license. 2. Allow; let; to give authorization.

PERPETUAL—Never-ending; continual; forever valid. Perpetual leases, for example, are generally for 99 years and renewal forever.

PERPETUITY—Endless; the quality of being perpetual.

PERSONAL LIABILITY—The personal responsibility to repay a debt, when the instrument of indebtedness is individually signed. This differs from one signed by a corporate officer, where the corporation can shield any personal obligation of the signer.

PERSONAL OBLIGATION BOND—(See OBLIGATION BOND.)

PERSONAL PROPERTY—All property other than real estate; personalty; chattels. Personal property refers to material of a movable nature and not permanently affixed to land or the buildings upon it.

PERSONALTY—A contraction of "personal property."

PEST CONTROL CLAUSE—A clause in a contract requiring the seller to eliminate any insect infestation, should such a condition be found to exist. (See TERMITE CLAUSE, for typical wording of such a provision.)

PETITION—A written request to an authority; a formal document asking that something be done or refrain from being done.

PHONE FATE—(See FATE.)

PHYSICAL DEPRECIATION—The decline in property value due to the action of time and the elements, as well as through usage; deterioration.

PHYSICAL LIFE—The lifespan of a building, from when it was built until the time it becomes structurally unsound.

PICK—A narrow strip of land.

PICTURE WINDOW—A large, fixed-pane window, usually made of plate glass, that affords a panoramic view of the outdoors. As a rule, on either side of the picture window are smaller windows that allow for ventilation and additional light.

PIECE OF THE ACTION—1. A slang expression meaning participating as part owner in a real estate venture. 2. In reference to a lender, if the terms of the mortgage include receiving a percentage of the profits, the mortgagee is said to have a KICKER, an equity position, or a piece of the action.

PIERCE THE CORPORATE VEIL—A corporation offers certain protective advantages, particularly the personal liability of acts done in the name of the corporation. Officers of a corporation have a "veil" of protection, as the corporation is looked upon as a separate entity, an "artificial person." In law, however, this anonymity does not always stand up and the protective veil can sometimes be lifted; when this occurs, the corporate veil is said to be "pierced."

PIGGY BACK FINANCING—A participation loan between two separate lenders for the same property. This technique most frequently occurs when a private lender is assigned a portion of a loan made by an institutional lender. If bank regulations prohibit making a loan over a certain percentage of the value, piggy back financing can act to overcome the barrier. Also, a lender might not want to participate so heavily in one venture. It is a means of spreading mortgage investments over a wider range.

PILASTER—A vertical column, attached to and part of a wall, a portion of which projects beyond the surface.

P.I.T.I.—Abbreviation for PRINCIPAL, INTEREST, TAXES and INSURANCE. It is frequently used when the terms of a mortgage payment are stated.

PLACE LANDS—Property, granted to railroads, comprising the land on each side of the tracks.

PLACE OF CONTRACT—The location where a contract was made. The laws of that jurisdiction may determine questions concerning the execution, validity and construction of the contract.

PLAINTIFF—A party bringing legal action against another. The one who sues; the complainant.

PLAN—1. An architectural drawing or diagram showing the proposed sections, elevations, dimensions, materials, etc. of a building. 2. A plot plan; a detailed map of an area, usually drawn to scale.

PLANNED UNIT DEVELOPMENT (PUD)—An overall land use concept that provides for residential, business and industrial projects, as well as park and recreation areas, school sites and public buildings. Though the housing units are frequently clustered and individual lots are of modest size, when properly engineered the overall density is generally less concentrated than most communities because of the required public areas. Strategically located shopping centers and outlying sections set aside for industry greatly reduce the possibility of haphazard, wasteful developnent. Many PUD projects provide for joint public area ownership or for public facilities to be deeded to the local government after being developed.

PLANNING COMMISSION—A government agency or committee responsible for planning an area's future development.

PLAT—A map or survey showing how a parcel of land has been subdivided into blocks and lots. A "plot plan."

PLAT BOOK—A public book of maps of the community showing the various subdivisions, the names of the owners of record and the present and future division of land into blocks, lots and parcels.

PLATTED LAND—Territory that has been surveyed and charted into lots, blocks and subdivisions, or otherwise legally described.

PLAZA—A public square; a market or meeting place usually in the center of town.

PLEDGE—1. Anything of value put up as security for a debt. 2. A promise; a solemn agreement to do or refrain from doing something.

PLOT—1. A small parcel of land; a lot. 2. A ground plan, map or plat. A diagram, scheme or chart, as of a building or of land.

PLOTTAGE—The assemblage of several plots of ground into a single unit.

PLOTTAGE INCREMENT—The overall increase in land value established by owners joining their properties together. The larger property thus formed is frequently more valuable than the sum of the parcels held separately.

PLOTTING COMMISSION—(See PLANNING COMMISSION.)

PLOW LAND—Tillable land; farmland especially suited for cultivation. Agricultural property.

P.M.M.—Abbreviation for PURCHASE MONEY MORTGAGE. (See that term.)

POCKET LISTING—An open listing that a real estate salesman "pockets" or keeps hidden from his associates. This is considered unethical in most offices, as listings within an office are generally made available to all.

POINT—1. A "point" represents 1 percent of the principal amount. The term is most frequently used when referring to mortgage premiums. It is a method used by lenders to obtain additional revenue over the interest rate. 2. As used in legal descriptions, it is the extreme end of a boundary line.

POLE STRUCTURE—A building method utilizing round columns or timbers as structural roof supports. Farm outbuildings and sheds are sometimes built in this manner.

POLICE POWER—The control that a government has over the life and property of its citizens. The exercising of police power should be in the best interest of the general public, and not in conflict with the Fourteenth Amendment to the United States Constitution, which protects the civil rights and freedom of the individual.

POLL DEED—A deed executed by, and the responsibility of, one party. It is also referred to in reverse order (Deed Poll).

PORTICO—A roofed area having columns and open at the sides, often found at the entrance to buildings. A front porch.

Portico

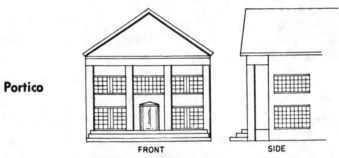

FRONT   SIDE

POSSESSION—The act or state of possessing; the holding and peaceful enjoyment of property. Ownership or physical control of property. In the case of a tenant, he is in physical or actual possession, but does not own the property. The owner has constructive possession by right of title. (See ACTUAL POSSESSION; ADVERSE POSSESSION; CONSTRUCTIVE POSSESSION; RIGHT OF POSSESSION.)

POSSESSION IS NINE-TENTHS OF THE LAW—An old adage that is not necessarily true according to law, though one in possession may have a substantial claim to it.

POSSESSORY ACTION—A legal action brought to regain possession of one's real estate. Lawsuits of this nature frequently occur when an owner seeks to obtain physical possession of his land and property by evicting a tenant.

POSSESSORY INTEREST—The rights and interest one has in possessing property: the use, benefits and enjoyment of it. (See QUIET ENJOYMENT.)

POST DATE—Placing a date on a document later than when it was prepared.

POUND OF LAND—An early English term meaning land containing approximately 52 acres. It is rarely used today.

POWER—The ability to act forcefully. In real estate law it is the authority to create, revoke, dispose of, or otherwise do something with or to property. (See RIGHT(S).)

POWER OF APPOINTMENT—A power given to one individual by another to dispose of property or of an interest held in it. This authority is confirmed by a deed or will and authorizes the appointee (called the donee) to act as a conduit through which title is passed. The power created does not constitute an estate or interest, and is legally referred to as "naked" power. However, the donee can himself be granted an interest in the subject property. If this occurs, he is said to have a "power coupled with an interest."

POWER OF ATTORNEY—A written authority for one to act as another's agent. The extent of the authority is limited to that stated in the instrument. A power of attorney is also known as an attorney-in-fact.

POWER OF SALE—1. An authority given by an owner for another to sell his property. The legal power to produce a change in ownership. 2. A statement written into a mortgage authorizing the mortgagee to sell the mortgaged property in the event of a default. The proceeds of such a sale would be used to satisfy the creditors. Any funds remaining would be given to the mortgagor who would then become completely divested of the property with no recourse to redeem it. (See also SHORT CUT FORECLOSURE.)

POWER OF SALE CLAUSE—The name given to the clause in a will, deed, trust or other document that authorizes the properly designated party to sell or transfer an interest in real estate. That authority is sometimes referred to as a POWER OF APPOINTMENT.

PRACTITIONER—A person engaged in an art, profession or occupation. One who actively practices a field of endeavor, as a lawyer, doctor, banker, real estate broker, accountant, artist, architect, etc.

PRECAST CONCRETE—Concrete segments that have been formed to size and shape prior to being delivered to a construction project.

PRECEDING ESTATE—An estate that came before an existing one. A prior estate.

PRE-CLOSING PREPARATIONS—The preparations that must be made before real estate can change ownership. Reading title reports, drawing of all necessary legal documents, calculating the closing statements and obtaining estoppel certificates are some of the matters that have to be completed prior to holding a closing.

PRECONTRACT—1. A contract previously entered into that would estop the entering into of another, similar agreement. A pre-existing agreement. 2. To establish by an agreement in advance.

PRECUT—Lumber and other materials that are cut to usable sizes before being delivered to the building site.

PRE-EMPT—1. To seize property before others can acquire it; take for oneself. Appropriate. 2. To settle on public lands.

PRE-ENGINEERED BUILDING—A factory-made, standard design building, such as the open-span, steel fabricated structure familiar to most industrial areas.

PREFABRICATE—To construct parts of a building prior to the time of installation. Portions of a building that are factory built and bolted into place or otherwise assembled at the building site; fabricated prior to being installed. Trusses, floor and wall panels and precast concrete slabs are some of the commonly used prefabricated materials. (See COMPONENT BUILDING.)

PREFERENCE AND PRIORITY CLAUSE IN MORTGAGE—(See PARITY CLAUSE IN MORTGAGE.)

PREFERRED DEBT—A debt that takes precedence over others; one that must be paid in full ahead of any other, such as a first mortgage.

PREFERRED STOCK—A classification of corporate stock that is subject to certain preferential treatment. Priority as to dividend distribution at a fixed rate is one of the main benefits. If a company's earnings are limited, the preferred stockholders receive dividends first. Only if there are additional profits still to be divided do the common stockholders benefit. In addition, preferred stockholders are in a superior position in the event of liquidation, missed dividends and voting rights.

PRELIMINARY SALES AGREEMENT—1. An agreement made before a more formal and detailed sales contract is drawn; a binder. A memorandum of agreement; a letter of intent. 2. An offer to buy; a unilateral contract.

PREMISES—1. That portion of a deed that appears before the *HABENDUM* clause and recites the names of the parties, the consideration given and the description of the property. 2. A parcel of land and the improvements upon it. A business or residential location; a place.

PREPAID INTEREST—Interest on a mortgage that is paid in advance for the tax advantage it provides. A tax-saving device used when investment real estate is sold. However, the Treasury Department substantially limits when and how it can be applied. By allocating a portion of the down payment as interest on the mortgage, to cover a period that does not extend beyond the following year, it may be considered a tax deductible expense. This is a controversial point of tax sheltering. A top-heavy prepaid interest down payment may be declared illegal. Both buyer and seller should consult competent tax advisors before entering into a transaction based on an advance interest payment being a part of the cash to close. (See also SOFT DOLLARS.)

PREPAYMENT CLAUSE—A clause in a mortgage permitting the mortgagor to pay all or part of the unpaid balance before it becomes due, thereby saving the interest or clearing the way for a new mortgage. A typical prepayment clause reads as follows: "The purchaser shall have the privilege at any time of paying any sum or sums in addition to the payments herein required upon the consideration, and it is understood and agreed that no such prepayment, except payment in full, shall stop the accrual of interest on the amount so paid until the next succeeding semiannual computation of interest after such payment is made as herein provided." A short form of this clause reads: "This mortgage may be prepaid in full or part at any time without penalty."

PREPAYMENT PENALTY—A penalty imposed upon a mortgagor for paying the mortgage before it becomes due, when there is no PREPAYMENT CLAUSE.

PREPAYMENT PRIVILEGE—(See PREPAYMENT CLAUSE.)

PRESCRIPTION—The term refers to the period of time required for one to open and continuously possess INCORPOREAL HEREDITAMENTS (intangible property that can be inherited, such as right of way easements, water rights, mortgages, options, etc.) before obtaining title. Ownership by prescription is evidenced by exclusive and continuous usage for 5 to 20 years, the fixed periods varying with different state statutes. While ADVERSE POSSESSION refers to acquiring title to land, prescription applies to any rights that can be inherited. (See ADVERSE POSSESSION.)

PRESUMPTIVE TITLE—Open occupation or possession of land which may lead others to presume ownership, where in fact ownership may not exist.

PREVENTIVE MAINTENANCE—Repairing and maintaining property before it shows signs of neglect or deterioration, in order to prevent major breakdowns or damage to the asset.

PRICE—The amount paid in legal tender, goods or services; the consideration; purchase price. The terms for which a thing is done. (See MARKET VALUE.)

PRIMA FACIE—(Latin) On the face of it; an obvious fact; on the surface. Evidence at first hand; presumably.

PRIMARY BONDSMAN—The mortgagor of real property.

PRIMARY MEMBERS—A builder's reference to load-bearing walls and large beams or columns that serve a major support function in a building.

PRIME LOCATION—A choice property site; one ideally suited for a specific purpose. (See HUNDRED PERCENT LOCATION.)

PRIME MERIDIAN—In GOVERNMENT SURVEY legal descriptions, the prime meridian is the main imaginary line, running north and south, from which other meridians (each 24 miles apart) are surveyed. Also called Principal Meridian. (See MERIDIAN LINES, GOVERNMENT SURVEY.)

PRIME RATE—A term referring to the interest rate reserved by banks for prime or preferred borrowers. Only the highest credit rated, public corporations are in this category. The ever-fluctuating, prime interest rate is generally established by the leading New York banks. The prime rate tends to set all other interest charges, and acts as a guideline for banking institutions throughout the nation.

PRINCIPAL—1. One of the main parties in a real estate transaction; the purchaser or the seller. 2. In the law of agency, the one giving the authority to another to act for him. The employer of a real estate broker; the broker's client; the one responsible for paying his commission. 3. The basic amount of money as distinguished from interest. The capital sum; the amount upon which interest is paid.

PRINCIPAL MERIDIAN—(See PRIME MERIDIAN.)

PRINCIPAL NOTE—A note that is secured by a mortgage.

PRINCIPLE—A fundamental truth. An accepted guide of conduct. A natural, basic law. Principles are a code of behavior that denotes the highest ideals. In the real estate profession the National Association of Realtors has adopted a comprehensive Code of Ethics. (See CODE OF ETHICS for a complete reproduction of the NAR Code.)

PRIOR LIEN—A lien that is senior to others; a first lien, though it may not necessarily have come first in time.

PRIORITY OF LIEN—The order in which a lien will be honored in relation to others.

PRIVACY—(See RIGHT OF PRIVACY.)

PRIVATE DWELLING—A single-family house.

PRIVATE LENDERS—A term used to distinguish individuals who lend money from institutional lenders (banks and insurance companies).

PRIVATE PLAT—An unrecorded map or survey of privately held land.

PRIVATE PROPERTY—All land not held by a government. Individually owned property.

PRIVITY—A mutual relationship of people having the same legal interest in a right or in property.

PRO—(Latin) 1. Acting as; in support of; for; in respect of. Favoring. In real estate it is used in forming compound words (either with or without a hyphen) such as *Pro Facto, Pro Forma; Pro Indiviso, Prorate; Pro Tempore*, etc. 2. Short for professional. An expert in a specific field of endeavor.

PROBATE—The act of verifying the authenticity of a will in a proper court of law, and the legal process of distributing its assets.

PROBATE COURT—A court dealing with wills, estate settlements, intestate succession and guardianships. It is also referred to as a Surrogate Court or County Judges Court.

PROCEDURE—An established method of doing something. A traditional, known way.

PROCURING CAUSE—In a real estate transaction, it is the broker or his salesman who produces a READY, WILLING AND ABLE buyer for the agreed upon price and terms who is the procuring cause of the transaction. He is the one entitled to receive the commission.

PRODUCING CAUSE—(See PROCURING CAUSE.)

PRO FACTO—(Latin) Considered as a fact. For or held as a fact.

PROFESSION—A practice or occupation often obtained only after years of academic preparation; one that, requires mental skills and knowledge, rather than manual ability.

PROFESSIONAL ORGANIZATIONS—(See ORGANIZATIONS.)

PROFILE—A side view; a sectional elevation of a building or other structure; a vertical section.

PROFIT—Earning; the sum of a business or other venture remaining after the expenses incurred have been paid. Net income; the tangible gains that are realized.

PROFIT AND LOSS STATEMENT—An itemized statement of the income and expenses of a business and the exact amount of profit or loss sustained.

PRO FORMA—(Latin) According to a prescribed form; as a matter of form.

PROGRESS PAYMENTS—Periodic payments made to a contractor as a building project advances. A builder usually receives partial payments of his building loan as each stage of construction is completed. (See BUILDING LOANS.)

PRO INDIVISO—(Latin) In common. Undivided interest. The joint occupancy of land, for example. Each party has an interest in the total parcel, but not of a specific portion. The parties have a joint interest in the undivided whole.

PROJECT FINANCING—In development housing projects, overall financing is often accomplished by the use of blanket mortgages. Release clauses are provided for in the mortgage and put into effect upon payment of a *pro rata* share by the developer. As each home in a section is completed, it can immediately be sold off. The purchaser of the home receives a new, permanent mortgage. In this manner a project helps finance itself as it progresses toward completion. (See BUILDING LOANS.)

PROJECTED INCOME—An estimate of the future income that can be expected from a business or property; the amount of income that an investor can logically anticipate.

PROMISSORY NOTE—A written evidence of indebtedness wherein the maker promises to pay a specified sum on demand to the party named or at a stated time in the future.

PROMONTORY—A peak or ridge that projects from a body of water. Headland. A bluff overlooking lower land.

PROMOTER—One who conceives, develops and advances a business or real estate project and is the motivating force behind its success or failure; an entrepreneur.

PROMULGATE—To make known. To disseminate. To spread widely. Publish, as printing and distributing points of law.

PROOF—Evidence required to substantiate a fact or establish the validity of something. In real estate proof is continually sought in the form of witnesses to DOCUMENTS, NOTARIZATIONS, AFFIRMATIONS, ACKNOWLEDG-MENTS and AFFIDAVITS.

PROPERTY—That which is legally owned by an individual or group and which may be kept and enjoyed or disposed of as the owner sees fit. The unrestricted rights to something owned which are guaranteed and protected by the government. Property is divided into two classes, real and personal. Real property is land and that which is permanently affixed to it such as buildings, fences, trees—anything immovable. Personal property is everything that is owned except real estate: chattels of a movable nature, such as goods, furniture, money, vehicles, livestock, etc.

PROPERTY BRIEF—An INFORMATION SHEET giving the salient points of a property being offered for sale.

PROPERTY DESCRIPTIONS—(See LEGAL DESCRIPTIONS.)

PROPERTY LINE—The boundary or border line of a parcel of land. The line described in a legal description of the land.

PROPERTY MANAGEMENT—The branch of real estate composed of renting, supervising, collecting, paying and the overall maintaining and managing of real estate for others. (See MANAGEMENT AGREEMENT or CONTRACT, page 356.)

PROPERTY MORTGAGE—(See MORTGAGE.)

PROPERTY TAX—A tax levied on real and personal property; *AD VALOREM* tax.

PROPOSAL—An offer presented for consideration. A prospectus; an offering; something proposed.

PROPOSITION OR PURCHASE AGREEMENT—1. In Indiana it is the name given the instrument used to submit an offer. It is similar to a BINDER, DEPOSIT RECEIPT or an OFFER TO PURCHASE. Upon acceptance by the seller, it becomes a valid contract. 2. A proposal; prospectus. (See PROPOSAL.)

PROPRIETARY INTEREST—Ownership interest. Of or pertaining to an owner's interest. The right and title that is exclusively held by a corporation or private party.

PROPRIETARY LEASE—A lease made between a tenant-owner and the operating corporation in a cooperative apartment building.

PROPRIETOR—The owner of property; the one who has lawful title to it.

PRO RATA—(Latin) In proportion. (See PRORATE.)

PRORATE—Proportion according to one's interest. In real estate contracts, for example, taxes, insurance, rents, interest and certain other annual expenses of the property are generally prorated at the time of closing or when the sale is recorded. A proportionate amount of these fixed expenses is charged to the seller and buyer.

PROSPECT—A possible buyer. A customer. A person who is shown real estate by an agent who hopes to have him purchase it.

PROSPECT CARDS—(See CUSTOMER RECORD CARDS.)

PROSPECTUS—A printed statement of a company or property describing its activities, financial condition, future plans and general outlook. An offering to investors; a written proposal.

PROTECTION OF TITLE—Safety measures that can be followed to assure that one is getting good title, such as having the CHAIN OF TITLE carefully examined by a competent attorney or title company before a closing, promptly recording the transaction in the proper public records and buying a TITLE INSURANCE policy.

PROTECTIVE COVENANTS—(See RESTRICTIVE COVENANTS; DEED RESTRICTIONS.)

PROVISIONAL—Temporarily provided for, but subject to change.

PROXY—1. A person designated to temporarily act in behalf of another; a written grant of authority for one person to vote the extent of another's stock interest on a pending corporation matter; a substitute. 2. The instrument giving another the limited power to act for him; a POWER OF ATTORNEY.

PUBLIC—1. People taken as a whole. The inhabitants of a state or area; the general public; the populace. 2. Activity having to do with the community in general rather than a private transaction or occurrence. Governmental.

PUBLIC ACCOUNTANT—One trained in the practice of accounting; a skilled auditor. A person whose profession it is to keep the books, records and accounts of a company and to advise their clients in business, tax and other specialized financial matters. Accountants who pass specified educational and state qualifications are licensed to use the title CERTIFIED PUBLIC ACCOUNTANT.

PUBLIC BUILDING—Any building open to the public including federal, state and local government buildings, as well as privately owned structures.

PUBLIC DOMAIN LAND—Land owned by the government. (See PUBLIC PROPERTY.)

PUD—Abbreviation for PLANNED UNIT DEVELOPMENT. (See that term.)

PURCHASE OFFER—An offer to buy; a unilateral contract signed by the buyer.

PURCHASE PRICE—The price paid; the amount for which the property sold. The total of money and mortgages given to obtain the property.

PURCHASER—The buyer. The one who acquires title to property other than by gift, decent or inheritance. The vendee.

PURE PROFIT—(See NET PROFIT.)

PURLIN—A horizontal, supporting beam of a roof frame, placed under rafters, that is parallel to the ridge line.

PYRAMID ROOF—A roof that forms a pyramid with four triangular sides coming to a point. Churches and public buildings, as well as some institutions, sometimes utilize this steeple-style construction. (See ROOF illustrations.)

PYRAMID ZONING—A zoning regulation allowing all the uses permitted in more restrictive zoning to be automatically applicable in the less restricted ones.

Q

QUADRANGLE—A rectangular area bordered on all sides by buildings.

QUALIFIED—Eligible; fit; entitled to be chosen; meeting the requirements. Legally competent or capable.

QUALIFIED FEE—(See FEE DETERMINABLE.)

QUALITY OF ESTATE—The manner in which an estate is to be owned as to type of possession (sole, jointly, tenancy-in-common, etc.) and time (present or future). The term does not allude to value or physical characteristics of the estate.

QUANTITY SURVEY—1. In building, it is an estimate of all materials and labor that would be required to complete construction of a building or other project. Estimators take such a survey when arriving at the amount of the bid price. 2. In appraising, it is an estimate of the replacement cost of a building by figuring the amount of labor and materials that have gone into it and determining what it would currently cost to construct.

QUARRY—An open land area used for the excavation of granite, limestone, marble or other stones.

QUARTER SECTION—A quarter section of land; 160 acres; 2640 feet by 2640 feet.

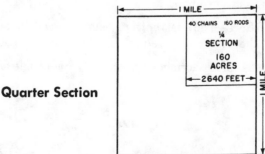

Quarter Section

QUARTERLY—Four times a year as in quarterly payment, quarterly dividend, quarterly report, etc. Consisting of four parts.

183

QUASH—Suppress; to annul; legally put an end to; to make void; stop; vacate; quell; lawfully overthrow.

QUASI—(Latin) As if. Having a limited legal status. Sufficiently similar but not actual; in some degree; almost. A combination form, familiar to the real estate field, with such words as quasi-contract; quasi-possession; quasi-corporation; quasi-official; quasi-judicial, etc.

QUEEN POSTS—Vertical beams extending from the base beam of a roof's framework to the roof line of either side of the peak. (See also KING POST.)

Queen Posts

QUICK ASSETS—Assets that can be readily turned into cash. Also called LIQUID ASSETS or current assets.

QUID PRO QUO—(Latin) Something of value given for something else of value. The valuable consideration that passes between parties to make a contract valid.

QUIET ENJOYMENT—The right an owner or tenant has to enjoy property in peace and without disturbance. When referring to ownership, quiet enjoyment means freedom from being disturbed by title defects. Applied to a tenant, it takes on the added meaning of his right of privacy and his not being unnecessarily disturbed.

QUIET TITLE SUIT—A suit to remove a defect, cloud or any questionable or conflicting claims against the title to property.

QUIT-CLAIM—Relinquish claim; release any hold or interest.

QUIT-CLAIM DEED—The instrument used to remove any and all claims or interest in ownership that an individual may have without his warranting the quality or validity of the title. In some sections of the country quit-claim deeds are used when there is a questionable interest in the property or to remove a cloud upon the title. In other areas it is more commonly used in ordinary transactions to transfer title without warranting it.

QUIT RENT—The final rental payment a tenant makes before leaving the property; no others are due or required.

QUOINS—Blocks forming the external corner angle of a building's outer wall. The cornerstones.

Quoins

QUONSET HUT—A prefabricated building having a semi-rounded metal roof that curves to the ground forming the structure's sides.

R

RACE RESTRICTION—A restrictive covenant running with the land preventing a racial group owning or occupying property in a given area. Race restrictive covenants have been declared unconstitutional by the United States Supreme Court. (See DISCRIMINATORY COVENANTS.)

RACK RENT—1. Rent charged that is beyond justification. The raising of rent far above its value. Oppressively high rent. 2. Rent that is past due.

RADIUS—The straight line distance from the center of a circle to any point on the circumference.

RAFTERS—Sloping parallel beams used as roof supports. (See HOUSE CROSS SECTION, page 412.)

RANCH—A large farm, typically containing many acres of grazing land, for raising livestock.

RANCH HOUSE—A one-story rambling-style home, usually having a low-pitched roof line.

Ranch

RANCHO—A small ranch.

RANGE—1. In the GOVERNMENT SURVEY method of describing property, it is one of the north-south divisions of land of townships that are six miles apart. Range lines are designated as being so many "ranges" east and west of the Principal Meridian. The first on either side is "range one east" and "range one west." The second on either side is "range two east" and "range two west," and so on. (See GOVERNMENT SURVEY illustrations.) 2. An open land area used for cattle grazing. Rangeland. 3. A series of mountains.

RATABLE—Able to be rated or estimated.

RATABLE PROPERTY—Real estate capable of being appraised or assessed. Taxable property that can be rated as to its true value. Property that can be readily compared to others and thereby evaluated.

RATE—1. A standardized charge, as in interest rate, commission rate, insurance rate, tax rate, etc. A fixed ratio. 2. Appraise; estimate, as when one assigns an evaluation or grade to an asset.

RATIFICATION—Confirmation; affirmation. Making something binding by formally approving it. Validation.

RATIO—Proportion; rate. The fixed relation of one thing to another.

RAVINE—A small valley having steep sides.

RAW LAND—Unimproved land; vacant land; land in or near its natural state. Virgin territory. (The term is relative, however, as for instance, cultivated farm land is considered raw land to the subdivider, but is improved land to the farmer.)

RE:—(Latin) Regarding. In the matter of.

READY—(See READY, WILLING AND ABLE.)

READY AND WILLING—(See READY, WILLING AND ABLE.)

READY, WILLING AND ABLE—The phrase means that a buyer is completely agreeable and fully qualified to enter into and consummate a transaction. "Ready" means that he is prepared at this time to enter into a contract. "Willing" refers to a person's own free choice and that he is of a mind to buy. "Able" has to do with his ability to meet the financial requirements of the agreement.

REAL—A general term of or relating to the land and what is permanently attached to it such as buildings, fences, landscaping, trees, etc.

REAL ESTATE—The land itself and everything below, growing upon or attached to it. The physical substance of real property. Houses, trees and shrubs, fences, and what is permanently affixed to the land are classified as real estate. Anything else is personal property.

REAL ESTATE AGENT—(See AGENT.)

REAL ESTATE BOARDS—Local, state and national associations of real estate brokers. Private real estate organizations formed to improve the real estate profession, to aid those in it, to better serve the public, and to promote cooperation and ethical practices among real estate agents. (See ORGANIZATIONS, REALTOR.)

REAL ESTATE BROKER—(See BROKER.)

REAL ESTATE DEALER—(See DEALER.)

REAL ESTATE INVESTMENT TRUST (REIT)—A group of real estate investors consisting of one or more trustees who hold title to the assets for the trust and control its acquisitions, management and sale. Though unincorporated, the trust must be owned in the form of shares by one hundred or more people (no five of whom are to possess over 50 percent interest). The major advantage of a business structure of this nature is the tax benefits, as no corporation tax need be paid. A disadvantage is the strict federal and state regulatory requirements as to the type of investments that can be made. When a real estate investment trust has shareholders in more than one state it is also subject to Security and Exchange Commission regulations.

REAL ESTATE MARKET—The buying and selling of real property that creates supply and demand resulting in the setting of market values and prices.

REAL ESTATE SALESMAN—(See SALESMAN.)

REAL ESTATE SETTLEMENT PROCEDURES ACT (RESPA)—A federal law first enacted in 1974 to protect the home buyer from paying excessive or unearned fees for closing real estate transactions. An outgrowth of the Department of Housing and Urban Development's 1972 proposed regulations establishing settlement cost ceilings, its controversial provisions have been repealed and revised to its present form that calls for the following:

A HUD information booklet covering settlement costs must be given to HUD-insured mortgage applicants within three business days of filing for the loan.

Applicants must be given a "good faith" estimate of the closing costs, also within three days after filing a written application for a HUD loan.

If the buyer requests it, a statement of the actual closing costs, to the extent the figures are known, must be given him at least one day before settlement.

A HUD-approved uniform settlement statement form, with the separation of buyer and seller information must be furnished the buyer. This latter requirement is left to the option of the settlement agent.

Transactions involving real estate brokers selling to other brokers are exempt from HUD settlement requirements.

REAL LAW—The area of law that deals with real property and related matters. Real estate is subject to local and state laws of the government in which it is situated.

REAL PROPERTY—Land itself, the improvements thereon, and the rights, title and interest one has in it. (See also REAL ESTATE.)

REAL PROPERTY LAWS—The series of federal, state and local government laws relating to real estate.

*REALTOR—"A professional in real estate who subscribes to a strict Code of Ethics as a member of the local and state boards and of the National Association of Realtors." The term Realtor is a service mark registered in the United States Patent Office. Only members of the National Association of Realtors and its state and local affiliates may use it and display its seal.

REALTY—A contraction of the term "real property."

*Definition of Realtor reproduced with permission of the National Association of Realtors.

REALTY BOARDS—(See REAL ESTATE BOARDS.)

REAPPRAISAL—1. An appraisal of property at a subsequent time, a second appraisal. 2. In assessment work the term is used to indicate a general, periodic reassessment of property.

REAPPRAISAL LEASE—A fluctuating lease based upon the current valuation of the property. If the reappraisal is higher or lower, the payments will proportionately reflect the change.

REASONABLE VALUE—Value placed on property that corresponds to the current market value or is in line with the physical value.

REASSESSMENT—A re-evaluation; a change in the assessed value of property; a reappraisal.

REBATE—A return of a portion of a payment made, as in a tax rebate, mortgage rebate, etc. In mortgage loans and other liens, it is a refund given when a debt is paid before it is due.

RECAPTURE CLAUSE—1. A clause in leases giving the landlord the right to terminate the lease if certain conditions or standards are not maintained, such as may occur in a percentage lease, where the landlord has the right to cancel if a specified minimum volume of business is not maintained. 2. A clause found in ground rents providing an option for the outright purchase of the land for a specific price and at a specified time in the future. (See GROUND RENT.)

RECASTING A MORTGAGE—The act of reconstructing an existing mortgage by increasing or decreasing its amount, interest rate or length of time.

RECEIPT—A written acknowledgment of having received something.

RECEIVER—A court-appointed, neutral party, who takes possession and manages the property of a bankrupt or of property being otherwise litigated. The receiver's function is to maintain the premises and its assets for the benefit and protection of those having an equity in it, until a court decision as to its disposition is reached.

RECEIVERSHIP—Being in the hands of a receiver.

RECIPROCAL CONTRACT—(See BILATERAL CONTRACT.)

RECIPROCITY—The mutual exchange of privileges between groups and states. Being reciprocal as in the case of license laws. In real estate, it is the automatic recognition of licensed real estate brokers and salesmen to practice in another state. In many states, however, no reciprocity exists and a new course of study must be taken and examination passed.

RECISSION OF CONTRACT—(See RESCISSION OF CONTRACT.)

RECLAIM—1. To recover, restore or receive again that which was once owned. To seek the return of something previously in one's possession; to redeem. 2. To reclaim land is to return or restore blighted areas to a more useful purpose. This can be done by slum clearance and the erection of new, modern buildings in its place.

The Department of Housing and Urban Development (HUD) has instituted a Model Cities program for this purpose. (See DEPARTMENT OF HOUSING AND URBAN DEVELOPMENT (HUD).) Deserts and marshes may also be reclaimed by drainage of the land. (See RECLAMATION.)

RECLAMATION—The restoring of worthless, arid land or swampy, saturated land. This may be accomplished by the installation of proper drainage canals, adding fill, making land accessible by roadbuilding, etc.

RECOMPENSE—To compensate for something done; to repay in kind; return an equivalent value.

RECONDITIONING PROPERTY—Enhancing a property's value by making repairs, remodeling, painting, cleaning, landscaping, etc.

RECONVEYANCE—To convey or return ownership of real estate to one who previously had title to it. The transfer of title back to its former owner.

RECORD—1. A written statement; to officially commit to writing; to transcribe for future use or reference. 2. Placing a document on the public records by recording it in the proper county office where the general public may examine it.

RECORDED MAP OR PLAT—A map of subdivided land that is publicly recorded and which thereafter may be used as a basis for legal descriptions and reference.

RECORDER OF DEEDS—A county official whose office officially records deeds, mortgages or other documents relating to real estate title transfers. In some states the office is called the REGISTER OF DEEDS or simply the RECORDER'S OFFICE.

RECORDER'S OFFICE—The governmental office which publicly records deeds, mortgages and all instruments relating to real estate title transfer.

RECORDING—(See RECORD.)

RECORDING OF CONVEYANCES—The act of giving constructive notice, in the proper county office, of ownership transfer of property by making the document a part of the public records.

RECORDING OF DEEDS—(See RECORDING OF CONVEYANCES.)

RECORDING OF LEASE—Recording a lease in the proper county office to serve as protection for the parties to a transaction. Recording of a lease is not generally done with residential leases, but is in more common practice with long-term, commercial leases.

RECORDING OF MORTGAGES—Mortgages are recorded in the proper county office so that there is public notice of the encumbrance, as a safeguard against subsequent mortgages claiming priority.

RECOUP—1. Regain; reimburse; to make up for. 2. In law, to deduct or withhold payment of all or part of a debt to insure reimbursement of another claim or counterclaim. Also spelled Recoupe.

RECOURSE—Seeking aid in an effort to protect one's interest. Taking a new line of action.

RECOVER—To regain; to possess again.

RECTANGULAR OR GOVERNMENT SURVEY—(See GOVERNMENT SURVEY.)

RECTIFICATION OF BOUNDARIES—The clarification or correction of variations in boundary lines between properties.

REDDENDUM CLAUSE—(Latin) A clause in a conveyance that reserves something to the grantor of what he has granted. In a lease, for example, it reserves the periodic rent payments to the lessor. It may also cause a future interest in land to be retained, as occurs in the granting of a life estate. It is the clause that first renders or yields, then reserves something out of it to be returned.

REDEEM—Repurchase; recover; reclaim, as when one liberates property from a lien by satisfactorily clearing that which encumbered it.

REDEEMABLE RENT—1. Rental payments that can be recovered, such as might occur in a rental agreement with an option to purchase. Upon exercising the option, all or a portion of the rents are refunded the purchaser or applied to the sale price. 2. In GROUND LEASES, a clause is sometimes agreed upon allowing the lessee to redeem (recapture) ownership of the ground. (See RECAPTURE CLAUSE.)

REDEEMABLE RIGHTS—Rights that may be given back to the grantor upon his repaying the amount of consideration for which they were taken away.

REDEMISE—The renewing of leased property.

REDEMPTION—1. The act of a party redeeming property he has put up as security for a loan by paying the indebtedness. (See EQUITY OF REDEMPTION; RIGHT OF REDEMPTION.) 2. A method of voiding or redeeming a conditional sales contract by the grantor himself performing the conditions, thereby preventing the intended purchaser from being able to complete the transaction.

REDEVELOPMENT—The demolition and clearing away of a structure to allow new facilities to be built.

REDISCOUNT RATE—The rate charged by the Federal Reserve Bank for loans made to member banks.

REDLINING—The practice of some banking institutions as well as private lenders of putting certain neighborhoods off limits for mortgages. Declining areas and ghettos are prime targets for this practice. It is illegal for savings institutions to discriminate in this manner. The law requires that such lenders periodically make public a list showing the locations of their mortgage loans.

REDUCTION OF MORTGAGE CERTIFICATE—A document stating the exact remaining balance of the mortgage at the time of writing. An ESTOPPEL CERTIFICATE (OR LETTER).

RE-ENTRY—A landlord's right to repossess leased property if rent payments are not made or other terms in the lease are broken. Such reservations for regaining possession by the landlord must be a written part of the lease.

REFEREE—A court-appointed, neutral party authorized to arbitrate, investigate or settle a legal matter; an arbiter.

REFEREE IN BANKRUPTCY—A court-appointed party vested with quasi-judicial powers to administer to or dispose of a bankrupt estate.

REFEREE'S DEED IN FORECLOSURE—A deed prepared by an official of the court which forecloses the mortgage on a property and temporarily conveys the title to the referee. Once foreclosed the property may then be sold.

REFEREE'S DEED IN PARTITION—This deed conveys title to property when co-owners decide to divide their interest. Similar in content to a REFEREE'S DEED IN FORECLOSURE, the manner of division is determined by the court-appointed referee.

REFERRAL—The act of referring. In real estate practice, a referral client or prospect is one who has been obtained through the recommendation of another broker.

REFINANCE—To renew or extend existing financing or obtain another source. To finance anew, as when a mortgage is retired in order that a new, larger one may be placed upon the property.

REFORMATION—The correcting or rewriting of a contract by mutual consent when the contract does not express the true agreement or intent of the parties. It is also the legal obligation of the parties to change the agreement when fraud or a mistake exists. The word differs from a Recision Of Contract, which is rescinding or annulling the entire agreement.

REFORMATION OF DEED—Rectification or modification of a deed by court order when a spelling or other mechanical error has been made in preparing it, a fraud has been perpetrated by one of the parties, or for any other reason wherein the true intentions of the deed have not been fulfilled. It is variously known as a Deed of Conformation, Correction Deed and Reformation Deed.

REFUND—The return of funds; repayment; the amount given back.

REFUNDING MORTGAGE—Refinancing a mortgage from the funds of a new loan.

REFUSAL—In law, declining to exercise one's legal rights. (See FIRST REFUSAL.)

REGIONAL PLAN—(See CITY PLANNING, PLANNING COMMISSION.)

REGIONAL SHOPPING CENTER—A large shopping complex serving an extensive, well-populated area. Usually one or two major department stores form the nucleus, with fifty to one hundred or more other stores, as well as a post office, bank, theatre, etc., furnishing the public with goods, services and facilities of all descriptions. Many are connected under one roof in elaborate, air-conditioned mall areas.

REGISTER—1. To duly record; enroll. 2. An authorized officer whose duties are to keep public records of legal instruments. In some areas he is called a RECORDER OF DEEDS. 3. The actual records or books of recorded documents.

REGISTER IN BANKRUPCY—(See REFEREE IN BANKRUPTCY.)

REGISTER OF LAND OFFICE—A district officer of the federal government's BUREAU OF LAND MANAGEMENT, whose duties include managing, selling, leasing and acquiring government lands.

REGISTER OF DEEDS: REGISTRAR OF DEEDS: REGISTRY OF DEEDS— (See RECORDER OF DEEDS.)

REGISTRATION OF TITLE—Placing upon the public records instruments that serve as proof of the transfer of ownership of real property.

REGISTRY OF DEEDS—1. The method of publicly recording deeds as well as all other instruments used to prove ownership or interest in real estate. 2. The place where such documents are recorded and filed.

REHABILITATE—Restore to former condition, as when buildings are repaired and modernized. Returning a structure to good use through proper maintenance and remodeling. Physically improving a property to take on the characteristics of a more up-to-date building.

REIMBURSEMENT—Repayment; recompensation.

REINFORCED CONCRETE—Concrete having embedded metal rods, wire mesh, steel or other strengthening material.

REINSTATE—Return to a former state or position.

REINSURANCE—A method used by insurance companies to spread their risk by assigning a portion of insurance they have become obligated for to one or more other insurors. It is the assignment of liability from one insuror to another.

R.E.I.T.—Abbreviation for REAL ESTATE INVESTMENT TRUST. (See that definition.)

RELEASE—To relinquish; discharge from responsibility. Freeing from any legal obligation; abandoning a claim or right.

RE-LEASE—(See RELET.)

RELEASE CLAUSE—1. A clause found in blanket mortgages providing for the payment of a portion of the indebtedness so that a proportionate part of the property can be released. 2. Any clause that releases a party from an agreement when a specified contingency arises.

RELEASE OF DEED—(See DEED OF RELEASE.)

RELEASE OF DEPOSIT—A form signed by the purchaser, seller and broker authorizing the distribution of escrow funds. (See page 382.)

RELEASE OF DOWER—A release clause written into instruments when a married woman joins her husband in selling their real estate. By this clause she automatically relinquishes her dower interest in the property.

RELEASE OF LIEN—An instrument signed by subcontractors, materialmen and anyone else who may have a lien on the property disclaiming any further debt. It affords only limited protection for a new owner, as other lien holders who have not signed the release can sue. A new owner's best safeguard is to have title insurance covering MECHANIC'S LIENS.

RELEASE OF MORTGAGE—(See DEED OF RELEASE.)

RELEASE OF PART OF MORTGAGED PREMISES—The form used to release a portion of property from the lien of a mortgage. (See page 386.)

RELET—Leasing the premises again, as occurs following an expired lease or when a lease is broken allowing the landlord to immediately attempt to rerent the property. The first tenant who abandoned the lease is still liable, though generally to a lesser degree, for the unused portion of the lease.

RELICTION—Land uncovered by the permanent receding of a water line. This can occur when a river changes course or a build-up of sand deposits takes place on sea or oceanfront properties. The new land thus formed becomes the property of the riparian owner. Also referred to as DERELICTION, or ACCRETION.

RELIEF MAP—A map showing the different elevations of a land area. A CONTOUR or TOPOGRAPHIC MAP.

RELINQUISH—To give up; abandon; renounce any interest.

REMAINDER ESTATE—An estate that comes into being upon the termination of a prior estate, such as when an owner grants a life estate to one party. Upon completion of the life estate, the property either reverts to the owner or goes to another (generally an heir). If the owner does not take it back, a remainder estate is created. The holder of such an estate is called a REMAINDERMAN.

REMAINDERMAN—The person who is to receive a remainder estate. If a contingency arises that may cause the estate never to come about, or if there is a question of who is to receive it, it is referred to as a CONTINGENT REMAINDER. (See REMAINDER ESTATE.)

REMISE—To grant, give up, or release.

REMISE, RELEASE AND QUIT-CLAIM—The words found in a QUIT-CLAIM DEED that state the grantor's intent to relinquish or discharge all interest or title he has in the property.

REMIT—1. To remand; to send something as money or goods. 2. Defer; postpone.

REMITTER—In law, the relationship of a person owning the same property at separate intervals where the title may now be defective, though when he formerly owned it, it was clear of defects. The owner is remitted or "sent back" to the old title by a court order and is awarded clear title again.

REMNANT RULE—A rule applying to lots in a platted block in which the frontage measurements of all but one are calculated. What is left over is called the remnant lot and all remaining footage is assigned to this parcel.

REMODELING—Modernizing. Improvements made to property to bring it up to date and extend its life.

REMOVING CLOUD FROM TITLE—The legal procedures necessary to render defective property marketable and/or insurable. Quieting title.

REMUNERATION—Payment. The act of paying for services rendered.

RENDERING—An artist's three-dimensional sketch of a structure.

RE-NEGOTIATION—Further attempts to bring about an agreement after original negotiations have broken off.

RENEWAL OF LEASE—(See LEASE RENEWAL.)

RENOUNCE—(See RENUNCIATION.)

RENOVATE—Restore; renew to its former condition; revive.

RENT—The income received from leasing real estate. What is given of value, whether it is money, goods, crops, services, etc. for the use of property.

RENTABLE AREA—The actual square footage of a building that can be rented—halls, lobbies, elevator shafts, maintenance rooms, lavatories, etc. excluded. When calculating rentable area, square footage is determined by measuring from the center line of the walls.

RENTAGE—Amount of rent.

RENTAL—Rent.

RENTAL APPLICATION—An application form filled out by a prospective tenant and submitted to a landlord for approval before the lease is drawn.

RENTAL DEPARTMENT—A separate department in real estate offices devoted exclusively to leasing properties.

RENTAL VALUE—A term meaning the value of property estimated by the gross rental it produces. Investors in income properties, for example, speak of a selling price based on five, six, seven, etc. times the annual gross income received from the property.

RENTAL VALUE INSURANCE—Coverage for the owner of property who is occupying it himself. It is insurance in the event of damages to the premises. He will be paid the equivalent amount of the rental value for the time he is unable to utilize it, or be paid a sufficient sum to cover renting similar quarters until the insured property is restored to usable condition.

RENT CONTROL—Limitations on the amount of rent a landlord can charge as established by government controls (usually local or state). Rent control regulations are enacted in order to freeze rents or set a ceiling upon them to protect the public against rent gouging.

RENT GOUGING—(See GOUGING.)

RENT INSURANCE—A policy that insures rental income to the owner in the event of fire or other damage to the property. (See also RENTAL VALUE INSURANCE.)

RENT ROLL—A roster of the tenants that includes such information as the term of the lease, the security being held on deposit and the amount of the rental.

RENUNCIATION—The unilateral act of relinquishing a right to or interest in property, usually without consideration and without transferring title. Abandonment.

REORGANIZATION—Organizing anew; the reconstruction of a business or other organization. A partial or complete change in ownership often accompanied by new financing, techniques and objectives.

REPAIRS AND MAINTENANCE—The keeping of property and equipment in good condition by painting, decorating, repairing, landscaping, etc. (See MAINTENANCE.)

REPAY—To pay back; recompense; refund.

REPLACEMENT COST—1. The amount of money that would be needed to replace the equivalent of a building, furnishings or other asset. 2. In appraising it is the estimated current cost to replace an asset similar or equivalent to the one being appraised. When this method is used, the cost of unnecessary or known undesirable features are not considered in arriving at the estimate.

REPLEVIN—Legal proceedings referred to as a possessory action to recover personal belongings that have been unlawfully taken (usually for nonpayment of rent).

REPORT OF TITLE—(See TITLE REPORT.)

REPRESENTATION—An allegation of fact; a position taken. A statement, written or implied, that is an influencing factor in a purchaser's entering into a contract.

REPRODUCTION COST—The cost to duplicate an asset. (See REPLACEMENT COST.)

REPUDIATION—Renunciation; rejection. The act of refusing to accept something.

REPUTABLE—Having a good reputation; held in high esteem; estimable.

REPUTED OWNER—The one who the public believes to be the owner, though in fact he may not be.

RESALE—To sell again; a second sale.

RESCIND—Call back; to make void; repeal; cancel, as when one rescinds a contract.

RESCISSION OF CONTRACT—To rescind, abrogate or annul a contract. Also spelled Recision.

RESERVATION—1. To reserve something in a deed or other instrument for the benefit of the grantor. The act of a grantor holding something back from the estate which he has given. Setting something aside for future use, such as mineral rights, rental income or an easement. 2. An expanse of public land set apart for a specific purpose, as a tract for use by Indians, a military installation or a park.

RESERVE—To hold something back; set aside for the future, as when financial resources are held in readiness for use in an emergency.

RESERVED LAND—Public land that is held out for a specific purpose or future use.

RESERVOIR—A natural or artificial body of water used as a holding area for a community's water supply.

RESIDENCE—The place where one lives; a person's home. His permanent legal dwelling.

RESIDENT FREEHOLD—A person who owns at least a FREEHOLD interest in his place of residence.

RESIDENTIAL BUILDING RATE—An area's housing starts per 1,000 population over a given period of time.

RESIDENTIAL LISTING FORM—A form specifically designed for taking house listings. (See page 346.)

RESIDENTIAL MARKET—The real estate house market. The prevailing conditions as to activity, supply, demand, prices, availability of mortgages, etc. relating to the sale of homes.

RESIDUAL—1. That which remains; the residue. 2. Certain real estate commissions are in the form of delayed payments, particularly in installment land contract sales or in notes taken by the broker as part of his fee. These are sometimes referred to as residuals.

RESIDUARY BEQUEST—A bequest of the remainder of an estate that has not been disposed of, after the payment of all debts and obligations.

RESIDUARY CLAUSE—A clause in a will which disposes of the remaining estate after all debts, bequests and devises have been satisfied.

RESIDUARY DEVISEE—The recipient by will of the remainder of real property after all other claimants have been paid.

RESIDUARY ESTATE—The remainder of an estate after all else has been legally disposed of according to the terms of a will.

RESIDUARY LEGACY—The remaining personal property of an estate after all claims to it have been disposed of satisfactorily.

RESIDUARY LEGATEE—The recipient of the remaining personal property of an estate after all other specific bequests of personal property have been provided for in the will.

RESIDUE—1. The remainder; the part left after a portion has been taken. 2. That portion of an estate still remaining after all debts, charges, devises and bequests have been paid.

RESIDUUM—Remainder; residue. The balance remaining after deductions are made. In wills, that which remains after all else has been paid.

RESORT PROPERTY—Property particularly suited for vacationing and recreation. Mountainous areas, ocean and lake frontage, country retreats having scenic beauty, locales offering special climate conditions and those having sports facilities such as hunting, fishing, skiing, golfing, swimming, boating, etc. are some that readily lead themselves to resort development.

R.E.S.P.A.—REAL ESTATE SETTLEMENT AND PROCEDURES ACT. (See that definition.)

RESTITUTION—The act of making good for a loss or restoring something taken. Indemnification; reparation.

RESTORATION—1. Restoring a building by repairing and remodeling to its former appearance. In addition to an extension of their useful life, structures of historical significance are thus preserved for future generations to view and study. 2. Revitalizing land to its former state by replanting cut timber areas, leveling strip mines, sand and gravel sites, etc.

RESTRAIN—To limit; to curb; prohibit from doing something; to hold back; prevent.

RESTRAINT OF TRADE—Business alliances or practices that act to eliminate competition by controlling the supply of raw material, merchandise, property or prices. (See also CARTEL, MONOPOLY.)

RESTRAINT ON ALIENATION—Limiting the power to alienate property. (See ALIENATION, PERPETUITY.)

RESTRICTED LAND—Land that is limited by laws or by deed restrictions as to its utilization. (See RESTRICTIVE COVENANTS.)

RESTRICTED LANDS—Lands protected by the government as in the case of Indian reservations and national forests.

RESTRICTION—A limitation on the use of real estate. (See DEED RESTRICTIONS, DISCRIMINATORY COVENANTS, RACE RESTRICTIONS, RESTRICTIVE COVENANTS, ZONING)

RESTRICTIVE COVENANTS—Agreements written into instruments that curtail the full use of the property. As for example, imposing limitations on the density of buildings per acre, permitting only certain sizes and styles of structures to be erected, preventing particular businesses from operating or barring minority groups from owning or occupying homes in a given area. (This latter discriminatory covenant has been declared unconstitutional by the United States Supreme Court.) Also referred to as Protective Covenants.

RETAIN—1. To keep possession; continue in possession. 2. To have in one's service. To employ by paying or agreeing to pay a fee, as when a person engages the services of an attorney. (The sum of money given in advance is called a Retainer.)

RETAINING WALL—A wall built to hold the earth in place, where there is a difference in elevations, or to keep water from flooding, as with a seawall or dam.

RETIRE—To withdraw or to take out of service; to cease activity. Remove from circulation as retiring a note, bill of sale or money.

RETROACTIVE—Reverting to a prior time. Making a date on an instrument effective as a time in the past.

RETROSPECTIVE ASSESSMENT—(See OMITTED ASSESSMENT.)

RETURN—Profit from an investment; the sum of money that a property brings after expenses are paid; the yield.

REVALUATION—The reappraisal of an entire taxation jurisdiction in order to establish more up-to-date and equitable assessed values.

REVALUATION LEASE—(See REAPPRAISAL LEASE.)

REVENUE—1. The monetary return from an investment. The income that a property brings. 2. Money received by a government through taxation.

REVENUE STAMPS—(See DOCUMENTARY STAMPS, FEDERAL STAMPS).

REVERSION—(See ESTATE IN REVERSION.)

REVERSIONARY INTEREST—The future interest a person has in property that is presently in another's possession. (See ESTATE IN REVERSION.)

REVERSIONARY RIGHT—(See ESTATE IN REVERSION.)

REVERTER—That which reverts; reversion. That portion of an estate which returns to an owner or his heirs at the end of an ESTATE IN REVERSION.

REVEST—To revert to a prior owner; invest again; reinstate possession. The opposite of DIVEST.

REVOCABLE—Able to be revoked; capable of being annulled, repealed, or canceled; reversible.

REVOCATION OF AGENCY—A client's termination of an agent's employment.

REZONE—The change of land from one zoning classification to another.

RIBBON DEVELOPMENT—Land development that takes the form of a long, narrow strip. Such development occurs when housing or commercial projects are built alongside a highway that may extend for miles. Because of accessibility and the economy of building along an existing road, ribbon developments lack depth.

RIDER—An addition or amendment to an existing document. It generally takes the form of a separate paper that is attached to and made a part of the original instrument. An addendum.

RIDGEPOLE—The highest horizontal beam in the construction of a roof, it forms the topmost part when joined by the rafters. Also referred to as a ridgepiece, ridge beam, or ridge girder. (See HOUSE CROSS SECTION, page 410.)

RIGHT(S)—1. That which is just, proper and lawful. 2. The democratic concept that power, privilege and free action are born to all men. 3. An interest in or title to property. A well founded, established legal claim.

The word is in continual use in connection with real estate in such terms as Exclusive Right, Riparian Rights, Vested Rights, Right of Privacy, Right of Possession, Right of Property, Right of Redemption, Right of Survivorship, Right, Title and Interest, Right of Way, Squatter's Rights, and so on.

RIGHT OF FIRST REFUSAL—(See FIRST REFUSAL.)

RIGHT OF OCCUPANCY—The legal right to occupy and utilize land and the improvements upon it, as granted in a lease.

RIGHT OF POSSESSION—1. The right that one has to real property even if he is not in physical possession of it. If he has the right of possession, he has the legal power to remove from the premises anyone in actual possession. 2. The right to possess property, but not necessarily to have title to it, such as with leased premises. (See POSSESSION, ACTUAL POSSESSION, ADVERSE POSSESSION, CONSTRUCTIVE POSSESSION.)

RIGHT OF PRIVACY—The right to be left alone and free from observation. The right to enjoy seclusion.

RIGHT OF PROPERTY—An owner's right to the land by holding title to it, though he may not be in actual possession. The free use, maintenance or disposition of one's property.

RIGHT OF REDEMPTION—A reserved right, granted by statute, to free a property from foreclosure by paying the debts, fees and other accumulated charges that are causing it to be encumbered. This differs from EQUITY OF REDEMPTION which does not exist by statute and in which the property's debts must be cleared prior to a sale being made. Statutory right of redemption begins when Equity of Redemption ends. Also called STATUTORY REDEMPTION.

RIGHT OF SURVIVORSHIP—A right held by a surviving joint owner giving him sole title to the property. This right is found in JOINT TENANCIES and TENANCIES BY THE ENTIRETY.

RIGHT OF WAY—The right to pass over another's property. It is an easement that can be either private or public. A private right of way is created by the specific agreement of an owner. A public right of way is that right the public has to the use of highways, streets, parks, sidewalks, etc.

RIGHT PATENT—An absolete term meaning FEE SIMPLE ownership of land.

RIGHT, TITLE AND INTEREST—A term used in deeds to denote that the grantor is conveying all of what he held claim to.

RIGHT TO REDEEM—(See RIGHT OF REDEMPTION.)

RIPARIAN—Of or relating to land comprising the shore line of a watercourse.

RIPARIAN DOCTRINE—A theory that RIPARIAN RIGHTS should be based on fair and equitable usage as it relates to the public at large and to riparian property owners.

RIPARIAN OWNER—An owner of property having frontage on a river or other watercourse.

RIPARIAN PROPRIETOR—(See RIPARIAN OWNER.)

RIPARIAN RIGHTS—An owner's natural rights in regard to the banks of a river, stream or other watercourse, including access rights, accretion rights, abutting rights, reasonable use of the water and the right to the soil under the water. The rights of owners in connection with ocean and sea-front property, though sometimes referred to as riparian rights, should more accurately be called LITTORAL RIGHTS.

RIPARIAN WATER—Water below the high point of the normal flow of a river or other watercourse.

RISK CAPITAL—Invested capital that is speculative in nature and the least secured, consequently offering the greatest chance of loss.

RIVER BANKS—The water line of a river at high tide.

RIVERBED—The area between the banks of a river that is either covered or at one time was covered by water.

R. M.—Abbreviation for the designation of the AMERICAN INSTITUTE OF REAL ESTATE APPRAISERS meaning Residential Member. The American Institute is an affiliate of the National Association of Realtors.

ROAD—An open tract of land used by the public for travel. A route; highway; pathway.

ROADSIDE DEVELOPMENT—(See RIBBON DEVELOPMENT.)

ROD—A unit for measuring length that equals 16½ feet, 5½ yards or 5.029 meters.

ROOD OF LAND—An obsolete term meaning ¼ of an acre.

ROOF—The top, exterior, protective covering of a building, including the framing and roof boards.

Roof Styles

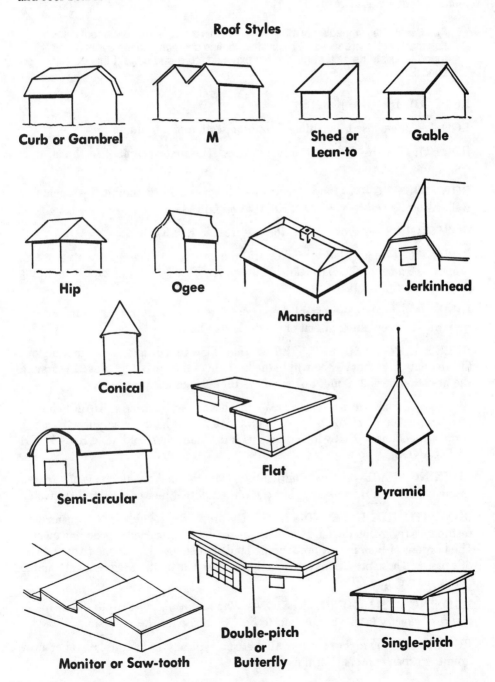

Curb or Gambrel   M   Shed or Lean-to   Gable

Hip   Ogee   Mansard   Jerkinhead

Conical   Flat

Semi-circular   Pyramid

Monitor or Saw-tooth   Double-pitch or Butterfly   Single-pitch

ROOF INSPECTION CLAUSE—A clause sometimes included in sales contracts providing for an independent inspection and report of the roof by a qualified expert. If the roof is found to be faulty, it will be repaired at the seller's expense. A typical roof inspection clause reads:

> Purchaser shall immediately after signing of this agreement have a roof inspection made of the premises by a qualified roofing company. In the event a leak is found to exist, the seller shall, at his expense, cure and correct this defective condition.

ROOF JOISTS—(See JOISTS.)

ROOM—An enclosed, partitioned interior section of a building.

ROOT OF TITLE—Where the title begins. The first document in the abstract concerning the property.

ROW HOUSING—A group of houses each connected to another by a common wall. Also referred to as CLUSTER DEVELOPING.

ROW STORES—A group of adjoining stores. STRIP STORES.

ROYALTIES—As applied to real estate, they are percentage payments made to property owners for the extraction of minerals, oil, gas, sand, gravel, or for cutting timber from the land.

RULE—A regulation; an established procedure by an authority; a court order; a prescribed, acceptable pattern of conduct; standard.

RULE AGAINST PERPETUITIES—A rule of law that disallows the granting of a future estate if it is not vested within the life or lives then in being, plus 21 years and the gestation period (9 months) from the time the estate was created.

RUN—1. To continue in force, as a lease that has a specified time still to go before its term is completed. 2. To lie as one boundary line in relation to another. To take a certain direction. 3. That which passes with the land when sold. (See RUN WITH THE LAND.)

RUNNING LEASE—A type of agricultural lease in which the tenant is not limited to any portion of a tract of land, but can utilize all that he can clear and cultivate.

RUN WITH THE LAND—The law of real property provides for covenants and restrictions regarding the land becoming incumbent upon each succeeding owner. The burdens or benefits (or both) of the land are conveyed from one to another as title passes. These provisions of ownership as the chain of title progresses are said to "run with the land."

RUNNING WITH THE REVERSION—When a covenant passes to the recipient of a reversionary interest, it is said to be "running with the reversion."

RURAL—Relating to the country. All the area, typically agricultural, that lies away from the urban centers. Farming country.

RURAL HOMESTEAD—(See HOMESTEAD.)

RURBAN—A contraction of rural and urban meaning that area between a metropolitan center and farming country that retains some of the characteristics of both (See EXURBAN; SUBURBAN; RURAL; URBAN.)

S

SALE—1. The change in ownership of property for a specified sum and under stipulated terms and conditions. A contract for the transfer of title to property, from one party to another. The making of an agreement (contract) to do so. 2. The offering for sale of property to the public. 3. Selling something at a reduced price. 4. An auction.

SALEABLE—Property that can be readily sold; marketable because of location, demand, price or some other desirable factor; capable of being sold. Also spelled Salable.

SALE AND LEASEBACK—A transaction in which the seller remains in occupancy by simultaneously signing a lease (usually of long duration) with the purchaser at the time of the sale. By so doing the seller receives cash for the transaction, while the buyer is assured a tenant and thus a fixed return on his investment.

SALE IN GROSS—Land transactions that are sold by the tract or otherwise in bulk without a warranty as to actual acreage or footage involved. Outlying, remote areas having limited commercial value are sometimes conveyed in this way.

SALE, LEASEBACK, BUYBACK—A SALE AND LEASEBACK transaction in which a further provision is made for the leaseholder to have the option to buy back his original property after a specified period of time as the lessee. In this type of transaction, with its tax shelter and profit benefits for both parties, the final "buyback" option usually takes effect at least five and sometimes ten or more years after the lease has commenced.

SALE OF LEASE—(See ASSIGNMENT OF LEASE.)

SALE OF LEASED PROPERTY—A sale of property that has tenants occupying the premises, as in the case of office buildings, stores, apartment houses, shopping centers, etc. The new owner cannot terminate the existing leases. They survive the sale. In the absence of an agreement to the contrary, a lease will continue in force without change or interruption.

SALE OF MORTGAGE—(See ASSIGNMENT OF MORTGAGE.)

SALE OF MORTGAGED PROPERTY—Consent of the mortgagee generally need not be obtained in such a sale. The property itself is the security for the debt and not the individual who owns it. Property can be sold subject to or assuming the mortgage. If the purchaser buys the property *subject to,* he is not personally responsible for the satisfaction of the mortgage. If, however, he takes title *assuming* the mortgage he is then liable for its payments in case of default.

SALES AGREEMENT: SALES CONTRACT—(See CONTRACT.)

SALES DEPOSIT RECEIPT—(See DEPOSIT RECEIPT.)

SALESMAN—As applied to real estate, an individual, usually required by state law to be licensed, who is employed by a broker or property owner to offer for sale, sell, list, lease, exchange or manage real estate. (See BROKER-SALESMAN CONTRACT.)

SALES PUFF—(See PUFF.)

SALINE LAND—Land that is high in salt content and therefore unsuited for growing crops.

SALT BOX—(See NEW ENGLAND COLONIAL ARCHITECTURE.)

SALVAGE VALUE—The price someone will pay for removing a structure or its parts from the land.

SANDWICH BUILDING—A building that utilizes the walls of the structures on either side.

SANDWICH LEASE—In subleasing property, when the holder of a sublease in turn sublets to another, his position is that of being sandwiched between the original lessee and the second sublessee.

SATELLITE COMMUNITY—A separate community situated near a large city that is closely tied economically, politically and socially to the metropolitan area it borders.

SATELLITE TENANT—In commercial real estate jargon, a non-rated, local tenant.

SATISFACTION—The paying of a debt; paying a claim or demand; settling an obligation; discharging by performance.

SATISFACTION OF LIEN—The instrument used as proof that a lien has been paid.

SATISFACTION OF MORTGAGE—An instrument acknowledging payment in full of a mortgage, that any further obligations concerning it are discharged.

SATISFACTION PIECE—A document acknowledging payment of a debt.

SAVINGS AND LOAN ASSOCIATION—A financial institution that is state or federally chartered and privately owned by the depositors or stockholders. Its prime functions are to furnish mortgage loans on real estate and to provide government insured, interest bearing savings accounts. (See FEDERAL SAVINGS AND LOAN ASSOCIATIONS.)

SCAVENGER SALE—Property taken over by the state due to non-payment of taxes.

SCENIC EASEMENT—A land use restriction imposed to maintain scenic beauty, or preserve historical landmarks. An example of scenic easements is restrictions against billboards.

SCHEMATIC—1. Relating to a scheme, plan or diagram. 2. An architect's three-dimensional, detailed drawing.

SCILICET—(Latin) To wit; that is to say. It is abbreviated as "SS."

SCRAP VALUE—(See SALVAGE VALUE.)

SCRIVENER—A writer. One who prepares documents. A scribe; notary.

SEAL—1. A device for making an embossed impression on paper to authenticate a document or attest to a signature, as a notary or corporate seal. 2. To sign a document followed by the letters L. S. which is a Latin abbreviation meaning *under seal* or *the place of the seal* (see *LOCUS SIGILLI*). 3. To ratify, confirm; an indication of approval.

Seal

SEA LEVEL—The sea's surface between high and low tides. All land elevations are calculated from sea level.

SEASHORE—The line where a sea or ocean meets dry land; seacoast.

SEASONED MORTGAGE—A mortgage in which periodic payments have been made, for a relatively long period of time, and the borrower's payment pattern is well established.

SEATED LAND—All land that is being put to use, such as farm land under cultivation, business property, land occupied by a community of homes, or for any other use. The term originated and is used almost exclusively in Pennsylvania. The opposite of UNSEATED LAND.

SEAWALL—A wall erected to separate water from land; an embankment to prevent erosion.

SECONDARY BUILDING—(See OUTBUILDING.)

SECONDARY FINANCING—(See SECOND MORTGAGES.)

SECONDARY LOCATION—A location that may be satisfactory for certain usage, but is in some way inferior and not classified as prime or a "hundred percent" location. A location away from the center of business activity.

SECONDARY MORTGAGE MARKET—In the field of mortgage banking, institutions such as banks, savings and loan associations, insurance companies, trust and mortgage companies, etc. often sell off a portion of the mortgages they are holding. For example, the Federal National Mortgage Association, a function of the Department of Housing and Urban Development, buys large quantities of such mortgages in order to make available funds to these lending institutions. They in turn can then provide additional mortgages to the public. This process of lenders selling their mortgages in bulk, with its continually fluctuating interest rates, comprises the Secondary Mortgage market.

SECONDARY RENTAL—A lease based partly on the landlord's costs. If taxes or utility rates increase, the rent will be proportionately raised.

SECOND DEED OF TRUST—Deeds of trust are used in some areas of the country in place of mortgages. One subordinate to a first DEED OF TRUST.

SECOND HOME—(See LEISURE HOME.)

SECOND LIEN—The lien that ranks behind the first and is next in order to be satisfied.

SECOND LOAN: SECOND MORTGAGE—A mortgage that is second in rank and subordinate to a first mortgage. Also called a JUNIOR MORTGAGE.

SECONDS—A subdivision of a degree of circular measurement used in Metes and Bounds legal descriptions. It is 1/60th of a degree or 1/3600 part of a circle. Seconds are symbolized by the mark ". For example, 21° 30′ 20″ means 21 degrees, 30 minutes, *20 seconds*.

SECTION OF LAND—As used in the Government Survey of public lands, it is an area one mile square containing 640 acres. A section is 1/36th of a township.

SECTION, TOWNSHIP AND RANGE DESCRIPTION—(See GOVERNMENT SURVEY.)

SECTIONAL HOUSE—A house put together at the job site in ready-made sections. (See also COMPONENT BUILDINGS, PREFABRICATE, and MODULE CONSTRUCTION.)

SECURITY—A deposit or personal pledge to guarantee payment of an obligation, insure against damages, or the faithful performance of an agreement, such as a security deposit given with a lease

SECURITY INTEREST—Any interest in real or personal property that serves to insure the payment of an indebtedness. All forms of mortgages, installment sales contracts and pledges are examples.

SEGREGATION—(See DEED RESTRICTIONS; DISCRIMINATORY COVENANTS.)

SEISIN—To seize property; taking legal possession of it. Actual possession of property by one who claims to have rightful ownership. Also spelled Seizin.

SEIZE—In real estate, it is to possess and own a freehold estate. To have RIGHT, TITLE and INTEREST IN FEE SIMPLE.

SEIZURE—The action of dispossessing. Seizing or taking possession of property by legal or apparently legal process. In CONDEMNATION, for example, it is the first step in the legal proceedings against the property holder.

SELF-SUPPORTING WALL—A wall that does not support the structure, but just its own weight. A NONBEARING WALL.

SELL—1. To transfer property and ownership to another for an agreed upon price and terms. 2. To cause or attempt to make a sale.

SELL AND LEASE AGREEMENT—(See SALE AND LEASEBACK.)

SELLER—The one offering property for sale or who has sold his property. The party successful in finding a buyer; the vendor, the grantor.

SELLER'S LIEN—A mortgage or note held by the seller for an amount still outstanding when he had relinquished title to the property. A PURCHASE MONEY MORTGAGE.

SELLER'S MARKET—When any commodity including real estate is in short supply, the seller is in a more commanding position. Within reason, an owner can generally name his price and terms. He holds a great advantage over the buyer, as he can sometimes choose the best of several offers. When these conditions prevail, it is referred to as a seller's market.

SEMI-DETACHED DWELLING—A home that is attached to another on one side by a party wall, as in a duplex or townhouse.

SEMI-PUBLIC PROPERTY—Property that is maintained by a private, generally non-profit, organization for use by the public.

SENIOR MORTGAGE—A first mortgage; one that is superior to all others.

SENTIMENTAL VALUE—A value a person places on real estate and its improvements because of personal attachment. It has no validity when estimating market value.

SEPARATE PROPERTY—Property owned individually as distinguished from what is jointly held. As an example, real estate owned by a wife that was obtained prior to her marriage. Also, privately owned property of one member of a business partnership.

SEPTIC TANK—An underground, enclosed tank used to hold sewage solids as they decompose by bacterial action. (See also CESSPOOL.)

SEQUESTRATION (IN EQUITY)—Legally taking possession of a defendant's real or personal property until what he owes has been paid. To seize by a writ of sequestration is to separate a person from his property and hold it in custody.

SERIATIM—(Latin) One by one; in succession; separately.

SERVICE CHARGE—A fee charged for services rendered.

SERVICE PROPERTY—Real estate that is being used primarily to serve the public and not meant for commercial gain. Such structures as churches, museums, historic sites, libraries and schools are considered service properties, as are national and state parks and recreational facilities provided by local governments.

SETBACK LINE—A zoning regulation prohibiting the construction of a building, beyond a prescribed distance from the property line. Most local zoning ordinances require structures to be set back specified distances from the street, as well as from rear and side lines.

SET-OFF—A legal demand against a plaintiff that is independent of the plaintiff's cause of action. Where a counter-claim arises out of the same complaint, a set-off is a separate action. If the set-off prevails, it lessens the plaintiff's eventual amount of recovery.

SETTLEMENT—1. The process of making adjustments in a business transaction, an estate or in a legal dispute. 2. In real estate, it is the transfer of title with the resulting financial prorations and adjustments. A CLOSING.

SETTLOR—1. The grantor who gives an asset to a trustee for the benefit of a third party. The one who thus causes a trust to be created by donating real or personal property for a beneficiary. 2. The donor in a deed of a settlement.

SEVERABLE CONTRACT—A divisible contract. One in which the parties can be separated in the event of a breach. It is a contract looked upon as a series of independent agreements. If one of the agreements is breached, only that part may be in default. The remainder of the agreement would remain in force.

SEVERALLY—Separately and apart. The term "severally liable," or "jointly and severally liable," as used in legal documents, means that parties to the agreement are individually responsible.

SEVERALTY—Sole ownership. An estate held by one person only; no other individual has any part or interest in the estate.

SEVERANCE—The act of severing; separating something from the land, such as the taking of natural resources (oil, minerals, gas, lumber, game, etc.) from property.

SEVERANCE DAMAGE—1. The lowering in market value due to something being taken from the land, as when timber or minerals are removed. 2. The decrease in value of land when it is divided. A lot, for example, because of its utility for a specific purpose may be worth more as one large parcel than the sum of the divided parts.

SEVERANCE TAX—A tax for the removal of certain natural resources from the land, such as timber, minerals, fish and game, oil, gas, etc.

SEXTERY LANDS—Property given to and maintained by the church.

SERVIENT ESTATE: SERVIENT TENEMENT—In relation to an EASEMENT, an estate can be either dominant or servient. A servient estate is one that is subject to use by the holder of the dominant estate. It is said to be "burdened with a servitude." Something is owed. An owner of a dominant estate, for example, may have the right of ingress and egress over the land that comprises the servient property.

SHARECROPPING—The payment of rent in the form of crops or grain. Also called GRAIN RENT.

SHARE OF OWNERSHIP AGREEMENT—In mortgages and other forms of real estate interest, two or more people combine funds to share ownership. An agreement is drawn stating the extent each is a participant in the transaction.

SHED—1. A small, single-storied building either free-standing or lean-to, usually used for storage. 2. A structure open on one or more sides for storage or shelter.

SHELL HOUSE—A home that has only the exterior completed when sold. Wiring, plumbing, heating and other interior facilities are not installed and are left to the purchaser to complete. A prefabricated or manufactured home. (See also COMPONENT BUILDING.)

SHELTER—Protection; refuge. Certain types of income property, for example, offer great tax savings by allowing the owner to deduct depreciation of the improvements from otherwise taxable income. This is referred to as a TAX SHELTER.

SHERIFF'S DEED—The form of deed used when the court orders the conveyance of property to satisfy a judgment. In some jurisdictions it is referred to as a MASTER'S DEED.

SHOPPING CENTER—A group of separately owned, retail businesses and other establishments, under a common roof, that provide off-street parking and maximum customer convenience. The larger, modern centers offer enclosed air-conditioned malls and a complete selection of goods and services for one-stop shopping. (See NEIGHBORHOOD SHOPPING CENTER, REGIONAL SHOPPING CENTER, SUBURBAN SHOPPING CENTER.)

SHORE—Land that ends with the waterline of an ocean, river, sea, lake or other watercourse.

SHORE LANDS—The land situated between the high and low water marks.

SHORTCUT FORECLOSURE—A time-saving method of the foreclosure process, allowed in some states, in which a "power of sale" clause in the mortgage permits the lender to sell the property if it goes into default. While the borrower must be notified, the issuing of a public notice and notification of the junior mortgage holders need not be done. Upon the foreclosure of the property, the junior mortgage holders' positions are normally wiped out, unless the sale produces more than the outstanding first mortgage. (See also POWER OF SALE.)

SHORT FORM—Legal instruments that do not actually contain the usually lengthy statute laws, but are nevertheless implied and have the same effect as if they were included. (See STATUTORY DEED.)

SHORT FORM MORTGAGE CLAUSE—This clause in a mortgage provides for the purchaser to take it over subject to and not assuming liability for its payment. (See SALE OF MORTGAGED PROPERTY.)

SHORT LEASE—A residential lease for a month or up to a year is considered a short lease, but otherwise the term is relative. Some commercial leases for five or even ten years are thought of as being of short duration.

SHORT-TERM LOAN—A loan of short duration. In banking, it is generally considered that a mortgage of ten to twelve years is a short term. Mortgage loans for twenty years or more are referred to as long-term loans.

SHORT RATE—When an insurance policy is canceled, the rate for the time that it was in force will increase, as the premium originally charged was calculated on the full period of the policy. This increased premium is known as the "short rate." It is a rate based on a period of less than a year.

SHOTGUN FLOORPLAN—An expression for a simplified interior design having a straight center hall from front to rear, with rooms off to each side. It is so named because one could presumably fire a shotgun from one end to the other without hitting any partition.

Shotgun Floorplan

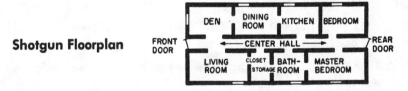

SHYSTER—An unscrupulous, generally dishonest lawyer.

SIDEWALK—A lateral paved strip running parallel with the street for pedestrian use.

SIDING—The material used for surfacing the outside walls of a building.

SIGHT DRAFT—A draft that is payable on presentation or demand. (See LETTER OF CREDIT.)

SIGHT LINE EASEMENT—A sight line is the distance from which another property can be clearly seen without visibility obstructions. An easement for such a sight line prevents construction that would block out the view of the property.

SIGN—1. To write a signature; to signify approval by affixing one's name to a document. 2. A printed display used for advertising; a signboard.

SIGNATORY—A signer of a document. One of a group of signers. One bound by what he signed.

SIGN RIGHTS—The rights given by the owner of property to have billboards or other type signs displayed upon the exterior of a building. It may be given to a tenant, as part of the lease agreement, or leased to others.

SILENT PARTNER—An inactive, non-participating partner in a business. One who has a monetary interest but does not work for the company. He is "silent" as to the management, the running of the business and as far as the general public is concerned. Also called a dormant or sleeping partner.

SILO—A tall, windowless, cylindrical structure used as a bin for the storage of grain.

SIMPLE CONTRACT—A contract that is not under seal. It may be in writing or oral.

SIMPLE INTEREST—Interest that is computed on the principal amount of a loan only. No amount need be paid for amassing interest, as occurs with a loan containing COMPOUND INTEREST.

SIMPLE LISTING—An OPEN LISTING; one being offered to the public by more than one broker at a time; not an EXCLUSIVE RIGHT OF SALE or EXCLUSIVE AGENCY LISTING.

SIMULATED CONTRACT—A contract that outwardly has the appearance of being valid, but in fact is a sham, having little if any basis in fact. It is not enforceable and has no validity.

SINGLE FAMILY DWELLING (OR RESIDENCE)—A house designed for occupancy by one family; a private home.

SINGULAR TITLE—Title granted to one person; sole ownership. A singular successor to property.

SINKING FUND—A gradually accumulated fund created to diminish a debt. At the end of a given period, the fund will have a sufficient amount, including interest earned, to replace the loss or satisfy the obligation that has fallen due.

SITE—The location or position of something. A parcel of land set aside for a specific use.

SITE PLAN—A map showing the location of improvements in relation to the parcel of land.

SITING—Planning the location of a building or lot. The placement of a structure as it relates to other improvements.

SITUS—(Latin) A site, place, location or position. Where something is.

SKY LEASE—1. A lease of the air rights above a property. 2. A lease given to a tenant to erect upper floors on an existing building or roadway. The lease is usually of long duration, for upon its termination the improvements remain with the property.

SKYSCRAPER—A tall building. By inference, a structure so tall that it scrapes the sky. (See HIGH-RISE.)

SLAB—A level layer of material, generally of poured concrete. Slab foundations are a familiar building technique. They may be built directly on the ground or on supported floors.

SLANDER OF TITLE—Disparaging or false statements (written or oral) concerning one's lawful title to property. Malicious intent must be proved in an action for slander of title.

SLEEPER—A slang expression meaning a property with hidden values. One that seems destined for unexpected appreciation.

SLUM—A poorly kept, run-down section of a city or suburb. It is marked by dilapidated buildings, over-crowded, squalid and unsanitary living conditions, as well as poverty and depressed social standards.

SLUM CLEARANCE—The razing and removing of old, run-down buildings so that the land can be put to new and better use. It is an effort to eliminate the existence of substandard living conditions. Usually such programs are federally, state and locally subsidized. On the national level the Department of Housing and Urban Development (HUD) is working to clear slum and blighted areas and replace them with low-rent housing projects. (See DEPARTMENT OF HOUSING AND URBAN DEVELOPMENT (HUD) and URBAN RENEWAL.)

SLUMLORD—An owner who rents out slum property.

SOCIAL OBSOLESENCE—(See ECONOMIC OBSOLESCENCE.)

SOFIT—The underside of any portion of a building, such as a staircase, protruding wall, cave, archway, etc.

SOFT DOLLARS—A jargon term meaning any deferred payments such as mortgages, notes, etc. The opposite of HARD MONEY, which is cash or its equivalent.

SOFT SELL—Low-pressure selling. Selling by the use of logic and reasoning rather than loud, overly aggressive tactics.

SOIL—The surface covering of the land. The upper layer of the earth's crust.

SOIL RIGHTS—A landowner's right to the ground on and beneath the earth's surface.

SOLD—Purchased property that has changed hands. The past tense of sell.

SOLDIERS AND SAILORS CIVIL RELIEF ACT—This act provides protection to men in military service against loss of real estate in the event of failure to pay taxes. If they or their dependents owned the property when they entered the service, the property cannot be sold without their express approval.

SOLD NOTICE—A written notice from a broker or owner that a particular property has been sold and is no longer on the market.

SOLE OWNER OR PROPRIETOR—The only one possessing title to a particular piece of property or ownership of a business.

SOLVENT—The position of being able to pay one's financial and legal obligations; the ability to meet one's debts.

SOUND INVESTMENT—An investment that shows good judgment; one that is logical and valid. An investment in which the present or future prospect of making a profit is apparent.

SOUTH—A directional description that is pointing toward the south pole; due south; 180 degrees on a compass. One of the four cardinal points of direction.

SOUTHERN COLONIAL—A style of architecture familiar to the southern United States, featuring a rectangular frame house with large, two-story pillars at the entrance.

Southern Colonial

SPECIAL ASSESSMENT—A special levy on property to pay for a specific public improvement to the property or in the immediate area, such as for road construction, sidewalks, sewers, street lights, etc.

SPECIAL BENEFITS—Benefits accruing to a particular parcel of land that others in the area do not enjoy. Direct benefits resulting from public improvements to a particular property or properties. Also called OFFSETTING BENEFITS.

SPECIAL LIEN—A lien that binds only a specified piece of property. It creates a right to retain something of value belonging to another as compensation for labor, material or money expended in that person's behalf. It is unlike a GENERAL LIEN which is levied against all of one's assets. Also called PARTICULAR or SPECIFIC LIEN.

SPECIAL PURPOSE PROPERTIES—Properties suitable only for a specific use;

for example, cemeteries, churches, clubs, railroad properties, sports arenas, theatres, etc.

SPECIAL TAX ASSESSMENT—(See SPECIAL ASSESSMENT.)

SPECIAL WARRANTY DEED—In this type of deed the grantor will defend the title against claims brought only by the grantee, his heirs, administrators and those claiming by, through or under him. The grantor assumes no other liability. It is the type of deed often used by trustees in transferring title and, pursuant to court orders, to convey tax titles.

SPECIFICATIONS—Detailed information covering exact measurements, elevations, type of materials, workmanship, and other elements that go into a structure.

SPECIFIC LIEN—(See SPECIAL LIEN.)

SPECIFIC PERFORMANCE—1. Performing exactly, or as reasonably as possible, the terms of a contract. Fulfilling specifically as agreed. 2. In the event of a default by one of the parties, it is the name given the lawsuit brought for failure to perform as stated in the agreement.

SPECULATIVE BUILDER—(See CUSTOM BUILDER.)

SPECULATOR—An individual engaged in speculating in real property. A knowledgeable party who studies the real estate market and its trends, and invests for his own account. If he foresees a rise in prices, he will acquire properties and hold them for the most opportune time to sell.

SPENDABLE INCOME—Usable income. The cash flow.

SPINOFF—A term meaning a company's transfer of a portion of its assets to a newly formed subsidiary.

SPIT—A narrow strip of land extending into a body of water. A long shoal extending from the shoreline.

SPLIT-LEVEL HOUSE—A home so designed that a portion of the upper and lower floor levels are located part way between the main floors. This compact architectural style is most effectively used on sloping terrain.

Split-Level

SPREADING AGREEMENT—An agreement to extend or spread the lien of a mortgage over additional properties in order to give the lender further security for his loan.

SPOIL—Excavated or dredged rock, debris or earth.

SPOT BUILDER—A builder who erects one or two houses at a time in a chosen "spot" on speculation. (See CUSTOM BUILDER.)

SPOT ZONING—Areas where inconsistent zoning or a zoning variance is permitted. Nonconforming zoning that differs from the general pattern of the surrounding area.

SQUARE—1. A city block; land having streets on all sides. 2. An open public area in a city or town set aside near the center of activity of the community. 3. In the GOVERNMENT SURVEY of public lands, it is an area measuring 24 miles by 24 miles; sometimes referred to as a check.

SQUARE FOOT VALUE—To estimate square foot value, find the square footage of the building (length × width), then multiply it by the estimated cost per square foot of replacing it.

SQUATTER—A person who illegally occupies land belonging to another. As a general rule a squatter cannot obtain title to property; the exception being that if he openly and notoriously occupies it for a required statutory period, he may possibly obtain title by adverse possession. (See ADVERSE POSSESSION; SQUATTER'S RIGHTS.)

SQUATTER'S RIGHTS—A squatter may begin to obtain rights when his occupancy is considered in ADVERSE POSSESSION. Occupancy must be in "actual, open, notorious, exclusive and continuous" possession for a prescribed statutory period. State laws vary as to the amount of time, some require as short a period as five or seven years, with others up to twenty.

S.R.A.—A designation of the Society of Real Estate Appraisers meaning Senior Residential Appraiser.

S.R.E.A.—A designation of the Society of Real Estate Appraisers meaning Senior Real Estate Analyst.

SS—(Latin) An abbreviation for the word *scilicet*, meaning "to wit," "namely," "that is to say."

STANDARD DEPTH—The depth of a lot that is common to an area.

STANDARD PARALLELS—In the Government Survey of public lands, standard parallels are survey lines running east and west, generally spaced 24 miles apart and located north and south of, and parallel to, the Base Line. (See GOVERNMENT SURVEY.)

STAND-BY COMMITMENT—A loan pledge for use sometime in the future. The term is used in financing construction projects. A builder generally obtains two separate loans. One is a short-term building loan, given for the duration of the construction period. The other is the long-term permanent loan. This is the stand-by commitment. It is pledged by the lender to be placed in the future. It takes the form of a commitment letter. The financing is said to be in a "stand-by" position until the construction is completed.

STATE—A body of people living in the same described territory and having their own governing system.

STATEMENT—1. A declaration; an assertion. 2. A written account of the amount of money due for services rendered or materials furnished. A typical real estate broker's commission statement is shown.

STATEMENT

Date _____

From: _____
_____

To: _____
_____

Re: The following described property:
_____

For services in bringing about the above captioned transaction.

$ _____
Received payment _____
_____

STATE STAMPS—(See DOCUMENTARY STAMPS.)

STATUTE—1. A written law of a government's legislative body. 2. An act of a corporation, university, society, etc. setting forth its rules, by-laws or regulations.

STATUTE OF FRAUDS—Nearly every state recognizes the early English statute (enacted in the year 1677) which provides that real estate contracts must be in writing and duly signed to be enforceable. In general, oral contracts pertaining to real property are not enforceable by law. This statute was founded to prevent frauds and perjuries, and has been enlarged to become a basic concept and foundation of real estate and contract law.

STATUTE OF LIMITATIONS—A statute placing a time limit on the right of action in certain cases where a remedy is sought in a court of law.

STATUTORY—Relating to statute law; having to do with the written law.

STATUTORY BOND—A bond that meets the statutory requirements.

STATUTORY DEED—Most states recognize an abbreviated form of deed in which certain customary provisions and covenants are not written out in full, but are nevertheless implied and have the same force as if they were completely written. When this short form is used, it is referred to as a statutory deed.

STATUTORY LAW—Law enacted by the legislature. Statutory laws are created to form governmental bodies, define crimes, prescribe conduct, allocate money and, in general, to promote the welfare of the public.

STATUTORY LIEN—A lien that arises under the rules of a statute. TAX LIENS, street improvement liens, JUDGMENT LIENS and ATTACHMENT LIENS are examples.

STATUTORY MORTGAGE—A mortgage that meets the requirements of statute.

STATUTORY REDEMPTION—(See RIGHT OF REDEMPTION.)

STEERING—The practice of directing a prospective buyer away from a certain property. Steering is the reluctance to sell or negotiate for the sale of real estate because of a person's race, color, religion, national origin or sex. Both the Department of Justice and the Department of Housing and Urban Development prohibit this by law. It is clearly discriminatory. The Fair Housing Law contains guidelines against both BLOCK BUSTING and the steering of buyers in this fashion.

Many Boards of Realtors and their member affiliates throughout the country have adopted a meaningful policy in support of this position. Signs stating fair housing policies are prominently displayed and pocket cards are carried by salespersons proclaiming their company's civil rights position. A typical sign reads:

"Please do not ask, or expect to be shown homes according to the racial, religious or ethnic characteristics of the neighborhood in which the homes are located. Company policy, as well as Federal Law, prohibits us from placing any such restrictions on showings or information about the availability of homes for sale or rent."

STEP LEASE—(See ESCALATOR CLAUSE.)

STEP-UP CLAUSE—(See ESCALATOR CLAUSE.)

STOCK—1. An inventory of material; merchandise; supplies. To fill with goods. 2. The capital or money assets of a company. 3. A share or capital interest one has in a corporation. (See also COMMON STOCK; PREFERRED STOCK.)

STOCK CERTIFICATE—A certificate duly signed and sealed showing ownership of a share or shares in a corporation.

STOCK COMPANY—A corporation or other form of business organization whose assets are represented by stock.

STOCK DIVIDEND—The payment of additional shares of stock to a stockholder in proportion to his holdings as a method of distributing profits.

STOCKHOLDER—An owner of a share or shares of stock.

STORE—1. A retail business establishment where merchandise is kept and displayed for sale to the public. 2. Accumulate for future use; stock.

STORE LEASE—A lease agreement worded specifically for the rental of a store.

STORY—A floor level of a building usually divided into rooms, hallways, etc.

STRAIGHT LEASE—A lease with regular periodic payments (monthly, quarterly, etc.) of equal amounts. Also called a FLAT LEASE.

STRAIGHT LINE DEPRECIATION—A method of calculating an allowance for depreciation of a building by deducting a fixed sum annually over the anticipated life of the building. It allows the owner to regain his investment in the property during its useful life. The fixed sum is calculated by dividing the total cost of the structure by its estimated economic life.

STRAIGHT LOAN—A loan in which only interest payments are periodically made with the entire principal amount becoming due at maturity.

STRAW MAN—A person who buys property for another to conceal the identity of the true purchaser. He holds naked title on behalf of another. More commonly called a "dummy" purchaser.

STREET—A dedicated public roadway or thoroughfare in or near a city or other developed community.

STREET LOT LINE—A line demarking the street frontage of a lot.

STREET RIGHTS—The inherent rights of ingress and egress possessed by land owners to the use of streets abutting their property.

STRIP STORES—A group of stores under one roof, bordering a thoroughfare.

STRUCTURE—1. Something built or constructed. A building, bridge, dam, tunnel, dock, highway, etc. 2. Make up; manner of construction. The parts or elements that go into making the finished product.

STUDIO APARTMENT—(See EFFICIENCY.)

STUDS—Vertical structural members used in the framing of a building.

SUBAGENT—A salesman working for an agent. A person employed by an agent to perform under his direction and supervision.

SUB-CHAPTER S—A federal corporate designation having unique tax advantages for qualifying business firms. Smaller corporations may, for tax purposes, be considered as if they were partnerships. The individual stockholder still benefits by having only limited personal liability, and needs to pay only individual, not corporate, taxes. Only corporations with certain limited earnings qualify for the Sub-Chapter S designation.

SUB-CONTRACT—A contract given out by one holding the original or general contract to perform all or any portion of the work. It is common practice to "sub" out specialized construction work such as heating, air conditioning, foundation and cement work, wiring, plumbing, and so on, to experts in their fields.

SUB-CONTRACTOR—The individual or firm agreeing to perform all or a part of the work of a principal or general contract.

SUBDIVIDE—To divide into smaller parts, as a tract of land that is made into blocks, lots and streets.

SUBDIVIDER—A developer or builder who divides land and makes the necessary improvements to it so as to be saleable for building sites.

SUBDIVISION—A parcel of land divided into smaller lots for homesites or other use.

SUBDIVISION TRUST—This type of trust is used when a company or corporation that owns a subdivision empowers a trustee to act in its behalf. The trustee handles such matters as sales to the public, physical improvements to the subdivision, paying and supervising contractors, further division of the land, collecting debts, etc. He is usually placed in complete charge and may act without consulting the officers of the corporation.

SUBJECTIVE VALUE—Value that exists in a person's mind. The intangible evaluation formed by personal opinion or feeling. The opposite of objective.

SUBJECT TO MORTGAGE—The term subject to means limiting, qualifying or subordinate to. When used in mortgages, it refers to taking title to property having an existing mortgage, but without assuming personal liability for its payment. If liability is to be assumed it must be so stated and agreed upon. (See SALE OF MORTGAGED PROPERTY.)

SUBLEASE—The letting of premises by a tenant to a third party, but still retaining some portion or interest in it. Either all or part of the premises may be subleased and it may be for the whole term of the original lease or for a portion of it. (Also called an UNDERLEASE or UNDERLYING LEASE.) If, however, the tenant relinquishes his entire interest, it is no longer considered a sublease but an ASSIGNMENT OF LEASE.

SUBLESSEE—(See SUBTENANT.)

SUBLET—(See SUBLEASE.)

SUB-MARGINAL LAND—Property of little or no economic value. Land unable to produce enough to warrant cultivation or other development. Swamps, deserts and remote mountain areas are examples of sub-marginal lands.

SUBMERGE LAND—The disappearance of land under water; to overflow by flooding, causing land to go permanently under water.

SUBMIT—1. The act of presenting or submitting something for consideration, as when property is offered to a prospect. To make available. 2. An agreement to offer something for arbitration usually in a court of law.

SUBMITTAL NOTICE—A written notice of record, from a broker to an owner, stating that his property has been shown and listing the prospect's name, address and the price quoted.

SUBMITTAL NOTICE

_____, 19__

Mr. _____

_____

_____

Please be advised that today we submitted to _____

_____

your property listed with this office, located at _____

_____Price quoted $_____

We will endeavor to interest this prospect further. If they return to examine same, or call by phone, please notify us at once, as your co-operation will greatly assist in the sale of your property. Thank you.

By _____Salesman

_____, Realtors

SUBMORTGAGE—When a lender pledges a mortgage he holds as collateral for obtaining a loan for himself, he creates a submortgage.

SUBORDINATED INTEREST—An interest or right in property that is inferior to another, such as a second mortgage being subordinate to a first.

SUBORDINATION—When a lien holder agrees to place his interest in lesser rank than another. This frequently occurs when the seller of vacant land, in order to make the sale, takes back a mortgage and agrees to lower its rank to second position behind a construction or permanent loan.

SUBORDINATION CLAUSE—The clause in an instrument which states that a lien or mortgage shall be inferior to that of another.

SUBPOENA—(Latin) A legal order directing a witness to appear and testify before a court of law, a commission or other legal body.

SUBROGATION—Replacing one person with another in regard to a legal right, interest or obligation. Substitution, such as a mortgage holder selling his rights and interest to another.

SUBROGEE—The person who is substituted for another and succeeds to his rights as well as obligations.

SUBSCRIBE—To put one's signature to a document; to sign. To agree to in writing. Giving consent by endorsing an instrument.

SUBSCRIBING WITNESS—One who attests to witnessing someone's signature on a document by signing his name to that effect.

SUBSIDIARY COMPANY—A company under the control of a parent company, though usually having its own officers and directors and performing its functions independently. An auxiliary company.

SUBSOIL—The ground lying immediately below the surface layer of the earth.

SUBSTANTIAL PERFORMANCE—When virtually all the provisions of a contract are met, with the possible exception of minor technicalities or inadvertent omissions. If there are no departures from the basic terms, and in essence the spirit of the contract is unchanged, it is considered as being performed.

SUBSURFACE EASEMENT—1. An easement permitting the use of space below the ground, for a tunnel, underground cable, electric line, pipe line, etc. It is also called a subsurface right. 2. The right to extract minerals, gas, coal, oil or other substances from below the surface of the land.

SUBSURFACE RIGHT—(See SUBSURFACE EASEMENT.)

SUBTENANT—A tenant who leases from another tenant. A sublessee; undertenant.

SUBURBAN SHOPPING CENTER—A shopping center, outside a city, that often serves several surrounding communities. (See SHOPPING CENTER.)

SUBURBIA—Having to do with the suburbs; the area around a metropolis referred to as suburban.

SUBURBS—The communities or towns near a larger city which are tied economically and socially to the city. Property located at the outskirts of a city.

SUCCESSION—The legal act or right of acquiring property by descent. Succeeding to an asset by will or inheritance.

SUCCESSION TAX OR DUTY—(See INHERITANCE TAX.)

SUCCESSOR—An individual who succeeds to an estate or business. The one who takes over where a predecessor left off.

SUE—To seek legal means to recover one's rights.

SUFFERANCE—1. Consent by inaction; implied permission by failing to enforce or act upon; passive consent; negative permission by not trying to prevent. A tenant at sufferance, for example, is one who remains in legal possession after the expiration of a lease if there was no action to remove him. 2. Patient endurance.

SUFFICIENT CONSIDERATION—An ample amount of consideration for the particular transaction covered. Consideration that has enough value to compensate the grantor should the grantee fail to perform.

SUIT—A court action to recover one's legal rights.

SUMMARY PROCEEDINGS—Short legal proceedings without a jury, indictments, subpoenaed witnesses or the usual and often lengthy requirements of a regular course of law. Summary proceedings are commonly used in such instances as a landlord's action to regain possession, probating a will, bankruptcy hearings, enforcing local ordinances, etc.

SUMMATION APPRAISAL—(See COST APPROACH TO VALUE.)

SUM OF THE YEARS' DIGITS DEPRECIATION—A method of taking depreciation for newly constructed buildings. This formula takes into account the total years of useful life of the property, and divides it by the sum of these digits. For example, if the estimated life of an asset is 15 years, the first year's depreciation would be expressed in the formula of $^{15}/_{120}$. The denominator of the fraction is totaled: $1+2+3+4+5+6+7+8+9+10+11+12+13+14+15=120$. The second year's depreciation would be $^{14}/_{120}$, the third $^{13}/_{120}$, then $^{12}/_{120}$, and so on. The denominator represents the cost of the asset, less any estimated salvage value.

SUMP—A low lying, drainage area or pit designed to receive fluid waste material.

SUMP PUMP—A pump used to drain a sump pit.

SUNDAY CONTRACTS—A contract made and signed on Sunday. Such contracts in some states are void, while in others they are considered as being no different from those made on any other day.

SUPERFICIARIUS—(Latin) A GROUND RENT tenant.

SUPERSEDE—To replace or supplant. To cause to set aside; displace.

SUPPLY AND DEMAND—A business axiom or "law" which holds that price and sometimes value vary directly with supply. An oversupply reduces price, and vice versa.

SUPPORT DEED—The deed used when property is conveyed, with the consideration being that the grantee will support the grantor for the rest of his life. This frequently occurs when a parent deeds land to a child or when elderly people designate a retirement home or a friend to care for them. If proper support ceases, a court may disavow the deed.

SURETY—A personal guarantee to fulfill an obligation. An individual who has legally committed himself to the fidelity, obligations or debts of another, should that party fail to perform as agreed.

SURETY BOND—A bond used when employees are entrusted with sums of money or are held responsible for valuable assets. They are insured by bonding and insurance companies guaranteeing that they will honestly carry out their responsibilities.

SURFACE RIGHTS—The right to use the surface area of the land. Such rights might be granted to others, for example, by a mining company whose work is below ground.

SUR MORTGAGE—A type of writ used in certain states which requires one who has defaulted on mortgage payments to show cause why the mortgagee should not foreclose.

SURPLUS LAND—Extra land; land not needed for the purpose for which it was originally acquired; superfluous land.

SURRENDER DEED—(See DEED OF SURRENDER.)

SURRENDER OF LEASE—A mutual agreement between tenant and landlord to terminate a lease before its normal expiration period.

SURRENDER OF PREMISES—Physical removal from property. At the expiration of a lease, for example, the lessee is expected to promptly vacate and surrender the premises.

SURTAX—An additional tax. A tax on something already being taxed.

SURVEY—1. Determining the dimensions and elevations of a parcel of land by taking its perimeter and topographic measurements. 2. A map or plat showing the results of measuring the land with its elevations and improvements shown and its relationship to surrounding tracts of land. 3. To inspect the condition of something with regard to evaluating it.

SURVEYOR—An individual qualified and usually licensed to practice the art of land surveying.

SURVIVAL CLAUSE—A clause in a lease making a tenant, who has been evicted because of default, liable for the balance of the rent.

SURVIVORSHIP—The right one acquires as the remaining, live member of a joint ownership. (See RIGHT OF SURVIVAL.)

SUSPEND—To stop temporarily. To set aside a decision or planned course of action. Defer. Cease for the time being.

SWALE—A small, low-lying area in otherwise level terrain.

SWAMP LAND—Marsh land; land that is sometimes covered with water; moist, spongy soil. Overflowed land.

SWEAR—To make a solemn statement. To state under oath, to a supreme being, either in a court of law, before a NOTARY or other officer, that a statement or testimony is correct.

SWEAT EQUITY—Labor or services put into improving real property to gain possession and title in lieu of money. It is good and valuable consideration, the same as money.

SYNDICATE—An association of investors who undertake to successfully transact business for a limited period of time. A short-term partnership. A group of individuals who combine abilities and finances in a business venture. Similar to a joint venture.

SYSTEM—An established, orderly method of doing something. Organized procedure; order.

T

TACIT—Inferred. Implied. Not spoken. A tacit law, for example, derives its authority from common and frequently long-standing acceptance by the people, and not from judicial or legislative enactment.

TACIT MORTGAGE—A term used in Louisiana indicating that in certain instances a creditor has an automatic mortgage on the property of a debtor. Nothing written or oral need transpire to create the mortgage. It is also referred to as a legal or judicial mortgage.

TACKING—Adding on something, such as a supplement; annexing. The term is used in mortgaging in such instances as when a third mortgage holder acquires the first mortgage and unites (tacks) them to assume a senior position over the second mortgage holder.

The term is also used when an individual holding property in adverse possession sells or passes on by descent any rights he may have acquired to the property. The time spent toward creating adverse possession that passes to the new holder is called tacking. The recipient adds the time spent to that of his own.

TAIL—(See ENTAIL.)

TAKE BACK A MORTGAGE—A reference found in contracts to an owner taking back a PURCHASE MONEY MORTGAGE (a mortgage in lieu of all or part of the money) when selling property.

TAKEOUT COMMITMENT—A commitment by a lending institution to take over a short term construction loan and issue a more permanent mortgage.

TANGIBLE PROPERTY—Property that is material in form. Real or personal property that can be perceived or touched such as a house, furnishings or the land itself. The opposite of intangible or incorporeal assets, which include franchises, rents, notes, stocks, bonds, accounts receivable, etc.

TAX—As applied to real estate, it is an enforced charge imposed on persons, property or income to be used to support the state. The governing body in turn utilizes the funds in the best interest of the general public.

TAX ABATEMENT—Tax reduction. A lowering of the tax assessment.

TAXABLE INCOME—Income that is subject to government taxation. In the instance of investment real estate, taxable income is the net return a property generates after subtracting depreciation and interest paid on the mortgage.

TAXABLE VALUE—The ASSESSED VALUE of property. This evaluation usually represents only a percentage of the MARKET VALUE and is placed on the asset for purposes of taxation.

TAXATION—(See TAX.)

TAX BASE—The value assigned to property for purposes of taxation. In the case of income tax, the base is the net taxable income. For determining property tax, it is the assessment.

TAX BOOK—(See TAX ROLL.)

TAX CERTIFICATE—A certificate issued to the purchaser of tax-delinquent land prior to the delivery of a TAX DEED. If the back taxes are not paid within the time specified by law, the holder of the tax certificate becomes the owner.

TAX CLAUSE—(See TAX PARTICIPATION CLAUSE.)

TAX CONSULTANT—An expert on tax matters. In real estate, there are specialists who help individuals and private companies obtain tax reductions. Because of the complexities of tax assessments that are based on arbitrary evaluations, a tax consultant's specialized knowledge can often result in substantial savings. Their payment is sometimes based on a percentage of the reduction they obtain—no reduction, no fee.

TAX DEED—The form of deed used when land is sold for non-payment of taxes. Sometimes the Tax Certificate itself in effect becomes the deed. It is deemed to pass FEE SIMPLE title to the holder. (See TAX CERTIFICATE.)

TAX EXEMPTION—1. The elimination of tax payments for certain classifications of ownership, as for example, church properties, non-profit organizations, schools. 2. Partial tax exemptions occur in some states on homesteads and for widow's benefits.

TAX LEASE—A long-term lease given to the purchaser of tax-delinquent land, where the law prohibits an outright sale.

TAX LEVY—1. The amount of taxes to be imposed in a given district or area. 2. The formal action of a legislative body imposing a tax on a person, property or income.

TAX LIEN—An unpaid tax; a legal encumbrance placed upon real estate or chattel for nonpayment of taxes. It is a STATUTORY LIEN in favor of a governing body.

TAX PARTICIPATION CLAUSE—A clause in a lease providing for the *prorata* payment by the tenant of any increase in taxes during the term of the lease.

TAXPAYER—1. A property owner who pays taxes. 2. A one-story building, typically a store, originally so called because the revenue from it was sufficient only to pay the taxes on the property. Though still called taxpayers, stores as income-producing real estate are now often highly profitable forms of investment, bringing far greater returns to the owner than just the taxes.

TAX RECEIVER—A court-appointed or statute-designated office that receives possession of property upon default of taxes.

TAX ROLL—The official record book of the property owners of an area giving their addresses, assessed valuation and the amount of taxes to be paid. Also referred to as a tax book.

TAX SALE—A sale of property that is in default due to non-payment of taxes. (See also TAX CERTIFICATE; TAX DEED.)

TAX SEARCH—A search of the records to determine if there are any unpaid taxes on a property.

TAX SHELTER—Tax protection. (See SHELTER.)

TAX STOP—A clause in a lease that provides for the tenant to assume payment of the taxes over a certain established base. (See TAX PARTICIPATION CLAUSE.)

TAX TITLE—Title to property obtained by buying land that is up for public sale due to unpaid taxes.

TEMPORARY LOANS—(See BUILDING LOANS.)

TENANCY—1. The act of occupying property belonging to another. 2. Possession of land by any of numerous forms of title. (See specific tenancy definitions immediately following.)

TENANCY AT WILL—A tenant who is legally occupying a property but has no fixed term or lease. Also called a periodic tenancy, it is based on the express or implied permission of the owner.

TENANCY BY THE ENTIRETY (ENTIRETIES)—A joint estate equally owned by husband and wife, with the one surviving receiving the entire estate. It cannot be terminated without the consent of each party.

TENANCY IN COMMON—The condition existing when two or more individuals own property each possessing a separate, undivided interest and there being no RIGHT OF SURVIVORSHIP.

TENANCY IN PARTNERSHIP—A tenancy created when property is purchased with funds of a business partnership.

TENANCY, JOINT—(See JOINT TENANCY.)

TENANT—A party who has legal possession and use of property belonging to another. The one to whom a lease is made. The lessee.

TENANT AT SUFFERANCE—A tenant who originally lawfully occupied property but remained in possession after the tenancy had expired; a holdover tenant. A tenant at sufferance has no rights whatsoever in the premises.

TENANT BY THE CURTESY—A tenancy held for life by a husband who survives his wife and who has designated an heir or heirs; upon the death of the husband they inherit the estate.

TENANT FOR LIFE—One who possesses property for the term of his life, or during the life or lives of others.

TENANT FOR YEARS—A lease for one year or more.

TENANT FROM YEAR TO YEAR—A holdover tenant whose yearly lease has expired and who automatically remains and continues under the same terms and conditions.

TENANT IN COMMON—(See TENANCY IN COMMON.)

TENANT IN DOWER—This tenancy arises when a husband, who has himself inherited an estate, dies; the wife then receives one-third of his inherited estate for her lifetime.

TENANT IN FEE SIMPLE (TENANCY IN FEE)—A tenancy by one who holds land in absolute possession for himself and his heirs forever, with no mention of who the heirs may be. He can dispose of his interest as he elects or, in the absence of a choice, the assets are turned over to a court of law for disposition.

TENANT IN SEVERALTY—A tenancy held by one person only. No other person has any part or interest.

TENANT IN TAIL—(See ENTAIL.)

TENANT OWNERSHIP CORPORATION—(See COOPERATIVE APARTMENT OR BUILDING.)

TENDER—1. An offer, without conditions, of money or services to settle a claim. 2. Making a bid for a contract.

TENEMENT—1. An apartment house; a structure occupied as a multiple dwelling; a residence. The term's common meaning refers to older, run-down, city apartment buildings. 2. Land or corporeal and incorporeal property being held by one person though owned by another. Tenement refers to everything of a permanent nature.

TENEMENTS AND HEREDITAMENTS—(See LAND, TENEMENTS AND HEREDITAMENTS.)

TENENDUM—(Latin) That portion of a deed that is united with the HABENDUM CLAUSE, indicating that the grantee is "to have and to hold" the subject land.

TENURE—1. Legally holding and occupying real property. Tenure, in accordance with the American concept of real estate ownership, means that all rights and title of the land rest with the owner. 2. The right of occupancy or tenancy of the land.

TENURIAL OWNERSHIP—Ownership of land that is subject to fullfilment of an obligation owed to another. The word "tenurial" (from tenure) originated in feudal ages when land was held in subordination to a king or lord.

TERM—1. An established, fixed period of time. 2. A provision in an agreement. A condition in a contract that must be agreed upon by all parties before being signed. (Usually used in the plural form.)

TERMINATE—To end; to cease; close; to come to a conclusion; finish.

TERMITE CLAUSE—A clause in a contract providing that the property be free of termite infestation. In the event termites are found to exist on the property, it is often the responsibility of the seller to eliminate it before the time of title closing. A typical such clause reads:

"Seller shall furnish to the buyer prior to closing a written statement of a licensed and bonded termite company showing whether there is any active, live termite infestation on the premises. The seller shall pay all costs of the treatment and repairs required to remedy such infestation so reported."

TERM MORTGAGE—A mortgage having a stipulated duration, usually under five years, in which only interest is paid. At the expiration of the term, the entire principle amount becomes due.

TERM OF LEASE OR MORTGAGE—The duration of time that a lease or mortgage is in force.

TERRA FIRMA—Land; the earth; dry ground.

TERRE-TENANT—1. The owner of land formerly bound by a judgment lien. The party in possession and ownership of land in which there is a lien against a prior grantor. 2. The owner of land that has an existing mortgage or mortgages upon it.

TERRITORY—An established geographical area. A large expanse of land such as a country, region, district or province. The word's meaning is indefinite as to size. Puerto Rico, for example, is referred to as a territory (as was Alaska before it became a state). It can also mean a comparatively small local region or district.

TESTAMENT—A will.

TESTAMENTARY—Regarding a will.

TESTAMENTARY TRUST—A trust created by a will.

TESTATOR—The person making a will.

TESTATRIX—A female maker of a will.

TESTIMONY CLAUSE—A clause at the end of a document that reads, "In witness whereof, I hereunto set my hand and official seal at said County and State, this __ day of __, A.D. 19_."

THENCE—A connective word used in legal descriptions to denote the next direction in which a property line proceeds. From one place to another.

THIRD LOAN: THIRD MORTGAGE—A mortgage that is inferior in rank to two others.

THIRD PARTY—As applied to contracts and other instruments, a third party is someone besides the principals, such as a real estate broker or escrow agent.

THREE-QUARTER SECTION—Seventy-five percent of a section of land; 480 acres. (See SECTION; GOVERNMENT SURVEY.)

THREE-WAY EXCHANGE—A real estate exchange involving three separate properties and usually three different traders. (See EXCHANGE OF REAL ESTATE.)

THROUGH LOT—A lot having frontage on two streets. Same as a MERGED LOT.

THROW-OFF—A slang reference to the income that a property will bring.

TIDE LAND—Land between high and low tides that is covered and uncovered by the ebb and flow of the tides.

TIDEWATER LANDS—The land beneath the ocean from lowtide mark to the outer territorial limits of a country.

TIE-IN DEAL—A transaction whereby a less desirable piece of property must be bought or leased in order to obtain the desired one.

TIERCE—A third. In mortgage parlance, a third mortgage is one said to be in a tierciary position.

TILLABLE LAND—Land that can be put under cultivation; plowable land, productive land.

TILT-UP WALLS—A precast construction method utilizing sections of concrete that are brought to the site and lifted into position forming the sides.

TIME IS OF THE ESSENCE CLAUSE—The clause in a contract that places great importance on completing the terms and conditions exactly when specified. It means the specific date is an essential element of the agreement.

TITLE—As applied to real estate, title indicates lawful ownership and right to property. It is the fee position. Title to property is that BUNDLE OF RIGHTS an owner possesses.

TITLE BY ADVERSE POSSESSION—(See ADVERSE POSSESSION.)

TITLE CLOSING—(See CLOSING.)

TITLE COMPANY OR AGENCY—A company that examines the records to determine if title to property is clear. In addition, title companies offer to sell title insurance to the owner.

TITLE DEED—A deed is evidence of land ownership. As such, the document is sometimes referred to as a title deed.

TITLE EXAMINATION—(See EXAMINATION OF TITLE.)

TITLE GUARANTEE—(See TITLE INSURANCE.)

TITLE INSURANCE—1. Insuring the title to property. An insurance policy issued to the landowner indemnifying him up to a specified amount against having a defective or unmarketable title as long as he owns the property. 2. Title policies are also issued to the mortgagee as protection against loss in the event title to the mortgaged property proves defective. These are referred to as mortgage policies or loan policies.

TITLE INSURANCE BINDER—Temporary title insurance coverage in force until the formal policy is issued. This occurs at the time of title closing so the new owner is immediately covered.

TITLE I LOAN—A Federal Housing Administration (FHA) insured loan given to improve and repair residential properties. The maximum that can be borrowed under this program is $3,500.

TITLE II LOAN—This encompasses the main loan insurance program of the Federal Housing Administration (FHA). (See FEDERAL HOUSING ADMINISTRATION.)

TITLE POLICY—(See TITLE INSURANCE.)

TITLE REPORT—A report of the condition of the title to a specific piece of property after an examination of the abstract has been made.

TITLE SEARCH—An examination of the public records tracing the chain of title to a specific property to the present owner, and determining if it is clear and marketable or is in any way defective.

TITLE THEORY STATES—States in which legal emphasis is placed on protecting the lender of mortgage money should a mortgage go into default. In these states he is assumed to have some lawful title to the mortgaged property. Having a title interest, it is easier for him to recover the property should there be a default. Other states protect the borrower to a greater degree and are referred to as LIEN THEORY STATES. (See that title.)

TO HAVE AND TO HOLD CLAUSE—The clause in a deed showing the extent and quality of ownership to be conveyed. (See *HABENDUM* CLAUSE, *TENENDUM*.)

TONNAGE RENT—A rental based on the tons of ore, coal, sand, soil, gravel, crops or other natural or produced resources removed from the land.

TOPO—An abbreviation of TOPOGRAPHY.

TOPOGRAPHIC MAP—A surveyor's map of land areas showing its elevations by means of contour lines. It is also called a relief or CONTOUR MAP.

TOPOGRAPHY—The variations in elevations of the earth's surface.

TOPPING-OFF—A builder's reference to the highest point of construction. It means the reaching of a significant stage of the project and is marked for all to see by nailing a tree branch to the topmost point.

TORRENS CERTIFICATE—A certificate of title issued to a landowner in those states or countries that have adopted the TORRENS TITLE SYSTEM.

TORRENS TITLE SYSTEM—A system of title registration, in use in several states and throughout many parts of the world, to modernize and speed up the process of title searches and proof of ownership to land. Named for its founder, Sir Robert Torrens, it is explained by him as follows:

> "The person or persons in whom single or collectively the fee simple is vested, either in law or in equity, may apply to have the land placed on the register of titles. The applications are submitted for examination to a barrister and to a conveyancer, who are styled 'examiners of titles.' These gentlemen report to the register: First: Whether the description of land is definite and clear. Second: Is the applicant in undisputed possession of the property? Third: Does he appear in equity and justice rightfully titled thereto? Fourth: Does he produce such evidence of title as leads to the conclusion that no other person is in position to succeed against him in an action for ejectment?"

TORT—A civil wrong. A wrongful act, other than by breach of contract, committed against a person or his property for which a remedy can be sought in a court of law.

TOTAL EVICTION—Physical removal from the premises and all rights to it; actual eviction. (See EVICTION.)

TO WIT—Namely; that is to say; as follows. It is sometimes abbreviated as "SS."

TOWN—A moderately populated community generally smaller than a city and larger than a village, hamlet or settlement.

TOWNHOUSE—1. Literally a house in town. The term originated as the city residence of one whose main house was in the country. A typical townhouse today is a two-story attached dwelling. 2. A type of apartment unit having two floors, typically with the living area and kitchen on the ground floor and the bedrooms located on the second level.

TOWNSHIP—1. A town. A geographical area having its own local government. Often abbreviated, in legal descriptions, "Tp." or "T." 2. As used in the Government Survey of public lands, a township is 6 miles square, containing 36 sections

Township

6	5	4	3	2	1
7	8	9	10	11	12
18	17	16	15	14	13
19	20	21	22	23	24
30	29	28	27	26	35
31	32	33	34	35	36

each 1 mile square and consisting of 23,040 acres. Sections are numbered beginning with "1" in the upper right hand corner and proceeding numerically to the left across the top of the township. Thence crossing back and forth until the last (36th) section at the bottom right corner of the township. It should be noted that townships occasionally are irregular and can be larger or smaller than the standard 36 sections. This occurs when they abut bodies of water or when corrections were made to allow for the earth's curvature. (See GOVERNMENT SURVEY.)

TRACT—A parcel of land of undefined size. A tract usually infers acreage and therefore denotes a larger area. A single body of land legally described in one deed.

TRACT BOOK—(See PLAT BOOK.)

TRACT HOUSE—A house in a development.

TRACT SUBDIVISION—(See SUBDIVISION.)

TRADE—(See EXCHANGE OF REAL ESTATE.)

TRADE-IN PLAN—A plan by which a broker or builder guarantees to purchase the real estate of a customer who is buying another property from him. (See EXCHANGE OF REAL ESTATE.)

TRADE NAME—An adopted name of a business firm, to distinguish and identify it from others. The name by which the public knows the company.

TRADER—1. One who deals in real estate exchanges. 2. The agent who brings about a real estate trade. Exchanger.

TRAILER PARK—A tract of land zoned for trailer homesites. Facilities such as paved streets and sidewalks, electricity, water, gas lines, septic tanks, laundry, recreation facilities, shopping, etc. are made available to the residents. It is also called a mobile home park.

TRANSFER CLAUSE—A clause in a lease that cancels the agreement upon the lessee receiving a job transfer. A typically worded transfer clause reads:

> In the event the lessee is transferred to an area beyond 50 miles of this city, the lessor will allow the lessee to cancel the lease if the following conditions are met: 1. The lessor is given 30 days prior written notice of such a transfer. 2. The lessor is given proof that such a transfer is being made by lessor's employer. 3. The lessee's rent is current and no rent is past due.

TRANSFER FEE—A charge made by a lending institution holding a mortgage on real estate to change their records indicating a different owner.

TRANSFER OF TITLE—The change in the title to property from one owner to another. (See CLOSE; CLOSING OF TITLE.)

TRANSFER TAX—A tax levied on the transfer of property in an estate or a valuable interest to the heirs. An inheritance tax. It is also a tax on certain assets such as stocks, bonds, etc. when given by a living person to another.

TRANSPORTED SOIL—Soil materials that have been transported to their present location by the forces of nature, such as by winds, floods, tides, glacial movements, etc.

TREASURER'S SALE—A sale made for unpaid taxes. It is more commonly referred to as a tax sale.

TRESPASS—The unauthorized, unlawful entry upon the property of another.

TRIBAL LANDS—Indian reservation lands belonging to the various tribes of the area.

TRI-LEVEL HOUSE—A split-level home having three floor elevations off the main floor. (See SPLIT-LEVEL HOMES.)

TRIPLE-A TENANT—(See AAA TENANT.)

TRIPLEX—A three-unit apartment building or other dwelling in which three families reside.

TRUE VALUE—Actual value. Market value. The price a property will bring under normal conditions when on the market for a reasonable period of time.

TRUSS—A building's open structural member, made of wood or metal framework, for the support of a floor, roof, wall or other portion of the structure.

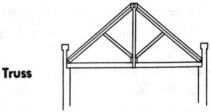

Truss

TRUST—A position of responsibility given to one to act in the best interests of another. A trust can be either expressed or implied. It is a right that is enforceable in a court of equity. (See BUSINESS TRUST, *CESTUI QUE* TRUST, TRUST ACCOUNT, PUBLIC TRUST.)

TRUST ACCOUNT—(See ESCROW ACCOUNT.)

TRUST AND CONFIDENCE—A term indicating a fiduciary relationship. (See FIDUCIARY.)

TRUST DEED or TRUST DEED MORTGAGE—(See DEED OF TRUST.)

TRUSTEE—1. A party who legally holds property in trust for others. 2. One placed in a position of responsibility.

TRUSTEE IN BANKRUPTCY—An individual, appointed by the court, who is entrusted with handling the assets of a party in bankruptcy.

TRUST ESTATE—An estate that is being held in trust by one person for the benefit of another.

TRUST FUND—A fund set up by one party for the benefit of another. An escrow account.

TRUST INDENTURE—The document that serves as evidence of a trust agreement. (See DEED OF TRUST.)

TRUST IN REAL ESTATE—(See REAL ESTATE INVESTMENT TRUST.)

TRUSTOR—The originator or creator of a trust.

TURN-KEY JOB—A building term indicating a complete construction job, from groundbreaking to the final turning over of the key after the last structural detail is completed; the implication being that nothing else need be done but turn the key and move in.

TURNOVER—1. As applied to real estate, it is the frequency with which a given property or an entire area is sold and resold. 2. In regard to leasing, it refers to the average length of occupancy of the tenants.

TURPITUDE—A vile act. Baseness. Contrary to good moral principles.

TWO-FAMILY HOUSE—(See DUPLEX.)

TWO-STORY—Any structure having two floors of approximately standard height.

U

U.C.C.—Abbreviation for UNIFORM COMMERCIAL CODE. (See that definition.)

ULTIMATUM—The ultimate, final statement of one's terms and position. The word implies serious consequences will ensue if the provisions are not met.

ULTRA VIRES—(Latin) Beyond its powers. A corporation's powers, for example, are limited to those given it by law and what is implied. When a corporate act exceeds such powers, it is said to be performing *ultra vires*. As a rule such actions are voidable. Those dealing with a corporation should know the general powers of the corporation in the jurisdiction in which it acts, or where a contract is made. If a corporation acts beyond its powers, its stockholders may, by injunction, prevent the action from occurring. As a remedy, a corporation may lose its charter for acts *ultra vires*.

UNACCRUED—Without periodic accumulation; not developing or continuing to grow. Not becoming due.

UNBALANCED IMPROVEMENT—An improvement to land that does not represent its highest and best use. When a property is not put to its most logical, productive or esthetic use, whether it be over or under developed, it is said to be an unbalanced improvement.

UNDER AND SUBJECT—A term sometimes used in contracts and deeds when the buyer obtains the property *subject to* a mortgage. It does not make him personally liable, as would occur if he obtained it *assuming* a mortgage.

UNDER COLOR OF TITLE—(See COLOR OF TITLE.)

UNDERIMPROVED LAND—1. Land needing further development in order to realize its highest and best use. 2. Land that has improvements upon it that prevent its being utilized to its highest and best use. For example, a one-family house situated on a valuable commercial parcel.

UNDER-IMPROVEMENT—An improvement to property that is not sufficiently extensive for the purpose intended or for the needs of a given community. As an example, an area where a housing shortage exists is under-improved in this type of real estate. The opposite of OVER-IMPROVEMENT.

UNDER LEASE: UNDERLYING LEASE—A lease of property, by a tenant to a third party; a SUBLEASE.

UNDERLESSEE—(See UNDERTENANT.)

UNDERLYING MORTGAGE—A mortgage that is senior to a larger one, such as a building with a first mortgage of $50,000 and a second of $100,000.

UNDERSIGNED—The parties who sign their names to a document. The signatories.

UNDERTENANT—(See SUBTENANT.)

UNDERWRITE—Insure something against loss, thus assuming liability for its payment. To financially guarantee.

UNDERWRITER—1. An expert who evaluates insurance policies that have been solicited and accepts or rejects insurance risks. 2. One who guarantees the sale of a security issue with the intention of distributing it to the public.

UNDISCLOSED PRINCIPAL—When one of the parties to a transaction is not made known. This might occur when a broker is instructed to keep the identity of his client or prospect secret, or when one of the principals has a dummy act in his behalf.

UNDIVIDED RIGHT—A right that a party owner in property has that cannot be separated from the rights of the other owners. This undivided interest occurs with tenants in common and joint tenants.

UNDUE INFLUENCE—The exerting of excessive pressure upon a person. When a contract, deed, will or any other legal instrument results from such pressure, a court of equity can declare it void.

UNDULATING LAND—Gently sloped terrain. Land having gradual rises and dips. Land with elevation changes of 3 percent to 8 percent.

UNEARNED INCREMENT—An increase in property value that came about because of outside factors and not necessarily through any knowledgeable acts of the owner. It is often due to an increase in population, normal economic growth and real estate appreciation that follows. When value increases through an owner's skill and efforts it is called EARNED INCREMENT. (See that title.)

UNENCUMBERED PROPERTY—Property free and clar of mortgages, liens and assessments of any kind.

UNETHICAL—Lacking in moral principles. Not conforming to an accepted, honorable and fair manner of conduct.

UNGRADED LEASE—(See FLAT LEASE.)

UNIFORM BUILDING CODE—-Published by the International Conference of Building Officials, this model code has been adopted by more than 1,000 municipalities throughout the United States and abroad. The organization annually publishes texts and conducts courses of study for its members. The construction industry recognizes this code as one of, if not, the most comprehensive and influential in existence. (See NATIONAL BUILDING CODE.)

UNIFORM COMMERCIAL CODE—A federal act that has the following underlying purposes and policies:

(a) to simplify, clarify and modernize the law governing commercial transactions;
(b) to permit the continued expansion of commercial practices through custom, usage and agreement of the parties;
(c) to make uniform the law among the various jurisdictions.

According to the official text of the Uniform Commercial Code (as prepared by the National Conference of Commissioners on Uniform State Laws and The American Law Institute) this comprehensive, wide-ranging act covers sale transactions, commercial paper, bank deposits and collections, letters of credit, bulk transfers, documents of title, investment securities and secured transactions. The UCC greatly influences business throughout the country by bringing uniformity and clarity to state laws governing commerce.

UNILATERAL CONTRACT—A contract in which only one party expressly agrees to something. Unlike a fully executed (bilateral) contract, just one principal is bound by the terms of the agreement. As an example, a contract that has been signed by the purchaser but not as yet by the seller. It can be recalled and declared void at any time prior to its becoming a bilateral agreement.

UNILATERAL LISTING AGREEMENT—An open listing. A listing that does not obligate a broker to advertise, promote or in any way attempt to sell the property. The owner, on the other hand, is responsible for paying a commission, if a sale is effected through the broker's efforts.

UNIMPROVED LAND—Land without buildings or other man-made improvements. Raw, uncleared land. Land in its natural state. Also, land once improved but later abandoned and left to the ravages of the elements.

UNINSURABLE TITLE—Property that a title insurance company will not insure. It may or may not be good title, but the risk against claims of ownership by others renders it uninsurable as it stands.

UNIT—1. Any single portion of something larger. 2. A word which, when used as plural, refers to the number of apartments or offices in a building, or the number of rooms in a motel or hotel.

UNITY—As applied to a joint tenancy, each principal is said to have the same extent of an estate comprising unity of interest, unity of possession, unity of title and unity of time.

UNIVERSAL AGENT—A party designated by another to legally act in his behalf.

UNIVERSAL LEGACY—A legacy in which the entire property of the testator is given to one or more persons.

UNMARKETABLE TITLE—Title that is not necessarily bad, but one in which sufficient doubt as to its validity may be found, which renders it unsalable until it is cured.

UNPAID RENT NOTICE—(See NOTICE OF UNPAID RENT.)

UNRECORDED INSTRUMENT—Any document that has not been publicly recorded.

UNRECORDED PLAT—A land survey that has not been made a part of the public record.

UNSEATED LAND—Privately owned land that is left in its natural state. Unimproved, unoccupied, virgin land. The opposite of SEATED LAND. (The term originated, and is used almost exclusively, in Pennsylvania).

UPLAND—A region having a high elevation, in comparison to the surrounding countryside.

UP-RENT POTENTIAL—The amount that rentals can reasonably be expected to increase in the predictable future due to expanding economic conditions or other factors.

UPSET DATE—A date stipulated in a contract when a building must be ready for occupancy or the buyer has the option to rescind the contract.

UPSET PRICE—The price at which bidding begins at an auction sale. One which represents the lowest price the seller will accept.

URBAN—Pertaining to the metropolitan area and its immediate environs.

URBAN HOMESTEAD—(See HOMESTEAD.)

URBAN RENEWAL—The acquisition of slum or run-down city areas for purposes of redevelopment. Federal, state and local governments are working cooperatively to eliminate blighted sections throughout some of our most heavily populated communities. The Department of Housing and Urban Development (HUD) has instituted programs of redevelopment in certain major cities throughout the country to clear and replace slum areas with low-rent, public housing. It is called the Model Cities program. (See DEPARTMENT OF HOUSING AND URBAN DEVELOPMENT (HUD) SLUM CLEARANCE.)

USABLE FLOOR AREA—The portions of a building that can be utilized. (See RENTABLE AREA.)

USABLE INCOME—Cash flow. Spendable income. The money that can be taken from an asset after all financial obligations are met.

USE DENSITY—1. The amount of land that can be built upon in a given parcel. 2. The ratio of allowable square footage of floor space to land area.

U.S. DEPARTMENT OF HOUSING AND URBAN DEVELOPMENT (HUD)—(See DEPARTMENT OF HOUSING AND URBAN DEVELOPMENT (HUD).)

USEFUL LIFE—A property's life as long as it proves of utility to the owner. (See DEPRECIATION; ECONOMIC LIFE.)

USE VALUE—An evaluation of property that takes into consideration a structure's specific purpose. Because of the design, a building may have limited or no value for other purposes. Appraisers refer to this as "value-in-use," and evaluate it for present usefulness, though its actual MARKET VALUE may be entirely different. (See also SPECIAL PURPOSE PROPERTIES.)

U.S. FEDERAL HOUSING AUTHORITY—(See FEDERAL HOUSING AUTHORITY.)

U.S. GOVERNMENT BUREAU OF LAND MANAGEMENT—(See BUREAU OF LAND MANAGEMENT.)

U.S. GOVERNMENT PUBLIC LAND DESCRIPTION—(See GOVERNMENT SURVEY.)

U.S. GOVERNMENT SURVEY—(See GOVERNMENT SURVEY.)

USUFRUCTUARY RIGHT—The right to reasonable use and enjoyment of property though one does not own it.

USURY—The charging of excessively high or unlawful interest rates for the use of money.

U.S. VETERANS ADMINISTRATION—(See VETERANS ADMINISTRATION.)

UTILITY—1. The usefulness of a property; its ability to satisfactorily function for its intended purpose. 2. A government-franchised, privately owned company serving the general public. Any public service such as water, electricity, telephone, gas. (See PUBLIC UTILITY.)

UTILITY BUILDING—An outbuilding, usually small, used to store tools and supplies.

UTILITY EASEMENT—A right-of-way easement granted to utility companies for the use of another's land. Telephone poles, electric lines, sewer and gas mains on and under private property, are examples of utility easements.

UTILITY ROOM—A handy room designed to house laundry machines, heating and air conditioning units, storage, tools, or other equipment.

UXOR—(Latin) Wife. (See *ET UXOR*.)

V

VA—(See VETERANS ADMINISTRATION.)

VACANCY FACTOR—The percentage of a building's unrented space during a given period. It is sometimes figured as the gross income that a building loses due to vacancies. In estimating rental income, the vacancy factor is deducted from the gross rental when at capacity.

VACANT LAND—Land without buildings or other improvements; land in its natural state. Unimproved or uninhabited property.

VACANT LOT LISTING FORM—A form for listing unimproved lots. (See page 406.)

VACATE—To give up occupancy; to make vacant; move out of a premises.

VACATED STREET—A street that has been officially abandoned by a public agency. Normally, dedicated streets revert one half to each abutting owner.

VADIUM—(Latin) A pledge of property as security.

VADIUM MORTUUM—(Latin). A pledge by a mortgagor which grants the lender the right to FEE SIMPLE ownership if the mortgage goes into default.

VALID—Legally in force; binding by law; sound; authoritative.

VALLEY—1. A low land area situated between elevated ground such as a hill or mountain. 2. The depression formed by the juncture of the sides of sloping roofs.

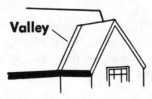

VA LOAN—(See G.I. LOAN.)

VALUABLE CONSIDERATION—(See CONSIDERATION.)

VALUABLE IMPROVEMENTS—Additions made to real estate that enhance its worth. The term refers to improvements of a more permanent nature. (See IMPROVEMENTS.)

VALUATION—A term synonymous with appraising. An opinion of an asset's worth; the act of setting a value; evaluation.

VALUATOR—An APPRAISER. One skilled in the art of evaluating property. An estimator of value.

VALUE—The worth of one thing in comparison with another. The market value. Something desirable and therefore having worth. Usefulness; importance.

VALUE IN USE—A reference to the value of a building that is designed for a specific purpose. (See SPECIAL PURPOSE PROPERTIES; USE VALUE.)

VARA—A Spanish unit of measure varying in length from 32.993 inches to 33.87 inches.

VARIABLE INTEREST RATE—An interest rate that increases or decreases with the mortgage market. Instead of the interest on a loan being fixed as of the time of issuance, a variable rate mortgage is subject to periodic examination by the lending institution and is raised or lowered in accordance with availability of funds and the mortgage market in the area. (See FLOATING INTEREST RATE.)

VARIANCE—As applied to real estate, it is a special request to do something with property which is an exception to the existing zoning laws. A change from that which is in existence.

VEND—To sell.

VENDEE—A buyer; purchaser. In a contract he is usually called the party of the second part.

VENDEE'S LIEN—A vendee may become a lien holder when the seller defaults on the contract. The lien is for the return of his deposit money and sometimes for additional sums spent on the property in anticipation of ownership.

VENDIBLE—Able to be sold. Merchantable.

VENDOR—A seller. In a contract he is usually referred to as the party of the first part.

VENDOR'S LIEN—When all or a portion of the purchase price is not paid, the amount still due the seller at closing constitutes a vendor's lien. The lien is automatically discharged upon paying the sum due and transferring title. Also called Grantor's Lien.

VENDUE—1. An auction sale. 2. A sale made under the authority of law for back taxes, to settle an estate, to satisfy creditors, etc.

VENEER—A thin surface layer of wood, plastic or other material applied for beauty and finish, covering an unfinished, undersurface material.

VENTURE—A speculative business undertaking. (See JOINT VENTURE.)

VENTURE CAPITAL—Risk capital. Money invested that is unsecured. Because of the risks involved it usually offers the highest percentage of return for the investment.

VERBAL CONTRACT—An oral contract.

VERIFICATION—The act of verifying or confirming something. A sworn statement attesting to the correctness of a document. Substantiation.

VESTED—Placed in possession and control. Given or committed to another. Authorized, fixed, absolute, as a VESTED ESTATE, VESTED INTEREST, VESTED REMAINDER, VESTED RIGHT, etc.

VESTED ESTATE—An interest in an estate carrying present and future legal rights, but with the existing interest able to be transferred to another.

VESTED INTEREST—An interest in which there is an established right or title, both present and future, to an asset. One holding a vested interest possesses an existing right to transfer property from one person to another. Also referred to as VESTED ESTATE.

VESTED REMAINDER—A current interest in an estate that passes on to another for that party's future use and enjoyment.

VESTED RIGHT—A person's immediate, fixed legal right that cannot be taken from him without his consent.

VESTIBULE—An ante-room or passage hall located inside the front door and leading to other rooms in a building. A small lobby.

VESTURE OF LAND—A term referring to all the vegetation and plant growth that covers the surface of land.

VETERANS ADMINISTRATION (VA)—An agency of the federal government organized in 1930 to administer the laws that were enacted for veterans and their dependents or beneficiaries. The VA's function in real estate is to guarantee mortage loans made by lending institutions to veterans. (See G. I. LOAN.)

VETERANS ADMINISTRATION LOAN—(See G. I. LOAN.)

VIA—(Latin) Way. A right of way. Road. In civil law, the right to traverse another's land.

VICINAGE—Vicinity. Neighborhood. A region within an area.

VIDELICET—(Latin). To wit, that is to say, namely. Usually abbreviated "Viz."

VIRGATA—An old English word meaning a quarter (¼) acre.

VIRGIN LAND—Vacant land that has not been farmed or used in any way. Untouched land in its natural state; unimproved property. An uncut forest.

VIRGIN LEASE—The first lease. Not a sublease.

VISIBLE AMENITIES—The visual, apparent attractiveness, pleasantness and desirability that a property possesses. Its outward appearance. (See also AMENITIES; HIDDEN AMENITIES.)

VISUAL RIGHTS—1. The right to restrict billboard signs where they obstruct a scenic view. 2. The right to prevent a structure from being built where it could interfere with clear vision at intersections or other points along a public way.

VIZ—(Latin) An abbreviation of *videlicet* meaning to wit, that is to say, namely.

VOID—Nullify; of no legal significance, force or effect. Not binding. Worthless in a court of law. A contract so adjudged cannot be enforced and has no effect whatsoever.

VOIDABLE—Able to be nullified.

VOLUNTARY ALIENATION—The normal transfer of interest and title when real estate changes ownership, such as when an owner, of his own free will, sells and relinquishes his rights, title and interest for an agreed upon consideration. The opposite of involuntary alienation.

VOLUNTARY CONVEYANCE—A voluntary transfer of an owner's rights and title to property conveyed to the lien holder, generally to avoid the legal entanglement of a deficiency judgment. It occurs without the transfer of a valuable consideration.

VOLUNTARY DEED—(See VOLUNTARY CONVEYANCE.)

VOUCHER—A stamped receipt or signed document serving as proof that a debt has been paid, or the terms of a transaction met.

VS—An abbreviation for *versus*. Against, as in legal proceedings (Jones vs Smith).

W

WAINSCOT—The lower portion of an inside wall made of other material than that of the upper. For example, the tiled half of a bathroom, or the partial wood-paneling of the wall surface in a den.

WAIVER—1. To relinquish or abandon a claim or right of one's free will. 2. A written instrument stating what is being voluntarily relinquished.

WAIVER OF DEFENSES—(See CERTIFICATE OF NO DEFENSE.)

WALK-UP—A building of any kind consisting of two or more stories that does not have an elevator.

WALL—1. The upright exterior sides of a building as well as the vertical portions partitioning the interior. 2. A fence of masonry or other material used to enclose property. (See also PARTY WALL.)

WALL BEARING—A wall that helps carry the weight of the structure itself. A supporting wall.

WANT OF CONSIDERATION—1. A promise to give something of value that was never performed. A bargained for and agreed upon, valuable consideration that was not fulfilled. 2. Transactions in which no consideration was intended.

WAREHOUSE—A storehouse. A building where merchandise or other materials are kept under the protective cover of a roof.

WARRANT—To promise, represent as a fact or to guarantee something; to assure. A warranty may be expressed, as in oral agreements or implied statements, when written into a contract.

WARRANTIES OF TITLE—(See WARRANTY DEED.)

WARRANTY DEED—A deed in which the grantor guarantees that he is giving the grantee and his heirs good title free of encumbrances. It is recognized as the highest form of deed, as the grantor agrees to defend the title and possession against all claims. Also called a full covenant or general warranty deed.

WASTE LAND—Unproductive, uncultivated, unimproved, barren land. Deserts, remote mountainous regions and swamp lands are classified as waste lands until some useful purpose can be found for them.

WASTING PROPERTY—Diminishing property. In real estate, the depletion of oil, gas or coal from the land are examples, as is the cutting of timber. However, timber land need not be considered wasting property if an adequate program of reforestation is instituted.

WATERCOURSE—The path through which water flows, whether natural or man-made.

WATERFRONT PROPERTY—Any land that has frontage on an ocean, river, lake, canal or other watercourse.

WATER LEVEL—(See WATER TABLE.)

WATER LINE EASEMENT—An easement permitting a waterline through one's property.

WATERPOWER RIGHTS—The rights to utilize or channel water on one's property for purposes of creating power.

WATER RIGHTS—The rights a land owner has in the use of a body of water that abuts or lies near his property. (See also RIPARIAN RIGHTS, LITTORAL RIGHTS.)

WATERSHED—Waterparting. A land elevation separating the waters flowing into two river basins. A narrow ridge between drainage areas.

WATER TABLE—The level, above or below the surface of the ground, at which water will be found.

WAY, RIGHT OF—(See RIGHT OF WAY.)

WEAR AND TEAR—The depreciation of an asset due to ordinary use.

WEST—A directional description that is due west; the direction where the sun sets; 270 degrees on a compass. Toward the west. Opposite to east. One of the four cardinal points of the compass.

WETLAND—Marshland. Land containing a large percentage of water in the soil. Swampland; a bog; or quagmire.

WHEELER-DEALER—A speculator who rapidly buys and sells properties. A knowledgeable investor always seeking fast, profitable deals.

WHITE ACRE—(See BLACK ACRE AND WHITE ACRE.)

WHITE ELEPHANT—Property difficult to dispose of.

WIFE'S EQUITY—A wife's vested interest in her husband's estate.

WIFE'S SEPARATE PROPERTY—Property owned by a wife in her own name, as distinguished from that which she holds with her husband. (See also FREE-DEALER.)

WILD LAND—Wilderness. (See VIRGIN LAND.)

WILL—A person's written legal declaration of how he directs his estate to be disposed of after death.

WILLING—Consenting of one's own free choice and without reluctance. (See READY, WILLING AND ABLE.)

WINDFALL—A fortunate occurrence that comes about through no particular wisdom, foresight or effort of the recipient. (See also UNEARNED INCREMENT.)

WIRE FATE—(See FATE.)

WIT—(See TO WIT.)

WITH PREJUDICE—In law, when an adverse decision is made "with prejudice," it means that the court has issued a final decision and no further appeal to that court will be heard, nor will the opinion rendered be altered. The judge's decision is final.

WITHOUT PREJUDICE—In law, when a decision is handed down "without prejudice," it means that an individual's right to amend his appeal or seek a different verdict has not been jeopardized.

WITHOUT RECOURSE—This term is most frequently found in endorsements of negotiable instruments, and means that the endorser does not assume responsibility or liability for its collection.

WITH RIGHT OF SURVIVORSHIP—(See RIGHT OF SURVIVORSHIP.)

WITNESS—1. To add one's name to a document to verify the fact that the principal has signed it. 2. To attest; give evidence; the one who saw something occur. A party giving testimony.

WITNESS CORNER—An identification mark such as a MONUMENT that indicates a change in direction of a property line. A surveyor's mark showing a corner point.

WOOD FRAME CONSTRUCTION—The frame of a structure that is made of wood, usually including the studs, walls, roof line and floors.

WOODLAND—Forest; land covered with trees. A wooded parcel.

WORKING CAPITAL—Usable capital. The excess of assets over liabilities of a business that can be readily converted into cash.

WORKING DRAWING—A mechanical drawing, usually in blueprint or whiteprint form, giving detailed dimensions and instructions for a construction job.

WORTH—The value of property. What something is equal to in money, goods or services.

WRAP-AROUND MORTGAGE—A refinancing technique in which the lender assumes payment of the existing mortgage and gives a new, increased mortgage to the borrower at a higher interest rate. As defined by its name, the new mortgage "wraps around" the original one. This method of refinancing was first introduced in Canada in the late 1930's. When the trend in the mortgage market is toward rising interest rates and appreciating property values, wrap-around mortgaging invariably gains increased acceptance.

WRIT—A court order, under seal, directing a person or group to do or refrain from doing something.

WRIT OF *CERTIORARI*—(See *CERTIORARI*.)

WRIT OF ENTRY—A legal action to regain possession of property once a party has been dispossessed.

WRIT OF EXECUTION—A court order directing a duly appointed officer to implement a decision of the court; as for example, when a sheriff is directed to dispossess a tenant.

WRIT OF MANDAMUS—A court order directing that a specific thing be done. It is the result of an original proceeding to enforce a legal right.

WRITTEN CONTRACT—A contract in writing. (See CONTRACT.)

WRITTEN INSTRUMENT—A document reduced to writing that serves as evidence, or is proof of an agreement. A formal expression.

X

X—In signing legal documents, individuals who cannot write should affix an "X" where the signature would ordinarily go. A witness writes the person's name around the mark as follows:

$$\text{Robert } \overset{\text{his}}{(\mathsf{X})} \underset{\text{mark}}{\text{ Jones}}$$

X—A jargon expression for an EXCLUSIVE LISTING.

X-BRACING—Cross-member bracing used between underflooring joists, columns, partitions, etc.

Y

YARD—1. A parcel of land, usually fenced, that surrounds a building. Also, an enclosed vacant plot of land used for storing materials or for parking vehicles. 2. A unit of measure 3 feet long.

YEARLY TENANCY—A lease for one year. Upon completion of the initial year, and in the absence of a new lease, the tenancy automatically continues from year to year, unless notice is given by either party to the contrary.

YIELD—1. What an investment or property will return; the profit or income. The money derived from any given business venture. Expressed in formula as follows:

$$\text{YIELD} = \frac{\text{Annual Net Income, Interest or Dividends}}{\text{Cost or Market Value}}$$

2. To turn over or surrender possession.

YIELDING AND PAYING—Part of the phraseology used in leases where the amount of the rent is set forth and reserved.

Z

ZANGERLE CURVE—A generally obsolete formula for appraising corner lot, commercial properties. It takes into consideration a corner lot's side-street depth and assigns a percentage to be added to the overall value. Professional appraisers and assessors agree that it has little validity in today's real estate market.

ZONE—A region or district set off from other areas.

ZONE CONDEMNATION—When entire areas are marked for demolition and clearance to make way for new construction. Slum clearance projects are the most notable examples of zone condemnation.

ZONING—The division of an area into separate districts reserved for different real property usages such as business, residential, light, medium or heavy industry, etc., as well as regulating the type and density of the improvements upon it.

ZONING APPEALS BOARD—A quasi-judicial committee or board formed to hear parties appealing zoning decisions or asking for variances in existing regulations.

ZONING BOARD OR COMMISSION—A board authorized by a local government to prepare and promulgate zoning rules and regulations and to effect changes in them according to statutory requirements.

ZONING MAP—A map of a community showing existing zoning and land use regulations.

ZONING ORDINANCES—The acts of an authorized local government establishing building codes and setting forth regulations for proper land usage.

ZONING REGULATIONS—(See ZONING ORDINANCES.)

ZONING RESTRICTIONS—(See ZONING ORDINANCES.)

ZONING VARIANCE—(See VARIANCE.)

Portfolio
of
Forms

PORTFOLIO OF FORMS

ACKNOWLEDGMENT
(General)

State of _____, County of _____, ss.

I HEREBY CERTIFY, that on this day, before me an officer duly authorized in the State aforesaid and in the County aforesaid to take acknowledgments, personally appeared _____, to me known to be the person described in and who executed the foregoing instrument and _____ ACKNOWLEDGED before me that __ he executed the same.

WITNESS my hand and official seal in the County and State last aforesaid this _____ day of _____ A.D., 19__.

_____
Notary Public
My Commission expires _____

(NOTARY SEAL)

ACKNOWLEDGMENT
(Of a Corporation)

State of _____, County of _____, ss. On the _____ day of _____, 19__, before me personally came _____ to me known, who being by me duly sworn, did depose and say that __ he is _____ of _____, the corporation described in, and which executed the above instrument; that __ he knows the seal of the said corporation; that the seal affixed to said instrument is such corporation seal; that it was so affixed by order of the Board of Directors of said corporation, and that __ he signed his (her) name thereto by like order.

_____
Notary Public
My Commission expires _____

(NOTARY SEAL)

FORM C

ACREAGE

NO. OF ACRES_____   PRICE PER ACRE $_____

SIZE_____X_____   TOTAL PRICE $_____

ZONED_____   DOWN PAY. $_____

LOCATION_____

LEGAL DESCRIPTION_____ SEC_____T_____R_____

N

W   E

S

FIRST MORTGAGE $_____HELD BY_____

PAYABLE $_____INTEREST_____%

SECOND MORTGAGE $_____HELD BY_____

PAYABLE $_____INTEREST_____%

ELEVATION_____TAXES $_____PAVED ROAD_____

_____INCOME $_____
GROVE. PINE. SCARIFIED. ETC.

EXISTING BUILDING_____

_____

OWNER_____   LISTED BY_____

ADDRESS_____   DATE LISTED_____

TELEPHONE_____   EXCLUSIVE_____

APPROVED BY_____
(OWNER)

Acreage Listing Form

General Affidavit

State of Florida
County of   }

     Before the undersigned, an officer duly commissioned by the laws of Florida, on this

day of   *19*   *personally appeared*

who having been first duly sworn depose   and say   :

Sworn to and subscribed before me this   *day of*   *. A.D. 19*

(SEAL)

_____

_____

Affidavit (General)

Standard N. Y. B. T. U. Form 8051 • 8-65-10M— Affidavit of Title

Affidavit of Title

State of New York ⎰ *ss.:*
County of ⎱

Title No.............

I reside at No.

I am the *

owner in fee simple of premises

and

Register's Office of

.... the grantee .... described in a certain deed of said premises recorded in the .... County in Liber .... of Conveyances, page .

Said premises have been in my possession since 19 ; that my possession thereof has been peaceable and undisturbed, and the title thereto has never been disputed, questioned or rejected, nor insurance thereof refused, as far as I know. I know of no facts by reason of which said possession or title might be called in question, or by reason of which any claim to any part of said premises or any interest therein adverse to me might be set up. There are no federal tax claims or liens assessed or filed against me . There are no judgments against me unpaid or unsatisfied of record entered in any court of this state, or of the United States, and said premises are, as far as I know, free from all leases, mortgages, taxes, assessments, water charges, sewer rents and other liens and encumbrances, except

Said premises are now occupied by

No proceedings in bankruptcy have ever been instituted by or against me in any court or before any officer of any state, or of the United States, nor have I at any time made an assignment for the benefit of creditors, nor an assignment, now in effect, of the rents of said premises or any part thereof.

.... , being duly sworn, says:

*If owner is a corporation, fill in office held by deponent and name of corporation.

260

*I am a citizen of the United States, and am more than 21 years old. I am by occupation   who is   . I am married to   over the age of 21 years and is competent to convey or mortgage real estate. I was married to her on the   day of   19   . I have never been married to any other person now living. I have not been known by any other name during the past ten years.

*That the charter of said corporation is in full force and effect and no proceeding is pending for its dissolution or annulment. That all license and franchise taxes due and payable by said corporation have been paid in full.

There are no actions pending affecting said premises. That no repairs, alterations or improvements have been made to said premises which have not been completed more than four months prior to the date hereof. There are no facts known to me relating to the title to said premises which have not been set forth in this affidavit.

This affidavit is made to induce   of   said premises, and to induce The Title Guarantee to accept a   on   premises numbered above covering said premises knowing that they will Company to issue its policy of title insurance rely on the statements herein made.

Sworn to before me this

day of   , 19

_____

Consult Your Lawyer Before Signing This Instrument—This Instrument Should Be Used By Lawyers Only.

Affidavit of Title

(Reproduced with permission of New York Board of Title Underwriters)

261

Agreement for Deed

This Agreement, *Made this* _____ *day of* _____, *A. D. 19* ____.

by and between _____

of _____, *County,* _____, *hereinafter called Sellers, and* _____

_____, *hereinafter called Buyers, witnesseth:*

That if the said Buyers shall first make the payments and perform the covenants hereinafter mentioned on their part to be performed, the said Sellers hereby covenant and agree to convey and assure to the Buyers or their heirs or assigns, in fee simple, clear of all incumbrances whatever, by good and sufficient Warranty Deed of conveyance, the lot ____, piece ____, or parcel ____ of ground situated in the County of _____

_____ and State of _____, known and described as follows, to-wit:

And the Buyers hereby covenant and agree to pay to the Sellers the sum of $ _____, to be paid as follows: $ _____ cash in hand, the receipt of which is hereby acknowledged, and $ _____ or more per month on or before the _____ day of each and every month after the date of this instrument, to be mailed to Sellers' address given herein, with interest at the rate of _____ per cent, per annum on the whole sum remaining from time to time unpaid, the interest to be payable:

And the Buyers agree to pay all taxes, assessments, or impositions that may be legally levied or imposed upon said land subsequent to the year

In case of the failure of the Buyers to make any of the payments herein designated, or any part thereof, or failure to perform any of the covenants on their part hereby made and entered into for a period of _____ days after maturity, this contract shall be forfeited and terminated, and the Buyers shall forfeit all payments made by them on this contract, and such payments shall be retained by the Sellers in full satisfaction and in liquidation of all damages by them sustained; and the Sellers shall have the right to re-enter and take possession of the premises aforesaid without being liable to any action therefor. Notice to quit and of forfeiture are each hereby waived.

It is agreed that the Buyers shall have the privilege at any time of paying in advance the unpaid balance under this contract, together with interest, taxes and other assessments that may be due, and procuring a deed from the Sellers.

It is further agreed by the parties hereto that this contract is not to be recorded, and that no assignment or transfer of said contract or the rights thereunder of the Buyers shall be valid and binding as against the Sellers, unless the Sellers shall consent in writing to such recording or assignment.

IT IS MUTUALLY AGREED by and between the parties hereto that the time of payment shall be an essential part of this contract, and that all covenants and agreements herein contained shall extend to and be obligatory upon the heirs, executors, administrators, and assigns of the respective parties.

IN WITNESS WHEREOF, the parties to these presents have hereunto set their hands and seals effective the day and year first above written.

1. _____ (Seal)

2. _____ (Seal)

3. _____ (Seal)

4. _____ (Seal)

Agreement for Deed
(Reproduced with permission of Official Legal Forms, Hialeah, Fla.)

Agreement of Sale

CALIFORNIA REAL ESTATE ASSOCIATION STANDARD FORM

This Agreement, made and entered into this _____ day of _____, 19 ____

between _____, hereinafter called Seller,

and _____, hereinafter called Buyer.

WITNESSETH, that the Seller, in consideration of the payments to be made by the Buyer and the conditions and covenants to be kept and performed by him, as hereinafter set forth, agrees to sell and the Buyer agrees to buy, the real property, situated in the _____, State of California, described as follows,

County of _____

to-wit:

for the sum of _____ Dollars, in lawful money of the United States of America, and the Buyer, in consideration of the premises, promises and agrees to pay the Seller the aforesaid sum of money, for all of said real property, as follows, to-wit:

....Dollars

upon the execution and delivery hereof, the receipt whereof is hereby acknowledged, and the balance of

....Dollars

in installments, including interest on all unpaid principal from date hereof until date of payment at the

rate of...per centum per annum. The first installment of

....Dollars

to be paid...................., 19........, and a like amount shall be paid on the same day

of each.................thereafter until the balance of principal and interest has been paid in full.

The amount of the final payment, however, shall be the total of the principal and interest then due. All

payments to be made by the Buyer shall be paid with lawful money of the United States of America.

IN ADDITION IT IS AGREED AS FOLLOWS. TO-WIT:

FIRST: Possession shall be delivered to the Buyer upon the execution and delivery of this agreement, unless otherwise provided herein.

SECOND: The Buyer shall pay all taxes and assessments from date hereof and assessed and levied against said property hereafter, unless otherwise specified herein. Taxes for the fiscal year ending June 30th following the date of this agreement shall be prorated, unless otherwise specified herein.

THIRD: The Seller on receiving payment of all amounts of money mentioned herein shall execute a grant deed for said property in favor of said Buyer and shall deliver said deed to said Buyer. As of the date of delivery of deed the Seller shall supply the Buyer with a Policy of Title Insurance or Certificate of Title, to be issued by a reliable title company, which shall show the title to said property to be merchantable and free from taxes, assessments, liens and encumbrances, except such thereof as are set forth herein and such thereof as may be suffered or created hereafter by the Buyer. The Seller shall pay for said evidence of title unless otherwise set forth herein.

FOURTH: Should the Buyer fail to make said payments or any thereof when due or fail to comply with the conditions, covenants and agreements set forth herein, the amounts paid hereon may be retained by the Seller as the consideration for making this agreement and thereupon the Seller shall be released from all obligation in law or equity to convey said property and any occupancy of said property thereafter by said Buyer shall be deemed to be and be a tenancy at the pleasure of the Seller and said Buyer shall never acquire and expressly waives any and all rights or claims of title because of such possession.

Agreement of Sale

(Reproduced with permission of the California Real Estate Assn.)

FIFTH: Should the Seller sue the Buyer to enforce this agreement or any of its terms, the Buyer shall pay a reasonable attorney fee and all expenses in connection therewith.

SIXTH: The Seller reserves the right to deliver the deed, at any time during the term hereof, and the Buyer, in lieu of this agreement, shall execute and deliver to said Seller, or his nominee, a note for all amounts of money then unpaid and said note shall be secured by a Deed of Trust on said property and said Buyer shall likewise execute and deliver said Deed of Trust concurrently with the delivery of said note.

SEVENTH: The waiver by the Seller of any covenant, condition or agreement herein contained shall not vitiate the same or any other covenant, condition or agreement contained herein and the terms, conditions, covenants and agreements set forth herein shall apply to and bind the heirs, successors, and assigns of each of the parties hereto. Time is the essence of this agreement.

EIGHTH: All words used in this agreement, including the words Buyer and Seller, shall be construed to include the plural as well as the singular number and words used herein in the present tense shall include the future as well as the present and words used in the masculine gender shall include the feminine and neuter.

NINTH: The Buyer shall insure the buildings now on said property, if any, or such buildings as may be placed thereon, against fire, for not less than 75% of the value thereof, with some Fire Insurance Company to be approved by the Seller and any loss thereunder shall be paid to the Buyer and the Seller as their interests may appear. Should said property be not insured as aforesaid the Seller may insure said property and the cost thereof shall be paid by the Buyer, upon demand, including interest thereon from the date the premium is paid by the Seller. All insurance policies to be issued as aforesaid shall be delivered to and held by the Seller until all amounts of money to be paid by the Buyer have been paid in full.

TENTH: The number of years required to complete payment under this contract:_____

ELEVENTH: Tax estimate: $_____ (Based on taxes for year_____.)

IN WITNESS WHEREOF said parties have executed this agreement as of the day and year first above written.

_____

_____

_____

For these forms address the California Real Estate Association,
520 So. Grand Ave., Los Angeles 90017. Revision Approved 11-15-43
Copyrighted, California Real Estate Association. All Rights Reserved

FORM AS 14

Agreement of Sale (Continued)

PAPCO'S FORM 30

PAPCO PUBLISHING CORPORATION
MIAMI 45, FLORIDA

Apartment Lease

THIS LEASE, made this   day of   A.D., 19   , by and

between

proprietor of the   or   , owner and

his duly authorized agent, both of

                                    Florida, hereinafter called the Lessor, and

hereinafter called the Lessee

WITNESSETH, That in consideration of the sum of   Dollars
paid by the Lessee......, which said sum is hereby acknowledged to have been received as part payment of rents
accruing under this lease, and in the further consideration of the covenants, agreements and conditions herein contained, on the part of the Lessee....... to be kept, done and performed, the said Lessor does hereby lease to the
Lessee....... Apartment No.   on   floor in the

            , situated   , Florida, with the full under-
standing that   family consists of   adults and   child   and no more.

TO HAVE AND TO HOLD THE SAME for the full term of
the   day of   A.D., 19   , to the   day of   from
the said Lessee   yielding and paying to the Lessor therefor the total rent of   ,19
            And the said Lessee   covenant   with the Lessor to pay said rent in advance in   Dollars.
the first payment of   Dollars on the   day of   , A. D., 19   payments,
which said sum has been paid and acknowledged herein, and the remaining payments as follows, namely:

AND THE SAID LESSEE   further covenant   and agree   not to use nor permit to be used the
premises leased for any illegal, immoral or improper purposes; not to make nor permit any disturbance, noise or
annoyance whatsoever detrimental to the premises or to the comfort and peace of any of the inhabitants of said
building or its neighbors, and particularly, said Lessee   agree   that under no circumstances will
allow or permit their child or children to play in the halls, lobby, porches or stair-cases of said building or in any
other way to annoy the tenants of other Apartments, and the Lessor does hereby reserve the right to terminate
this lease at any time this condition is permitted to exist; not to assign this lease nor sub-let any part of the premises
here leased, except with the written consent of the owner and only at a price which shall be an amount not less
than the proportional rate for the full term; not to use said premises for any other purpose than as a private dwel-

Apartment Lease
(Reproduced with permission of Official Legal Forms, Hialeah, Fla.)

267

ling for the members of .... family; to pay the cost of repairing all damage to the apartment occasioned by the Lessee .... or any of .... family; and especially the cost of removing foreign substances from toilets and sinks.

AND THE LESSEE .... hereby covenant .... and agree .... that if default is made in the payment of rent as above set forth or any part thereof, or if said Lessee .... or .... family shall violate any of the covenants, agreements and conditions of this lease, then the Lessee .... shall become a tenant at sufferance, hereby waiving all right of notice to vacate said premises, and the Lessor shall be entitled to reenter and retake possession immediately of the demised premises, and the entire rent for the rental period next ensuing shall at once be due and payable and may forthwith be collected by distress or otherwise as provided by law; and will at the end of h term without demand quietly and peaceably deliver up the possession of said premises in as good condition as they now are (ordinary wear and the decay and damage by fire or the elements only excepted).

SAID LESSEE .... hereby acknowledges receipt of the articles enumerated on the reverse side of this lease and by agreement made a part hereof and further covenants and agrees to assume full responsibility for said articles and to make good any damage or deficiency therein at the expiration of this lease; to return all linens clean and pay for cleaning of same upon termination of lease.

And the Lessor, upon performance of the said covenants, agreements and conditions by said Lessee .... hereby covenants that the said Lessee .... shall have the quiet and peaceable enjoyment of said premises, herein reserving the right to inspect said premises so often as shall be deemed necessary and to show the apartment at reasonable hours to prospective tenants during the thirty days next prior to the expiration of this lease.

Lessee agrees that if the Lessee is in default of any of the other terms, covenants or conditions of this lease, other than the default in payment of rent, and as a result thereof the Lessor reacquires possession of the demised premises, then all unearned rentals shall be retained by the Lessor as agreed upon and liquidated damages, the parties being unable to ascertain the exact amount of the damages that may be sustained by the Lessor as a result of breach of this lease by the Lessee. However, the Lessor agrees that in the event he can mitigate his damages by releasing of the demised premises, then and in that event, any monies that the Lessor may receive in mitigation of the damages shall be payable to the Lessee. In enforcing the terms, covenants and conditions of this lease, the Lessee shall be responsible for all court costs and attorney's fees incurred in connection therewith. All of the remedies under this lease and rider hereto shall be considered cumulative.

Witness our hands and seals this .... day of .... , A.D., 19........

Signed and sealed in the presence of:

.... (Seal)
                                              Lessor.

.... (Seal)
                                              Agent for Lessor.

.... (Seal)
                                              Lessee.

.... (Seal)
                                              Lessee.

Apartment Lease (Continued)

APARTMENT HOUSE LISTING FORM

Name of Apartment _____

Address _____

Units _____ Stories _____ Type of Construction _____

Age _____ Pool _____ × _____ Lot size _____

Total Units _____ Number Furnished _____ Number Unfurnished _____

    Efficiencies   _____
    One Bedroom   _____
    Two Bedrooms   _____
    Hotel Rooms   _____
    Other   _____

Roof _____ Windows _____ Floors _____ Shopping _____

Bus _____ Children Allowed _____ Pets Allowed _____

Elevator _____ Parking _____ Carpeting _____

Air Conditioning _____ Heating _____ Laundry Facilities _____

Recreation Area _____ Utilities _____

Miscellaneous _____

Square ft. rentable area and size of each apartment:

    Efficiences   _____ _____
    One Bedroom   _____ _____
    Two Bedrooms   _____ _____
    Hotel Rooms   _____ _____
    Other   _____ _____

First Mortgagee _____

Second Mortgagee _____

Other Lienholders _____

Ground Lease Information _____

Insurance Company _____

Legal Description _____

_____

Remarks _____

_____

_____

Price $_____ Terms _____

_____

Mortgage Information:

    Balance 1st Mtg. $_____ Payable $_____ Int. _____%

Yrs. to pay out _____

    Balance 2nd Mtg. $_____ Payable $_____ Int. ___% Yrs. to pay out _____

    Other Liens $_____ Payable $_____ Int.___%

Payable $_____ Int. _% Yrs. to pay out   Total

    Ground Lease $_____ per _____

    Recapture between_____and_____@ $_____

Commitments _____

Purchase Money Mortgage Terms _____

	Expenses		Income	
County RE Taxes	_____	Eff. Furn.	@	_____
City RE Taxes	_____	Eff. Unfurn.	@	_____
County PP Taxes	_____	1 Bdrm. Furn.	@	_____
City PP Taxes	_____	1 Bdrm. Unfurn.	@	_____
Electricity	_____	2 Bdrm. Furn.	@	_____
Water	_____	2 Bdrm. Unfurn	@	_____
Gas	_____		@	_____
Oil	_____		@	_____
Pool	_____		@	_____
Elevator	_____	Gross Total		_____
Exterminator	_____	Less Vacancy Factor (___%)		_____
Licenses	_____	Balance		_____
Management	_____	Misc. Income		_____
Air Cond.	_____	Grand Total		_____
Advertising	_____	Less Cash Out		_____
Insurance	_____	Net Cash Income		_____
Repairs	_____			
Maintenance	_____	Total Mortgages		_____
Supplies	_____	Owner's Equity		_____
Accounting	_____	PURCHASE PRICE		_____
Garbage	_____			
Landscaping	_____	Cash Required		_____
Ground Rent	_____	Balance as purchase		_____
Other	_____	money mt. @___% with		
Mortgage Payments	_____	payments of $___ per___		_____
Total Cash Out	_____	Owner's Equity		_____

Owner _____ Listing Salesman _____

Address _____ Tel. _____ Exclusive _____ Open _____

Manager _____ Date _____, 19_____

Manager's Tel. _____ To Show _____

Apartment House Listing Form (Continued)

RESIDENTIAL APPRAISAL REPORT

File No. _____

To be completed by Lender

Borrower/Client	Census Tract _____ Map Reference _____
Property Address	
City _____ County _____	State _____ Zip Code _____
Legal Description	
Sale Price $ _____ Date of Sale _____ Property Rights Appraised ☐ Fee ☐ Leasehold ☐ DeMinimis PUD(FNMA only) ☐ Condo ☐ PUD	
Actual Real Estate Taxes $ _____ (yr) Loan charges to be paid by seller $ _____ Other sales concessions _____	
Lender _____ Lender's Address _____	
Occupant _____ Appraiser _____ Instructions to Appraiser _____	

TAX FOLIO NO. _____   **ASSESSED VALUE $** _____

NEIGHBORHOOD

	Urban	Suburban	Rural
Location	☐	☐	☐
Built Up	☐ Over 75%	☐ 25% to 75%	☐ Under 25%
Growth Rate ☐ Fully Dev.	☐ Rapid	☐ Steady	☐ Slow
Property Values	☐ Increasing	☐ Stable	☐ Declining
Demand/Supply	☐ Shortage	☐ In Balance	☐ Over Supply
Marketing Time	☐ Under 3 Mos.	☐ 4–6 Mos.	☐ Over 6 Mos.

Present Land Use ___% 1 Family ___% 2–4 Family ___% Apts. ___% Condo ___% Commercial ___% Industrial ___% Vacant ___%

Change in Present Land Use ☐ Not Likely ☐ Likely (*) ☐ Taking Place (*)
(*) From _____ To _____

Predominant Occupancy ☐ Owner ☐ Tenant ___% Vacant

Single Family Price Range $ _____ to $ _____ Predominant Value $ _____

Single Family Age _____ yrs to _____ yrs Predominant Age _____ yrs

	Good	Avg.	Fair	Poor
Employment Stability	☐	☐	☐	☐
Convenience to Employment	☐	☐	☐	☐
Convenience to Shopping	☐	☐	☐	☐
Convenience to Schools	☐	☐	☐	☐
Quality of Schools	☐	☐	☐	☐
Recreational Facilities	☐	☐	☐	☐
Adequacy of Utilities	☐	☐	☐	☐
Property Compatibility	☐	☐	☐	☐
Protection from Detrimental Conditions	☐	☐	☐	☐
Police and Fire Protection	☐	☐	☐	☐
General Appearance of Properties	☐	☐	☐	☐
Appeal to Market	☐	☐	☐	☐

Note: FHLMC/FNMA do not consider the racial composition of the neighborhood to be a relevant factor and it must not be considered in the appraisal.

Comments (including those factors adversely affecting marketability) _____

SITE

Dimensions _____ - _____ Sq. Ft or Acres ☐ Corner Lot

Zoning classification _____ Present improvements ☐ do ☐ do not conform to zoning regulations

Highest and best use: ☐ Present use ☐ Other (specify) _____

	Public	Other (Describe)	OFF SITE IMPROVEMENTS	Topo _____
Elec.	☐	_____	Street Access: ☐ Public ☐ Private	Size _____
Gas	☐	_____	Surface _____	Shape _____
Water	☐	_____	Maintenance: ☐ Public ☐ Private	View _____
San.Sewer	☐	_____	☐ Storm Sewer ☐ Curb/Gutter	Drainage _____
	☐ Underground Elect. & Tel.		☐ Sidewalk ☐ Street Lights	Is the property located in a HUD identified Flood Hazard Area? ☐ No ☐ Yes

Comments (favorable or unfavorable including any apparent adverse easements, encroachments or other adverse conditions) _____

IMPROVEMENTS

☐ Existing (approx. yr. blt.) 19___ No. Units ___ Type (det, duplex, semi/det, etc.) _____ Design (rambler, split level, etc.) _____ Exterior Walls _____

☐ Proposed ☐ Under Construction No. Stories ___

Roof Material _____	Gutters & Downspouts ☐ None	Window (Type): _____	Insulation ☐ None ☐ Floor
		☐ Storm Sash ☐ Screens ☐ Combination	☐ Ceiling ☐ Roof ☐ Walls

Foundation Walls _____

BSMT. ___% Basement ☐ Floor Drain Finished Ceiling _____
☐ Outside Entrance ☐ Sump Pump Finished Walls _____
☐ Concrete Floor ___% Finished Finished Floor _____
Evidence of: ☐ Dampness ☐ Termites ☐ Settlement

☐ Crawl Space
☐ Slab on Grade

Comments _____

ROOM LIST

Room List	Foyer	Living	Dining	Kitchen	Den	Family Rm.	Rec. Rm.	Bedrooms	No. Baths	Laundry	Other
Basement											
1st Level											
2nd Level											

Total _____ Rooms _____ Bedrooms _____ Baths in finished area above grade.

INTERIOR FINISH & EQUIPMENT

Kitchen Equipment: ☐ Refrigerator ☐ Range/Oven ☐ Disposal ☐ Dishwasher ☐ Fan/Hood ☐ Compactor ☐ Washer ☐ Dryer ☐

HEAT: Type _____ Fuel _____ Cond. _____ AIR COND: ☐ Central ☐ Other _____ ☐ Adequate ☐ Inadequate

Floors	☐ Hardwood ☐ Carpet Over _____ ☐
Walls	☐ Drywall ☐ Plaster _____
Trim/Finish	☐ Good ☐ Average ☐ Fair ☐ Poor
Bath Floor	☐ Ceramic _____
Bath Wainscot	☐ Ceramic _____

Special Features (including fireplaces): _____

ATTIC: ☐ Yes ☐ No ☐ Stairway ☐ Drop-stair ☐ Scuttle ☐ Floored
Finished (Describe) _____ ☐ Heated

CAR STORAGE: ☐ Garage ☐ Built-in ☐ Attached ☐ Detached ☐ Car Port
No. Cars ___ ☐ Adequate ☐ Inadequate Condition _____

PROPERTY RATING

	Good	Avg.	Fair	Poor
Quality of Construction (Materials & Finish)	☐	☐	☐	☐
Condition of Improvements	☐	☐	☐	☐
Rooms size and layout	☐	☐	☐	☐
Closets and Storage	☐	☐	☐	☐
Plumbing—adequacy and condition	☐	☐	☐	☐
Electrical—adequacy and condition	☐	☐	☐	☐
Kitchen Cabinets—adequacy and condition	☐	☐	☐	☐
Compatibility to Neighborhood	☐	☐	☐	☐
Overall Livability	☐	☐	☐	☐
Appeal and Marketability	☐	☐	☐	☐

Effective Age ___ Yrs. Est. Remaining Economic Life ___ Yrs.

PORCHES, PATIOS, POOL, FENCES, etc. (describe) _____

COMMENTS (including functional or physical inadequacies, repairs needed, modernization, etc.) _____

FHLMC Form 70 Rev. 9/75
CF 1112   ATTACH DESCRIPTIVE PHOTOGRAPHS OF SUBJECT PROPERTY AND STREET SCENE   FNMA Form 1004 Rev. 9/75

VALUATION SECTION

Purpose of Appraisal is to estimate Market Value as defined in Certification & Statement of Limiting Conditions (FHLMC Form 439/FNMA Form 1004B). If submitted for FNMA, the appraiser must attach (1) sketch or map showing location of subject, street names, distance from nearest intersection, and any detrimental conditions and (2) exterior building sketch of improvements showing dimensions.

COST APPROACH

Measurements		No. Stories		Sq. Ft.	ESTIMATED REPRODUCTION COST — NEW — OF IMPROVEMENTS:
x	x	=			Dwelling _____ Sq. Ft. @ $ _____ = $ _____
x	x	=			_____ Sq. Ft. @ $ _____ = _____
x	x	=			Extras _____ = _____
x	x	=			_____ = _____
x	x	=			Porches, Patios, etc. _____ = _____
x	x	=			Garage/Car Port _____ Sq. Ft. @ $ _____ = _____

Total Gross Living Area (List in Market Data Analysis below) _____

Comment on functional and economic obsolescence: _____

Site Improvements (driveway, landscaping, etc.) = _____

Total Estimated Cost New . . . . = $ _____

Less | Physical | Functional | Economic

Depreciation $ _____ | $ _____ | $ _____ = $ (_____)

Depreciated value of improvements . . . . . . = $ _____

ESTIMATED LAND VALUE . . . . . . = $ _____
(If leasehold, show only leasehold value)

INDICATED VALUE BY COST APPROACH . . . $ _____

The undersigned has recited three recent sales of properties most similar and proximate to subject and has considered these in the market analysis. The description includes a dollar adjustment, reflecting market reaction to those items of significant variation between the subject and comparable properties. If a significant item in the comparable property is superior to, or more favorable than, the subject property, a minus (-) adjustment is made, thus reducing the indicated value of subject; if a significant item in the comparable is inferior to, or less favorable than, the subject property, a plus (+) adjustment is made, thus increasing the indicated value of the subject.

MARKET DATA ANALYSIS

ITEM	Subject Property	COMPARABLE NO. 1		COMPARABLE NO. 2		COMPARABLE NO. 3	
Address							
Proximity to Subj.							
Sales Price	$	$		$		$	
Price/Living area	$	$		$		$	
Data Source							
Date of Sale and Time Adjustment	DESCRIPTION	DESCRIPTION	+(−)$ Adjustment	DESCRIPTION	+(−)$ Adjustment	DESCRIPTION	+(−)$ Adjustment
Location							
Site/View							
Design and Appeal							
Quality of Const.							
Age							
Condition							
Living Area Room Count and Total	Total B-rms Baths	Total B-rms Baths		Total B-rms Baths		Total B-rms Baths	
Gross Living Area	Sq.Ft.	Sq.Ft.		Sq.Ft.		Sq.Ft.	
Basement & Bsmt. Finished Rooms							
Functional Utility							
Air Conditioning							
Garage/Car Port							
Porches, Patio, Pools, etc.							
Other (e.g. fireplaces, kitchen equip., heating, remodeling)							
Sales or Financing Concessions							
Net Adj. (Total)		☐ Plus; ☐ Minus $		☐ Plus; ☐ Minus $		☐ Plus; ☐ Minus $	
Indicated Value of Subject		$		$		$	

Comments on Market Data _____

INDICATED VALUE BY MARKET DATA APPROACH . . . . $ _____

INDICATED VALUE BY INCOME APPROACH (If applicable) Economic Market Rent $ _____ /Mo. x Gross Rent Multiplier _____ = $ _____

This appraisal is made ☐ "as is" ☐ subject to the repairs, alterations, or conditions listed below ☐ completion per plans and specifications.

Comments and Conditions of Appraisal: _____

Final Reconciliation: _____

INSURABLE VALUE: _____

This appraisal is based upon the above requirements, the certification, contingent and limiting conditions, and Market Value definition that are stated in

☐ FHLMC Form 439 (Rev. 9/75)/FNMA Form 1004B filed with client _____ 19 _____ ☐ attached.

If submitted for FNMA, the report has been prepared in compliance with FNMA form instructions.

I ESTIMATE THE MARKET VALUE, AS DEFINED, OF SUBJECT PROPERTY AS OF _____ 19 _____ to be $ _____

Appraiser(s) _____ Review Appraiser (If applicable) _____

☐ Did ☐ Did Not Physically Inspect Property

Residential Appraisal Report (Continued)

APPRAISAL REPORT
In Letter Form

Date _____

Dear Sirs:

I, _____(Appraiser's Name)_____ do hereby state that upon the

request of _____(Name of the one ordering the appraisal)_____

_____, I have made an investigation and analysis of the following described

property:

(Here follows the legal description and
common known address of the property)

and that I am of the opinion that on _____19_____,

when a detailed inspection of the premises was made, the Market Value of the land

and improvements thereon was:

$_____Total

allocated as Land: $_____ Improvements $_____

I further state that, to the best of my knowledge and belief, the evaluations

contained in this appraisal are correct.

I have no present or contemplated future interest in the property appraised and

compensation for making this appraisal is in no manner contingent upon the value

reported.

The physical condition of the improvements described herein was based on visual

inspection. No liability is assumed for the soundness of structural members since no

engineering tests were made of same.

Respectfully submitted,

_____

Realtor—Appraiser

(Here include highlights of the appraiser's qualifications. For example:
Member, Society of Real Estate Appraisers; V. A. appraiser 19__ to 19__;
Senior Member, National Society of Fee Appraisers, etc.)

Appraisal

APPRAISED FOR _____ ADDRESS _____

PROPERTY _____ TYPE _____

SECTION _____ BLOCK _____ LOT _____ VOLUME _____ PAGE _____

19 ___ ASSESSED VALUATION: LAND $ _____ BUILDING $ _____ TOTAL $ _____

SIZE OF LAND _____ AREA _____ SIZE OF BUILDING _____ EXTENSION _____

HEIGHT _____ MATERIALS _____ HEAT _____

CONDITION _____ USE _____

PRESENT MORTGAGE $ _____

This is to Certify

THAT THE PROPERTY DESCRIBED ABOVE HAS BEEN PERSONALLY EXAMINED BY THE INDIVIDUAL
WHOSE SIGNATURE APPEARS BELOW AND WHO ESTIMATES ITS VALUE AS FOLLOWS:

PRESENT MARKET VALUE OF LAND $ _____ ⎫
                                       ⎬ TOTAL $ _____
PRESENT MARKET VALUE OF BUILDING $ _____ ⎭

RENTAL ESTIMATED AT $ _____

REMARKS

_____ SIGNATURE _____
DATE

Form 235   S. S. Clarkson Mfg Corp 17 Bergen Street, Brooklyn, N. Y 11201   (212) MAin 5-2624

Certificate of Appraisal
(*Reproduced with permission of S. S. Clarkson Mfg. Corp., Brooklyn, N.Y.*)

ASSIGNMENT
General Form

For Value Received, I _____, of _____ Street, City of _____, State of _____, hereby assign, transfer and set over to _____, of _____ Avenue, City of _____, State of _____, all my right, title and interest in a certain agreement dated _____, 19__, by and between _____ and _____ subject to all the terms and conditions thereof and hereby remise, release and quit claim unto _____, all my right, title and interest in and to the said property.

Dated _____ 19__.

_____

ASSIGNMENT OF CONTRACT
Annexed To Contract

For Value Received, I _____ hereby assign all my rights, title and interest in the certain contract entered into by me with _____ on _____, 19__, a copy of which is hereto annexed as a part hereof.

In witness whereof I have hereunto set my hand and seal in the City of ____, State of _____, on this _____ day of _____, 19__.

_____

ASSIGNMENT OF CHATTEL MORTGAGE

THIS INSTRUMENT, made this _____ day of _____19__
BETWEEN _____
residing at _____
_____of the first part, and
residing at _____
of the second part.
WITNESSETH, That the part _____ of the first part, for a good and valuable
consideration to _____ in hand paid by the part _____ of the
second part, ha__ sold, assigned and transferred, and do _____ hereby sell,
assign, and transfer to the part _____ of the second part, a certain Chattel
Mortgage in the sum of _____
Dollars dated _____ 19__ and made by _____ payable to
_____ and filed in the Office of the _____ of
_____ County, on the _____ day of _____ 19__ at _____ o'clock
_____. M. under file number _____ together with all in-
debtedness and moneys owing by virtue of said Mortgage or secured thereby, and
together with all the right, title and interest of the part_____ of the first part in
and to the chattels therein described and claimed by virtue thereof, kept at
premises _____
to wit the following chattels:

AND the part _____ of the first part hereby covenants that there is due and
unpaid on said Mortgage the sum of _____ Dollars, with interest at
_____ per centum from _____ 19__.

AND the part _____ of the first part do _____ hereby make, constitute and
appoint the said part _____ of the second part _____ true and lawful
attorney, irrevocable, in _____ name or otherwise, but at the proper costs and
charges of the part _____ of the second part, to have, use and take, all lawful
means for the recovery of the said money and interest; and in case of payment to
discharge the same as fully as _____ might or could do if these presents were
not made.

IN WITNESS WHEREOF, the part _____ of the first part ha__ set
_____ hand __ and seal or caused these presents to be signed by its proper
corporate officers and caused its proper corporate seal to be hereto affixed, the
_____ day of _____ one thousand nine hundred and _____.

Signed, sealed and delivered
in the presence of

_____   _____L.S.
_____

Assignment of Contract

Know All Men By These Presents, That

of   County, State of ,

part   of the first part, in consideration of the sum of

and other valuable considerations to   in hand paid by

                              , State of   , of the County of

part   of the second part, at or before the ensealing and delivery of these presents, the receipt where-

of is hereby acknowledged, ha   granted, bargained, sold, assigned, transferred and set over, and

by these presents do   grant, bargain, sell, assign, transfer and set over unto the said part

of the second part,   heirs and assigns, forever, a certain land contract bearing date

the   day of   , A. D. 19   ,

made by   upon the

to   County,

following described piece or parcel of land, situate and being in

State of   , to-wit:

Assignment of Contract

(Reproduced with permission of Official Legal Forms, Hialeah, Fla.)

277

A portion of the consideration of this assignment being that the part   of the second part herein

assume   all the obligations and agree   to pay all the payments described in said contract now due

or to become due, together with all interest specified in said contract.

And upon the performance of all the terms and conditions and the completion of all payments as set

forth in said contract, by the said part   of the second part,

heirs or assigns, the part   of the first part do   hereby authorize the said

to make, execute and deliver a good and sufficient deed to the property hereinabove described, in like man-

ner as though the original contract had been made and executed by the said

                                                         with the said part   of the second part,

instead of with

TO HAVE AND TO HOLD the same unto the said part   of the second part,

heirs and assigns forever.

IN WITNESS WHEREOF, the said part   of the first part has   hereunto set

hand   and seal   this   day of   , A. D. 19

Signed, sealed and delivered in presence of us:

_____ (Seal)

_____ (Seal)

Assignment of Contract (Continued)

ASSIGNMENT OF MORTGAGE

Know All Men By These Presents, That _____, (I, We) _____ _____ part of the first part, in consideration of the sum of _____ Dollars, and other valuable considerations, received from or on behalf of _____ _____, part _____ of the second part, at or before the ensealing and delivery of these presents, the receipt whereof is hereby acknowledged, do hereby grant, bargain, sell, assign, transfer and set over unto the said part _____ of the second part a certain mortgage bearing date the _____ day of _____ A.D. 19_____ made by _____ in favor of _____ and recorded in Official Records Book _____, page _____, public records of _____County, _____, upon the following described piece or parcel of land, situate and being in said County and State, to-wit:

TOGETHER with the note ___ or obligation ___ described in said mortgage, and the moneys due and to become due thereon, with interest from the _____ day of _____, 19___

TO HAVE AND TO HOLD the same unto the said part _____ of the second part, _____ heirs, legal representatives, successors and assigns forever.

IN WITNESS WHEREOF, _____ have herunto set _____ hand _____ and seal _____, this day of _____, A.D., 19___

Signed, sealed and delivered in presence of:

_____   _____SEAL

_____   _____SEAL

BARGAIN AND SALE DEED

With Covenants Against Grantor's Acts

THIS INDENTURE, made the _____ day of _____, nineteen hundred and _____.

BETWEEN _____, residing at No. _____ Street, City of _____, State of _____, herein called the party of the first part and _____, residing at No. _____ Avenue, City of _____, State of _____, herein called the party of the second part.

WITNESSETH, that the party of the first part, in consideration of _____ dollars ($_____) lawful money of the United States, paid by the party of the second part does hereby grant and release unto the party of the second part, the heirs or successors and assigns of the party of the second part forever.

ALL that certain plot, piece, or parcel of land with the buildings and improvements thereon erected, situate, lying and being in the

TOGETHER with the buildings, improvements, woods, ways, streets, alleys, passages, waters, water course, rights, liberties, privileges, tenements, hereditments and appurtenances thereto belonging.

TOGETHER with the appurtenances and all the estate and rights of the party of the first part in and to said property.

TO HAVE AND TO HOLD the premises herein granted together with the appurtenances unto the party of the second part his successors and assigns forever.

AND THE SAID party of the first part covenants that he has not done or suffered anything whereby the premises have been encumbered in any way whatsoever.[1]

THE GRANTOR, in compliance with Section 13 of the Lien Law of the State of New York, covenants that the grantor will receive the consideration for this conveyance and will hold the right to receive such consideration as a trust fund to be applied first for the purpose of paying the cost of the improvement and that the grantor will apply the same first to the payment of the cost of the improvement before using any part of the total of the same for any other purpose.[2]

IN WITNESS WHEREOF, the party of the first part has hereunto set his hand and seal the day and year first above written. In the presence of:

_____   _____ (SEAL)
                                              Grantor

_____

---

1. The contents of a Bargain and Sale Deed *without* covenants against grantor's acts differs only in that this clause is omitted.
2. Clause applicable in New York State only.

BILL OF SALE
(Absolute)

KNOW ALL MEN BY THESE PRESENTS, That _____
of the _____ of _____, in the County of _____ and State of_____
of the first part, for and in consideration of the sum of _____
_____ Dollars lawful money of the United States, to _____
paid by _____
_____ of _____of the second
part, the receipt whereof is hereby acknowledged, ha__ granted, bargained, sold,
transferred and delivered, and by these presents do __ grant, bargain, sell, transfer
and delivery unto the said part __ of the second part, _____
executors, administrators and assigns, the following goods and chattels:

TO HAVE AND TO HOLD the same unto the said part _____ of the second
part, _____ executors, administrators and assigns forever.

AND _____ do _____, for _____and
_____ heirs, executors and administrators, covenant to and with
the said part _____ of the second part, _____
executors, administrators and assigns, that _____ the lawful own-
ers_____ of the said goods and chattels; that they are free from all encumbrances; that_____ ha__ good right to sell the same aforesaid, and
that _____ will warrant and defend the sale of the said property, goods and
chattels hereby made, unto the said part _____ of the second part
_____ executors, administrators and assigns against the lawful
claims and demands of all persons whomsoever.

IN WITNESS WHEREOF _____ ha__ hereunto set _____ hand
_____ and seal _____ this _____ day of_____, one thousand
nine hundred and_____. Signed, sealed and delivered in presence
of us:

_____   _____(Seal)

_____   _____(Seal)

257—Conditional Bill of Sale of Business.

w

JULIUS BLUMBERG, INC. LAW BLANK PUBLISHERS
80 EXCHANGE PLACE AT BROADWAY, NEW YORK

Know all Men by these Presents,

THAT

hereinafter designated as the Seller, for and in consideration of the sum of $ lawful money of the United States, received by the Seller, and the sum of $ to be paid in instalments as is evidenced by   promissory notes, more particularly hereinafter set forth, the receipt of the above is hereby acknowledged, does hereby conditionally grant, and conditionally bargain and conditionally sell unto

of

hereinafter designated as the Buyer, and by these presents does conditionally grant, conditionally grant, conditionally bargain and conditionally sell unto the said Buyer and the Buyer's executors, administrators and assigns, all the right, title and interest that the Seller has in and to all

also the good will of the said business and the lease of the premises, and all other chattels and fixtures now found in

of the premises now known as No.

all of which chattels and fixtures are free and clear from any and all incumbrances.

TO HAVE AND TO HOLD all and singular the business, stock, goods, chattels and fixtures above conditionally bargained, conditionally granted or intended so to be, unto the said Buyer and the Buyer's executors, administrators and assigns on the following terms and conditions:

THE CONDITION of the above is such: That if the Buyer shall and do well and truly pay unto the Seller the just, true and full sum of $, lawful money of the United States, in instalments, and which sum of $ is evidenced by   promissory notes each bearing even

date herewith, made payable in the sum and manner following:
The first note of $ _____ to be paid on the _____ day of _____ , 19 ___ ,
and the remaining _____ notes, monthly thereafter
until all shall have been paid for, the last note for the sum of $ _____ is to be due and payable on
the _____ day of _____ , 19 ___ , then this agreement is to be
in full force and effect, otherwise to be null, void, inoperative and without any effect.

The Buyer covenants and agrees to and with the Seller that in the event default be made in the payment of any of the instalments as hereinbefore mentioned, that it shall be lawful for, and the Buyer does hereby authorize and empower the Seller to enter any dwelling house, store or other premises where the said goods and chattels are, or may be found, and to take and carry away said goods and chattels and to sell and dispose of them at public or private sale for the best price that the Seller can obtain, and out of the proceeds of the said sale, retain the amount remaining unpaid, together with any and all charges and expenses that may be incurred by the Seller, rendering the surplus (if any) unto the Buyer.

The Buyer does hereby agree to and with the Seller, that in the event default be made in the payment of any of the instalments as the same become due, that the amount remaining unpaid shall then, at the option of the Seller, become immediately due and payable after such default; it being understood and agreed between the parties hereto that the lease of the store aforesaid, and the good will, and the right, title and interest in and to the stock, merchandise, and fixtures of said business shall in no event pass unto the Buyer until the Buyer has fully complied with all the conditions herein, and has made the payments mentioned herein, and in accordance with the terms of this agreement, this being a condition precedent before the title to these premises shall pass from the Seller to the Buyer.

The Seller in consideration of the Buyer fully complying with the terms aforesaid, agrees to and with the Buyer, that the Seller will not engage in a business similar to the one mentioned in this agreement, either directly or indirectly, as principal, agent, servant or employee, or act for any other person, firm or corporation whatsoever for a period of _____ years from the date hereof, and not within a radius of
(_____) square blocks from the premises aforesaid.

The Buyer also agrees to keep said business fully insured against loss or damage by fire for the benefit of the Seller, in a sum not less than $ _____ , and if the Buyer fails to procure or effect such insurance within ten (10) days from date hereof, the Seller may effect such insurance and charge the cost thereof to the Buyer, and which charge the Buyer agrees to pay on demand, or upon the failure or refusal of the Buyer to pay said premium, then the Seller may, at Seller's option, take immediate possession of the said business, anything herein contained to the contrary notwithstanding.

The Buyer in consideration of the above, agrees to keep, during the continuance of this agreement, stock in a sum not less than the amount of stock now contained in the aforesaid premises, the value thereof to be not less than $ _____ , and in the event that the Buyer fails to comply therewith, the balance remaining unpaid shall then, at the option of the Seller, become due and payable, and the possession of the business herein mentioned is to revert back to the Seller, and the Buyer agrees that the Seller may maintain an action to eject the Buyer as trespasser on said premises.

Bill of Sale of Business (Conditional)

(Forms by courtesy of Julius Blumberg, Inc., 80 Exchange Place, New York, N.Y. 10004)

The Buyer in consideration of the sum of one dollar to the Buyer in hand paid by the Seller, the receipt whereof is hereby acknowledged, hereby agrees to and with the Seller, that in the event the Buyer fails to comply with any and all the terms and conditions of this agreement, or in the event the Buyer fails to pay any and all of the instalments at the time and in the manner hereinbefore mentioned, then the Buyer authorizes the Seller to re-take possession of said business, stock, chattels, fixtures, and the good will thereof, and any sum of money paid hereunder shall belong to the Seller, as liquidated, fixed and stipulated damages, and not as a penalty because the parties herein cannot ascertain the exact amount of damages sustained by the Seller for a breach of the conditions of this agreement by the Buyer, and the Buyer agrees to and with the Seller, in the event the Buyer shall default in the payment of the instalments hereinbefore mentioned, or in the event the Buyer fails to comply with any and all the terms and conditions of this agreement, that the Buyer will not engage in a business similar to the one mentioned in this agreement, either directly or indirectly, as principal, agent, servant, or employee, for any person, firm or corporation whatsoever, neither will the Buyer establish a business of a like nature, nor cause the same to be established, for a period of   years from date hereof, within a radius of   (   ) square blocks from the aforesaid premises, and the parties hereto agree that in the event of a breach of the aforementioned condition, the Seller will be entitled to an injunction restraining the Buyer for violating the terms of the agreement hereinbefore mentioned.

If more than one person joins in the execution of this agreement, and if any be of the feminine sex, or if this agreement is executed by a corporation, the relative words herein shall be read as if written in the plural, or in the feminine or neuter gender, as the case may be.

This agreement may not be changed or terminated orally. This agreement shall bind and enure to the benefit of the parties hereto, their respective heirs, personal representatives, successors and assigns.

IT IS ALSO UNDERSTOOD between the parties hereto, that upon full compliance by the Buyer of all the terms, covenants and conditions herein contained, that the Buyer is to have, hold and enjoy the above business unto Buyer and the Buyer's heirs, executors, administrators and assigns forever.

IN WITNESS WHEREOF, the parties hereto have hereunto set their hands and seals this day of 19

In presence of

Bill of Sale of Business-Conditional (Continued)

285

BINDER

Agreement, Between _____ and purchaser subscribing hereto. Purchaser agrees to purchase _____ 19___

at price of $ _____ with a deposit of $ _____ for which this is a receipt, and $ _____ when a more formal contract, such as is used by Title Companies, is signed by owner and purchaser, which is to be signed within _____ days, at _____. When warranty deed is delivered on _____ 19___ at _____ the purchaser agrees to pay $ _____, and $ _____ by assuming and agreeing to pay mortgage for that amount now on property above described. Balance $ _____ to be paid by purchaser _____

_____ In case the owner is not willing to accept the amount and terms as outlined above, the deposit is to be returned. If owner accepts and purchaser fails to comply, deposit shall be forfeited.

_____

_____

Above agreement approved and accepted by owner, who agrees to pay _____ _____% of the purchase price as commission.

Broker _____

Owner _____ _____ *Purchaser*

_____ *Purchaser Address*

FORM 245   S. S. Clarkson Mfg. Corp. 17 Bergen Street, Brooklyn, N. Y. 11201   (212) MAin 5-2624

Binder

(Reproduced with permission of S. S. Clarkson Mfg. Corp., Brooklyn, N.Y.)

BOND

KNOW ALL MEN BY THESE PRESENTS,

THAT _____
_____
hereinafter designated as the obligator ___, do ___ hereby acknowledge _____
to be _____ indebted to _____
_____
hereinafter designated as the obligee, in the sum of _____
dollars, lawful money of the United States, which sum_____ said obligor__
_____ do hereby _____
covenant to pay to said obligee, _____ or assigns, on the
_____ day of_____ nineteen hundred and_____ with interest thereon, to be computed from the _____ day of_____, 19___, at the rate of
_____ per centum, per annum and to be paid on the _____ day of
_____ next ensuing the date hereof, and_____ thereafter.

AND IT IS HEREBY EXPRESSLY AGREED THAT the whole of the said principal sum shall become due at the option of said obligee after default in the payment of
interest for days, or after default in the payment of any tax, water rate or assessment
for _____ days after notice and demand. All of the covenants and agreements
made by the said obligator _____ in the mortgage covering premises therein
described and collateral hereto, are hereby made part of this instrument.

Signed and sealed this _____ day of _____ 19___,
In the presence of

_____   _____(Seal)

_____   _____(Seal)

BOND AND MORTGAGE

With Additional Clauses
Individual or Corporation

THIS BOND AND MORTGAGE, made the ____ day of ____ 19 ____ BETWEEN ____

____, herein referred to as the mortgagor, and ____

____, herein referred to as the mortgagee,

WITNESSETH, that the mortgagor, does hereby acknowledge himself to be indebted to the mortgagee in the sum of

____ ($ ____) Dollars lawful money of the United States, which the mortgagor does hereby agree and bind himself to repay to the mortgagee ____

____

____

to secure the payment of which the mortgagor hereby mortgages to the mortgagee ALL ____

____

TOGETHER with all right, title and interest, if any, of the mortgagor of, in and to any streets and roads abutting the above-described premises to the center lines thereof

TOGETHER with all fixtures and articles of personal property, now or hereafter attached to, or contained in and used in connection with, said premises, including but not limited to all apparatus, machinery, plumbing, heating, lighting and cooking fixtures, fittings, gas ranges, bathroom and kitchen cabinets, ice boxes, refrigerators, food freezers, air-conditioning fixtures and units, pumps, awnings, shades, screens, storm sashes, aerials, plants and shrubbery.

TOGETHER with any and all awards heretofore and hereafter made to the present and all subsequent owners of the mortgaged premises by any governmental or other lawful authorities for taking by eminent domain the whole or any part of said premises or any easement therein, including any awards for any changes of grade of streets, which said awards are hereby assigned to the holder of this bond and mortgage, who is hereby authorized to collect and receive the proceeds of any such awards from such authorities and to give proper receipts and acquittances therefor, and to apply the same toward the payment of the amount owing on account of this bond and mortgage, notwithstanding the fact that the amount owing hereon may not then be due and payable; and the said mortgagor hereby covenants and agrees, upon request, to make, execute and deliver any and all assignments and other

288

instruments sufficient for the purpose of assigning the aforesaid awards to the holder of this bond and mortgage, free, clear and discharged of any and all encumbrances of any kind or nature whatsoever.

AND the mortgagor covenants with the mortgagee as follows:

1. That the mortgagor will pay the indebtedness as hereinbefore provided.

2. That the mortgagor will keep the buildings on the premises insured against loss by fire for the benefit of the mortgagee; that he will assign and deliver the policies to the mortgagee; and that he will reimburse the mortgagee for any premiums paid for insurance made by the mortgagee on the mortgagor's default in so insuring the buildings or in so assigning and delivering the policies.

3. That no building on the premises shall be removed or demolished without the consent of the mortgagee.

4. That the whole of said principal sum and interest shall become due at the option of the mortgagee: after default in the payment of any instalment of principal or of interest for   days; or after default in the payment of any tax, water rate, sewer rent or assessment for thirty days after notice and demand; or after default after notice and demand either in assigning and delivering the policies insuring the buildings against loss by fire or in reimbursing the mortgagee for premiums paid on such insurance, as hereinbefore provided; or after default upon request in furnishing a statement of the amount due on the bond and mortgage and whether any offsets or defenses exist against the mortgage debt, as hereinafter provided.

5. That the holder of this bond and mortgage, in any action to foreclose it, shall be entitled to the appointment of a receiver.

6. That the mortgagor will pay all taxes, assessments, sewer rents or water rates, and in default thereof, the mortgagee may pay the same.

7. That the mortgagor within six days upon request in person or within fifteen days upon request by mail will furnish a written statement duly acknowledged of the amount due on this bond and mortgage and whether any offsets or defenses exist against the morgage debt.

8. That notice and demand or request may be in writing and may be served in person or by mail.

9. That the mortgagor warrants the title to the premises.

10. That the mortgagor will receive the advances secured hereby and will hold the right to receive such advances as a trust fund to be applied first for the purpose of paying the cost of the improvement and will apply the same first to the payment of the cost of the improvement before using any part of the total of the same for any other purpose.

11. That fire insurance policies which are required by paragraph No. 2 above shall contain the usual extended coverage endorsement; in addition thereto the mortgagor, within thirty days after notice and demand will keep the buildings on the premises insured against loss by other insurable hazards for the benefit of the mortgagee, as may reasonably be required by the mortgagee; that he will assign and deliver the policies to the mortgagee; and that he will reimburse the mortgagee for any premiums paid for insurance made by the mortgagee on the mortgagor's default in so insuring or in so assigning and delivering the policies.

12. That in case of a sale, said premises, or so much thereof as may be affected by this bond and mortgage, may be sold in one parcel.

13. That in the event of any default in the performance of any of the terms, covenants or agreements herein contained, it is agreed that the then owner of the mortgaged premises, if he is the occupant of said premises or any part thereof, shall immediately surrender possession of the premises so occupied to the holder of this bond and mortgage, and if such occupant is permitted to remain in possession, the possession shall be as tenant of the holder of this bond and mortgage and such occupant shall, on demand, pay monthly in advance to the holder of this bond and mortgage a reasonable rental for the space so occupied and in default thereof, such occupant may be dispossessed by the usual summary proceedings. In case of foreclosure and the appointment of a receiver of rents, the covenants herein contained may be enforced by such receiver.

14. That the whole of said principal sum shall become due at the option of the mortgagee after default for thirty days after notice and demand, in the payment of any instalment of any assessment for local improvements heretofore or hereafter laid, which is or may become payable in annual instalments and which has affected, now affects or hereafter may affect the said premises, notwithstanding that such instalment be not due and payable at the time of such notice and demand, or upon the failure to exhibit to the mortgagee, within thirty days after demand, receipts showing payment of all taxes, assessments, water rates, sewer rents and any other charges which may have become a prior lien on the mortgaged premises.

15. That the whole of said principal sum shall become due at the option of the mortgagee, if the buildings on said premises are not maintained in reasonably good repair, or upon the failure of any owner of said premises to comply with the requirement of any governmental department claiming jurisdiction within three months after an order making such requirement has been issued by any such department.

16. That in the event of the passage after the date of this mortgage of any law, deducting from the value of land for the purposes of taxation any lien thereon, or changing in any way the laws for the taxation of mortgages or debts secured by mortgage for state or local purposes, or the manner of the collection of any such taxes, so as to affect this bond and mortgage, the holder of this bond and mortgage and of the debt which it secures, shall have the right to give thirty days' written notice to the owner of the mortgaged premises requiring the payment of the mortgage debt. If such notice be given the said debt shall become due, payable and collectible at the expiration of said thirty days.

17. That the whole of said principal sum shall immediately become due at the option of the mortgagee, if the mortgagor shall assign the rents or any part of the rents of the mortgaged premises without first obtaining the written consent of the mortgagee to such assignment, or upon the actual or threatened demolition or removal of any building erected or to be erected upon said premises.

18. That if any action or proceeding be commenced (except an action to foreclose this bond and mortgage or to collect the debt secured thereby), to which action or proceeding the holder of this bond and mortgage is made a party, or in which it becomes necessary to defend or uphold the lien of this mortgage, all sums paid by the holder of this bond and mortgage for the expense of any litigation to prosecute or defend the rights and lien created by this bond and mortgage (including reasonable counsel fees), shall be paid by the mortgagor, together with interest thereon at the rate of six per cent, per annum, and any such sum and the interest thereon shall be a lien on said premises, prior to any right, or title to, interest in or claim upon said premises attaching or accruing subsequent to

the lien of this mortgage, and shall be deemed to be secured by this bond and mortgage. In any action or proceeding to foreclose this mortgage, or to recover or collect the debt secured thereby, the provisions of law respecting the recovering of costs, disbursements and allowances shall prevail unaffected by this covenant.

19.   That the whole of said principal sum shall immediately become due at the option of the mortgagee upon any default in keeping the buildings on said premises insured as required by paragraph No. 2 or paragraph No. 11 hereof, or if after application by any holder of this bond and mortgage to two or more fire insurance companies and issuing policies of fire insurance upon buildings situate in the place where the mortgaged premises are situate, the companies to which such application has been made shall refuse to issue such policies, or upon default in complying with the provisions of paragraph No. 11 hereof, or upon default, for five days after notice and demand, either in assigning and delivering to the mortgagee the policies of fire insurance or in reimbursing the mortgagee for premiums paid on such fire insurance as hereinafter provided in paragraph No. 2 hereof.

If more than one person joins in the execution of this instrument, and if any of the feminine sex, or if this instrument is executed by a corporation, the relative words herein shall be read as if written in the plural, or in the feminine or neuter gender, as the case may be, and the words "mortgagor" and "mortgagee" where used herein shall be construed to include their and each of their heirs, executors, administrators, successors and assigns.

This bond and mortgage may not be changed orally.

IN WITNESS WHEREOF, this bond and mortgage has been duly executed by the mortgagor.

In presence of :

_____

_____ (Seal)

Bond and Mortgage (Continued)

BROKER-SALESMAN AGREEMENT

This Agreement made this _____ day of _____ by and between _____, Party of the First Part, herein after referred to as Broker, and _____, Party of the Second Part, hereinafter referred to as Salesman, for and in consideration of their mutual promises and agreements and for their mutual benefits, Witnesseth:

Whereas, said Broker is now, and has for many years, been engaged in business as a general real estate broker in the City of _____, and is qualified to and does operate a general real estate business and is duly qualified and does procure the listings of real estate for sale, lease or rental and prospective purchasers, lessees and renters thereof and has and does enjoy the good will of, and reputation for fair dealing with the public, and,

Whereas, said broker maintains an office in said County, properly equipped with furnishings and other equpment necessary and incidental to the proper operation of said business, and staffed with employees, suitable to serving the public as a real estate broker, and,

Whereas, said salesman is now, and has been engaged in business as a real estate salesman, has enjoyed and does enjoy a good reputation for fair and honest dealing with the public as such, and,

Whereas, it is deemed to be to the mutual advantage of said Broker and said Salesman to form the association hereinafter agreed to under the terms and conditions hereinafter set out, Therefore:

1. LISTINGS. The Broker agrees to make available to the Salesman all current listings of the office and agrees to assist the Salesman in his work by advice, instruction, and full cooperation in every way possible.

2. OFFICE FACILITIES. The Broker agrees that the Salesman may share with other Salesmen all the facilities of the office now operated by said Broker in connection with the subject matter of this contract, which office is now maintained at _____

3. SALESMAN'S DILIGENCE. The Salesman agrees to work diligently and with his best efforts to sell, lease or rent any and all real estate listed with the Broker, to solicit additional listings and customers of said Broker, and otherwise promote the business of serving the public in real estate transactions to the end that each of the parties hereto may derive the greatest profit possible.

4. CONDUCT. The Salesman agrees to conduct his business and regulate his habits, so as to maintain and to increase the good will and reputation of the Broker, and the parties hereto agree to conform to and abide by all laws, rules and regulations, and codes of ethics that are binding upon or applicable to real estate brokers and real estate salesmen.

5. COMMISSIONS. The usual and customary commissions shall be charged for any service performed hereunder, and the Broker shall advise the Salesman of any special contract relating to any particular transaction which he undertakes to handle. When the Salesman shall perform any service hereunder, whereby a commission is earned, said commission shall, when collected, be divided between the Broker and Salesman, in which division the Salesman shall receive a proportionate share as set out below:

Basic Commission Division	_____% to Salesman
	_____% to Broker
When Salesman Sells own Listing to own Buyer	_____% to Salesman
	_____% to Broker

In the event of special arrangements with any client of the Broker or the Salesman, a special division or commission may apply, such rate of division to be agreed upon by the Broker and the Salesman. In the event that two or more Salesmen participate in such a service, or claim to have done so, the amount of the commission over that accruing to the Broker shall be divided betwen the participating salesmen according to agreement between them or by arbitration. In no case shall the Broker be personally liable to the Salesman for any commission, nor shall said Salesman be personally liable to said Broker for any commissions, but when the commission shall have been collected from the party or parties for whom the service was performed, said Broker in the event such commissions are paid to him, shall hold the same in trust for said Salesman and himself to be divided according to the terms of this agreement, and in the event such commissions are paid to said Salesman, said Salesman shall pay over to said Broker said Broker's proportionate share of such commission according to the terms of this agreement.

6. DISTRIBUTION OF COMMISSION. The division and distribution of the earned commissions as set out in paragraph five hereof, which may be paid to or collected by said Broker, shall take place as soon as practicable after collection of such commissions from the party or parties for whom the services may have been performed.

7. BROKER NOT LIABLE FOR SALESMAN'S EXPENDITURES. The Broker shall not be liable to the Salesman for any expense incurred by him, or for any of his acts, nor shall the Salesman be liable to the Broker for office help or expense, and the Salesman shall have no authority to bind the Broker by any promises or representation, unless specifically authorized in a particular transaction; but expenses for attorney's fees, costs, revenue stamps, title abstracts and the like which must, by reason of some necessity, be paid from the commission, shall be paid by the parties in the same proportion as provided for herein the division of the commissions. Suits for commissions shall, agreeable to the law, be maintained only in the name of the Broker, and the Salesman shall be construed to be a sub-agent

only with respect to the clients and customers for whom services shall be performed, and shall otherwise be deemed to be an independent contractor and not a servant, employee, or partner of the Broker.

8. TERMINATION. This contract and the association created hereby, may be terminated by either party hereto, at any time upon notice given to the other, but the rights of the parties to any commission which accrued prior to said notice, shall not be divested by the termination of this contract.

9. INDEPENDENT CONTRACTOR. The parties hereto specifically agree that Salesman is an Independent Contractor, and not an employee, or partner of the Broker. That the provisions of this contract shall be construed to be directing the end result of Salesman's efforts, and not the methods by which they are accomplished. Broker is directed to not withhold from commissions Income Tax, Social Security, Workmen's Compensation or Unemployment Tax. In the event the courts shall decide, notwithstanding this provision, that such sums are due, or should Salesman be deemed to be an employee, Salesman shall be personally liable for all such taxes or sums that may be due thereby, and agrees to not be bound by the Workmen's Compensation Act. This provision shall be binding upon the heirs, executors, and administrators of the parties hereto.

10. USE OF MATERIAL BY SALESMAN AFTER TERMINATION. The Salesman shall not, after the termination of this contract, use to his own advantage, or the advantage of any other person or corporation, any information gained for or from the files or business of the Broker.

In Witness Whereof, the parties hereto have signed, or cause to be signed, these presents, this _____ day of _____, 19__.

By _____
Party of the First Part

_____
Party of the Second Part

Broker-Salesman Agreement (Continued)

BUILDING LOAN BOND

Individual Or Corporation

KNOW ALL MEN BY THESE PRESENTS, _____

That _____

hereinafter designated as the obligor does hereby acknowledge the obligor to be justly indebted to _____

hereinafter designated as the obligee, in the sum of _____

Dollars, lawful money of the United States, or so much thereof as may be advanced, which sum said obligor does hereby _____ covenant to pay the said obligee, and the executors, administrators, successors or assigns of the obligee, _____ with interest thereon to be computed from the date of each advance at the rate of _____ per centum per annum and to be paid on the _____ day of _____ 19___, next ensuing and _____ thereafter.

IT IS HEREBY EXPRESSLY AGREED, that the said principal sum shall at the option of the obligee become due on the happening of any default or event by which, under the terms of the mortgage securing this bond or of the building loan contract mentioned in said mortgage, said principal sum may or shall become due and payable; also, that all of the covenants, conditions and agreements contained in said mortgage and building loan contract are hereby made part of this instrument.

This bond may not be changed or terminated orally. The word "obligor" or "obligee" shall be construed as if it read "obligors" or "obligees" whenever the sense of this instrument so requires.

DATED the _____ day of _____ 19___.

In PRESENCE OF:

_____   _____

_____   _____

BUILDING LOAN MORTGAGE

Individual or Corporation

THIS MORTGAGE, made the   day of   , nineteen hundred and

BETWEEN

and   , the mortgagor,

                                                                                                                        , the mortgagee,

WITNESSETH, that to secure the payment of an indebtedness in the sum of   dollars,

lawful money of the United States or so much thereof as may be advanced, to be paid with interest thereon to be computed from the date of each advance, at the rate of per centum per annum, and to be paid on the 19 , next ensuing and thereafter,

according to a certain bond, note or obligation bearing even date herewith, the mortgagor hereby mortgages to the mortgagee

ALL that certain plot, piece or parcel of land, with the buildings and improvements thereon erected, situate, lying and being in the

Building Loan Mortgage

(Reproduced with permission of New York Board of Title Underwriters)

TOGETHER with all right, title and interest of the mortgagor in and to the land lying in the streets and roads in front of and adjoining said premises;

TOGETHER with all fixtures, chattels and articles of personal property now or hereafter attached to or used in connection with said premises, including but not limited to furnaces, boilers, oil burners, radiators and piping, coal stokers, plumbing and bathroom fixtures, refrigeration, air conditioning and sprinkler systems, wash-tubs, sinks, gas and electric fixtures, stoves, ranges, awnings, screens, window shades, elevators, motors, dynamos, refrigerators, kitchen cabinets, incinerators, plants and shrubbery and all other equipment and machinery, appliances, fittings, and fixtures of every kind in or used in the operation of the buildings standing on said premises, together with any and all replacements thereof and additions thereto;

TOGETHER with all awards heretofore and hereafter made to the mortgagor for taking by eminent domain the whole or any part of said premises or any easement therein, including any awards for changes of grade of streets, which said awards are hereby assigned to the mortgagee, who is hereby authorized to collect and receive the proceeds of such awards and to give proper receipts and acquittances therefor, and to apply the same toward the payment of the mortgage debt, notwithstanding the fact that the amount owing thereon may not then be due and payable; and the said mortgagor hereby agrees, upon request, to make, execute and deliver any and all assignments and other instruments sufficient for the purpose of assigning said awards to the mortgagee, free, clear and discharged of any encumbrances of any kind or nature whatsoever.

AND the mortgagor covenants with the mortgagee as follows:

1. That the mortgagor will pay the indebtedness as hereinbefore provided.

2. That the mortgagor will keep the buildings on the premises insured against loss by fire for the benefit of the mortgagee; that he will assign and deliver the policies to the mortgagee; and that he will reimburse the mortgagee for any premiums paid for insurance made by the mortgagee on the mortgagor's default in so insuring the buildings or in so assigning and delivering the policies.

3. That no building on the premises shall be altered, removed or demolished without the consent of the mortgagee.

298

4. That the whole of said principal sum and interest shall become due at the option of the mortgagee: after default in the payment of any instalment of principal or of interest for fifteen days; or after default in the payment of any tax, water rate, sewer rent or assessment for thirty days after notice and demand; or after default after notice and demand either in assigning and delivering the policies insuring the buildings against loss by fire or in reimbursing the mortgagee for premiums paid on such insurance, as hereinbefore provided; or after default upon request in furnishing a statement of the amount due on the mortgage and whether any offsets or defenses exist against the mortgage debt, as hereinafter provided. An assessment which has been made payable in instalments at the application of the mortgagor or lessee of the premises shall nevertheless, for the purpose of this paragraph, be deemed due and payable in its entirety on the day the first instalment becomes due or payable or a lien.

5. That the holder of this mortgage, in any action to foreclose it, shall be entitled to the appointment of a receiver.

6. That the mortgagor will pay all taxes, assessments, sewer rents or water rates, and in default thereof, the mortgagee may pay the same.

7. That the mortgagor within five days upon request in person or within ten days upon request by mail will furnish a written statement duly acknowledged of the amount due on this mortgage and whether any offsets or defenses exist against the mortgage debt.

8. That notice and demand or request may be in writing and may be served in person or by mail.

9. That the mortgagor warrants the title to the premises.

10. That the fire insurance policies required by paragraph No. 2 above shall contain the usual extended coverage endorsement; that in addition thereto the mortgagor, within thirty days after notice and demand, will keep the premises insured against war risk and any other hazard that may reasonably be required by the mortgagee. All of the provisions of paragraphs No. 2 and No. 4 above relating to fire insurance and the provisions of Section 254 of the Real Property Law construing the same shall apply to the additional insurance required by this paragraph.

11. That in case of a foreclosure sale, said premises, or so much thereof as may be affected by this mortgage, may be sold in one parcel.

12. That if any action or proceeding be commenced (except an action to foreclose this mortgage or to collect the debt secured thereby), to which action or proceeding the mortgagee is made a party, or in which it becomes necessary to defend or uphold the lien of this mortgage, all sums paid by the mortgagee for the expense of any litigation to prosecute or defend the rights and lien created by this mortgage (including reasonable counsel fees), shall be paid by the mortgagor, together with interest thereon at the rate of six per cent. per annum, and any such sum and the interest thereon shall be a lien on said premises, prior to any right, or title to, interest in or claim upon said premises attaching or accruing subsequent to the lien of this mortgage, and shall be deemed to be secured by this mortgage. In any action or proceeding to foreclose this mortgage, or to recover or collect the debt secured thereby, the provisions of law respecting the recovering of costs, disbursements and allowances shall prevail unaffected by this covenant.

Building Loan Mortgage (Continued)

13.   That the mortgagor hereby assigns to the mortgagee the rents, issues and profits of the premises as further security for the payment of said indebtedness, and the mortgagor grants to the mortgagee the right to enter upon and to take possession of the premises for the purpose of collecting the same and to let the premises or any part thereof, and to apply the rents, issues and profits, after payment of all necessary charges and expenses, on account of said indebtedness. This assignment and grant shall continue in effect until this mortgage is paid. The mortgagee hereby waives the right to enter upon and to take possession of said premises for the purpose of collecting said rents, issues and profits, and the mortgagor shall be entitled to collect and receive said rents, issues and profits until default under any of the covenants, conditions or agreements contained in this mortgage, and agrees to use such rents, issues and profits in payment of principal and interest becoming due on this mortgage and in payment of taxes, assessments, sewer rents, water rates and carrying charges becoming due against said premises, but such right of the mortgagor may be revoked by the mortgagee upon any default, on five days' written notice. The mortgagor will not, without the written consent of the mortgagee, receive or collect rent from any tenant of said premises or any part thereof for a period of more than one month in advance, and in the event of any default under this mortgage will pay monthly in advance to the mortgagee, or to any receiver appointed to collect said rents, issues and profits, the fair and reasonable rental value for the use and occupation of said premises or of such part thereof as may be in the possession of the mortgagor, and upon default in any such payment will vacate and surrender the possession of said premises to the mortgagee or to such receiver, and in default thereof may be evicted by summary proceedings.

14.   That the whole of said principal sum and the interest shall become due at the option of the mortgagee: (a) after failure to exhibit to the mortgagee, within ten days after demand, receipts showing payment of all taxes, water rates, sewer rents and assessments; or (b) after the actual or threatened alteration, demolition or removal of any building on the premises without the written consent of the mortgagee; or (c) after the assignment of the rents of the premises or any part thereof without the written consent of the mortgagee; or (d) if the buildings on said premises are not maintained in reasonably good repair; or (e) after failure to comply with any requirement or order or notice of violation of law or ordinance issued by any governmental department claiming jurisdiction over the premises within three months from the issuance thereof; or (f) if on application of the mortgagee two or more fire insurance companies lawfully doing business in the State of New York refuse to issue policies insuring the buildings on the premises; or (g) in the event of the removal, demolition or destruction in whole or in part of any of the fixtures, chattels or articles of personal property covered hereby, unless the same are promptly replaced by similar fixtures, chattels and articles of personal property at least equal in quality and condition to those replaced, free from chattel mortgages or other encumbrances thereon and free from any reservation of title thereto; or (h) after thirty days' notice to the mortgagor, in the event of the passage of any law deducting from the value of land for the purposes of taxation any lien thereon, or changing in any way the taxation of mortgages or debts secured thereby for state or local purposes; or (i) if the mortgagor fails to keep, observe and perform any of the other covenants, conditions or agreements contained in this mortgage or of those contained in the building loan contract hereinafter mentioned.

15.   That the mortgagor will, in compliance with Section 13 of the Lien Law, receive the advances secured hereby and will hold the right to receive such advances as a trust fund to be applied first for the purpose of paying the cost of the improvement and will apply the same first to the payment of the cost of the improvement before using any part of the total of the same for any other purpose.

16.   This mortgage is made pursuant to a certain building loan contract between the mortgagor and the mortgagee dated   19   , and intended to be filed in the office of the Clerk of the County of   on or before the date of the recording of this mortgage, and is subject to all the provisions of said contract as if they were fully set forth herein and made part of this mortgage.

17.   That the execution of this mortgage has been duly authorized by the board of directors of the mortgagor.

Strike out clause
17 if inapplicable.

This mortgage may not be changed or terminated orally. The covenants contained in this mortgage shall run with the land and bind the mortgagor, the heirs, personal representatives, successors and assigns of the mortgagor and all subsequent owners, encumbrancers, tenants and subtenants of the premises, and shall enure to the benefit of the mortgagee, the personal representatives, successors and assigns of the mortgagee and all subsequent holders of this mortgage. The word "mortgagor" shall be construed as if it read "mortgagors" and the word "mortgagee" shall be construed as if it read "mortgagees" whenever the sense of this mortgage so requires.

IN WITNESS WHEREOF, this mortgage has been duly executed by the mortgagor.

IN PRESENCE OF:

Building Loan Mortgage (Continued)

301

BUILDING LOAN MORTGAGE NOTE

Individual or Corporation

$ New York,   19

FOR VALUE RECEIVED,

promise   to pay to

or order, at

or at such other place as may be designated in writing by the holder of this note, the principal sum of

                                       Dollars, or so much thereof as may be advanced, on

with interest thereon to be computed from the date of each advance, at the rate of   per centum per annum and to be paid on the   day of   19   , next ensuing and thereafter.

IT IS HEREBY EXPRESSLY AGREED, that the said principal sum secured by this note shall at the option of the holder thereof become due on the happening of any default or event by which, under the terms of the mortgage securing this note or of the building loan contract mentioned in said mortgage, said principal sum may or shall become due and payable; also, that all of the covenants, conditions and agreements contained in said mortgage and building loan contract are hereby made part of this instrument.

Presentment for payment, notice of dishonor, protest and notice of protest are hereby waived.

This note is secured by a mortgage made by the maker to the payee of even date herewith, on property situate in the

This note may not be changed or terminated orally.

Building Loan Mortgage Note
(Reproduced with permission of New York Board of Title Underwriters)

BUSINESS PROPERTY

LOCATION   SECTION

LEGAL

SIZE PLOT   ZONE

BUILDING

SIZE   CONSTRUCTION   NO. STORIES

DETAILS

INSURED FOR   BY

LEASES

SPACE   TENANT   RENTAL   EXPIRES

TAXES   19   CITY   S & C   TOTAL

INSURANCE RATE   FIRE   BLDG.   CONTENTS,

                    WINDSTORM   BLDG.   CONTENTS

ANNUAL PREMIUMS

OPERATING EXPENSES

CASH PRICE $ TERM PRICE $

TERMS

WILL CONSIDER EXCHANGE FOR

OWNER   DATE LISTED

ADDRESS   EXCLUSIVE BY

                                   LISTED BY

Business and Industrial Property Listing Form

BUSINESS LEASE

THIS AGREEMENT, made this _____ day of _____ ,
19_____ , by and between_____
_____ ,
as Landlord, and_____a corporation of the State of
_____ , with its principal office and place of business in_____
_____ as Tenant:

WITNESSETH: That the said Landlord does hereby demise and lease to Tenant and Tenant does hereby hire from Landlord the following described premises:

together with all appurtenances thereto and with easements of ingress and egress necessary and adequate for the conduct of Tenant's business as hereinafter described, for the term of_____years, running from and including the_____
day of_____ , 19_____up to and including the_____
day of_____ , 19_____ , for use in Tenant's regular business of
_____
_____
or in any other legitimate business, subject to the terms and conditions of this lease.

AMOUNT OF RENTAL

Tenant covenants to pay to Landlord at Landlord's office at_____
_____
or such other place in_____
as Landlord shall designate in writing as rent for said premises, the sum of $_____
per month, payable in advance commencing_____ .
In addition to the above, Landlord and Tenant mutually covenant and agree as follows:

TENANT'S MAINTENANCE AND REPAIR OF PREMISES

1. Except as hereinafter provided, Tenant shall maintain and keep the interior of the premises in good repair, free of refuse and rubbish and shall return the same at the expiration or termination of this lease in as good condition as received by Tenant, ordinary wear and tear, damage or destruction by fire, flood storm, civil commotion or other unavoidable cause excepted; provided, however, that if alterations, additions and/or installations shall have been made by Tenant as provided for in this lease, Tenant shall not be required to restore the premises to the condition in which they were prior to such alterations, additions and/or installations except as hereinafter provided.

TENANT'S ALTERATIONS, ADDITIONS, INSTALLATIONS, AND REMOVAL THEREOF

2. Tenant may, at its own expense, either at the commencement of or during the term of this lease, make such alterations in and/or additions to the leased premises including, with-

out prejudice to the generality of the foregoing, alterations in the water, gas, and the electric wiring system, as may be necessary to fit the same for its business, upon first obtaining the written approval of Landlord as to the materials to be used and the manner of making such alterations and/or additions. Landlord covenants not to unreasonably withhold approval of alterations and/or additions proposed to be made by Tenant. Tenant may also, at its own expense, install such counters, racks, shelving, fixtures, fittings, machinery and equipment upon or within the leased premises as Tenant may consider to the conduct of its business. At any time prior to the expiration or earlier termination of the lease, Tenant may remove any or all such alterations, additions or installations in such a manner as will not substantially injure the leased premises. In the event Tenant shall elect to make any such removal, Tenant shall restore the premises, or the portion or portions affected by such removal, to the same condition as existed prior to the making of such alteration, addition or installation, ordinary wear and tear, damage or destruction by fire, flood, storm, civil commotion or other unavoidable cause excepted.

All alterations, additions or installations not so removed by Tenant shall become the property of Landlord without liability on Landlord's part to pay for the same.

LANDLORD'S MAINTENANCE AND REPAIR OF PREMISES

3. Landlord shall, without expenses to Tenant, maintain and make all necessary repairs to the foundations, load bearing walls, roof, gutters, downspouts, heating system, air conditioning, elevators, water mains, gas and sewer lines, sidewalks, private roadways, parking areas, railroad spurs or sidings, and loading docks, if any, on or appurtenant to the leased premises.

UTILITIES

4. Tenant shall pay all charges for water, gas and electricity consumed by Tenant upon the leased premises.

OBSERVANCE OF LAWS

5. Tenant shall duly obey and comply with all public laws, ordinances, rules or regulations relating to the use of the leased premises; provided, however, that any installation of fire prevention apparatus, electric rewiring, plumbing changes or structural changes in the building on the leased premises, required by any such law, ordinance, rule, or regulation shall be made by Landlord without expense to Tenant.

DAMAGE BY FIRE, ETC.

Damage Repairable Within One Hundred Twenty (120) Days

6. In the event the said premises shall be damaged by fire, flood, storm, civil commotion, or other unavoidable cause, to an extent repairable within one hundred twenty (120) days from the date of such damage, Landlord shall forthwith proceed to repair such damage. If such repair shall not have been completed within one hundred twenty (120) days from

the date of such damage, delays occasioned by causes beyond the control of Landlord excepted, this lease may, at the option of Tenant, be terminated. During the period of repair, Tenant's rent shall abate in whole or in part depending upon the extent to which such damage and/or such repair shall deprive Tenant of the use of said premises for the normal purposes of Tenant's business. In the event that Landlord shall fail to promptly commence repair of such damage, or, having commenced the same shall fail to prosecute such repair to completion with due diligence, Tenant may at Tenant's option upon five (5) days' written notice to Landlord, make or complete such repair and deduct the cost thereof from the next ensuing installment or installments of rent payable under this lease.

Damage Not Repairable Within One Hundred Twenty (120) Days

7. In the event the said premises shall be damaged by fire, flood, storm, civil commotion, or other unavoidable cause, to an extent not repairable within one hundred twenty (120) days from the date of such damage, this lease shall terminate as of the date of such damage.

SIDEWALK ENCUMBRANCES

8. Tenant shall neither encumber nor obstruct the sidewalk in front of, or any entrance to, the building on the leased premises.

SIGNS

9. Tenant shall have the right to erect, affix or display on the roof, exterior or interior walls, doors and windows of the building on the leased premises, such sign or sign advertising its business as Tenant may consider necessary or desirable, subject to all applicable municipal ordinances and regulations with respect thereto.

TERMINATION BY REASON OF DEFAULT

10. In the event that either of the parties hereto shall fail to perform any covenant required to be performed by such party under the terms and provisions of this lease, including Tenant's covenant to pay rent, and such failure shall continue unremedied or uncorrected for a period of fifteen (15) days after the service of written notice upon such party by the other party hereto, specifying such failure, this lease may be terminated, at the option of the party serving such notice, at the expiration of such period of fifteen (15) days; provided, however, that such termination shall not relieve the party so failing from liability to the other party for such damages as may be suffered by reason of such failure.

CONDEMNATION

11. In the event that the leased premises shall be taken for public use by the city, state, federal government, public authority or other corporation having the power of eminent domain, then this lease shall terminate as of the date on which possession thereof shall be taken for such public use, or, at the option of Tenant, as of the date on which the premises shall become unsuitable for Tenant's regular business by reason of such taking; provided,

however, that if only a part of the leased premises shall be so taken, such termination shall be at the option of Tenant only. If such a taking of only a part of the leased premises occurs, and Tenant elects not to terminate the lease, there shall be a proportionate reduction of the rent to be paid under this lease from and after the date such possession is taken for public use. Tenant shall have the right to participate, directly or indirectly, in any award for such public taking to the extent that it may have suffered compensable damage as a Tenant on account of such public taking.

ASSIGNMENT

12. Tenant may assign this lease or sub-let the premises or any part thereof for any legitimate use, either with or without the consent of Landlord. If any assignment or sub-lease is made by Tenant without Landlord's consent, Tenant shall remain liable as surety under the terms hereof notwithstanding such assignment or sub-lease.

TAXES

13. Landlord shall pay all taxes, assessments, and charges which shall be assessed and levied upon the leased premises or any part thereof during the said term as they shall become due.

TENANT'S LIABILITY INSURANCE

14. During the term of this lease, Tenant at his own expense shall carry public liability insurance in not less than the following limits:
bodily injury $100,000/$300,000
property damage $50,000

LANDLORD'S RIGHT TO ENTER PREMISES

15. Tenant shall permit Landlord and Landlord's agents to enter at all reasonable times to view the state and condition of the premises or to make such alterations or repairs therein as may be necessary for the safety and preservation thereof, or for any other reasonable purposes. Tenant shall also permit Landlord or Landlord's agents, on or after sixty (60) days next preceding the expiration of the term of this lease, to show the premises to prospective tenants at reasonable times, and to place notices on the front of said premises, or on any part thereof, offering the premises for lease or for sale.

RENEWAL OF LEASE

16. Tenant shall have the option to take a renewal lease of the demised premises for the further term of_____( ) years from and after the expiration of the term herein granted at a monthly rent of _____
_____dollars ($_____) and under and subject to the same covenants, provisos and agreements as are herein contained. In the event Tenant desires to exercise the

option herein provided, Tenant shall notify Landlord of such desire in writing not less than sixty (60) days prior to the expiration of the term hereby granted.

AND IT IS MUTUALLY UNDERSTOOD AND AGREED that the covenants and agreements herein contained shall insure to the benefit of and be equally binding upon the respective executors, administrators, heirs, successors and assigns of the parties hereto.

IN WITNESS WHEREOF, the parties hereto have executed this lease the day and year first above written.

_____ (L. S.)

_____ (L. S.)

Signed, Sealed and   _____ (L. S.)

Delivered in the   _____ (L. S.)

presence of   Landlord (s)

_____

_____

Attest:

_____   _____
        Assistant Secretary   Vice President

                                (Tenant)

(Reproduced with permission of PPG Industries, Inc., Pittsburgh, Pa.)

BUSINESS OPPORTUNITY

Name..

Location...Section...

Type of Business...

INCOME & EXPENSES			GENERAL INFORMATION

INCOME & EXPENSES

Gross Inc. $..............

Expenses

    Taxes $................   ....

    Ins. $................   ....

    Elec. $................   ....

    Gas $................   ....

    Water $................   ....

    Rent $................   ....

         $................   ....

         $................   ....

         $................   ....

         $................   ....

    Misc. $................   ....

Total Expense $..............

Net Income $..............

GENERAL INFORMATION

Replacement Value..

....

Income Value..

....

Cash Price..

Terms..

....

Mortgages..

....

Size of Business Location...................................

REMARKS...

....

....

Lease...

Type.............................Length..............

Owner's Name...

Address..Tel...

Date Listed...Exclusive by:..

Signature...Listed by:..

            (Proprietor)

Business Opportunity Listing Form

CHATTEL MORTGAGE

$_____ 19_____

ON OR BEFORE, the_____day of_____, 19_____,_____
_____promise to pay to_____
or order,_____Dollars with interest at the rate of
_____percent, per annum from date until paid. Value received.

WITNESS:

_____   _____ (SEAL)

_____   _____ (SEAL)

_____   _____ (SEAL)

And said_____as mortgagor for the purpose of securing
the prompt and full payment of the same at maturity, do give unto the mortgagee,_____
_____, heirs, successors and assigns, a mortgage lien upon the
following property, now in _____possession, custody
and control, in the County of_____ and State of_____
_____, to wit:

And said mortgagor_____do_____hereby warrant
and represent that_____has_____full rights and power
to encumber said property as above set forth, and that the same is free and clear of all other
mortgages, liens or encumbrances, of any kind or nature whatsoever.
And the said mortgagor_____do_____hereby agree
that if said note or any part thereof remains unpaid at maturity, to pay all costs, charges
and expenses together with an attorney's fee of_____per cent, on the amount of
the claim that the said_____heirs, successors, or assigns, may
incur or be put to in collecting said money by law or otherwise.
And the said mortgagor_____hereby waive the benefit of the
Homestead and Exemption Laws of the State of_____upon the above
described property.

IN WITNESS WHEREOF,_____have hereunto set_____

hand-and-seal this_____day of_____, A.D., 19_____.

_____   _____ (SEAL)

_____   _____ (SEAL)

_____   _____ (SEAL)

_____   _____ (SEAL)

CLAIM OF LIEN

STATE OF _____
COUNTY OF _____

Before me, the undersigned authority, personally appeared _____
who, being duly sworn, says that he is the lienor herein or (the agent, the attorney)
of the lienor herein, _____
(Lienor's Name

whose address is _____
(Lienor's Address)

and that in pursuance of a contract with _____,
_____
lienor furnished labor, services or materials consisting of: (Describe specially
fabricated materials separately) of a total value of _____dollars
($_____) of which there remains unpaid $_____, for which amount he
claims a lien on the followiong described real property in _____
County, _____ owned by _____

He further says that lienor furnished the first of said labor, services or materials on
_____, 19__, and the last of the same on _____, 19__, and (if the lien is
claimed by one not in privity with the owner) that the lienor served his notice to
owner on _____, 19__, by _____
(Method of Service)

_____

By _____
Lienor, Agent or Attorney

Sworn to and subscribed before me this _____ day of _____, 19__.

_____
Notary Public

CLOSING STATEMENT
TO

Lot _____ Block _____ Subdivision _____

_____ 19 _____

Our File No. _____

CHARGES FOR WATER, RENTS, GAS, ELECTRICITY, TAXES ON PERSONAL PROPERTY, LICENSE OR GARBAGE TAXES NOT ADJUSTED THIS COMPANY ASSUMES NO LIABILITY FOR THESE ITEMS.

DESCRIPTION OF PROPERTY	CREDITS	DEBITS
PURCHASE PRICE		
DEPOSIT		
DEPOSIT IN ESCROW		
PROCEEDS OF LOAN		
ABSTRACTING		
RECORDING		
U.S. REVENUE STAMPS		
FLORIDA DOCUMENTARY STAMPS		
TITLE INSURANCE		
ESCROW FEE		
SURVEY		
INSPECTION SURVEY		
MORTGAGE		
MORTGAGE		
MORTGAGE		
PRORATION OF TAXES—REAL ESTATE		

PRORATION OF TAXES—PERSONAL PROPERTY:

CERTIFIED MUNICIPAL LIENS

ALLOWANCE FOR PENDING MUNICIPAL LIENS

PRORATION OF INTEREST

PRORATION OF INSURANCE

PRORATION OF RENTS

INSURANCE, FIRE

INSURANCE, TORNADO

BROKER'S COMMISSION

TAXES PAID, REAL AND PERSONAL PROPERTY, MUNICIPAL,

STATE AND COUNTY, DRAINAGE, ETC., TO-WIT:

I have read the foregoing statement and hereby approve the same.

Date _____

Closing Statement

COMMERCIAL AND INDUSTRIAL BUILDINGS

FORM I

TYPE BLDGS. _____   PRICE $ _____

NO. OF UNITS _____   DOWN PAY. $ _____

LOCATION _____

LOT _____ , BLOCK _____ , SUBDIVISION _____

LOT SIZE _____ X _____ , ZONED _____ , CITY _____ COUNTY _____

NO. STORIES _____ SQ. FT. _____ RAILROAD _____

TYPE CONST. _____ BLDG. SIZE _____ PAVED STREET _____

FLOORS _____ YEAR BUILT _____ SIDEWALKS _____

ROOF _____ WATER _____ CITY TAXES _____

TYPE HEAT _____ SEWAGE _____ COUNTY TAXES _____

AIR COND. _____ CANAL _____ INSURANCE _____

OTHER FEATURES _____

UNITS	SIZE	TENANT	RENTAL	LEASE EXPIRES
1	____ X ____	_____	$ _____	_____
2	____ X ____	_____	$ _____	_____
3	____ X ____	_____	$ _____	_____
4	____ X ____	_____	$ _____	_____
5	____ X ____	_____	$ _____	_____
6	____ X ____	_____	$ _____	_____
7	____ X ____	_____	$ _____	_____
8	____ X ____	_____	$ _____	_____

TERMS:

FIRST MORTGAGE $ _____ , HELD BY _____

PAYABLE $ _____ , PER MO., INTEREST _____ %

SECOND MORTGAGE $ _____ , HELD BY _____

PAYABLE $ _____ , PER MO., INTEREST _____ %

LISTED BY _____

DATE LISTED _____

EXCLUSIVE _____

OWNER _____

ADDRESS _____

PHONE _____

Commercial and Industrial Buildings Listing Form
(*Reproduced with permission of Florida Forms, Homestead Fla.*)

CONDITIONAL SALES CONTRACT

_____ _____, 19____

RECEIVED FROM _____   _____

ADDRESS _____

THE SUM OF $ _____ Sales Price $ _____

Received $ _____

Balance $ _____

The balance of $_____ is to be paid in equal monthly installments of $_____ until paid in full, on the first day of each month. This amount includes principal and interest of_____% per annum on the unpaid balance, the interest to be deducted from each payment as made.

This agreement is made betweeen_____, party of the first part, a corporation of the State of_____, and_____ _____, party of the second part.

WITNESSETH: That if the party of the second part shall first make the payments and perform the covenants mentioned herein on part to be performed, the party of the first part hereby covenants and agrees to convey and assure to the party of the second part, in fee simple, clear of all encumbrances whatsoever, by good and sufficient_____ _____deed, the lot_____ of ground situated in the County of_____ _____, State of_____, known and described as follows:

(Here include legal description)

In case of the failure of the party of the second part to make any of the payments herein designated, or any part thereof, or failure to perform any of the covenants for a period of_____ days after maturity, this agreement shall be forfeited and terminated within_____days after receipt of declaration of intent to forfeit and terminate by the Seller via registered or certified mail, and the party of the second part shall forfeit all payments made on this contract, and such payments shall be retained by the said party of the first part as due or accumulated rent on the property, and shall become liable to the party of the first part for monthly rental of $_____per month payable on the first day of each month; and in case of nonpayment of such rent, the party of the first part shall have the right to re-enter and take possession of the premises aforesaid without being liable to any action therefor, or any costs incurred.

In addition the party of the second part agrees to pay all taxes, subsequent to year_____.

Construction shall be limited to residences built of new materials. Residences must be located at least fifteen feet from front lot line. No shacks or unsightly structures allowed. Structures of a temporary nature used during normal construction must be removed within one year. Sewage disposal systems must include septic tanks of currently acceptable design and construction.

It is further agreed by the parties hereto that this contract or any assignment thereof is not to be recorded without permission of the owners. If this contract or assignment thereto is recorded contrary to the above provision then any existing balance shall become due and payable.

Conditional Sales Contract *(Continued)*

It is mutually agreed by and between the parties that the time of payment shall be an essential part of this contract, and that all covenants and agreements herein contained shall extend to and be obligatory upon the heirs executors, administrators, and assigns of the respective parties.

It is agreed that the party of the second part shall have the privilege and right to examine a master abstract.

IN WITNESS WHEREOF, the parties to these presents have hereunto set their hands and seals the day and year first above written.

WITNESS OF BUYERS:　　　　　　　　　BUYERS:

_____ _____　　　_____ (Seal)

_____　　_____ ___ (Seal)

　　　　　　　　　　　　　　　　　　　ACCEPTED:

ATTEST　　　　　　(Seal)

_____　　_____ - _____

　　　Assistant Secretary　　　　　　　　　　　　　President

125 — Improved Contract for Sale of Property. ■

JULIUS BLUMBERG, INC., LAW BLANK PUBLISHERS
80 EXCHANGE PLACE AT BROADWAY, NEW YORK

THIS AGREEMENT, made the   day of   19

BETWEEN

hereinafter described as the seller, and

hereinafter described as the purchaser,

WITNESSETH, that the seller agrees to sell and convey, and the purchaser agrees to purchase, all that certain plot, piece or parcel of land, with the buildings and improvements thereon, situate, lying and being in the

This sale includes all right, title and interest, if any, of the seller in and to any land lying in the bed of any street, road or avenue opened or proposed, in front of or adjoining said premises, to the center line thereof, and all right, title and interest of the seller in and to any award made or to be made in lieu thereof and in and to any unpaid award for damage to said premises by reason of change of grade of any street; and the seller will execute and deliver to the purchaser, on closing of title, or thereafter, on demand, all proper instruments for the conveyance of such title and the assignment and collection of any such award.

Contract

(Form by courtesy of Julius Blumberg, Inc., 80 Exchange Place, New York, N.Y. 10004)

The price is Dollars, payable as follows:

on the signing of this contract, by check subject to collection, the receipt of which is hereby acknowledged; Dollars,

in cash or good certified check on the delivery of the deed as hereinafter provided; Dollars,

by taking title subject to a mortgage now a lien on said premises in that amount, bearing interest at the rate of per cent per annum, the principal being due and payable Dollars,

by the purchaser or assigns executing, acknowledging and delivering to the seller a bond or note satisfactory to the seller secured by a purchase money mortgage on the above premises, in that amount, payable

together with interest at the rate of per cent per annum payable

Any bond or note and mortgage to be given hereunder shall contain the clauses usually employed by Title Companies in New York City in such instruments for mortgages of like lien; and shall be drawn by the attorney for the seller at the expense of the purchaser, who shall also pay the mortgage recording tax and recording fees and pay for and affix to such instruments any and all revenue stamps that may be necessary.

If such purchase money mortgage is to be a subordinate mortgage on the premises it shall provide that it shall be subject and subordinate to the lien of the existing mortgage of $, any extensions thereof and to any mortgage or consolidated mortgage which may be placed on the premises in lieu thereof, and to any extensions thereof provided (a) that the interest rate thereof shall not be greater than per cent per annum and (b) that, if the principal amount thereof shall exceed the amount of principal owing and unpaid on said existing mortgage at the time of placing such new mortgage or consolidated mortgage, the excess be paid to the holder of such purchase money mortgage in reduction of the principal thereof. Such purchase money mortgage shall also provide that such payment to the holder thereof shall not alter or affect the regular installments, if any, of principal payable thereunder and shall further provide that the holder thereof will, on demand and without charge therefor, execute, acknowledge and deliver any agreement or agreements further to effectuate such subordination.

If this sale is subject to the Real Property Transfer Tax imposed by Title I of Chapter 46 of the Administrative Code of the City of New York, at the closing of the title the seller shall deliver to the purchaser a certified check to the order of the City Treasurer for the amount so imposed and will also deliver to the purchaser the return required by the said statute and the regulations issued pursuant to the authority thereof, duly signed and sworn to by the seller; the purchaser agrees to sign and swear to the said return and to cause the said check and the said return to be delivered to the City Register promptly after the closing of the title.

Said premises are sold and are to be conveyed subject to:

1. Zoning regulations and ordinances of the city, town or village in which the premises lie which are not violated by existing structures.

2. Consents by the seller or any former owner of premises for the erection of any structure or structures on, under or above any street or streets on which said premises may abut.

3. Encroachments of stoops, areas, cellar steps, trim and cornices, if any, upon any street or highway.

If there be a mortgage on the premises the seller agrees to deliver to the purchaser at the time of delivery of the deed a proper certificate executed and acknowledged by the holder of such mortgage and in form for recording, certifying as to the amount of the unpaid principal and interest thereon, date of maturity thereof and rate of interest thereon, and the seller shall pay the fees for recording such certificate.

All notes or notices of violations of law or municipal ordinances, orders or requirements noted in or issued by the Departments of Housing and Buildings, Fire, Labor, Health, or other State or Municipal Department having jurisdiction against or affecting the premises at the date hereof, shall be complied with by the seller and the premises shall be conveyed free of the same, and this provision of this contract shall survive delivery of the deed hereunder. The seller shall furnish the purchaser with an authorization to make the necessary searches therefor.

If, at the time of the delivery of the deed, the premises or any part thereof shall be or shall have been affected by an assessment or assessments which are or may become payable in annual installments, of which the first installment is then a charge or lien, or has been paid, then for the purposes of this contract all the unpaid installments of any such assessment, including those which are to become due and payable after the delivery of the deed, shall be deemed to be due and payable and to be liens upon the premises affected thereby and shall be paid and discharged by the seller, upon the delivery of the deed. Westchester County Sewer System Taxes shall be excluded from the provisions of this paragraph and the installments thereof not due and payable at the time of the delivery of the deed hereunder shall be assumed by the purchaser without abatement of the purchase price.

Contract (Continued)

The following are to be apportioned:

(1) Rents as and when collected. (2) Interest on mortgages. (3) Premiums on existing transferable insurance policies or renewals of those expiring prior to the closing. (4) Taxes and sewer rents, if any, on the basis of the fiscal year for which assessed. (5) Water charges on the basis of the calendar year. (6) Fuel, if any.

If the closing of the title shall occur before the tax rate is fixed, the apportionment of taxes shall be upon the basis of the tax rate for the next preceding year applied to the latest assessed valuation.

If there be a water meter on the premises, the seller shall furnish a reading to date not more than thirty days prior to the time herein set for closing title, and the unfixed meter charge and the unfixed sewer rent, if any, based thereon for the intervening time shall be apportioned on the basis of such last reading.

The deed shall be the usual

deed in proper statutory short form for record and shall be duly executed, acknowledged, and have revenue stamps in the proper amount affixed thereto by the seller, at the seller's expense, so as to convey to the purchaser the fee simple of the said premises, free of all encumbrances, except as herein stated, and shall also contain the covenant required by subdivision 5 of Section 13 of the Lien Law.

The seller shall give and the purchaser shall accept a title such as   will approve and insure.

All sums paid on account of this contract, and the reasonable expenses of the examination of the title to said premises and of the survey, if any, made in connection therewith are hereby made liens thereon, but such liens shall not continue after default by the purchaser under this contract.

All fixtures and articles of personal property attached or appurtenant to or used in connection with said premises are represented to be owned by the seller, free from all liens and encumbrances except as herein stated, and are included in this sale; without limiting the generality of the foregoing, such fixtures and articles of personal property include plumbing, heating, lighting and cooking fixtures, air conditioning fixtures and units, ranges, refrigerators, radio and television aerials, bathroom and kitchen cabinets, mantels, door mirrors, venetian blinds, shades, screens, awnings, storm windows, window boxes, storm doors, mail boxes, weather vanes, flagpoles, pumps, shrubbery and outdoor statuary.

The amount of any unpaid taxes, assessments, water charges and sewer rents which the seller is obligated to pay and discharge, with the interest and penalties thereon to a date not less than two business days after the date of closing title, may at the option of the seller be allowed to the purchaser out of the balance of the purchase price, provided official bills therefor with interest and penalties thereon figured to said date are furnished by the seller at the closing. If at the date of closing title there may be any other liens or encumbrances which the seller is obligated to pay and discharge, the seller may use any portion of the balance of the purchase price to satisfy the same, provided the seller shall have delivered to the purchaser at the closing of title instruments in recordable form and sufficient to satisfy such liens and encumbrances of record, together with the cost of recording or filing said instruments. The purchaser, if request is made within a reasonable time prior to the date of closing of title, agrees to provide at the closing separate certified checks as requested, aggregating the amount of the balance of the purchase price, to facilitate the satisfaction of any such liens or encumbrances. The existence of any such taxes or other liens and encumbrances shall not be deemed objections to title if the seller shall comply with the foregoing requirements.

If a search of the title discloses judgments, bankruptcies or other returns against other persons having names the same as or similar to that of the seller, the seller will on request deliver to the purchaser an affidavit showing that such judgments, bankruptcies or other returns are not against the seller.

In the event that the seller is unable to convey title in accordance with the terms of this contract, the sole liability of the seller will be to refund to the purchaser the amount paid on account of the purchase price and to pay the net cost of examining the title and the net cost of any survey made in connection therewith incurred by the purchaser, and upon such refund and payment being made this contract shall be considered canceled.

The deed shall be delivered upon the receipt of said payments at the office of

at   o'clock on   19

The parties agree that

brought about this sale and the seller agrees to pay the commission at the rates established or adopted by the Board of Real Estate Brokers in the locality where the property is situated.

It is understood and agreed that all understandings and agreements heretofore had between the parties hereto are merged in this contract, which alone fully and completely expresses their agreement, and that the same is entered into after full investigation, neither party relying upon any statement or representation, not embodied in this contract, made by the other. The purchaser has inspected the buildings standing on said premises and is thoroughly acquainted with their condition.

This agreement may not be changed or terminated orally. The stipulations aforesaid are to apply to and bind the heirs, executors, administrators, successors and assigns of the respective parties.

If two or more persons constitute either the seller or the purchaser, the word "seller" or the word "purchaser" shall be construed as if it read "sellers" or "purchasers" whenever the sense of this agreement so requires.

IN WITNESS WHEREOF, this agreement has been duly executed by the parties hereto.

In presence of:

Contract (Continued)

321

BUYER	Section		PROPERTY	
		Garage		
Name		Material		
Address		Stories		
Phone		Rooms		
		Price		
Other Info.		Cash		
How Interviewed				
Salesman		Date		(over)

FRONT

Date	Property Shown	No. Fams.	If not interested, Why?
Prospect Good Fair			Nat.
Form 345 S. J. Clark's Sons, Inc. 135 Union Street, Brooklyn, N. Y. 11231			

BACK

Customer or Prospect Card
(Reproduced with permission of S. J. Clark's Sons, Inc., Brooklyn, New York)

WARRANTY DEED IN TRUST

THIS INDENTURE WITNESSETH, That the Grantor

of the County of   and State of

of

and valuable considerations in hand paid, Convey   and warrant   unto the CHICAGO TITLE

AND TRUST COMPANY, a corporation of Illinois, as Trustee under the provisions of a trust agreement

dated the   day of   19   , known as Trust Number

the following described real estate in the County of   and State of Illinois, to-wit:

for and in consideration

Dollars, and other good

TO HAVE AND TO HOLD the said premises with the appurtenances upon the trusts and for the uses and purposes herein and in said trust agreement set forth.

Full power and authority is hereby granted to said trustee to improve, manage, protect and subdivide said premises or any part thereof, to dedicate parks, streets, highways or alleys and to vacate any subdivision or part thereof, and to resubdivide said property as often as desired, to contract to sell, to grant options to purchase, to sell on any terms, to convey either with or without consideration, to convey said premises or any part thereof to a successor or successors in trust and to grant to such successor or successors in trust all of the title, estate, powers and authorities vested in said trustee, to donate, to dedicate, to mortgage, pledge or otherwise encumber said property, or any part thereof, to lease said property, or any part thereof, from time to time, in possession or reversion, by leases to commence in praesenti or futuro, and upon any terms and for any period or periods of time, not exceeding in the case of any single demise the term of 198 years, and to renew or extend leases upon any terms and for any period or periods of time, to amend, change or modify leases and the terms and provisions thereof at any time or times hereafter, to contract to make leases and to grant options to lease and options to renew leases and options to purchase the whole or any part of the reversion and to contract respecting the manner of fixing the amount of present or future rentals, to partition or to exchange said property, or any part thereof, for other real or personal property, to grant easements or charges of any kind, to release, convey or assign any right, title or interest in or about or easement appurtenant to said premises or any part thereof, and to deal with said property and every part thereof in all other ways and for such other considerations as it would be lawful for any person owning the same to deal with the same, whether similar to or different from the ways above specified, at any time or times hereafter.

Deed of Trust (Warranty)

(Reproduced with permission of the Chicago Title and Trust Co.)

In no case shall any party dealing with said trustee in relation to said premises, or to whom said premises or any part thereof shall be conveyed, contracted to be sold, leased or mortgaged by said trustee, be obliged to see to the application of any purchase money, rent, or money borrowed or advanced on said premises, or be obliged to see that the terms of this trust have been complied with, or be obliged to inquire into the necessity or expediency of any act of said trustee, or be obliged or privileged to inquire into any of the terms of said trust agreement; and every deed, trust deed, mortgage, lease or other instrument executed by said trustee in relation to said real estate shall be conclusive evidence in favor of every person relying upon or claiming under any such conveyance, lease or other instrument, (a) that at the time of the delivery thereof the trust created by this indenture and by said trust agreement was in full force and effect, (b) that such conveyance or other instrument was executed in accordance with the trusts, conditions and limitations contained in this indenture and in said trust agreement or in some amendment thereof and binding upon all beneficiaries thereunder, (c) that said trustee was duly authorized and empowered to execute and deliver every such deed, trust deed, lease, mortgage or other instrument and (d) if the conveyance is made to a successor or successors in trust, that such successor or successors in trust have been properly appointed and are fully vested with all the title, estate, rights, powers, authorities, duties and obligations of its, his or their predecessor in trust.

The interest of each and every beneficiary hereunder and of all persons claiming under them or any of them shall be only in the earnings, avails and proceeds arising from the sale or other disposition of said real estate, and such interest is hereby declared to be personal property, and no beneficiary hereunder shall have any title or interest, legal or equitable, in or to said real estate as such, but only an interest in the earnings, avails and proceeds thereof as aforesaid.

If the title to any of the above lands is now or hereafter registered, the Registrar of Titles is hereby directed not to register or note in the certificate of title or duplicate thereof, or memorial, the words "in trust", or "upon condition", or "with limitations", or words of similar import, in accordance with the statute in such case made and provided.

And the said grantor_____ hereby expressly waive_____ and release_____ any and all right or benefit under and by virtue of any and all statutes of the State of Illinois, providing for the exemption of homesteads from sale on execution or otherwise.

In Witness Whereof, the grantor_____ aforesaid ha_____ hereunto set_____ hand_____ and seal_____ this_____ day of_____ 19_____

_____(Seal) _____(Seal)

_____(Seal) _____(Seal)

State of_____ }
County of_____ } ss.

I,_____ a Notary Public in and for said County, in the state aforesaid, do hereby certify that_____

personally known to me to be the same person_____ whose name_____ subscribed to the foregoing instrument, appeared before me this day in person and acknowledged that_____ signed, sealed and delivered the said instrument as_____ free and voluntary act, for the uses and purposes therein set forth, including the release and waiver of the right of homestead.

Given under my hand and notarial seal this_____ day of_____ 19_____

_____
Notary Public

Chicago Title and Trust Co.
Box 533

For information only insert street address of above described property.

Deed of Trust (Continued)

REALTOR®

THE MIAMI BOARD OF REALTORS

of the National Association of Real Estate Boards

Realtors adhere to a code of professional ethics

PURCHASE AND SALE CONTRACT
AND RECEIPT FOR DEPOSIT

Miami, Florida _____ , 19 ____

Receipt is hereby acknowledged of the sum of:

_____ (check/cash) Dollars ($ _____)

from _____

proceeds to be held in escrow by _____

subject to the terms hereof, as a deposit on account of the purchase price of the following described property:

Purchase price:

_____ Dollars ($ _____)

Terms and conditions of sale:

Seller agrees to surrender possession of herein described premises to purchaser on _____
Seller agrees to assume risk of any and all damage to above described premises prior to closing of this transaction, ordinary wear and tear excepted.

Taxes based on 19_____ assessments, insurance, interest, rents and other expenses or revenue of said property shall be
_____
_____

Certified liens, if any, shall be paid in full by the seller. Pending liens, if any, shall be assumed by the purchaser. It is understood and agreed that this property is being sold and purchased subject to the zoning restrictions, reservations and limitations of record, if any. Seller agrees to convey title free and clear of all encumbrances, except as herein set forth, by a good and sufficient
_____ deed.

Seller agrees to deliver to purchaser within _____ days from the date hereof a complete abstract to said property, brought to date showing his title to be good, marketable and/or insurable, and in the event such abstract is not delivered within said time, seller hereby authorizes the undersigned broker to have an abstract made at seller's expense and delivered to purchaser; but, in the event title shall not be found good, marketable and/or insurable, seller agrees to use reasonable diligence to make the said title good, marketable and/or insurable and shall have _____ days so to do, but if after reasonable diligence on his part, said title shall not be made good, marketable and/or insurable within _____ days, the money this day paid and all monies that may have been paid under this contract shall be returned to purchaser and the purchaser and seller shall be released from all obligations hereunder to each other. Or, upon request of the purchaser, the seller shall deliver the title in its existing condition.

It is mutually agreed that this transaction shall be closed and the purchaser shall pay the balance of the cash to close and execute all papers necessary to be executed by him for the completion of his purchase within _____ days from the delivery of the aforementioned abstract.

Checks issued for the deposit on this contract will be deposited promptly for clearance and the holder of the deposit will not be responsible for non-payment of checks received. Deposit checks will be deposited and the funds held in an escrow account until the sale is closed. If the seller does not execute the contract, the deposit will be returned to the purchaser upon notification by the bank to the holder of the deposit that checks received have cleared.

When this contract is executed by the purchaser and the seller and the sale is not closed due to any default or failure on the part of the purchaser, the seller, at his option, may seek to enforce this contract; in which event, the purchaser shall be obligated to pay reasonable attorney's fee and court costs to the seller, or else the seller may direct the holder of the deposit to pay the broker his brokerage fee not to exceed one-half of the deposit and to pay the balance of the deposit to the seller as consideration for execution of this agreement, and the holder of the deposit shall be held harmless by all parties for disbursement in accordance with this agreement.

When the contract is executed by the purchaser and the seller and the sale is not closed due to default or failure on the part of the seller, the purchaser, at his option, may take action to enforce this contract; in which event, the seller shall be obligated to pay reasonable attorney's fees and court costs to the purchaser, and the seller shall be obligated to pay the full real estate brokerage fee to the broker. In the event it shall be necessary for the broker or brokers to enforce collection of the payment of the real estate brokerage fee, the seller shall be obligated to pay reasonable attorney's fees and court costs to the broker or brokers.

Time shall be of the essence and this contract shall be binding on both parties, their heirs, personal representatives, and/or assigns when this contract shall have been signed by both parties or their agents.

Singular pronouns of the first person shall be read as plural when the agreement is signed by two or more persons.

By _____

Purchase and Sale Contract and Receipt for Deposit (Continued)

I, or we, agree to purchase the above described property on the terms and conditions stated in the foregoing contract, and do hereby approve, ratify, and confirm said contract in all respects.

Witness as to Purchaser:

_____ (SEAL)
Purchaser

_____ (SEAL)
Purchaser

I, or we, agree to sell the above described property on the terms and conditions stated in the foregoing contract, and do hereby approve, ratify and confirm said contract in all respects. The undersigned acknowledges the employment of the broker named herein and agrees to pay said broker _____ % of the purchase price of the said property as a brokerage fee for finding the above signed purchaser. Said brokerage fee for finding the above signed purchaser shall be paid at time of closing of this transaction, except as otherwise provided herein.

Witness as to Sellers:

_____ (SEAL)
Seller

_____ (SEAL)
Seller

Purchase and Sale Contract and Receipt for Deposit (Continued)

FORM H

DUPLEX

I   II

BEDROOMS _____   _____   PRICE $ _____

BATHS   _____   _____   DOWN PAY. $ _____

LOCATION _____

LOT _____ , BLOCK _____ , SUBDIVISION _____

LOT SIZE _____ X _____ , ZONED _____ , CITY _____ , COUNTY _____

DESCRIPTION:

I   II

	I	II		
LIVING ROOM	_____	_____	NO. STORIES	_____
FLORIDA ROOM	_____	_____	SWIM POOL	_____
KITCHEN	_____	_____	FLOORS	_____
DINING ROOM	_____	_____	ROOF	_____
UTILITY ROOM	_____	_____	TYPE CONST.	_____
GARAGE	_____	_____	SQUARE FT.	_____
CAR PORT	_____	_____	WATER	_____
PORCH	_____	_____	SEWAGE	_____
FURNISHED	_____	_____	PAVED ST.	_____
STOVE	_____	_____	SIDEWALKS	_____
REFRIG.	_____	_____	TYPE WINDOWS	_____
AIR COND.	_____	_____	CITY TAXES	_____
HEAT	_____	_____	COUNTY TAXES	_____
FIREPLACE	_____	_____	INSURANCE	_____
AWNINGS	_____	_____	BUILDER	_____
H.W. SYSTEM	_____	_____	YEAR BUILT	_____
MONTHLY RENT	_____	_____	KEY AT	_____
OCCUPANT	_____	_____	WILL TRADE FOR	_____

OTHER FEATURES _____

TERMS:

FIRST MORTGAGE $ _____ , HELD BY _____

PAYABLE $ _____ , PER MO., INTEREST _____ %

SECOND MORTGAGE $ _____ HELD BY _____

PAYABLE $ _____ , PER MO., INTRESTE _____ %

OWNER _____   LISTED BY _____

ADDRESS _____   DATE LISTED _____

TELEPHONE _____   EXCLUSIVE _____

APPROVED BY _____
                                              (OWNER)

FLORIDA FORMS, P.O. BOX 406, HOMESTEAD, FLA.

Duplex Listing Form

ESTOPPEL CERTIFICATE

Date_____19_____

Re: Mortgage being held by the undersigned relating to the following legally described property:

_____

_____

Gentlemen:

Be it known that we are the owners of a certain indenture of mortgage and bond bearing the date of_____day of_____, 19_____, made and executed by_____ to secure the payment of the principal sum of $_____and interest and duly recorded in the office of the County Clerk, County of_____, State of_____ _____, in Liber # _____of Mortgages of Section_____page _____, on the_____day of_____19_____and covering premises situated in _____County as above legally described. More commonly known as a two-story dwelling at_____Avenue, City of_____, State of_____.

The undersigned hereby certifies that the amount now due on said mortgage and bond has been reduced by monthly principal and interest payment of $_____, and that there is now due upon said mortgage and bond the principal sum of $_____. with interest thereon at the rate of_____ % per annum from _____day of_____ 19_____.

_____

_____

EXCHANGE AGREEMENT

Date_____   _____, Florida

The undersigned, as First Party (1)_____

_____

does agree to transfer and convey to, as Second Party (2)_____

_____

the following described property (show Legal of (1))

(show mortgages and amounts, if any)

and (pay) (accept) $_____upon

closing in consideration of the transfer and conveyance of the following described property

to him or his assigns (show legal of (2))
(show mortgages and amounts, if any)

TERMS AND CONDITIONS

The parties hereto shall execute and deliver within_____days from the date of acceptance, all instruments, in writing, necessary to transfer title to said properties and complete this exchange. Conveyance shall be by warranty deed. Abstracts_____
____shall be furnished by the owners showing their titles to be insurable in the usual form subject to easements and restrictions common to the subdivision. Liens of governmental agencies for work authorized or not completed at time of closing and the mortgages shown above which shall be_____, taxes, insurance, interest and rents shall be prorated to date of closing.

First Party agrees that the Real Estate Broker representing him in this exchange is:
_____ of_____Fla._____
Broker(s)   Address   Phone No.
First party agrees that Broker may cooperate with other Brokers and divide commissions in any manner satisfactory to them. The above Broker or (Brokers) is (are) authorized to act as Broker for all parties hereto and may accept commission therefrom. Should second party accept this offer, first party agrees to pay said Broker commission for services rendered as follows:

_____

_____

This offer shall be deemed revoked unless accepted in writing within_____days after date hereof and such acceptance is communicated to first party within said period. Broker is hereby given the exclusive and irrevocable right to obtain acceptance of second party within said period.

Time is of the essence of this contract, but Broker may, without notice, extend for a period of not to exceed one month the time for the performance of any act hereunder, except the time for the acceptance hereof by second party.

_____

_____

Signed, sealed and delivered in
presence of:

_____   _____(Seal)

_____   _____(Seal)
                                              First Party or Parties

Dated_____, 19_____.   Accepted:
                                         Broker:_____

                                         By_____

ACCEPTANCE

Second party hereby accepts the foregoing offer upon the terms and conditions stated and agrees to pay commission for services rendered to:

_____of_____Fla._____
            Broker   Address   Phone No.

as follows:_____

_____

Second party agrees that Broker may act as Broker for all parties hereto and may accept commission therefrom, and may co-operate with other Brokers and divide commission in any manner satisfactory to them.

_____

_____

Signed, sealed and delivered in
presence of:

_____   _____(Seal)

_____   _____(Seal)
                                              Second Party or Parties

Dated_____19_____   Accepted:

                                         Broker:_____

                                         By_____

(Copyright form of the Florida Association Of Realtors used with its permission in this publication and not for reprinting)

Exchange Agreement (Continued)

332

Exclusive Authorization to Exchange Property

CALIFORNIA REAL ESTATE ASSOCIATION STANDARD FORM

This listing expires_____, 196____.

_____

_____

(Owner) hereby irrevocably employs_____

_____

(Realtor) as Owner's exclusive agent for a period beginning_____, 19_____,

and ending_____, 19_____, at midnight, to solicit offers to exchange for other real property acceptable to Owner the property of the Owner described as follows:

SUBJECT TO:

Owner reserves the right to accept or reject any offer of property, but shall specify to Realtor the reason why any offer to exchange presented by Realtor is not satisfactory to Owner. In consideration of the services to be rendered by Realtor hereunder, Owner agrees to pay Realtor a fee of_____upon the occurrence of any of the following:

(a) The presentation by Realtor to Owner of a written offer to exchange for the property of Owner other property acceptable to Owner and the completion of the contemplated exchange. If the Owner accepts the offer but the exchange is not completed through his fault, the fee is nevertheless payable.

(b) The sale, lease or exchange of the property of Owner during the term of this Authorization and any extension hereof, whether the sale, lease or exchange is effected by Owner with or without the assistance of Realtor.

(c) The sale, exchange or lease of said property, within one year after termination of this Authorization and all extensions hereof, to parties with whom Realtor has negotiated before the termination, if Realtor before the said termination has notified Owner in writing personally or by mail of the negotiations and the identity of the parties to them.

Owner agrees that Realtor may act as agent for all parties to any transactions in connection with the above described property and may accept from any or all parties to consummated transactions fees for services rendered, may cooperate with other brokers, and divide with other brokers fees for services in any manner satisfactory to them.

I acknowledge receipt of a copy of this Authorization.

Dated_____, 19_____.

_____

_____

Owner

_____

Address of Owner

_____

City _____ Phone

In consideration of the execution of the foregoing, the undersigned Realtor agrees to use diligence in effecting an exchange.

_____   _____

Address of Realtor   Realtor

By_____

City _____ Phone

Exclusive Authorization to Exchange Property
(Reproduced with permission of the California Real Estate Assn.)

Exclusive Authorization to Lease or Rent

CALIFORNIA REAL ESTATE ASSOCIATION STANDARD FORM

In consideration of the services to be rendered by _____ ,
hereinafter called agent, I hereby employ said agent for a period of _____ days from date hereof, and ending at midnight
_____ ,19 _____ , to find a Lessee for the property situated in the _____
County of _____ State of California, described as follows, to wit:

_____

_____

_____

_____

_____

and I hereby grant to said agent the sole and irrevocable right to lease or rent said property within said time for _____
_____ DOLLARS ($_____) per _____ payable
in advance on the ____ _____
and I hereby authorize said agent to accept a deposit thereon.

_____

_____

_____

_____

Terms Lease

_____

_____

_____

_____

I hereby agree to pay a commission of _____ of the
total rental price to said agent whether said property is leased or rented through the efforts of said agent, or by me, or by another
agent, or through any other source. I further agree to pay such a commission to said agent in the event said property is transferred or
conveyed or withdrawn from said agent's authority during the time set forth herein. Said commission shall be payable_____
_____

In the event a lease is procured hereunder, and in the further event said lease is renewed, then I hereby agree to pay an
additional commission of _____ of the total rental price of the renewal lease to said agent.

Should a lease or rental be made within _____ days after the termination of this contract of employment
to parties whom said agent negotiated during its life and said agent notifies me personally or by mail, in writing, of such negotiation
within five (5) days after the termination of this contract, I agree to pay said agent the commission fixed herein.

In the event the lessee requests evidence of title, then the same shall be in the form of _____
_____ to be supplied by _____ and paid for by _____

Should a deposit be forfeited, one-half shall belong to said agent as commission and the other one-half thereof belong to
me, provided, however, the agent's share thereof shall not exceed the amount of commission which otherwise would be payable to
said agent. I hereby acknowledge receipt of a copy of this listing.

In consideration of the foregoing employment the undersigned agent agrees to use diligence in procuring a Lessee
for said property.

DATED: _____

SIGNED: _____

Listing Agent _____

ADDRESS: _____

By_____

PHONE: _____

(Form L-11) address California Real Estate Association,
520 So. Grand Ave., Los Angeles 90017. All rights reserved.
Copyright, 1962, by California Real Estate Association.

Exclusive Authorization to Lease
(Reproduced with permission of the California Real Estate Assn.)

EXCLUSIVE LISTING AGREEMENT

Date _____

1. In consideration of your agreement to list and to use your efforts to secure a purchaser for the property described as:

_____

_____

_____

_____

   I hereby give you for a period of _____ months from this date (and thereafter until this agreement is revoked by ten day's written notice delivered to you), the sole right and authority to find a purchaser for the above described property at the following price and terms, or at any other price and terms acceptable to me:

   Price: _____ Terms: _____

   _____

   _____

   _____

   Interest on encumbrances, taxes, insurance and rents shall be adjusted prorata at date of closing. Improvement liens are to be paid by me.

2. In case you secure a purchaser for the property, the usual and customary practice for the examination, curing title and for closing the transaction shall apply. I agree to deliver to the purchaser a good and sufficient warranty deed, free and clear of all liens and encumbrances except encumbrances of record and those which the purchaser shall assume as part of the purchase price and which are specifically detailed above.

3. For finding a purchaser for the above property:
   A. I agree to pay you a commission of _____% of the sales price.
   B. The commission is to be paid whether the purchaser be secured by you or me, or by any other person, at the price and upon the terms mentioned or at any other price or terms acceptable to me; of if the property is afterwards sold within three (3) months from the termination of this agency, to a purchaser to whom it was submitted by you, or a co-operating broker during the continuance of the agency, and whose name has been disclosed to me.
   C. In any exchange of this property, permission is given you to represent and receive commission from both parties.

4. In consideration of this exclusive listing, you agree:
   A. To carefully inspect my property and secure complete information regarding it.

B. To direct the concentrated efforts of your organization in bringing about a sale.

C. To advertise my property as you deem advisable in the local newspapers or other mediums of merit.

5. In consideration of the above, I agree to refer to you all inquiries of brokers or others interested in my property.

6. As my agent, you are authorized to accept, receipt for and hold all money paid or deposited as a binder thereon and if such deposit shall be forfeited by the prospective purchaser, you may retain one-half of such deposit, but not exceeding the total amount of your commission, as your compensation.

7. I understand that this agreement does not guarantee the sale of my property, but that it does guarantee that you will make an earnest and continued effort to sell same until this agreement is terminated.

WITNESS: OWNER:

_____   _____

_____   _____

ACCEPTED BY: SALESMAN:

_____   _____

The words "I", "MY" or "ME" shall be considered plural when applicable.

Exclusive Listing Agreement (Continued)

EXECUTOR'S DEED
Individual or Corporation

THIS DEED, made the_____day of_____, 19____,
between_____ of No._____ _____Street,
City of_____, State of_____, party of the
first part, and_____of No._____ _____Avenue,
City of_____, State of_____, party of the second
part,

WITNESSETH, that the party of the first part, by virtue of the power and authority given in and by said last will and testament, and in consideration of_____ _____dollars ($_____), lawful money of the United States, paid by the party of the second part, does hereby grant and release unto the party of the second part, the heirs or successors and assigns of the party of the second part forever.

ALL that certain plot, piece or parcel of land, with the buildings and improvements thereon erected, situate, lying and being in the

(Here include legal description)

TOGETHER with all right, title and interest, if any, of the party of the first part in any streets and roads abutting the above described premises to the center lines thereof. Together with the appurtenances, and also all the estate which the said decedent had at the time of decedent's death in said premises, and also the estate therein, which the party of the first part has or has power to convey or dispose of, whether individually, or by virtue of said will or otherwise.

TO HAVE AND TO HOLD the premises herein granted unto the party of the second part, the heirs or successors and assigns of the party of the second part forever.

AND the party of the first part covenants that the party of the first part has not done or suffered anything whereby the premises have been incumbered in any way whatsoever, except as aforsaid.

IN WITNESS WHEREOF, the party of the first part has duly executed this deed the day and year first above written.

In Presence of:

_____

_____   _____
                                                         Grantor

Standard N. Y. B. T. U. Form 8025 • 3-64-15M—Extension Agreement.

CONSULT YOUR LAWYER BEFORE SIGNING THIS INSTRUMENT—THIS INSTRUMENT SHOULD BE USED BY LAWYERS ONLY.

AGREEMENT, made the   day of   nineteen hundred and

BETWEEN

hereinafter designated as the party of the first part, and

hereinafter designated as the party of the second part,

WITNESSETH, that the party of the first part, the holder of the following mortgage and of the bond

or note   secured thereby:

Mortgage dated the   day of   , 19   , made by

to

and recorded in Liber   of section

in the principal sum of $, in the office of the   of the

of Mortgages, page

338

now a   lien upon the premises situate

and on which bond   or note   there is now due the sum of
dollars, with interest thereon, in consideration of one dollar paid by said party of the second part, and other valuable consideration, the receipt whereof is hereby acknowledged, does hereby extend the time of payment of the principal indebtedness secured by said bond or note   and mortgage   so that the same shall be due and payable

PROVIDED, the party of the second part meanwhile pay interest on the amount owing on said bond   or note
from the   day of   , 19   , at the rate of

per centum per annum on the   day of   , 19   , next ensuing and thereafter,

and comply with all the other terms of said bond   or note   and mortgage as hereby modified.

Extension Agreement
(Reproduced with permission of the New York Board of Underwriters)

AND the party of the second part, in consideration of the above extension, does hereby assume, covenant and agree to pay said principal sum and interest as above set forth and not before the maturity thereof as the same is hereby extended, and to comply with the other terms of said bond or note and mortgage as hereby modified.

AND the party of the second part further covenants with the party of the first part as follows:

1. That the party of the second part will pay the indebtedness as hereinbefore provided.

2. That the party of the second part will keep the buildings on the premises insured against loss by fire for the benefit of the party of the first part; that he will assign and deliver the policies to the party of the first part; and that he will reimburse the party of the first part for any premiums paid for insurance made by the party of the first part on default of the party of the second part in so insuring the buildings or in so assigning and delivering the policies.

3. That no building on the premises shall be altered, removed or demolished without the consent of the party of the first part.

4. That the whole of said principal sum and interest shall become due at the option of the party of the first part: after default in the payment of any instalment of principal or of interest for fifteen days; or after default in the payment of any tax, water rate, sewer rent or assessment for thirty days after notice and demand; or after default after notice and demand either in assigning and delivering the policies insuring the buildings against loss by fire or in reimbursing the party of the first part for premiums paid on such insurance, as hereinbefore provided; or after default upon request in furnishing a statement of the amount due on the mortgage and whether any offsets or defenses exist against the mortgage debt, as hereinafter provided. An assessment which has been made payable in instalments at the application of the party of the second part or lessee of the premises shall nevertheless, for the purpose of this paragraph, be deemed due and payable in its entirety on the day the first instalment becomes due or payable or a lien.

5. That the holder of this mortgage, in any action to foreclose it, shall be entitled to the appointment of a receiver.

6. That the party of the second part will pay all taxes, assessments, sewer rents or water rates, and in default thereof, the party of the first part may pay the same.

7. That the party of the second part within five days upon request in person or within ten days upon request by mail will furnish a written statement duly acknowledged of the amount due on this mortgage and whether any offsets or defenses exist against the mortgage debt.

8. That notice and demand or request may be in writing and may be served in person or by mail.

9. That the party of the second part warrants the title to the premises.

10. That the fire insurance policies required by paragraph No. 2 above shall contain the usual extended coverage endorsement; that in addition thereto the party of the second part, within thirty days after notice and demand, will keep the premises insured against war risk and any other hazard that may reasonably be required by the party of the first part. All of the provisions of paragraphs No. 2 and No. 4 above relating to fire insurance and the provisions of Section 254 of the Real Property Law construing the same shall apply to the additional insurance required by this paragraph.

11. That in case of a foreclosure sale, said premises, or so much thereof as may be affected by said mortgage, may be sold in one parcel.

12. That if any action or proceeding be commenced (except an action to foreclose said mortgage or to collect the debt secured thereby), to which action or proceeding the party of the first part is made a party, or in which it becomes necessary to defend or uphold the lien of said mortgage, all sums paid by the party of the

340

first part for the expense of any litigation to prosecute or defend the rights and lien created by said mortgage (including reasonable counsel fees), shall be paid by the party of the second part, together with interest thereon at the rate of six per cent. per annum, and any such sum and the interest thereon shall be a lien on said premises, prior to any right, or title to, interest in or claim upon said premises attaching or accruing subsequent to the lien of said mortgage, and shall be deemed to be secured by said mortgage. In any action or proceeding to foreclose said mortgage, or to recover or collect the debt secured thereby, the provisions of law respecting the recovering of costs, disbursements and allowances shall prevail unaffected by this covenant.

13. That the party of the second part hereby assigns to the party of the first part the rents, issues and profits of the premises as further security for the payment of said indebtedness, and the party of the second part grants to the party of the first part the right to enter upon the premises for the purpose of collecting the same and to let the premises or any part thereof, and to apply the rents, issues and profits, after payment of all necessary charges and expenses, on account of said indebtedness. This assignment and grant shall continue in effect until said mortgage is paid. The party of the first part hereby waives the right to enter upon said premises for the purpose of collecting said rents, issues and profits and the party of the second part shall be entitled to collect and receive said rents, issues and profits until default under any of the covenants, conditions or agreements contained in said mortgage, and agrees to use such rents, issues and profits in payment of principal and interest becoming due on said mortgage and in payment of taxes, assessments, sewer rents, water rates and carrying charges becoming due against said premises, but such right of the party of the second part may be revoked by the party of the first part upon any default, on five days' written notice. The party of the second part will not, without the written consent of the party of the first part, receive or collect rent from any tenant of said premises or any part thereof for a period of more than one month in advance, and in the event of any default under said mortgage will pay monthly in advance to the party of the first part, or to any receiver appointed to collect said rents, issues and profits, the fair and reasonable rental value for the use and occupation of said premises or of such part thereof as may be in the possession of the party of the second part, and upon default in any such payment will vacate and surrender the possession of said premises to the party of the first part or to such receiver, and in default thereof may be evicted by summary proceedings.

14. That the whole of said principal sum and the interest shall become due at the option of the party of the first part: (a) after failure to exhibit to the party of the first part, within ten days after demand, receipts showing payment of all taxes, water rates, sewer rents and assessments; or (b) after the actual or threatened alteration, demolition or removal of any building on the premises without the written consent of the party of the first part; or (c) after the assignment of the rents of the premises or any part thereof without the written consent of the party of the first part; or (d) if the buildings on said premises are not maintained in reasonably good repair; or (e) after failure to comply with any requirement or order or notice of violation of law or ordinance issued by any governmental department claiming jurisdiction over the premises within three months from the issuance thereof; or (f) if on application of the party of the first part two or more fire insurance companies lawfully doing business in the State of New York refuse to issue policies insuring the buildings on the premises; or (g) in the event of the removal, demolition or destruction in whole or in part of any of the fixtures, chattels or articles of personal property covered hereby, unless the same are promptly replaced by similar fixtures, chattels and articles of personal property at least equal in quality and condition to those replaced, free from chattel mortgages or other encumbrances thereon and free from any reservation of title thereto; or (h) after thirty days' notice to the party of the second part, in the event of the passage of any law deducting from the value of land for the purposes of taxation any lien thereon, or changing in any way the taxation of mortgages or debts secured thereby for state or local purposes; or (i) if the party of the second part fails to keep, observe and perform any of the covenants, conditions or agreements contained in said mortgage or in this agreement.

15. That the lien of said mortgage is hereby extended so as to cover all fixtures, chattels and articles of personal property now or hereafter attached to or used in connection with said premises, including but not limited to furnaces, boilers, oil burners, radiators and piping, coal stokers, plumbing and bathroom fixtures, refrigeration, air conditioning and sprinkler systems, wash-tubs, sinks, gas and electric fixtures, stoves, ranges, awnings, screens, window shades, elevators, motors, dynamos, refrigerators, kitchen cabinets, incinerators, plants and shrubbery and all other equipment and machinery, appliances, fittings, and fixtures of every kind in or used in the operation of the buildings standing on said premises, together with any and all replacements thereof and additions thereto.

16. That the party of the second part does hereby assign to the party of the first part all awards heretofore and hereafter made to the party of the second part for taking by eminent domain the whole or any part of said premises or any easement therein, including any awards for changes of grade of streets, which said awards are hereby assigned to the party of the first part, who is hereby authorized to collect and receive the proceeds of such awards and to give proper receipts and acquittances therefor, and to apply the same toward the payment of the mortgage debt, notwithstanding the fact that the amount owing thereon may not then be due and payable; and the said party of the second part hereby agrees, upon request, to make, execute and deliver any and all assignments and other instruments sufficient for the purpose of assigning said awards to the party of the first part, free, clear and discharged of any encumbrances of any kind or nature whatsoever.

17. That the party of the second part is now the owner of the premises upon which said mortgage is a valid lien for the amount above specified with interest thereon at the rate above set forth, and that there are no defenses or offsets to said mortgage or to the debt which it secures.

18. That the principal and interest hereby agreed to be paid shall be a lien on the mortgaged premises and be secured by said bond or note and mortgage, and that when the terms and provisions contained in said bond or note and mortgage in any way conflict with the terms and provisions contained in this agreement, the terms and provisions herein contained shall prevail, and that as modified by this agreement the said bond or note and mortgage are hereby ratified and confirmed.

342

This agreement may not be changed or terminated orally. The covenants contained in this agreement shall run with the land and bind the party of the second part, the heirs, personal representatives, successors and assigns of the party of the second part and all subsequent owners, encumbrancers, tenants and sub-tenants of the premises, and shall enure to the benefit of the party of the first part, the personal representatives, successors and assigns of the party of the first part and all subsequent holders of this mortgage. The word "party" shall be construed as if it reads "parties" whenever the sense of this agreement so requires.

IN WITNESS WHEREOF, this agreement has been duly executed by the parties hereto the day and year first above written.

IN PRESENCE OF :

Extension Agreement (Continued)

PERSONAL FINANCIAL STATEMENT

(Form suggested by Federal Reserve Bank of Atlanta for use by member banks in the Sixth Federal Reserve District)

Name_____   To:_____ BANK

Address_____   _____

I make the following statement of all my assets and liabilities as of the_____day of_____,

19._____, and give other material information for the purpose of obtaining credit with you on notes and bills bearing my signature, endorsement, or guarantee, and agree to notify you promptly of any change affecting my ability to pay.

(PLEASE ANSWER ALL QUESTIONS, USING "NO" OR "NONE" WHERE NECESSARY)

ASSETS		LIABILITIES AND NET WORTH	
Cash (See Sched. No. 1) On hand, and unrestricted in banks.	$	Notes Payable to Banks, Unsecured Direct borrowings only. (See Sched. No. 1)	$
U. S. Government Securities		Notes Payable to Banks, Secured Direct borrowings only. (See Sched. No. 1)	
Accounts and Loans Receivable (See Sched. No. 2)		Notes Receivable, Discounted With banks, finance companies, etc. (See Sched. No. 1)	
Notes Receivable, Not Discounted (See Sched. No. 2)		Notes Payable to Others, Unsecured	
Notes Receivable, Discounted With banks, finance companies, etc. (See Sched. No. 2)		Notes Payable to Others, Secured	
Life Insurance, Cash Surrender Value (Do not deduct loans.) (See Sched. No. 3)		Loans Against Life Insurance (See Sched. No. 3)	
Other Stocks and Bonds (See Sched. No. 4)		Accounts Payable	
Real Estate (See Sched. No. 5)		Interest Payable	
Automobiles Registered in Own Name.		Taxes and Assessments Payable (See Sched. No. 5)	
Other Assets (Itemize)		Mortgages Payable on Real Estate (See Sched. No. 5)	
		Brokers Margin Accounts (See Sched. No. 7)	
		Other Liabilities (Itemize)	
		Net Worth	$
Total Assets	$	Total Liabilities and Net Worth	$

SOURCE OF INCOME		PERSONAL INFORMATION	
Salary	$	Business or occupation	Age
Bonus and commissions	$		
Dividends	$	Partner or officer in any other venture	
Real Estate income	$		
Other income—itemize	$	Married	Dependent Children
		Single	Other Dependents
Total	$		

CONTINGENT LIABILITIES		GENERAL INFORMATION
As endorser or co-maker	$	Are any assets pledged?
On leases or contracts	$	Are you defendant in any suits or legal actions?
Legal claims	$	
Provision for Federal Income Taxes	$	Have you ever made a composition settlement? Explain:
Other special debt	$	Have you ever taken bankruptcy? Explain:

SUPPLEMENTARY SCHEDULES

No. 1. Banking Relations.   (A list of all my bank accounts, including savings, and loans)

Name and Location of Bank	Cash Balance	Amt. of Loan	Maturity of Loan	How Endorsed, Guaranteed, or Secured

(SEE OTHER SIDE)

Financial Statement
(Reproduced with permission of the Federal Reserve Bank of Atlanta, Georgia)

No. 2. Accounts, Loans and Notes Receivable. (A list of the largest amounts owing to me.)

Name and Address of Debtor	Amount Owing	Age of Debt	Decription of Nature of Debt	Description of Security Held	Date Payment Expected

No. 3. Life Insurance.

Name of Person Insured	Name of Beneficiary	Name of Insurance Co.	Type of Policy	Face Amount of Policy	Total Cash Surrender Value	Total Loans Against Policy	Amount of Yearly Premium	Is Policy Assigned?

No. 4. Other Stocks and Bonds.

Face Value (Bonds) No. of Shares (Stocks)	Description of Security	Registered in Name of	Cost	Present Market Value	Income Received Last Year	To Whom Pledged

No. 5. Real Estate. The legal and equitable title to all the real estate listed in this statement is solely in the name of the undersigned, except as follows:_____

Description or Street No.	Dimensions or Acres	Improvements Consist of	Mortgages or Liens	Due Dates and Amounts of Payments	Assessed Value	Present Market Value	Unpaid Taxes Year	Amount

No. 6. I buy goods principally from:

Name	Address	Name	Address

No. 7. Brokers Margin Accounts. List the names and addresses of the brokers and indicate the net amount due to each:

_____

_____

No. 8. Insurance Coverage. Fire Insurance: Buildings $_____, Automobile(s), Household Effects, etc. $_____; Indicate if policies have extended coverage endorsement: _____; Liability Insurance: Automotive $_____, Personal $_____, General Public $_____; Other Insurance (describe): _____

Date of latest independent analysis of insurance: _____; Indicate adequacy of coverage: _____

The undersigned certifies that each side hereof and the information inserted herein have been carefully read and is true and correct.

Date_____   Signed_____

Financial Statement (*Continued*)

345

HOUSE LISTING FORM

PRICE $ _____

OWNER: _____ TEL.: _____

STREET: _____ BUS. TEL.: _____

CITY-TOWN: _____ AGE: _____

OWNER'S ADDRESS: _____

TYPE: _____ FINISH: _____ COND.: _____

COLOR: _____ NO. ROOMS _____ NO. BEDROOMS _____

LAND AREA: _____ FRONT: _____ DEPTH: _____

LANDSCAPING: _____

1ST FLOOR: _____
_____

2ND FLOOR: _____

KITCHEN: _____ RANGE: _____

BATHS: _____ OVEN: _____

FIREPLACE: _____ LAUNDRY: _____

TYPE FLOORS: _____ INSULATION: _____

TYPE HEAT: _____ YEARLY COST: _____

DOMESTIC HOT WATER: _____ OCCUPANCY: _____

SCREENS: _____ STORM WINDOWS: _____

GARAGE: _____ OTHER BLDGS.: _____

MORTGAGE: $ _____ BANK: _____

ASSESSMENT: $ _____ MONTHLY TAX: $ _____

BETTERMENTS: _____ ZONING: _____

BASEMENT: _____

APPLICANCES INCLUDED: _____
_____

TYPE SEWAGE: _____ GAS: _____ WATER: _____

SCHOOLS: _____ STORES: _____ TRANS.: _____

STAMPS: _____ BOOKS: _____ PAGE: _____ DATE: _____

WHY MOVING? _____ WILL YOU SELL F.H.A.? _____

F.H.A. APPROVED: $ _____ MAY G.I. BUY? _____

IF G.I., WILL YOU ASSIGN PRESENT MORTGAGE? _____

DATE LISTED: _____ BY: _____ SIGN: _____

SOURCE: _____ EXCLUSIVE: _____ EXPIRES: _____

KEYS OR ENTRY: _____

SPECIAL REMARKS: _____
_____
_____
_____
_____

LISTING AUTHORIZED BY: _____

INSTALLMENT NOTE – FORM R. E. 10 – OFFICIAL LEGAL FORMS   HIALEAH, FLORIDA

$ _____

_____ Place _____   Date _____ , 19 ____

On the _____ day of each month, hereafter for value received, I, we, or either of us, promise

to pay _____ or order _____ Dollars

at the office of _____ with interest at the rate of _____ per cent per

annum, payable monthly, on the sums remaining from time to time unpaid. Said payments to continue until

the aggregate amount paid on account of principal shall be equal to the amount of _____

_____ Dollars, with option to pay off at any time the entire

sum remaining unpaid, with interest to the date of payment only.

Now, should it become necessary to collect this note through an attorney, each of us, whether maker, security or endorser, hereby
agrees to pay all costs of such collection, including a reasonable attorney's fee and hereby waives presentment for payment, protest, and
notice of protest and non-payment of this note.

_____ (SEAL)

_____ (SEAL)

DATE OF PAYMENT	AMOUNT OF PAYMENT	INTEREST CHARGED	APPLIED ON PRINCIPAL	BALANCE DUE ON PRINCIPAL	RECEIVED PAYMENT

Installment Note
(Reproduced with permission of Official Legal Forms, Hialeah, Fla.)

347

STATE OF ARIZONA } ss.   I hereby certify that the within instrument was filed and recorded
County of

In DOCKET   page   and indexed in deeds

at the request of

When recorded, mail to:

Witness my hand and official seal.

, County Recorder,

By   Deputy Recorder

Fee No.

Compared
Photostated
Fee:

JOINT TENANCY DEED

For the consideration of Ten Dollars, and other valuable considerations,

hereafter called the Grantor, whether one or more than one, hereby conveys to

not as tenants in common and not as a community property estate, but as joint tenants with right of survivorship, the following described property situated in   County, Arizona, together with all rights and privileges appurtenant thereto, to wit:

Subject to current taxes and other assessments, reservations in patents and all easements, rights of way, encumbrances, liens, covenants, conditions, restrictions, obligations and liabilities as may appear of record, the Grantor warrants the title against all persons whomsoever.

The grantees by signing the acceptance below evidence their intention to acquire said premises as joint tenants with the right of survivorship, and not as community property nor as tenants in common.

Dated this............day of................, 19........

Accepted and approved:

....
Grantees   Grantors

STATE OF .... ss.
County of..............................

This instrument was acknowledged before me this..............day of ...., 19........, by

....
Notary Public

My commission will expire

STATE OF .... ss.
County of..............................

This instrument was acknowledged before me this..............day of ...., 19........, by

....
Notary Public

My commission will expire

FORM B-14

FURNISHED THROUGH THE COURTESY OF (🦅) TRANSAMERICA TITLE INSURANCE COMPANY

Joint Tenancy Deed

(Reproduced with permission of Transamerica Title Insurance Co., Phoenix, Arizona)

LEASE (COMMON) FORM

FORM 28

Lease

This Lease, Made this   day of   , A. D. 19

by and between

herein called the lessor   , and

herein called lessee   .

WITNESSETH that in consideration of the covenants herein contained, on the part of the said lessee to be kept and performed, the said lessor do   hereby lease to the said lessee   the following described property:

TO HAVE AND TO HOLD the same for the term of

from the   day of   , A. D. 19   the said lessee   paying therefor
the

And the said lessee   covenant   with the said lessor   to pay the said rent in
payments of

each on the   day of each and every   for the said term, the first payment
to be made on the   day of   ; to make no unlawful, improper, or
offensive use of the premises; nor to assign this lease or to sublet any part of said premises without the
written consent of the lessor   ; not to use said premises for any other purpose than as a
                                                      , and to quit and deliver up said premises
at the end of said term in as good condition as they are now (ordinary wear and decay and damage by the
elements only excepted). And the said lessee   hereby covenant   and agree   that if default shall
be made in the payment of the rent as aforesaid, or if the said lessee   shall violate any of the covenants
of this lease, then said lessee   shall become tenant   at sufferance, hereby waiving all right of notice,
and the lessor   shall be entitled immediately to re-enter and re-take possession of the demised premises.

WITNESS our hands and seals this   day of   , A. D. 19
Signed, sealed and delivered in the presence of us:

_____   _____ (Seal)

_____ (Seal)

Lease (Common)

(Reproduced with permission of Official Legal Forms, Hialeah, Fla.)

Lease

THIS LEASE, executed this   day of   , A. D. 19   in *consideration of the following covenants, agreements, limitations and conditions entered into by the parties hereto for themselves, their heirs, successors, legal representatives and assigns*

hereinafter called Landlord, doth lease unto

hereinafter jointly, severally and collectively called the tenant, the

to be occupied only
unless written consent of landlord to occupy for other purposes is first obtained, for the terms commencing
on the   day of   19   , and ending on

the   day of   19   , at the

Rent of   ($).

1—PROVIDING ALWAYS, and the tenant hereby covenants as follows to pay the rent punctually in advance on the   *day of each and every month during the said term to the Landlord, at*
office.

2—To make any and all repairs to the said premises, plumbing, fixtures, wiring, etc., when the damage was in any wise caused by the fault or negligence of the said tenant; will at the end of this lease surrender and deliver up said premises, without demand, in as good order and conditions as when entered upon, loss by fire, inevitable accident, ordinary wear and decay only excepted.

3—That in the event the premises are destroyed or so damaged by fire or other unavoidable casualty as to be unfit for occupancy or use, then the rent hereby reserved, or a fair and just proportion thereof, according to the nature and extend of the damage sustained, shall, until the said premises shall have been rebuilt or reinstated, be suspended and cease to be payable, or this lease shall, at the election of the landlord, there-

by be determined and ended, provided, however that this agreement shall not be construed so as to extend the term of this lease or to render the landlord liable to rebuild or replace the said premises.

4—To permit the landlord or his agent, at any reasonable time to enter said premises or any part thereof for the purpose of exhibiting the same or making repairs thereto.

5—To pay all charges for electricity, water and gas used on said premises; not to hold the landlord responsible for any delay in the installation of electricity, water, or gas, or meters therefor, or interruption in the use and services of such commodities.

6—Not to use the demised premises, or any part thereof, or permit the same to be used for any illegal, immoral or improper purposes; not to make, or permit to be made, any disturbance, noise or annoyance whatsoever detrimental to the premises or the comfort and peace of the inhabitants of the vicinity of the demised premises.

7—The tenant acknowledges receipt of the articles enumerated on the reverse side or attached to this Lease and covenants and agrees to assume full responsibility for same and to replace all missing or damaged articles and to have all linens used in the premises laundered, prior to vacating.

8—IT IS FURTHER UNDERSTOOD AND AGREED BETWEEN THE PARTIES HERETO, that if default is made in the payment of rent as above set forth, or any part thereof, or if said tenant shall violate any of the covenants and conditions of this lease, then the tenant shall become a tenant at sufferance, thereby waiving all right of notice to vacate said premises, and the said landlord shall be entitled to re-enter and re-take possession immediately of the demised premises; that if any installment of rent shall remain unpaid for three (3) days after written notice of such non-payment shall have been served on the said tenant, or posted in a conspicuous place on said premises, then the entire rental to the end of this lease shall become at once due and payable without demand and may be recovered forthwith by distress or otherwise, and in all proceedings under this lease for the recovery of rent in arrears, whether said rent accrued before or after the expiration of this lease, and whether by distress or other action at law, the said tenant hereby waives the benefit of homestead and other exemption laws, any law to the contrary notwithstanding, and agrees to pay the landlord an attorney's fee of 15% of any amount so collected, together with all costs of such collection and in the event tenant is evicted by suit at law said tenant agrees to pay to said landlord all costs of such suit, including a reasonable attorney's fee; that no assent, expressed or implied, to any breach of one or more of the covenants and agreements hereof shall be deemed or taken to be a waiver of any succeeding or other breach.

AND IT IS FURTHER UNDERSTOOD AND AGREED that all covenants and agreement of this lease shall be binding upon and apply to the heirs, executors, legal representatives, and assigns of the respective parties hereto.

IN WITNESS WHEREOF, the said parties have hereunto set their hands and seals the day and year first above written.
Signed and sealed in the presence of:

....(Seal)

....(Seal)

....(Seal)

....(Seal)

Lease (House)

LETTER OF INTENTION

_____ 19__

Seller's Name
Address

Re: (Here include description of subject property)

Dear _____:

The undersigned hereby offers to purchase your property described above with the following basic terms and conditions:

The selling price is $_____, of which $_____ in cash is to be paid at time of closing.

The purchase price is subject to an existing first mortgage of $_____, payable $_____ per month including_____% interest per annum until paid in full in 19__.

The balance of the purchase price is to be covered by a purchase money second mortgage payable in __ monthly payments of $_____ including __% interest per annum.

Included in the sale are the following items of personal property:
(Itemize)

As a show of good faith, I have this date deposited in the trust account of _____, Realtor, the sum of $_____.

If this letter of intention is not accepted on or before _____, 19__, it shall be declared null and void and of no further effect, and the deposit shall be immediately returned.

The terms of this letter shall be in force and effect until a more formal and detailed contract is drawn and signed by both parties.

Very truly yours,

_____
(Purchaser)

Agreed to and Accepted:

_____
(Seller)

LIEN AFFIDAVIT

STATE OF _____

COUNTY _____

On this _____ day of _____ 19___, personally appeared before me, an officer duly authorized to administer oaths and take acknowledgments, _____
who, after being duly sworn, depose(s) and say(s):

1. That _____ he _____ is (are) the owner(s) of the following described property, to-wit:
_____
_____
which _____ he _____ is (are) this day selling to _____
_____

2. That there are no liens or encumbrances of any kind against the above described property except:
_____
_____

3. The above described property is being sold free and clear of any and all encumbrances except those mentioned above

_____
(SEAL)

_____
(SEAL)

SWORN AND SUBSCRIBED TO this _____ day of _____ 19___

_____
NOTARY PUBLIC

My commission expires:
_____

MANAGEMENT AGREEMENT

PARTIES

In consideration of the covenants herein contained _____

_____

(hereinafter called "Owner"), and _____

(hereinafter called "Agent"), agree as follows:

EXCLUSIVE AGENCY

1. The Owner hereby employs the Agent exclusively to rent, lease, operate and manage the property known as

_____

_____

upon the terms hereinafter set forth for the period of _____ beginning on the _____

day of _____, 19____, and ending on the _____ day of _____,

19____, and thereafter for annual periods unless on or before sixty (60) days prior to the date last

RENEWAL

above mentioned, or on or before thirty (30) days prior to the expiration of any such renewal period, either

TERMINA-TION

party hereto shall notify the other in writing of an intention to terminate this agreement in which case this agreement may be terminated prior to the last mentioned date. Either party may terminate this agreement upon thirty (30) days written notice after the expiration of _____ months of the original term.

2. The Agent accepts the employment and agrees:

RENTING OF PREMISES AGENT TO NEGOTIATE LEASE

a) To use due diligence in the management of the premises for the period and upon the terms herein provided, and agrees to furnish the services of his/its organization for the renting, leasing, operating and managing of the herein described premises.

MONTHLY STATEMENTS

b) To render monthly statements of receipts, expenses and charges and to remit to Owner receipts less disbursements. In the event the disbursements shall be in excess of the rents collected by the Agent, the Owner hereby agrees to pay such excess promptly upon demand of the Agent.

SEPARATE OWNERS' FUNDS

c) To deposit all receipts collected for Owner (less any sums properly deducted or otherwise provided herein) in a Trust account in a national or state institution qualified to engage in the banking or trust business, separate from Agent's personal account. However, Agent will not be held liable in event of bankruptcy or failure of a depository.

BONDED EMPLOYEES

d) Agent's employees who handle or are responsible for Owner's monies shall be bonded by a fidelity bond in adequate amount.

AGENT'S AUTHORITY

3. The owner hereby gives to the Agent the following authority and powers and agrees to assume the expenses in connection herewith:

a) To advertise the availability for rental of the herein described premises or any thereof, and to display "for rent" signs thereon; to sign, renew and/or cancel leases for the premises or any part thereof; to collect rents due or to become due and give receipts therefor; to terminate tenancies and to sign and serve in the name of the Owner such notices as are appropriate; to institute and prosecute actions; to evict tenants and to recover possession of said premises; to sue for in the name of the Owner and recover rents and other sums due; and when expedient, to settle, compromise, and release such actions or suits or reinstate such tenancies. Any lease executed for the Owner by the agent shall not exceed _____ years.

REPAIRS

b) To make or cause to be made and supervise repairs and alterations, and to do decorating on said premises; to purchase supplies and pay all bills therefor. The Agent agrees to secure the prior approval of the Owner on all expenditures in excess of $_____ for any one item, except monthly or recurring operating charges and/or emergency repairs in excess of the maximum, if in the opinion of the Agent such repairs are necessary to protect the property from damage or to maintain services to the tenants as called for in their leases.

EMPLOYEES

c) To hire, discharge and supervise all labor and employees required for the operation and maintenance of the premises; it being agreed that all employees shall be deemed employees of the Owner and not the Agent, and that the Agent may perform any of its duties through Owner's attorneys, agents or employees and shall not be responsible for their acts, defaults or negligence if reasonable care has been exercised in their appointment and retention.

SERVICE CONTRACTS

d) To make contracts for electricity, gas, fuel, water, telephone, window cleaning, ash or rubbish hauling and other services or such of them as the Agent shall deem advisable; the Owner to assume the obligation of any contract so entered into at the termination of this agreement.

4. The Owner further agrees:

SAVE HARMLESS

a) To save the Agent harmless from all damage suits in connection with the management of the herein described property and from liability from injury suffered by any employee or other person whomsoever, and to carry, at his own expense, necessary public liability and workmen's compensation insurance adequate to protect the interests of the parties hereto, which policies shall be so written as to protect the Agent in the same manner and to the same extent they protect the Owner, and will name the Agent as co-insured. The Agent also shall not be liable for any error of judgment or for any mistake of fact of law, or for anything which it may do or refrain from doing hereinafter, except in cases of willful misconduct or gross negligence.

b) The agent is hereby instructed and authorized to pay mortgage indebtedness, property and employee taxes, special assessments, and to place fire, liability, steam boiler, pressure vessel, or any other insurance required, and the agent is hereby directed to accrue and pay for same from the Owner's funds, with the following exceptions: _____

c) Upon and after the termination of this agreement pursuant to the method described in Paragraph 1 hereof, Owner shall recognize Agent as the broker in any pending negotiations of said premises, or any part thereof, and in the event of the consummation thereof Owner shall pay to Agent a commission therefor at the rate prescribed on Paragraph 4 d) hereof.

Management Agreement

(Reproduced with permission of the Institute of Real Estate Management, Chicago, Ill.)

d) To pay the Agent:

(1) For Management _____

(2) For Leasing _____

(3) For Modernization _____

(4) For Refinancing _____

(5) For Sale _____

(6) For Fire Restoration _____

(7) Other _____

_____

_____

e) Other Items of Mutual Agreement. _____

This Agreement shall be binding upon the successors and assigns of the Agent, and the heirs, administrators, executors, successors and assigns of the Owner.

IN WITNESS WHEREOF the parties hereto have affixed or caused to be affixed their respective signatures this _____ day of _____ 19____.

WITNESS:

_____ _____
                              Owner

_____
                              Agent

(This is a STANDARD FORM OF THE INSTITUTE OF REAL ESTATE MANAGEMENT of the National Association of Real Estate Boards, 155 East Superior, Chicago, Illinois 60611. When placing your order specify FORM PM-7.)

Management Agreement (Continued)

MECHANIC'S LIEN AFFIDAVIT

STATE OF _____)

                                        : ss:

COUNTY OF _____)

BEFORE ME, the undersigned authority, duly authorized to administer oaths 'nd take acknowledgments, this day personally appeared _____ 1e ow1er(s) of the following described property, and who, after being first duly sow 1 depose(s) 1nd say(s):

That _____ he _____ the owner(s) of the following described property:

Affiant(s) state(s) that there are no unpaid bills for labor performed or materials furnished on the improvements on the above described property; that all taxes thereon have been paid except for the current year; and that there are no unpaid liens or encumbrances against the personal property hereinabove described; that no one, other than the undersigned, is entitled to, or claims possession of said above described property.

Affiant(s) state(s) that the purpose of this Affidavit is to induce _____ into purchasing this property.

Deponent(s) further state(s) that _____ he _____ familiar with the nature of an oath and with the penalties as provided by the laws of the State of _____ for falsely swearing to statements made in an instrument of this nature.

Further Affiant(s) Sayeth Not.

_____

_____

_____

SWORN TO AND SUBSCRIBED
before me this _____
day of _____ , 19___.
Notary Public, State of _____

My Commission expires: _____

Mortgage Deed

This Indenture, Made this   day of   , A.D. 19   .

BETWEEN

hereinafter called the Mortgagor , and

, hereinafter called the Mortgagee .

WITNESSETH, That the said Mortgagor , for and in consideration of the sum of One Dollar, in hand paid by the said Mortgagee , the receipt whereof is hereby acknowledged,   granted, bargained and sold to the said Mortgagee ,   heirs and assigns forever, the following described land situate, lying and being in the County of

, State of

to-wit:

and the said Mortgagor   do   hereby fully warrant the title to said land, and will defend the same against the lawful claims of all persons whomsoever.

PROVIDED ALWAYS, That if said Mortgagor   ,   heirs, legal representatives or assigns shall pay unto the said Mortgagee   ,   legal representatives or assigns,

certain promissory note   dated the   day of   , A.D. 19   , for

the sum of   Dollars

payable
per cent from   with interest at

and shall perform, comply with and abide by each

signed by

and every the stipulations, agreements, conditions and covenants of the said promissory note   and of this mortgage, and shall pay all taxes which may accrue on said land and all costs and expenses said Mortgagee   may be put to in collecting said promissory note   by foreclosure of this mortgage or otherwise, including a reasonable attorney's fee, then this mortgage and the estate hereby created shall cease and be null and void.

IN WITNESS WHEREOF, The said Mortgagor   hereunto set   hand   and seal   the day and year first above written.

Signed, sealed and delivered in presence of us:

.... (Seal)

.... (Seal)

Mortgage Deed

(Reproduced with permission of Official Legal Forms, Hialeah, Fla.)

361

27 —Mortgage Note. Individual or Corporation (Straight or Installment)

JULIUS BLUMBERG, INC., LAW BLANK PUBLISHERS
80 EXCHANGE PLACE AT BROADWAY, NEW YORK

MORTGAGE NOTE

New York,   19   .

$

FOR VALUE RECEIVED,

promise   to pay to the order of

at

or at such other place as may be designated in writing by the holder of this note, the principal sum of

Dollars

with interest thereon to be computed from the   day of   19   , at the
rate of   per centum per annum and to be paid

IT IS HEREBY EXPRESSLY AGREED, that the said principal sum secured by this note shall become due at the option of the holder thereof on the happening of any default or event by which, under the terms of the mortgage securing this note, said principal sum may or shall become due and payable; also, that all of the covenants, conditions and agreements contained in said mortgage are hereby made part of this instrument to the same extent and with the same effect as if fully set forth herein.

The makers and all others who may become liable for the payment of all or any part of this obligation do hereby severally waive presentment for payment, protest and notice of protest and non-payment.

This note is secured by a mortgage made by the maker   to the payee   of even date herewith, on property situate in the

This note may not be changed orally, but only by an agreement in writing and signed by the party against whom enforcement of any waiver, change, modification or discharge is sought.

....

....

Mortgage Note

(Form courtesy of Julius Blumberg, Inc., 80 Exchange Place, New York, N.Y. 10004)

THIS IS A STANDARD FORM OF THE MIAMI BOARD OF REALTORS

A Realtor Designates Only Professional Members of the National Association of Real Estate Boards

Realtors are required to meet rigid standards • *Realtors adhere to a code of professional ethics*

MULTIPLE LISTING AGREEMENT
for Homes, Improved Property

Date _____

1. In consideration of your agreement to use your efforts to find a purchaser for that property situate in Dade County, Florida, described as follows:

   LEGAL DESCRIPTION _____

   _____

   STREET ADDRESS _____

   and list it with other Realtors in accordance with the program outlined below, the undersigned hereby give you for

   a period of _____ days from this date the exclusive right and authority to find a purchaser for said property at the following price and terms, or at any other price and terms acceptable to the undersigned, to-wit:

   SALES PRICE: _____

   TERMS: _____

   _____

2. In case you find a purchaser for said property, the undersigned agrees to enter into a customary written deposit receipt with purchaser on a form the same as or similar to the Miami Board of Realtors Deposit Receipt Standard Form No. 1.

3. For finding a purchaser for the above property:
   (A) The undersigned jointly and severally agree to pay you a commission of 7½% of the sale price of said property.
   (B) Said commission is to be paid you whether the purchaser is found by you or by the undersigned or by any other person at the price and upon the terms set forth above or at any price or terms acceptable to the undersigned; or if the undersigned agree to sell said property within three months next after the termination of this agency to a purchaser to whom you or any cooperating broker submitted said property for sale during the continuance of said agency.
   (C) In any exchange of this property, permission is given you to represent and receive commissions from both parties.
   (D) For single family residences, it is understood that if the residence is leased during the term of this agreement, by the undersigned owner, then the Miami Board of Realtor recommended commission for such leasing shall be paid to you, the listing Realtor.
   (E) The undersigned have the option to cancel this listing prior to the termination date as set forth above by payment to you of 2½% of the above listed sale price of said property.

4. In consideration of this exclusive listing, the undersigned Realtor agrees:
   (A) To carefully inspect said property and secure adequate information regarding it.
   (B) To advertise said property as he deems advisable in the local newspaper or other media of merit.
   (C) To notify all participating members of the Miami Board of Realtors Multiple Listing Service by means of a photo listing that the property is for sale upon the above terms and conditions.
   (D) To furnish additional information when requested by any cooperating Realtor, and to assist cooperating Realtors in closing a sale of said property when requested to do so.
   (E) To promptly pay 2/3 of said commission to any cooperating participating Realtor who finds the purchaser for said property, when said commission is received by the Realtor below.

5. In consideration of the above, the undersigned agree to immediately refer to you for attention all inquiries relative to purchase of said property.

6. As my real estate broker, you or any cooperating Realtor are authorized to act as escrow agent at such time as a deposit receipt is drawn, and in case of dispute between purchaser and seller as to the final disposition of said deposit, may institute a suit including a reasonable attorney's fee, said fee shall be paid out of said deposit.

7. It is hereby certified that we are the owners of the property described above.

WITNESSES:

_____   _____ (SEAL)
                                        Sole Owner ( )   Joint Owner ( )

_____   _____ (SEAL)

ACCEPTED BY:

By _____   _____
         As Realtor   Salesman

White Copy to Realtor — Blue Copy to ML Service — Yellow Copy to Seller
MUST BE MAILED TO MLS OFFICE WITHIN 24 HOURS

Multiple Listing Agreement
(Reproduced with permission of the Miami Board of Realtors, Miami, Fla.)

Open Listing Agreement

In consideration of the services of _____,
hereinafter called broker, I hereby list with said broker for a period of_____days from
date hereof, the following described property and at the following described price and terms:

ADDRESS: _____

LEGAL DESCRIPTION: _____

SELLING PRICE: $_____ FURNISHED _____ UNFURN. _____

EXISTING MORTGAGE (S) _____

MORTGAGE COMMITMENTS: _____

MINIMUM CASH REQUIRED: _____

      I agree to pay to the broker a commission of_____per cent (_____%)
of the selling price should the broker find a purchaser ready, willing and able to buy at the
above price and terms, or if he sells the property at other price and terms agreeable to me.

      It is understood that this listing agreement in no way prohibits me from selling the
property direct. I retain the right to sell to any party not first contacted by the broker. I
also retain the right to list my property for sale with any other broker or brokers. I also have
the right to withdraw the property form the market upon notice to the broker.

      Should a sale be made within six months after this authorization terminates to
parties with whom the broker may negotiate during the term hereof, and whose name has
been disclosed to me, then I agree to pay said commission to said broker.

      Should the property be sold, I agree to furnish the purchaser a good and sufficient
Warranty Deed, and a complete abstract of title.

      Should deposit money paid on account of purchase be forfeited by the purchaser,
one half shall be retained by the broker, providing said amount does not exceed the commission.

      I hereby acknowledge receipt of a copy of this authorization to sell.

      Signed on the _____ day of _____, 19____ .

_____   _____ (Seal)
Witness   Owner

_____   _____ (Seal)
Witness   Owner

      In consideration of the foregoing listing and authorization, the undersigned broker
agrees to use diligence in procuring a purchaser.

_____
                                    Broker

Open Listing Agreement

T 487—Option for Purchase of Property.

JULIUS BLUMBERG, INC., LAW BLANK PUBLISHERS
80 EXCHANGE PLACE AT BROADWAY, NEW YORK

AGREEMENT made this   day of   19   between

hereinafter described as the Seller, and

hereinafter described as the Purchaser.

WITNESSETH, that for and in consideration of the sum of

Dollars ($), paid by the Purchaser, the receipt of which is

hereby acknowledged by the Seller, the Seller hereby gives and grants to the Purchaser the exclusive

option, right and privilege of purchasing,

ALL THAT TRACT OR PARCEL OF LAND with the buildings and improvements thereon,

situate in the   of   County of

State of   briefly described as follows:

for the sum of   Dollars

($) payable as follows: $ upon the execution and delivery of this option

as hereinbefore provided, which amount Seller agrees to apply on the purchase price if Purchaser elects

to exercise the option; $ upon the acceptance of this option by the Purchaser as here-

inafter provided; and the balance of the purchase price, to wit, $, in the following

manner:

366

Notice of election to purchase hereunder shall be given by the Purchaser in writing by registered mail, addressed to the Seller, at

on or before   19   , which said notice shall be accompanied by the payment

of $ hereinbefore specified, and title shall close and the deed shall be delivered at the

office of

at   o'clock   . M. on   19   , following the giving of such notice,

or at such time and upon such other date as shall be mutually agreed upon by the parties hereto.

Seller shall convey said premises to Purchaser in fee simple, free and clear of all liens, rights of dower or other encumbrances (unless herein otherwise specified), by a good and sufficient deed of conveyance, in the usual form of a warranty deed, except that if Seller conveys as executor, trustee, administrator or guardian, or in any trust capacity, the usual deed given in such cases shall be accepted. Said conveyance shall also be made subject to all restrictions, easements and conditions of record, if any.

If Purchaser gives a mortgage on the herein referred to premises, to secure to Seller any of the purchase money therefor, it shall be designated therein as being given for that purpose; it shall be accompanied by the usual bond; both shall contain the usual statutory interest, insurance, tax, assessment and receivership clauses, if Seller so requires. The mortgage recording tax, recording fee for the mortgage and the revenue stamps on the bond accompanying the same, shall be paid by the Purchaser as part of the consideration of the said purchase.

Purchaser is to have possession of the premises on the day of transfer of title, except

All rentals, insurance premiums, interest and all other matters affecting the property herein referred to, not herein otherwise provided for, shall be adjusted pro rata to the day of the transfer of title.

The transfer is to include, without further consideration and unless herein otherwise stated, all fixtures and appurtenances now in said premises, including the heating plant and all appliances connected therewith, ranges, service hot water heaters, gas and electric chandeliers and fixtures (excepting portable lamps), bathroom fixtures attached, outside shades, screens, awnings, storm sash and storm doors.

Option

(Form by courtesy of Julius Blumberg, Inc., 80 Exchange Place, New York, N.Y. 10004)

The buildings on said premises shall be kept insured by Seller against loss by fire for a sum not less than $ until the time of transfer, and any insurance, in case of loss, shall be allowed to Purchaser who shall take the property in accordance with this contract notwithstanding any injury or destruction of the said buildings by fire.

The Seller agrees that   brought about this sale and agrees to pay the broker's commission therefor, if this option is duly accepted and exercised by the Purchaser.

The stipulations aforesaid are to apply to and bind the heirs, executors and administrators of the respective parties hereto. This instrument may not be changed orally.

WITNESS the signatures and seals of the above parties.

_____ L. S.

_____ L. S.

_____ L. S.

STATE OF
COUNTY OF   } ss.:

On the   day of   19   before me came

to me known and known to me to be the individual   described in, and who executed, the foregoing instrument, and acknowledged to me that   he   executed the same.

Option (Continued)

368

Owner's Affidavit of No Liens

STATE OF

COUNTY OF
} SS

     On this date personally appeared before me, the undersigned authority,

who is known to me, and who, being by me first duly sworn, on oath depose(s) and say(s):

     That they are the owners in fee simple of that certain real estate, situate, lying and

being in   County, State of Florida, described as:

Owner's Affidavit of No Liens

That any and all work, labor, materials and supplies which have been furnished, used or applied upon the said property at any time during the ownership of your affiant have been fully paid for and discharged; and that there is no possible lien which may be filed against the said property for work, labor or materials furnished thereon, to the knowledge of your affiant.

Affiants further say that they are in undisputed possession of the above described property, and that any building thereon was completed and all work thereon done more than three months prior to the date of this affidavit.

Affiants further say that there are no liens, chattel mortgages or retain title contracts affecting any personal property which might have been sold together with the above described property.

That this affidavit is made for the purpose of inducing

to purchase said property, and that the purchasers relying upon this affidavit and upon the representations contained herein, and upon the assurance that no liens of the above nature exist, have paid all moneys and executed all instruments necessary to complete the purchase of said property.

_____ (Seal)

_____ (Seal)

Sworn to and subscribed before me this

_____ day of _____, 196 .

My commission expires:

_____
Notary Public

Owner's Affidavit of No Liens (Continued)

This Agreement Made and entered into this the _____ day of _____, A.D. 19____

Between _____, of _____

_____, of _____

and _____, of _____

Witnesseth, as follows: The said parties above named have agreed to become copartners in business and by these presents do agree to be copartners together under the firm name and style of _____

to do business together in the _____, State of _____, County of _____, and in such other places as the nature of their business shall require. The business to be conducted by them shall be _____

This Partnership Agreement shall commence on _____ day of _____, 19____, and shall continue for the term or period of _____ years, unless discontinued before the expiration of that period by mutual consent of the parties hereto. To the end and purpose in view, the said parties agree to contribute to said business as follows: _____

_____

_____

_____

The sums of money or other contributions to said business are to be used and employed in common between the said partners for the support, maintenance, and management of said business, and to the mutual benefit and advantage of the said partners.

It is agreed by and between the parties to these presents that at all times during the continuance of their Copartnership, they, and each of them will give their attendance and do their, and each of their, best endeavors, and to the utmost of their skill and power, exert themselves for their joint interest, profit, benefit and advantage in the business aforesaid, and also that they shall and will, at all times during the said Copartnership, bear, pay and discharge equally between them all rents and other expenses that may be required for the support and management of the said business, and that all gains, profits and increase that shall come, grow or arise from, or by means of this said business, shall be divided among them in the following proportion, to-wit:

Partnership Agreement
(Reproduced with permission of Official Legal Forms, Hialeah, Fla.)

All loss that shall happen to the said business by ill commodities, bad debts, or from any other cause, shall be borne and paid between them in like proportion.

It is agreed by and between the said parties that there shall be had and kept at all times during the continuance of their Copartnership, perfect, just and true books of account wherein each of the said Copartners shall enter and set down all money by them or either of them received, paid, laid out and expended in and about said business, as well as all other matters and things whatsoever to the said business and management thereof in anywise appertaining; which said books shall be used in common between the said copartners, so that either of them may have access thereto without any interruption or hindrance of the other. And also the said copartners shall, once in each year, or oftener if necessary, make, yield and render each to the other, a true, just and perfect inventory and account of all profits and increase by them, or either of them, made, and of all losses by them, or either of them, sustained; and also all payments, receipts, disbursements, and all other things by them made, received, disbursed, acted, done or suffered by the said copartnership and business, and, the said account so made, shall and will clear, adjust, pay and deliver, each to the other, at the time, their just share of the profits so made as aforesaid.

And the said parties hereby mutually covenant and agree to and with each other, that, during the continuance of the said Copartnership, neither of them shall nor will endorse any note, or otherwise become surety for any person or persons whomsoever, without the consent of the other of the said copartners. And at the end, or other sooner determination of their Copartnership, the said copartners, each to the other, shall and will make a true, just, and final account of all things relating to their said business, and in all things truly adjust the same; and all and every the stock and stocks, as well as the gains and increase thereof, which shall appear to be remaining, either in money, goods, wares, fixtures, debts, or otherwise, shall be divided between them, in the proportion aforesaid.

In Witness Whereof, the said parties have hereunto set their hands the day and year first above

written.

_____(SEAL)

_____(SEAL)

_____(SEAL)

Partnership Agreement (Continued)

POWER OF ATTORNEY

KNOW ALL MEN BY THESE PRESENTS:

THAT _____ ha_____ made, constituted and appointed, and by these presents do make, constitute and appoint _____ true and lawful attorney for _____ and in _____ name, place and stead _____

giving and granting unto _____ said attorney full power and authority to do and perform all and every act and thing whatsoever requisite and necessary to be done in and about the premises as fully, to all intents and purposes, as _____ might or could do if personally present, with full power of substitution and revocation, hereby ratifying and confirming all that _____ _____ said attorney or _____ _____

substitute shall lawfully do or cause to be done by virtue hereof.

IN WITNESS WHEREOF, _____have hereunto set _____ hand _____ and seal _____ the _____ day of _____ in the year one thousand nine hundred and _____.

Sealed and delivered in the presence of

_____   _____(Seal)

_____   _____(Seal)

LONG'S · FR 7-1551

NO. · PN-1

PROMISSORY NOTE

Miami, Fla.

$ _____ 19 ____

FOR VALUE RECEIVED I promise to pay to the order of

the principal sum of

_____ Dollars,

($ _____), together with interest thereon from _____

per centum per annum until maturity, said principal and interest being payable as follows :

Each maker and endorser severally waives demand, protest and notice of maturity, non-payment or protest and all requirements necessary
to hold each of them liable as makers and endorses.
    Each maker and endorser further agrees, jointly and severally, to pay all costs of collection, including a reasonable Attorney's fee in case
the principal of this note or any payment on the principal or any interest thereon is not paid at the respective maturity thereof, or in case it becomes necessary to protest the security hereof, whether suit be brought or not.
    Deferred principal and interest payments shall bear interest at the rate of _____ per centum per annum from their respective
maturities until paid.
    This note is to be construed and enforced according to the State of Florida.

_____ (Seal)

_____ (Seal)

374

PROSPECTS

NAME_____

ADDRESS_____

CITY_____STATE_____PHONE_____

PROSPECT DESIRES:

DATE	PROPERTY SHOWED	REACTION

SALESMAN_____   DATE:_____

Prospect Form
(Reproduced with permission of Florida Forms, Homestead, Fla.)

PURCHASE AGREEMENT

INDIANAPOLIS REAL ESTATE BOARD

STANDARD PROPOSITION FORM

By _____

Through _____

Indianapolis, Indiana _____ 19___

The undersigned, hereinafter called purchaser, having inspected the premises and relying entirely for its condition upon his own examination hereby agrees to purchase from the owner through you as his Realtor the real estate known as

_____

_____

located in _____, _____ County, Indiana. Purchaser hereby further agrees to pay for said property the sum of _____ ($_____) Dollars upon the following terms and or conditions, viz: _____

_____

_____

_____

_____

_____

_____

_____

_____

No more than _____ days after the acceptance of this purchase agreement shall be allowed for obtaining a favorable commitment for any financing required by this purchase agreement.

Purchaser to have complete possession _____

Rents, if any, to be prorated to date of closing. Insurance to be (prorated) (cancelled) at date of closing.

All risk of loss shall be borne by seller until time of transfer of title.

Interest on encumbrances assumed by the purchaser to be prorated to date of closing.

Purchaser will assume and agree to pay all installments of taxes on said real estate beginning with the installment due and payable in _____ 19___, and all installments subsequent thereto.

Purchaser will assume and agree to pay all assessments for municipal improvements which are completed after date of this Purchase Agreement.

Said real estate shall be conveyed in the same condition as it now is, ordinary wear and tear excepted, to purchaser by general warranty deed, and in support of title, purchaser shall be furnished at seller's expense:

☐ Owner's policy of title insurance in the amount of _____ ☐ Complete and merchantable abstract of title continued to the purchase price. to date.

Said policy or abstract to show respectively an insurable or merchantable title to said real estate in the seller, subject only to easements and restrictions of record, if any, and free and clear of all other liens and encumbrances, except as herein stated. If such abstract fails to show such merchantable title then such owner's title policy shall be furnished.

Provided, however, that in the event this Purchase Agreement provides for a conditional sale of said real estate, seller will execute to buyer a conditional sales contract upon standard form approved by the Indianapolis Real Estate Board.

The following clause applicable only if this agreement is contingent upon purchaser's securing an FHA insured loan.

"It is expressly agreed that, notwithstanding any other provisions of this contract, the purchaser shall not be obligated to complete the purchase of the property described herein or to incur any penalty by forfeiture of earnest money deposits or otherwise unless the seller has delivered to the purchaser a written statement issued by the Federal Housing Commissioner setting forth the appraised value of not less than $ _____ which statement the seller hereby agrees to deliver to the purchaser promptly after such appraised value statement is made available to the seller. The purchaser shall, however, have the privilege and option of proceeding with the consummation of this contract without regard to the amount of the appraised valuation made by the Federal Housing Commissioner."

This transaction is to be closed within _____ days after said binder for title insurance or abstract showing merchantable title as provided for above is delivered to purchaser. Said title work to be ordered (immediately) (immediately) after loan approval).

This offer is void, if not accepted in writing on or before 12:00 o'clock noon of the _____ day of _____ 19____.
The above sales price includes all improvements permanently installed, such as electrical and/or gas fixtures, heating equipment and all attachments thereto, air-conditioning, (excluding window units), built in kitchen equipment, hot water heaters, incinerators, window shades, curtains, drapery poles and fixtures, Venetian blinds, storm doors and windows, linoleum, screens, awnings and TV antennas, _____

which belong to the above property and are now on the premises or elsewhere. All said items are now or will be at the date of closing fully paid for by seller. _____

Purchasers deposits herewith _____ ($_____) Dollars as earnest money to apply upon the cash payment provided herein.

The said earnest money deposit above mentioned shall be returned in full to purchaser promptly in event this purchase agreement is not accepted. In the event this purchase agreement is accepted, and purchaser shall, without legal cause, fail or refuse to complete the purchase of said real estate in accordance with the terms and conditions hereof, seller may pursue all legal or equitable remedies available to seller under the law, and said earnest money deposit shall be retained by the broker under his listing contract with said seller and shall be applied to the broker's and seller's damages.

It is expressly agreed that all terms and conditions are included herein, and no verbal agreements of any kind shall be binding or recognized.

_____   _____
Purchaser   Purchaser

As the owner(s) of the property described herein ____ hereby accept this Purchase Agreement this ____ day of _____ 19____.
and ____ agree to pay to _____ Realtor,
and licensed broker, the total sum of _____ ($_____) Dollars
commission for services rendered in this transaction.

Revised 11-67

_____   _____
Seller   Seller

Proposition or Purchase Agreement
(Reproduced with permission of the Indianapolis Real Estate Board, Indianapolis, Indiana)

377

Quit - Claim Deed

This Indenture, Made, this   day of   , A. D. 19   .

BETWEEN

of the County of

, part   of the first part, and

. and State of

of the County of   and State of   , part   of the

second part.

WITNESSETH, That the said part   of the first part, for and in consideration of the

sum of   Dollars,

in hand paid by the said part   of the second part, the receipt whereof is hereby acknowledged,

ha   remised, released and quit-claimed, and by these presents do   remise, release and quit-claim

unto the said part   of the second part and   heirs, and assigns forever,

all the right, title, interest, claim and demand which the part   of the first part ha   in and to

the following described lot   , piece   , or parcel   of land, situate, lying and being in the County of

. State of

to-wit:

TO HAVE AND TO HOLD the same together with all and singular the appurtenances thereunto belonging or in anywise appertaining, and all the estate, right, title, interest and claim whatsoever of the said part   of the first part either in law or equity, to the only proper use, benefit and behoof of the said part   of the second part,   heirs and assigns forever.

IN WITNESS WHEREOF, The said part   of the first part ha   hereunto set hand   and seal   the day and year first above written.

Signed, sealed and delivered in presence of us:

_____ (SEAL)

_____ (SEAL)

Quit-Claim Deed

(Reproduced with permission of Official Legal Forms, Hialeah, Fla.)

B 110—General Release—Individual.

JULIUS BLUMBERG, INC . LAW BLANK PUBLISHERS
80 EXCHANGE PLACE AT BROADWAY, NEW YORK

To all to whom these Presents shall come or may Concern,

Greeting: *KNOW YE. That*

for and in consideration of the sum of

dollars ($

)

in hand paid by

lawful money of the United States of America to

the receipt whereof is hereby acknowledged, have remised, released, and forever discharged and by these presents do   for   heirs, executors, and administrators and assigns, remise, release and forever discharge the said

heirs, executors, administrators, successors and assigns of and from all manner of actions, causes of action, suits, debts, dues, sums of money, accounts, reckoning, bonds, bills, specialties, covenants, contracts, controversies, agreements, promises, variances, trespasses, damages, judgments, extents, executions, claims and demands whatsoever, in law, in admiralty, or in equity, which against

ever had, now ha   or which   heirs, executors, or administrators, hereafter can, shall or may have for, upon or by reason of any matter, cause or thing whatsoever from the beginning of the world to the day of the date of these presents.

This release may not be changed orally.

In Witness Whereof, have hereunto set hand and seal

the

day of 19

Sealed and delivered in the presence of

_____ L.S.

State of **County of** ss.:

On the day of 19 before me personally came

to me known, and known to me to be the individual described in, and who executed the foregoing

instrument, and duly acknowledged to me that he executed the same

Release (General)

(Form by courtesy of Julius Blumberg, Inc., 80 Exchange Place, New York, N.Y. 10004))

F. A. R. STANDARD FORM NO. 9

RELEASE OF DEPOSIT RECEIPT

THIS RELEASE IS ENTERED INTO THIS _____ DAY OF _____ 19___, BETWEEN THE UNDERSIGNED PURCHASERS, THE UNDERSIGNED SELLERS AND THE UNDERSIGNED REALTOR, WHO WERE PARTIES TO THAT CERTAIN DEPOSIT RECEIPT DATED _____, 19___, COVERING THE FOLLOWING DESCRIBED PROPERTY:

WITNESSETH:

THAT EACH OF THE PARTIES HERETO IN CONSIDERATION OF EACH OF THE PARTIES RELEASING ALL OF THE OTHER PARTIES FROM THE AFORESAID DEPOSIT RECEIPT, DO HEREBY RELEASE EACH OF THE OTHER PARTIES TO SAID DEPOSIT RECEIPT FROM ANY AND ALL CLAIMS, ACTIONS OR DEMANDS WHATSOEVER WHICH EACH OF THE PARTIES HERETO MAY HAVE UP TO THE DATE OF THIS AGREEMENT AGAINST ANY OF THE OTHER PARTIES HERETO BY REASON OF SAID DEPOSIT RECEIPT.

IT IS THE INTENTION OF THIS AGREEMENT THAT ANY RESPONSIBILITY OR OBLIGATIONS OR RIGHTS ARISING BY VIRTUE OF SAID DEPOSIT RECEIPT ARE BY THIS RELEASE DECLARED NULL AND VOID AND OF NO FURTHER EFFECT.

THE ESCROW AGENT HOLDING THE DEPOSIT UNDER THE TERMS OF SAID DEPOSIT RECEIPT IS HEREBY DIRECTED AND INSTRUCTED FORTHWITH TO DISBURSE SAID DEPOSIT HELD IN ESCROW IN THE FOLLOWING MANNER:

$ _____ TO _____

$ _____ TO _____

$ _____ TO _____

IN WITNESS WHEREOF THE PARTIES HAVE HEREUNTO SET THEIR HANDS AND SEALS THE DAY AND YEAR FIRST ABOVE WRITTEN.

WITNESSED BY:

_____   _____ (SEAL)

_____ (SEAL)

AS TO PURCHASERS   PURCHASERS

_____   _____ (SEAL)

_____ (SEAL)

AS TO SELLERS   SELLERS

_____   _____ (SEAL)

AS TO REALTOR   REALTOR

Release of Deposit
(Reproduced with permission of the Florida Association of Realtors)

OFFICIAL FORM 105

OFFICIAL LEGAL FORMS
HIALEAH, FLORIDA

Release of Lien

STATE OF _____

County of _____ } ss

For and in consideration of the sum of _____ Dollars

to _____ in hand this day paid, the receipt of which is hereby acknowledged, _____ hereby

release the property hereinafter described from a certain lien filed by _____ me in the office of the

Clerk of the Circuit Court of _____ County, Florida, on the _____

day of _____, A. D. 19 _____ for the sum of _____ Dollars

due _____ for { labor and services and on said property; and _____ hereby declare said lien fully satisfied.
materials

Said property is described as follows:

WITNESS my hand and seal this _____ day of _____ A. D. 19 _____

Signed, sealed and delivered in the presence of:

_____ (SEAL)

_____ (SEAL)

STATE OF _____ } ss

County of _____

On this _____ day of _____ 19 ____ personally

appeared before me _____ and acknowledged that

executed the foregoing release of Lien for the purposes therein expressed.

WITNESS my hand and seal the day and year last above written.

_____

_____
NOTARY PUBLIC

My commission expires _____

Release of Lien

Partial Release of Mortgage

Know All Men By These Presents:

WHEREAS,

by Indenture of Mortgage dated the   day of   , A. D. 19   ,

and recorded in the office of the Clerk of the Circuit Court in and for the County of

State of Florida, in Mortgage Book   , Page   , granted and conveyed unto

and assigns, the premises therein particularly described, to secure the payment of the sum of

    Dollars,

with interest as therein mentioned:

AND WHEREAS THE SAID

requested, the said   to release the premises
hereinafter described, being part of said mortgaged premises, from the lien and operation of said Mortgage:

NOW, THEREFORE, KNOW YE, That the said

as well in consideration of the premises as of the sum of

    Dollars, to

at the time of execution hereof, the receipt whereof is hereby acknowledged, do remise, release, quit-claim, exonerate and discharge from the lien and operation of said mortgage unto the said

heirs and assigns, all that piece, parcel or tract of land, being a part of the premises conveyed by said mortgage, to-wit:

TO HAVE AND TO HOLD the same, with the appurtenances, unto the said

and assigns, forever, freed, exonerated and discharged of and from the lien of said mortgage, and every part thereof; Provided, always nevertheless, that nothing therein contained shall in anywise impair, alter or diminish the effect, lien or incumbrance of the aforesaid Mortgage on the remaining part of said mortgaged premises, not hereby released therefrom, or any of the rights and remedies of the holder hereof.

IN WITNESS WHEREOF, the said Mortgage   ha   hereunto set   hand   and seal   this   day of   , 19

Signed, sealed and delivered in the presence of:

_____   (Seal)

_____   (Seal)

Release of Part of Mortgaged Premises
(Reproduced with permission of Official Legal Forms, Hialeah, Fla.)

387

RENTAL APPLICATION

Name _____

Home Address _____
Street · City · State

Years at present address _____
Home Tel. No. _____

Firm Name
or Employer _____
Nature of
Business _____

Address _____
Street · City · State

Position _____
Years with
Firm · Business
Tel. No. _____

Bank Reference _____

Personal Reference _____
Name · Address

Marital Status _____
Number of Children · Pet _____ Yes or No

_____
Date

_____
Approved

231—Satisfaction of Lien

JULIUS BLUMBERG, INC. LAW BLANK PUBLISHERS
80 EXCHANGE PLACE AT BROADWAY, NEW YORK

STATE OF NEW YORK, COUNTY OF

ss.:

Do Hereby Certify, That a certain Mechanic's Lien, filed in the Office of the Clerk of the

County of

the   day of   19   at   o'clock, in the   noon, in favor of

on

claimant against the Building and Lot   situate   side of

Street,

Satisfaction of Lien

(Form by courtesy of Julius Blumberg, Inc., 80 Exchange Place, New York, N.Y. 10004)

and known as No.

claimed against

in said Street, for the sum of $

as owners

and

as

do hereby consent that the same be discharged of record.

is paid and satisfied, and

WITNESS the signature   and seal   of the above part   this

day of   nineteen hundred and

_____

_____

STATE OF NEW YORK, COUNTY OF   ss.:

On the   day of   19   , before me personally came

to me known and known to me to be the individual   described in, and who executed the above Certifi-

cate and   he   duly acknowledged to me that   he   had executed the same.

Satisfaction of Lien (Continued)

124B—Satisfaction of Mortgage—Individual   b   JULIUS BLUMBERG, INC., LAW BLANK PUBLISHERS
80 EXCHANGE PLACE AT BROADWAY, NEW YORK

THIS IS A LEGAL INSTRUMENT AND SHOULD BE EXECUTED UNDER SUPERVISION OF AN ATTORNEY.

Know all Men by these Presents,

THAT

*

DO   HEREBY CERTIFY that the following Mortgage   IS PAID, and do   hereby consent

that the same be discharged of record.

Mortgage dated the   day of   , 19   , made by

to

in the principal sum of $ and recorded on the   day of   19   ,

in Liber   of Section   of Mortgages, page   , in the office

of the   of the

Satisfaction of Mortgage

(Form by courtesy of Julius Blumberg, Inc., 80 Exchange Place, New York, N.Y. 10004)

which mortgage has not been † assigned of record.

Dated the day of , 19 .

IN PRESENCE OF:

* Insert residence, giving street and street number.
† Insert "further" when required.

Satisfaction of Mortgage (Continued)

Standard N. Y. B. T. U. Form 8029-12-60-1 M—Share of Ownership Agreement.

CONSULT YOUR LAWYER BEFORE SIGNING THIS INSTRUMENT—THIS INSTRUMENT SHOULD BE USED BY LAWYERS ONLY.

AGREEMENT, made the   day of   nineteen hundred and

BETWEEN

hereinafter designated as the party of the first part, and

hereinafter designated as the party of the second part.

WITNESSETH:—WHEREAS, the party of the second part is the holder of the following mortgage and of the bond   or note   secured thereby:

Mortgage dated the   day of   , 19   made by

to

in the principal sum of $ and recorded in Liber   of section   of
Mortgages, page   , in the office of the   of the

Share of Ownership Agreement

(Reproduced with permission of New York Board of Title Underwriters)

393

hereinafter referred to together as the mortgage, which covers premises situate

and

WHEREAS, there is unpaid on the mortgage the principal sum of

Dollars

and interest, and the party of the first part has an interest therein to the extent only as hereinafter set forth, and

WHEREAS, the parties hereto desire to declare their respective interests in the mortgage, and the terms upon which the mortgage is held by the party of the second part,

NOW THEREFORE, the parties hereto mutually certify and agree:

FIRST: The ownership of the party of the second part in the mortgage is now to the extent of

Dollars.

and the party of the first part is now the owner of the balance of the mortgage; but the ownership of the party of the second part is superior to that of the party of the first part, as if the party of the second part held a first mortgage and the party of the first part held a second and subordinate mortgage to secure their respective shares of the mortgage.

SECOND: The party of the second part is authorized to collect all the interest due and to become due on the mortgage and to give proper receipts therefor, and after deducting the amount thereof due under this agreement to the party of the second part, shall remit any balance remaining to the party of the first part by mailing the same to the party of the first part at the address herein given.

THIRD: The party of the second part or any assignee of the interest of the party of the second part in the mortgage is authorized to accept payment of the mortgage and to execute the proper release, satisfaction or assignment therefor, and the holder so releasing, satisfying or assigning the mortgage shall account to the party of the first part for all money received in excess of the ownership in the mortgage of said party of the second part of such assignee.

FOURTH: The party of the second part shall have the exclusive right to foreclose the mortgage, to exercise all options therein contained and to receive the proceeds of the sale in the foreclosure action, but shall account to the party of the first part for any money received by the party of the second part in excess of the interest of the party of the second part in the mortgage. The party of the second part shall be under no obligation to protect the interests of the party of the first part in the foreclosure action or at the foreclosure sale, except that the party of the first part shall be made a party in the action. If the party of the second part is the highest bidder at the foreclosure sale the party of the second part may take absolute title to the mortgaged property and resell the same without accounting at any time to the party of the first part for the proceeds of the resale of the property.

FIFTH: The interest of the party of the first part in the mortgage is not assignable as against the party of the second part except by an instrument duly executed in the manner required for the execution of a deed of real property to entitle it to be recorded, and by delivering to and leaving with the party of the second part a duplicate original thereof; this provision shall apply to each assignment of such interest. Any assignee of the interest of the party of the first part in the mortgage shall have no rights under this agreement, nor be entitled to any payment thereunder until such duplicate original assignment shall have been delivered to and left with the party of the second part and the receipt of the same shall have been noted by the party of the second part on this agreement. Whenever the proceeds of the ownership of the party of the first part in the mortgage shall be paid to the holder thereof, this agreement and the original of all assignments thereof shall be surrendered to the party of the second part with a satisfaction piece or assignment to the party of the second part of the interest of the party of the first part in the mortgage in form satisfactory to the party of the second part, to whom the party of the first part shall also pay the fees for recording such documents. The interest of the party of the second part is assignable to any person or corporation, without liability on the part of the party of the second part, but the interest of any such assignee shall be subject to this agreement.

SIXTH: The party of the first part, for himself or itself, and his or its legal representatives, successors and assigns, hereby expressly waives any and all rights, claims and remedies under Section 1079-a of the Civil Practice Act as now enacted or as may hereafter be amended, and under any other law, State or Federal, now or hereafter enacted which in any manner is or may be inconsistent with the rights and remedies of the party of the second part as set forth in this agreement.

SEVENTH: All rights and authority given to the party of the second part under this agreement are irrevocable so long as the party of the second part or the assignee of the party of the second part has any interest in the mortgage, and shall pass to and apply to any assignee of the interest of the party of the second part in the mortgage.

Share of Ownership Agreement (Continued)

This agreement may not be changed or terminated orally. This agreement shall bind and enure to the benefit of the parties hereto, their respective heirs, personal representatives, successors and assigns, provided, however, that assignment of the interest of the party of the first part shall become effectual only upon compliance with the provisions of Paragraph Fifth hereof. The word "party" shall be construed as if it read "parties" whenever the sense of this agreement so requires.

IN WITNESS WHEREOF, this agreement has been duly executed by the parties hereto the day and year first above written.

IN PRESENCE OF:

STATE OF NEW YORK, COUNTY OF   ss.:

On the   day of   , nineteen hundred and before me personally came

to me known to be the individual   described in and who executed the foregoing instrument. and acknowl-edged that   executed the same.

Share of Ownership Agreement (Continued)

Warranty Deed

This Indenture, Made the   day of   , A.D. 19   ,

BETWEEN

of the County of   , and State of   . of the first part, and

whose permanent address is

, and State of   , of the County of

, of the second part,

Witnesseth, That, the said part   of the first part, for and in consideration of the sum of

Dollars,

lawful money of the United States of America, to   in hand paid by the said part

of the second part, at or before the ensealing and delivery of these presents, the receipt whereof is hereby

acknowledged,   granted, bargained, sold, aliened, remised, released, conveyed and confirmed,

and by these presents do   grant, bargain, sell alien, remise, release, convey and confirm unto the said

part   of the second part, and   heirs and assigns forever, all the following piece ,

parcel   or tract   of land, situate, lying and being in the County of   , State of

. and more particularly described as follows:

Special Warranty Deed

(Reproduced with permission of Official Legal Forms, Hialeah, Fla.)

397

Together with all and singular the tenements, hereditaments and appurtenances thereunto belonging or in anywise appertaining, and the reversion and reversions, remainder and remainders, rents, issues and profits thereof, and also all the estate, right, title, interest, dower and right of dower, separate estate, property, possession, claim and demand whatsoever, as well as in equity, of the said part   of the first part, of, in and to the same, and every part and parcel thereof, with the appurtenances.

To Have and To Hold the above granted, bargained and described premises, with the appurtenances, unto the said part   of the second part,   heirs and assigns, to own proper use, benefit and behoof forever.

And the said part   of the first part, for   and for   heirs, executors and administrators, do   covenant, promise and agree to and with the said part   of the second part,   heirs and assigns, that the said part   of the first part, at the time of the ensealing and delivery of these presents,   lawfully seized of and in all and singular the above granted, bargained and described premises, with the appurtenances, and   good right, full power and lawful authority to grant, bargain, sell and convey the same in manner and form aforesaid. And the said part   of the second part,   heirs and assigns, shall and may at all times hereafter peaceably and quietly have, hold, use, occupy, possess and enjoy the above granted premises and every part and parcel thereof, with the appurtenances, without any let, suit, trouble, molestation, eviction or disturbance of the said part   of the first part,   heirs or assigns, or of any other person or persons lawfully claiming or to claim the same, by, through and under the grantor   herein.

And the said part   of the first part, for,   and for   heirs, warrants the
above described and hereby granted and released premises, and every part and parcel thereof, with the
appurtenances, unto the said part   of the second part,   heirs and assigns, against
the said part   of the first part,   heirs, and against all and every person or persons whomsoever lawfully claiming or to claim the same, by, through and under the grantor herein, shall and will
warrant and by these presents forever defend.

In Witness Whereof, The said part   of the first part   hereunto set
hand   and seal   the day and year first above written.

Signed, sealed and delivered in presence of us:

_____   _____ (Seal)

_____   _____ (Seal)

State of Florida
County of _____ } ss.

On this day personally appeared before me,

vidual   described in and who executed the foregoing deed of conveyance, and acknowledged that
executed the same for the purpose therein expressed, whereupon it is prayed that the same
may be recorded.

                                                to me well known and known to me to be the indi-

In Witness Whereof, I have hereunto affixed my hand and official seal, this
day of   , A.D. 19

_____ (Seal)

_____
NOTARY PUBLIC

My commission expires:

Special Warranty Deed (Continued)

399

263—Sub-Contract,
Between Contractor and Sub-Contractor.

JULIUS BLUMBERG, INC., LAW BLANK PUBLISHERS
80 EXCHANGE PLACE AT BROADWAY, NEW YORK

This Agreement *made this*

a   day of   19

by and between

of   *hereinafter described*

as Contractor; and

of   *hereinafter described*

as Sub-Contractor, the said parties for the considerations hereinafter mentioned hereby agree to the following:

1. The Sub-Contractor agrees to provide all the materials and perform all the work for the following described parts and divisions of work and materials specified in a certain contract between the Contractor and

described therein as Owner, in accordance with the terms, conditions and covenants of said contract as far as the same are applicable to the work and materials hereinafter mentioned, and as shown on the drawings and as set forth in the specifications mentioned in said contract prepared by

hereinafter described as Architect as far as the same are applicable to the work hereinafter mentioned, which said contract and said drawings and specifications therein mentioned are identified by the signatures of the respective parties hereto and are made and form a part of this contract:

400

2. The several portions of said work mentioned in this contract shall be finished at the times hereinafter stated, to wit,—

Sub-Contract

(Form courtesy of Julius Blumberg, Inc., 80 Exchange Place, New York, N.Y. 10004)

and the entire work embraced in this agreement shall be complete on or before the day of   19   and if the said work is not completed by the said date last mentioned, the said Contractor shall be entitled to receive as damages from the said Sub-Contractor for any such delay, in the absence of any legal ground or justification therefor, the sum of   dollars per   , it being understood and agreed between said parties hereto that the said sum fixed as liquidated damages is a reasonable sum, considering the damages that the Owner will sustain in the event of any such delay, and said amount is herein agreed upon and fixed as liquidated damages, because of the difficulty of ascertaining the exact amount of damages that may be sustained by such delay.

If, however the said Sub-Contractor is delayed in the performance or completion of said work by any act or neglect of the Contractor, or of the Owner, or of the Architect, or of any other Sub-Contractor employed by this Contractor or of any Contractor employed by the Owner, or by changes ordered in the work, or by labor strikes, lockouts, unavoidable casualties or other causes beyond the control of the said Sub-Contractor, then the time of the performance or completion of said work shall be extended for such period as the said Contractor or the said Architect may decide, but no such extension for a period covering more than seven days shall be valid, unless the same is in writing signed by said Contractor or by said Architect.

3. The Contractor agrees to pay to the Sub-Contractor for the work to be done and the materials to be furnished under this agreement the sum of

dollars, subject to additions and deductions for changes that may be agreed upon and to make payments on account thereof as follows:—

but said payments shall be made only upon certificates signed by   , and the final payment shall be made within   days after the completion of the said work embraced in this contract and after the issuance of the Architects certificate to that effect. No certificate, however, given by said Architect, or payment made under this contract, shall be conclusive evidence of the full performance of this contract by the Sub-Contractor, either wholly or in part, and no payment shall be considered to be an acceptance of defective work or improper materials.

4. The said Sub-Contractor agrees to assume towards the Contractor all the obligations and responsibilities in so far as the same may be applicable to the work and materials mentioned in this contract, as the said Contractor assumes towards the Owner.

5. The Contractor agrees to be bound to the Sub-Contractor by all the obligations that the Owner assumes to the Contractor under the contract between them hereinbefore mentioned, and by the drawings and specifications mentioned thereunder, and by all the provisions thereof, as far as the same may be applicable to the work and materials mentioned in this contract.

Sub-Contract (Continued)

6. The Contractor agrees to pay the Sub-Contractor a just share of any fire insurance money that may be received by the Contractor under and pursuant to the provisions of said contract existing between the Contractor and the Owner.

7. The said Contractor agrees in the event of any arbitration involving the work and materials mentioned in this contract under the terms and provisions of said contract between the Contractor and the Owner, to give the Sub-Contractor an opportunity to be present and submit evidence in reference thereto and to name as arbitrator the person named by the said Sub-Contractor, if the sole cause of controversy is the work and materials, rights or responsibilities of the Sub-Contractor; or, if of the Sub-Contractor and any other Sub-Contractor jointly, to name as such arbitrator the person upon whom they agree.

The terms Sub-Contractor, Owner, Contractor and Architect shall be read as if in the plural, or in the feminine gender, wherever appropriate.

In Witness Whereof, the parties hereto have executed this agreement the day and year first above written.

In presence of

Sub-Contract (Continued)

SUBORDINATION AGREEMENT
Of Mortgage

KNOW ALL MEN BY THESE PRESENTS THAT:

_____, as present legal
holder and owner of that certain mortgage dated_____executed by_____
_____, as Mortgagors, to
_____, as Mortgagee, recorded
_____in Docket_____, page_____, records of_____
_____County, _____ and concerning the real property in_____
_____described as follows:

_____

for and in consideration of the sum of Ten Dollars and Other Valuable Consideration to
him in hand paid, the receipt of which is hereby acknowledged, has, and by these presents
does waive the priority of the lien of the said mortgage insofar as the following described
mortgage is concerned, but not otherwise:

That certain Mortgage dated_____, by_____
_____, as Mortgagor to_____, as Mort-
gagee securing payment of a note in the amount of $_____dated_____
_____, with interest from the date hereof on unpaid principal at the rate of_____
_____% per annum; principal and interest payable in installments of $_____
_____on the_____day of every month beginning_____
_____and continuing until_____on
which date the entire balance of principal and interest remaining unpaid shall be due and
payable.

The undersigned, _____, hereby consenting
that the lien of the mortgage first above described be taken as second and inferior to the
mortgage last above described.

WITNESS his hand this_____day of_____, 19_____ .

_____ _____(Seal)

_____ _____(Seal)

_____ _____(Seal)

_____ _____(Seal)

FLORIDA FORMS, P.O. BOX 466, HOMESTEAD, FLA.

FORM D

VACANT LOTS

NO. OF LOTS_____   PRICE $_____

SIZE_____ X _____   DOWN PAY. $_____

ZONED _____   PRICE PER FOOT $_____

LOCATION _____

LEGAL DESCRIPTION _____ SEC. _____ T _____ R _____

LOT _____, BLOCK _____, SUBDIVISION _____

EXISTING MORTGAGE $_____, HELD BY _____

PAYABLE $_____ INTEREST _____ %

SECOND MORTGAGE $_____, HELD BY _____

PAYABLE $_____ INTEREST _____ %

TAXES $_____ PAVED STREETS _____ ELEVATION _____

WATER $_____ SEWAGE _____ SIDEWALKS _____

REMARKS _____

OWNER _____   LISTED BY _____

ADDRESS _____   DATE LISTED _____

TELEPHONE _____   EXCLUSIVE _____

APPROVED BY _____
(OWNER)

Vacant Lot Listing Form

406

285—Statutory Form A.
Warranty Deed with Full Covenants, Individual.

JULIUS BLUMBERG, INC.; LAW BLANK PUBLISHERS
80 EXCHANGE PLACE AT BROADWAY, NEW YORK

This Indenture,

Made the   day of   nineteen hundred

and

Between

and

part   of the first part,

part   of the second part,

Witnesseth, that the part   of the first part, in consideration of

Dollars,

Warranty Deed

(Form by courtesy of Julius Blumberg, Inc., 80 Exchange Place, New York, N.Y. 10004)

lawful money of the United States,

do   hereby grant and release unto the part   of the second part,

paid by the part   of the second part

and assigns forever,

All

Together with the appurtenances and all the estate and rights of the party of the first part in and to said premises.

To have and to hold the premises herein granted unto the part   of the second part,

and assigns forever,

408

In Witness Whereof, the part   of the first part ha   hereunto set

hand   and seal   the day and year first above written.

In presence of:

.... L. S.

.... L. S.

.... L. S.

.... L. S.

State of

County of   } ss.:

On the   day of   nineteen hundred and

before me came

to me known and known to me to be the individual   described in, and who executed, the foregoing instrument, and acknowledged to me that   he   executed the same.

Warranty Deed (Continued)

409

ORGANIZATIONS

National Organizations Active in
Real Estate and Allied Fields

American Chapter, International
Real Estate Federation
777 14th Street, N.W.
Washington, D.C. 20005

American Hotel and Motel Association
888 Seventh Ave.
New York, NY 10106

American Institute of Architects (AIA)
1735 New York Ave., N.W.
Washington, D.C. 20006

American Institute of Real Estate Appraisers (AIREA)
430 N. Michigan Ave.
Chicago, IL 60611

American Land Title Association
1828 L Street, N.W., Suite 705
Washington, D.C. 20036

American Planning Association (APA)
1776 Massachusetts Ave., N.W.
Washington, D.C. 20036

American Resort and Residential Association
1220 L Street, N.W., Suite 510
Washington, D.C. 20005

American Society of Real Estate Counselors (ASREC)
430 N. Michigan Ave.
Chicago, IL 60611

Associated General Contractors of America
1957 East Street, N.W.
Washington, D.C. 20006

Building Owners and Managers Association (BOMA)
1250 Eye Street, N.W., Suite 200
Washington, D.C. 20005

Farm and Land Institute
430 N. Michigan Ave.
Chicago, IL 60611

Federal Home Loan Bank Board
1700 G Street, N.W.
Washington, D.C. 20552

Institute of Real Estate Management (IREM)
430 N. Michigan Ave.
Chicago, IL 60611

International Council of Shopping Centers
665 Fifth Ave.
New York, NY 10022

International Real Estate Federation
(See American Chapter, International Real Estate Federation)

Mortgage Bankers Association of America
1125 15th Street, N.W.
Washington, D.C. 20005

National Apartment Association
1101 14th Street, N.W., Suite 804
Washington, D.C. 20005

National Association of Corporate Real Estate Executives
471 Spencer Drive S., Suite 8
West Palm Beach, FL 33409

National Association of Home Builders of the U.S.
15th and M Street, N.W.
Washington, D.C. 20005

National Association of Housing and Redevelopment Officials
1320 18th Street, N.W.
Washington, D.C. 20036

National Association of Independent Fee Appraisers
7501 Murdoch
St. Louis, MO 63119

National Association of Industrial and Office Parks
1215 Jefferson Davis Hwy., Suite 100
Arlington, VA 22202

National Association of Real Estate Appraisers
853 Broadway
New York, NY 10003

National Association of Real Estate Brokers (NAREB)
1101 14th Street, N.W., Suite 1000
Washington, D.C. 20005

National Association of Real Estate Investment Trusts
1101 17th Street, N.W., Suite 700
Washington, D.C. 20036

National Association of Realtors (NAR)
430 N. Michigan Ave.
Chicago, IL 60611

National Institute of Farm and Land Brokers
430 N. Michigan Ave.
Chicago, IL 60611

Realtors National Marketing Institute
430 N. Michigan Ave.
Chicago, IL 60611

Society of Industrial Realtors (SIR)
777 14th Street, N.W.
Washington, D.C. 20005

Society of Real Estate Appraisers (SREA)
645 N. Michigan Ave.
Chicago, IL 60611

The Urban Land Institute (ULI)
1090 Vermont Ave.
Washington, D.C. 20005

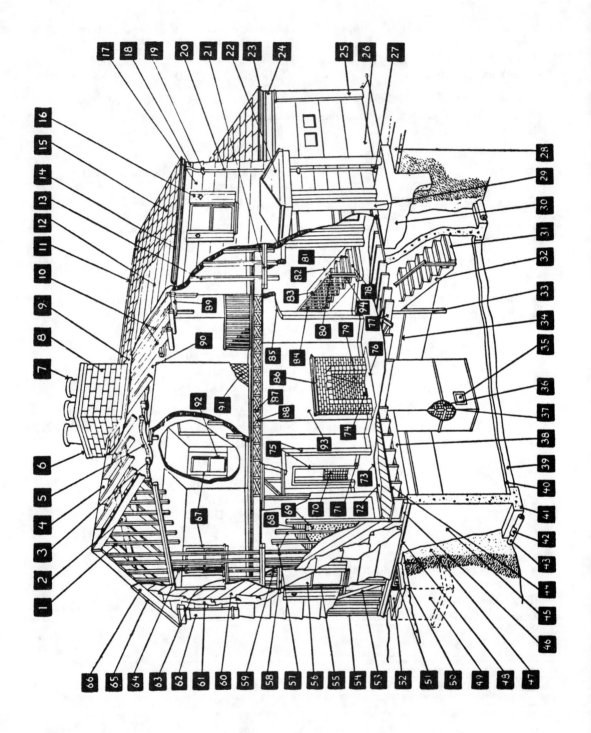

412

DESCRIPTION OF NUMBERED PARTS IN HOUSE CROSS SECTION

1—Gable stud	44—Diagonal subflooring	61—Building paper	78—Stair riser
2—Collar beam	45—Foundation wall	62—Pilaster	79—Fire brick
3—Ceiling joist	46—Sill	63—Rough header	80—Newel cap
4—Ridge board	47—Backfill	64—Window stud	81—Stair tread
5—Insulation	48—Termite shield	65—Cornice moulding	82—Finish stringer
6—Chimney cap	49—Areaway wall	66—Frieze or barge board	83—Stair rail
7—Chimney pots	50—Grade line	67—Window casing	84—Balusters
8—Chimney	51—Basement sash	68—Lath	85—Plaster arch
9—Chimney flashing	52—Areaway	69—Insulation	86—Mantel
10—Rafters	53—Corner brace	70—Wainscoting	87—Floor joists
11—Ridge	54—Corner studs	71—Baseboard	88—Bridging
12—Roof boards	55—Window frame	72—Building paper	89—Lookout
13—Stud	56—Window light	73—Finish floor	90—Attic space
14—Eave trough or gutter	57—Wall studs	74—Ash dump	91—Metal lath
15—Roofing	58—Header	75—Door trim	92—Window sash
16—Blind or shutter	59—Window cripple	76—Fireplace hearth	93—Chimney breast
17—Bevel siding	60—Wall sheathing	77—Floor joists	94—Newel
18—Downspout or leader gooseneck			
19—Downspout or leader strap			
20—Downspout, leader or conductor			
21—Double plate			
22—Entrance canopy			
23—Garage cornice			
24—Frieze			
25—Door jamb			
26—Garage door			
27—Downspout or leader shoe			
28—Sidewalk			
29—Entrance post			
30—Entrance platform			
31—Basement stair riser			
32—Stair stringer			
33—Girder post			
34—Chair rail			
35—Cleanout door			
36—Furring strips			
37—Corner stud			
38—Girder			
39—Cinder or gravel fill			
40—Concrete basement floor			
41—Footing for foundation wall			
42—Paper strip			
43—Foundation drain tile			

DIAGRAM SHOWING METHOD OF FIGURING LOADS FOR HOUSE FRAMING

Live load on roof = 30 lbs. per sq. ft. of horizontal surface
Dead load of roof of wood shingle construction = 10 lbs. per sq. ft.

Live load on Attic Floor, not used for living purposes = 20 lbs per sq. ft.
Dead load of Attic Floor, not floored = 10 lbs per sq. ft.
Dead load of Attic Floor when floored = 20 lbs. per sq. ft.

Dead load of partitions = 20 lbs per sq. ft of floor area

Live load on Second floor = 40 lbs. per sq. ft.
Dead load of Second floor = 20 lbs. per sq. ft.

Dead load of partitions = 20 lbs. per sq. ft. of floor area

Live load on First Floor = 40 lbs per sq. ft.
Dead load of First Floor, ceiling not plastered = 10 lbs. per sq. ft.
Dead load of First Floor, ceiling plastered = 20 lbs. per sq. ft.

Ceiling & Walls Plastered

Double Flooring

Girder

X = 12'-0"

24'-0"

House Cross Section (Description of Parts)
(Reproduced with permission of Building Materials Merchandiser, Chicago, Ill.)

413

MONTHLY PAYMENTS NECESSARY TO AMORTIZE
A LOAN FOR EACH $1,000 OF LOAN (*)

Yrs	5.5%	6%	6.5%	7%	8%	9%	10%
5	$19.11	$19.34	$19.57	$19.81	$20.28	$20.76	$21.25
10	10.86	11.11	11.36	11.62	12.14	12.67	21.25
15	8.18	8.44	8.72	8.99	9.56	10.15	10.75
20	6.88	7.17	7.46	7.76	8.37	9.00	9.66
25	6.15	6.45	6.76	7.07	7.72	8.40	9.09
30	5.68	6.00	6.33	6.66	7.34	8.05	8.78

Yrs	10.5%	11%	11.5%	12%	12.5%	13%	13.5%
5	$21.49	$21.74	$21.99	$22.25	$22.50	$22.75	$23.01
10	13.49	13.78	14.06	14.35	14.64	14.93	15.23
15	11.05	11.37	11.68	12.00	12.33	12.65	12.98
20	9.98	10.32	10.66	11.01	11.36	11.72	12.07
25	9.44	9.80	10.16	10.53	10.90	11.28	11.66
30	9.15	9.52	9.90	10.29	10.67	11.06	11.45

Yrs	14%	14.5%	15%	15.5%	16%	16.5%	17%
5	$23.27	$23.53	$23.79	$24.06	$24.32	$24.59	$24.86
10	15.53	15.83	16.13	16.45	16.76	17.07	17.38
15	13.32	13.66	14.00	14.34	14.96	15.04	15.40
20	12.44	12.80	13.17	13.54	13.92	14.29	14.67
25	12.04	12.42	12.81	13.20	13.59	13.99	14.38
30	11.85	12.25	12.64	13.05	13.45	13.86	14.26

Yrs	17.5%	18%	18.5%	19%	19.5%	20%	21%
5	$25.13	$25.40	$25.67	$25.95	$26.22	$26.50	$27.06
10	17.70	18.02	18.35	18.67	19.00	19.33	20.00
15	15.75	16.11	16.47	16.83	17.20	17.57	18.31
20	15.05	15.44	15.82	16.21	16.60	16.99	17.78
25	14.78	15.18	15.58	15.98	16.39	16.79	17.60
30	14.67	15.08	15.48	15.89	16.30	16.72	17.54

* (All payments shown hereon represent principal & interest only)

Amortization Table

NATIONAL ASSOCIATION OF REALTORS®
CODE OF ETHICS

Preamble ...

Under all is the land. Upon its wise utilization and widely allocated ownership depend the survival and growth of free institutions and of our civilization. The REALTOR® should recognize that the interests of the nation and its citizens require the highest and best use of the land and the widest distribution of land ownership. They require the creation of adequate housing, the building of functioning cities, the development of productive industries and farms, and the preservation of a healthful environment.

Such interests impose obligations beyond those of ordinary commerce. They impose grave social responsibility and a patriotic duty to which the REALTOR® should dedicate himself, and for which he should be diligent in preparing himself. The REALTOR®, therefore, is zealous to maintain and improve the standards of his calling and shares with his fellow-REALTORS® a common responsibility for its integrity and honor. The term REALTOR® has come to connote competency, fairness, and high integrity resulting from adherence to a lofty ideal of moral conduct in business relations. No inducement of profit and no instruction from clients ever can justify departure from this ideal.

In the interpretation of his obligation, a REALTOR® can take no safer guide than that which has been handed down through the centuries, embodied in the Golden Rule, "Whatsoever ye would that men should do to you, do ye even so to them."

Accepting this standard as his own, every REALTOR® pledges himself to observe its spirit in all of his activities and to conduct his business in accordance with the tenets set forth below.

Article 1

The REALTOR® should keep himself informed on matters affecting real estate in his community, the state, and nation so that he may be able to contribute responsibly to public thinking on such matters.

Article 2

In justice to those who place their interests in his care, the REALTOR® should endeavor always to be informed regarding laws, proposed legislation, governmental regulations, public policies, and current market conditions in order to be in a position to advise his clients properly.

Article 3

It is the duty of the REALTOR® to protect the public against fraud, misrepresentation, and unethical practices in real estate transactions. He should endeavor to eliminate in his community any practices which could be damaging to the public or bring discredit to the real estate profession. The REALTOR® should assist the governmental agency charged with regulating the practices of brokers and salesmen in his state.

Article 4

The REALTOR® should seek no unfair advantage over other REALTORS® and should conduct his business so as to avoid controversies with other REALTORS®.

Article 5

In the best interests of society, of his associates, and his own business, the REALTOR® should willingly share with other REALTORS® the lessons of his experience and study for the benefit of the public, and should be loyal to the Board of REALTORS® of his community and active in its work.

Article 6

To prevent dissension and misunderstanding and to assure better service to the owner, the REALTOR® should urge the exclusive listing of property unless contrary to the best interest of the owner.

Article 7

In accepting employment as an agent, the REALTOR® pledges himself to protect and promote the interests of the client. This obligation of absolute fidelity to the client's interests is primary, but it does not relieve the REALTOR® of the obligation to treat fairly all parties to the transaction.

Article 8

The REALTOR® shall not accept compensation from more than one party, even if permitted by law, without the full knowledge of all parties to the transaction.

Article 9

The REALTOR® shall avoid exaggeration, misrepresentation, or concealment of pertinent facts. He has an affirmative obligation to discover adverse factors that a reasonably competent and diligent investigation would disclose.

1

Article 10

The REALTOR® shall not deny equal professional services to any person for reasons of race, creed, sex, or country of national origin. The REALTOR® shall not be a party to any plan or agreement to discriminate against a person or persons on the basis of race, creed, sex, or country of national origin.

Article 11

A REALTOR® is expected to provide a level of competent service in keeping with the Standards of Practice in those fields in which the REALTOR® customarily engages.

The REALTOR® shall not undertake to provide specialized professional services concerning a type of property or service that is outside his field of competence unless he engages the assistance of one who is competent on such types of property or service, or unless the facts are fully disclosed to the client. Any person engaged to provide such assistance shall be so identified to the client and his contribution to the assignment should be set forth.

The REALTOR® shall refer to the Standards of Practice of the National Association as to the degree of competence that a client has a right to expect the REALTOR® to possess, taking into consideration the complexity of the problem, the availability of expert assistance, and the opportunities for experience available to the REALTOR®.

Article 12

The REALTOR® shall not undertake to provide professional services concerning a property or its value where he has a present or contemplated interest unless such interest is specifically disclosed to all affected parties.

Article 13

The REALTOR® shall not acquire an interest in or buy for himself, any member of his immediate family, his firm or any member thereof, or any entity in which he has a substantial ownership interest, property listed with him, without making the true position known to the listing owner. In selling property owned by himself, or in which he has any interest, the REALTOR® shall reveal the facts of his ownership or interest to the purchaser.

Article 14

In the event of a controversy between REALTORS® associated with different firms, arising out of their relationship as REALTORS®, the REALTORS® shall submit the dispute to arbitration in accordance with the regulations of their board or boards rather than litigate the matter.

Article 15

If a REALTOR® is charged with unethical practice or is asked to present evidence in any disciplinary proceeding or investigation, he shall place all pertinent facts before the proper tribunal of the member board or affiliated institute, society, or council of which he is a member.

Article 16

When acting as agent, the REALTOR® shall not accept any commission, rebate, or profit on expenditures made for his principal-owner, without the principal's knowledge and consent.

Article 17

The REALTOR® shall not engage in activities that constitute the unauthorized practice of law and shall recommend that legal counsel be obtained when the interest of any party to the transaction requires it.

Article 18

The REALTOR® shall keep in a special account in an appropriate financial institution, separated from his own funds, monies coming into his possession in trust for other persons, such as escrows, trust funds, clients' monies, and other like items.

Article 19

The REALTOR® shall be careful at all times to present a true picture in his advertising and representations to the public. He shall neither advertise without disclosing his name nor permit any person associated with him to use individual names or telephone numbers, unless such person's connection with the REALTOR® is obvious in the advertisement.

Article 20

The REALTOR®, for the protection of all parties, shall see that financial obligations and commitments regarding real estate transactions are in writing, expressing the exact agreement of the parties. A copy of each agreement shall be furnished to each party upon his signing such agreement.

Article 21

The REALTOR® shall not engage in any practice or take any action inconsistent with the agency of another REALTOR®.

Article 22

In the sale of property which is exclusively listed with a REALTOR®, the REALTOR® shall utilize the services of other brokers upon mutually agreed upon terms when it is in the best interests of the client.

Negotiations concerning property which is listed exclusively shall be carried on with the listing broker, not with the owner, except with the consent of the listing broker.

Article 23

The REALTOR® shall not publicly disparage the business practice of a competitor nor volunteer an opinion of a competitor's transaction. If his opinion is sought and if the REALTOR® deems it appropriate to respond, such opinion shall be rendered with strict professional integrity and courtesy.

Article 24

The REALTOR® shall not directly or indirectly solicit the services or affiliation of an employee or independent contractor in the organization of another REALTOR® without prior notice to said REALTOR®.

Where the word REALTOR® is used in this Code and Preamble, it shall be deemed to include REALTOR® ASSOCIATE. Pronouns shall be considered to include REALTORS® and REALTOR® ASSOCIATES of both genders

The Code of Ethics was adopted in 1913. Amended at the Annual Convention in 1924, 1928, 1950, 1951, 1952, 1955, 1956, 1961, 1962, 1974, and 1982.

2

NATIONAL ASSOCIATION OF REALTORS®

STANDARDS OF PRACTICE
RELATING TO ARTICLES OF THE CODE OF ETHICS

EXPLANATION

Standards of Practice relating to Articles of the Code of Ethics of the NATIONAL ASSOCIATION OF REALTORS® approved in May and November of 1975 are published below. These Standards of Practice are defined by the Committee on Professional Standards, National Association, as "interpretations" of various Articles of the Code of Ethics. It will be noted that such Standards of Practice have not been adopted for each and every Article. This does not indicate that such Standards may not be adopted at some point in time, but as of the date of this publication, only those set forth below have been adopted. From time to time, additional Standards of Practice will be adopted by the Committee on Professional Standards, subject to approval of the Board of Directors of the National Association. These "interpretations" (Standards of Practice) are **in addition to,** and **are not replacements for the "numbered cases"** found in Interpretations of the Code of Ethics. Thus, Standard of Practice 7-1 relates to Article 7 of the Code, but is not to be confused with **Case #7-1** which also relates to Article 7.

A Standard of Practice is a statement of general principle to guide the REALTOR® as to professional conduct required in the particular situation described by the Standard, whereas each of the "numbered cases" presents a **set of particular facts alleging a violation of the Code of Ethics, and describes a conclusion** reached by the Committee on Professional Standards in the light of the particular set of facts given.

It is emphasized that a Standard of Practice is, in fact, an "interpretation" of an Article of the Code, and is not to be construed as a part of the Code itself. The Appropriate relationship between a Standard of Practice and an Article of the Code is noted in the following advisory opinion adopted by the Committee on Professional Standards, and approved by the Board of Directors, National Association:

"In filing a charge of an alleged violation of the Code of Ethics by a REALTOR®, the charge shall read as an alleged violation of one or more Articles of the Code. A Standard of Practice may only be cited in support of the charge."

The system of "cross-referencing" the Standards of Practice is to be noted. For example, Standard of Practice 7-4 cites a cross-reference to Standard of Practice 22-1, which indicates that **Standard of Practice 22-1 relates primarily to Article 22** of the Code of Ethics, but is also relates to Article 7 of the Code.

As additional Standards of Practice are adopted from time to time, Member Boards and Board members will be advised of their adoption, and such Standards will then be included in the next revision or printing of the Interpretations of the Code of Ethics.

STANDARDS OF PRACTICE

STANDARD OF PRACTICE 7-1 — "The REALTOR® shall receive and shall transmit all offers on a specified property to the owner for his decision, whether such offers are received from a prospective purchaser or another broker."

STANDARD OF PRACTICE 7-2 — "The REALTOR®, acting as listing broker, shall submit all offers to the seller as quickly as possible."

STANDARD OF PRACTICE 7-3 — "The REALTOR®, in attempting to secure a listing, shall not deliberately mislead the owner as to market value."

STANDARD OF PRACTICE 7-4 — (Refer to Standard of Practice 22-1, which also relates to Article 7, Code of Ethics.)

STANDARD OF PRACTICE 7-5 — (Refer to Standard of Practice 22-2, which also relates to Article 7, Code of Ethics.)

STANDARD OF PRACTICE 9-1 — "The REALTOR® shall not be a party to the naming of a false consideration in any document, unless it be the naming of an obviously nominal consideration."

STANDARD OF PRACTICE 9-2 — "The REALTOR®, when asked by another broker, shall disclose the nature of his listing, i.e., an exclusive right to sell, an exclusive agency, open listing, or other."

STANDARD OF PRACTICE 9-3 — (Refer to Standard of Practice 7-3, which also relates to Article 9, Code of Ethics.)

3

STANDARD OF PRACTICE 9-4 — "The REALTOR⁸ shall not offer a service described as 'free of charge' when the rendering of a service is contingent on the obtaining of a benefit such as a listing or commission."

STANDARD OF PRACTICE 11-1 — "Whenever a REALTOR⁸ submits an oral or written opinion of the value of real property for a fee, his opinion shall be supported by a memorandum in his file or an appraisal report, either of which shall include as a minimum the following:
1. Limiting conditions
2. Any existing or contemplated interest
3. Defined value
4. Date applicable
5. The estate appraised
6. A description of the property
7. The basis of the reasoning including applicable market data and/or capitalization computation

"This report or memorandum shall be available to the Professional Standards Committee for a period of at least two years (beginning subsequent to final determination of the court if the appraisal is involved in litigation) to ensure compliance with Article 11 of the Code of Ethics of the NATIONAL ASSOCIATION OF REALTORS⁸."

STANDARD OF PRACTICE 11-2 — "The REALTOR⁸ shall not undertake to make an appraisal when his employment or fee is contingent upon the amount of appraisal."

STANDARD OF PRACTICE 12-1 — (Refer to Standard of Practice 9-4, which also relates to Article 12, Code of Ethics.)

STANDARD OF PRACTICE 16-1 — "The REALTOR⁸ shall not recommend or suggest to a principal or a customer the use of services of another organization or business entity in which he has a direct interest without disclosing such interest at the time of the recommendation or suggestion."

STANDARD OF PRACTICE 19-1 — "The REALTOR⁸ shall not submit or advertise property without authority, and in any offering, the price quoted shall not be other than that agreed upon with the owners."

STANDARD OF PRACTICE 19-2 — (Refer to Standard of Practice 9-4, which also relates to Article 19, Code of Ethics.)

STANDARD OF PRACTICE 21-1 — "Signs giving notice of property for sale, rent, lease, or exchange shall not be placed on property without the consent of the owner."

STANDARD OF PRACTICE 21-2 — "The REALTOR⁸ obtaining information from a listing broker about a specific property shall not convey this information to, nor invite the cooperation of a third party broker without the consent of the listing broker."

STANDARD OF PRACTICE 21-3 — "The REALTOR⁸ shall not solicit a listing which is currently listed exclusively with another broker."

STANDARD OF PRACTICE 21-4 — "The REALTOR⁸ shall not use information obtained by him from the listing broker, through offers to cooperate received through Multiple Listing Services or other sources authorized by the listing broker, for the purpose of creating a referral prospect to a third broker, or for creating a buyer prospect unless such use is authorized by the listing broker."

STANDARD OF PRACTICE 22-1 — "It is the obligation of the selling broker as subagent of the listing broker to disclose immediately all pertinent facts to the listing broker prior to as well as after the contract is executed."

STANDARD OF PRACTICE 22-2 — "The REALTOR®, when submitting offers to the seller, shall present each in an objective and unbiased manner. '

December 1975
‹ NATIONAL ASSOCIATION OF REALTORS⁸
All Rights Reserved

Form No. 111-811-1 (4/76)

4